Presenting the final issue of **FABLES** as told by

Bill Willingham writer/creator
Mark Buckingham penciller/inker
Steve Leialoha inker
Andrew Pepoy inker
Dan Green inker
Jose Marzan Jr. inker
Lee Loughridge colorist
Todd Klein letterer
Nimit Malavia cover
Rowena Yow assoc. editor
Shelly Bond editor

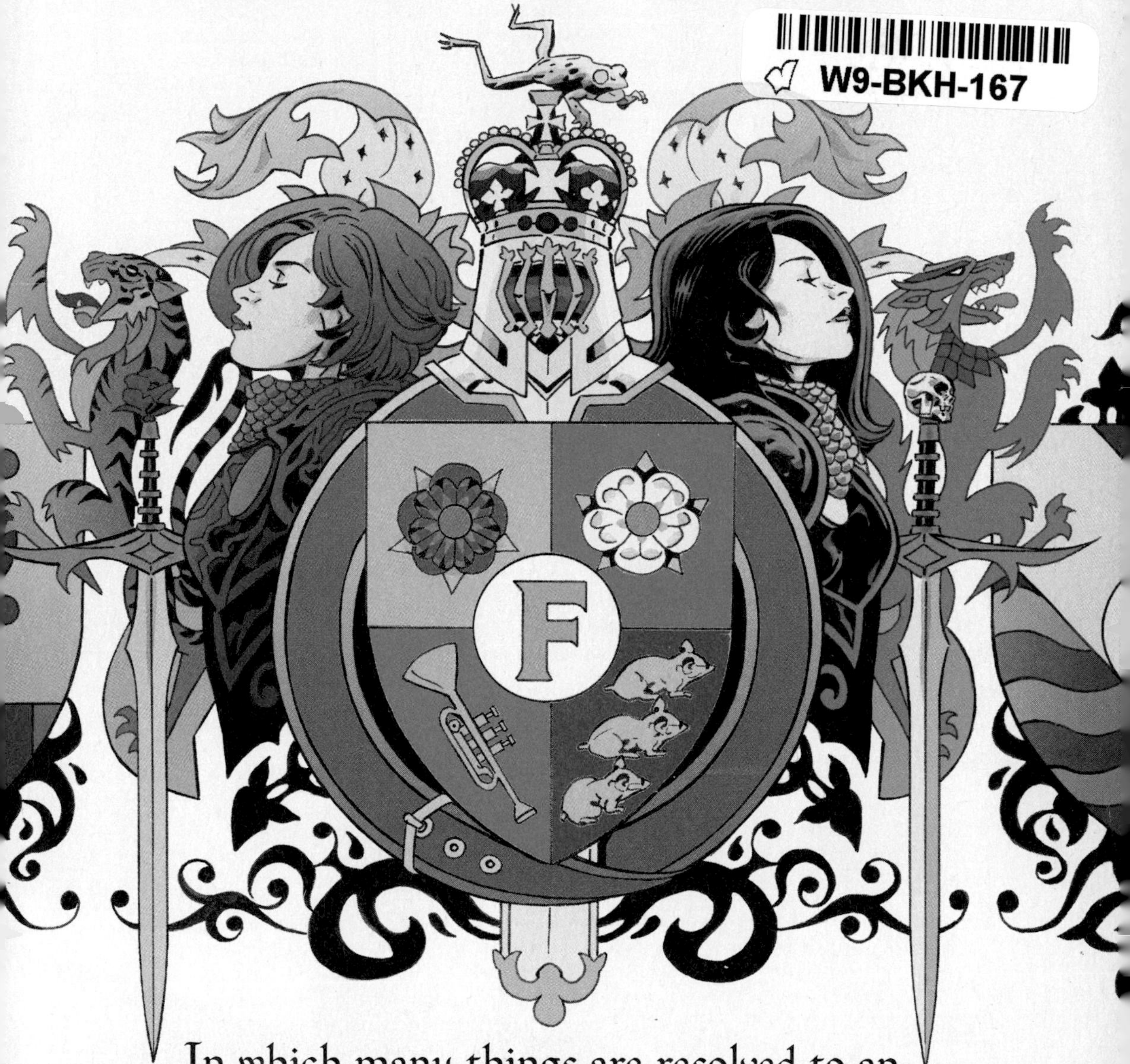
F

In which many things are resolved to an extent that the gentlewomen and gentlemen who've been privileged to bring you these tales in years past, and who proudly present this one today, can take the opportunity to wish you a fond, if somewhat troubling,

FAREWELL

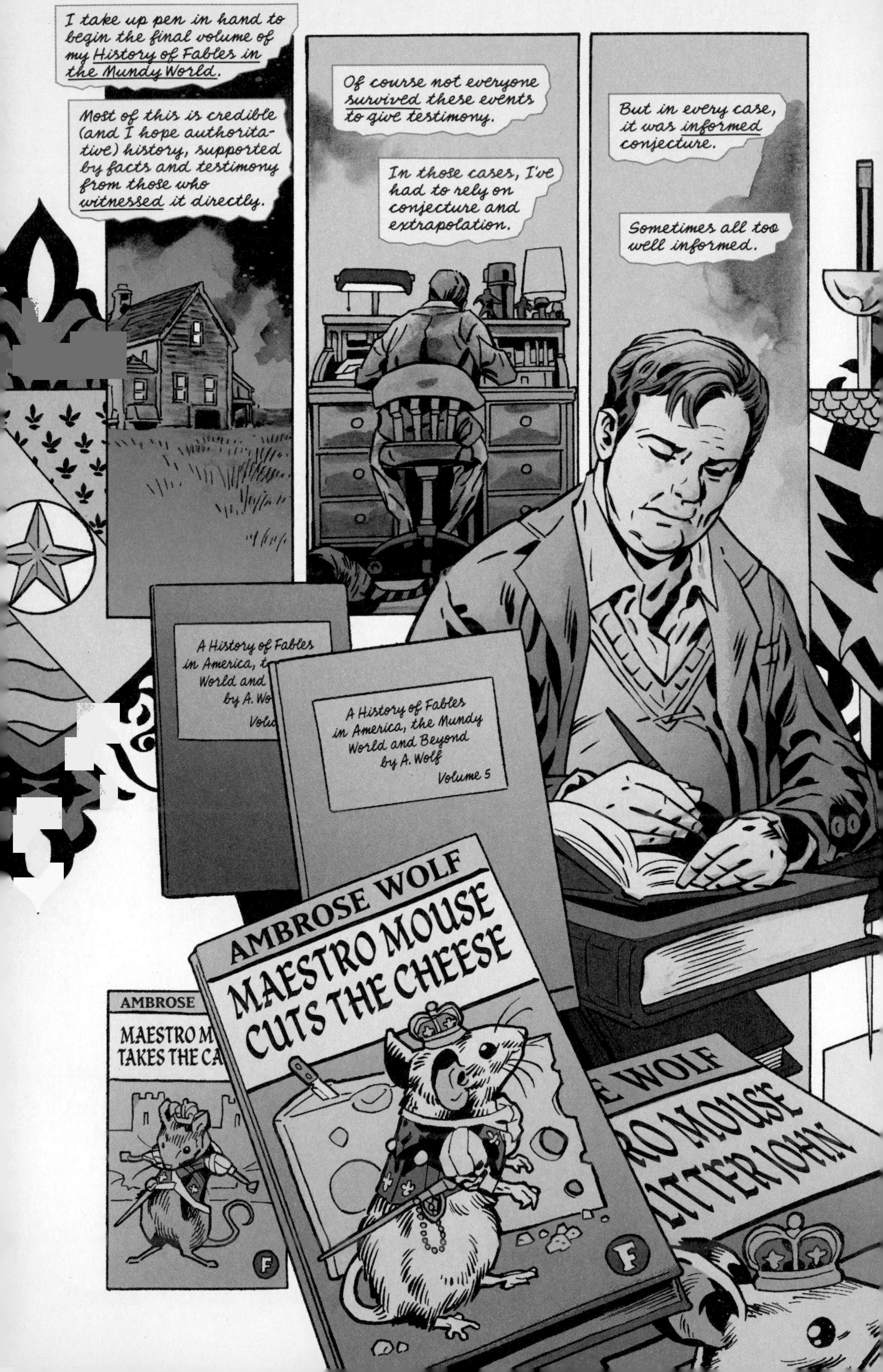
I take up pen in hand to begin the final volume of my History of Fables in the Mundy World.
Most of this is credible (and I hope authoritative) history, supported by facts and testimony from those who witnessed it directly.
Of course not everyone survived these events to give testimony.
In those cases, I've had to rely on conjecture and extrapolation.
But in every case, it was informed conjecture.
Sometimes all too well informed.
A History of Fables in America, the Mundy World and Beyond by A. Wolf Volume 5
AMBROSE WOLF
MAESTRO MOUSE CUTS THE CHEESE
AMBROSE

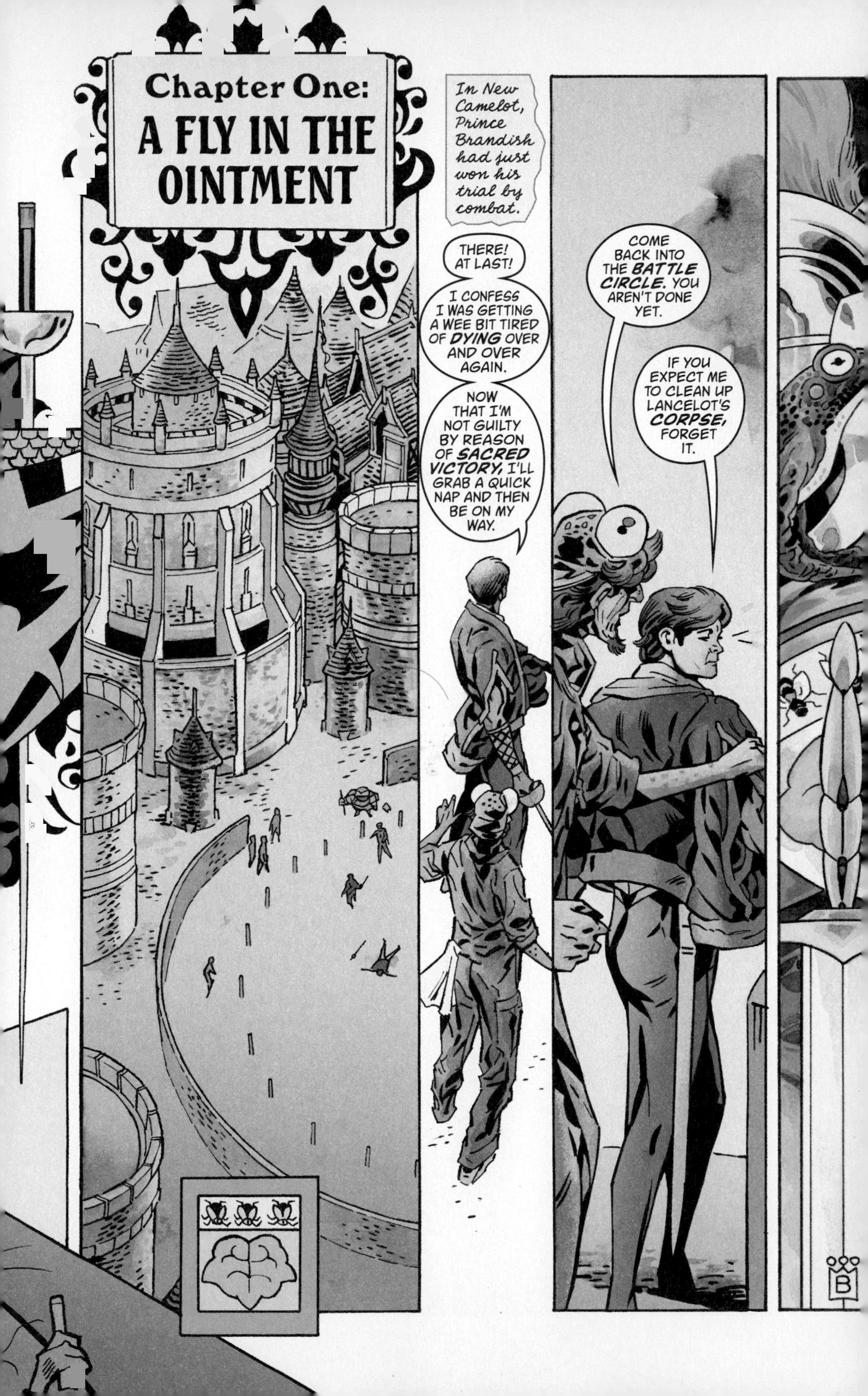

Chapter One:
A FLY IN THE OINTMENT
In New Camelot, Prince Brandish had just won his trial by combat.
THERE! AT LAST!
I CONFESS I WAS GETTING A WEE BIT TIRED OF DYING OVER AND OVER AGAIN.
NOW THAT I'M NOT GUILTY BY REASON OF SACRED VICTORY, I'LL GRAB A QUICK NAP AND THEN BE ON MY WAY.
COME BACK INTO THE BATTLE CIRCLE. YOU AREN'T DONE YET.
IF YOU EXPECT ME TO CLEAN UP LANCELOT'S CORPSE, FORGET IT.

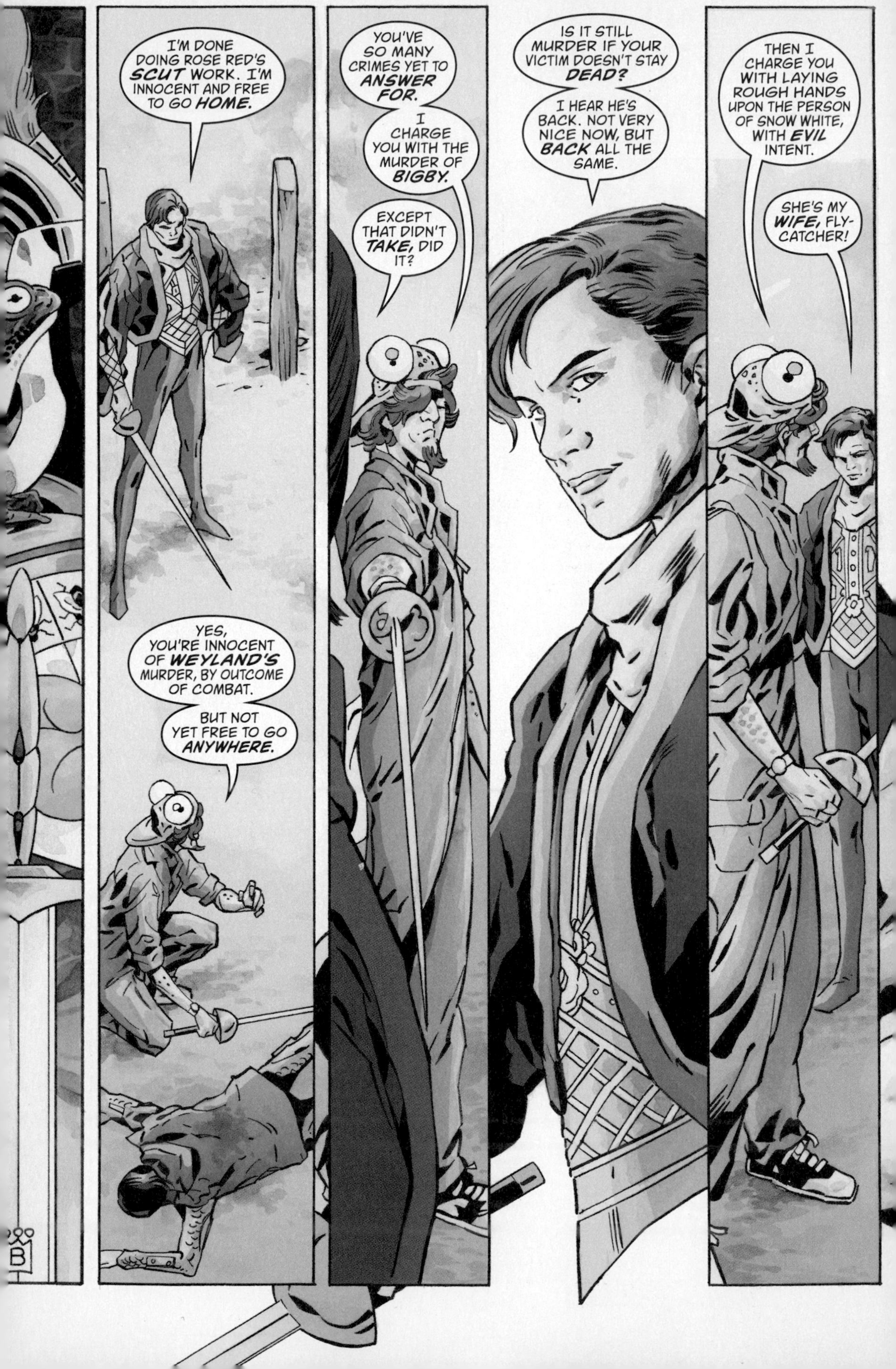

I'M DONE DOING ROSE RED'S SCUT WORK. I'M INNOCENT AND FREE TO GO HOME.
YES, YOU'RE INNOCENT OF WEYLAND'S MURDER, BY OUTCOME OF COMBAT.
BUT NOT YET FREE TO GO ANYWHERE.
YOU'VE SO MANY CRIMES YET TO ANSWER FOR.
I CHARGE YOU WITH THE MURDER OF BIGBY.
EXCEPT THAT DIDN'T TAKE, DID IT?
IS IT STILL MURDER IF YOUR VICTIM DOESN'T STAY DEAD?
I HEAR HE'S BACK. NOT VERY NICE NOW, BUT BACK ALL THE SAME.
THEN I CHARGE YOU WITH LAYING ROUGH HANDS UPON THE PERSON OF SNOW WHITE, WITH EVIL INTENT.
SHE'S MY WIFE, FLY-CATCHER!

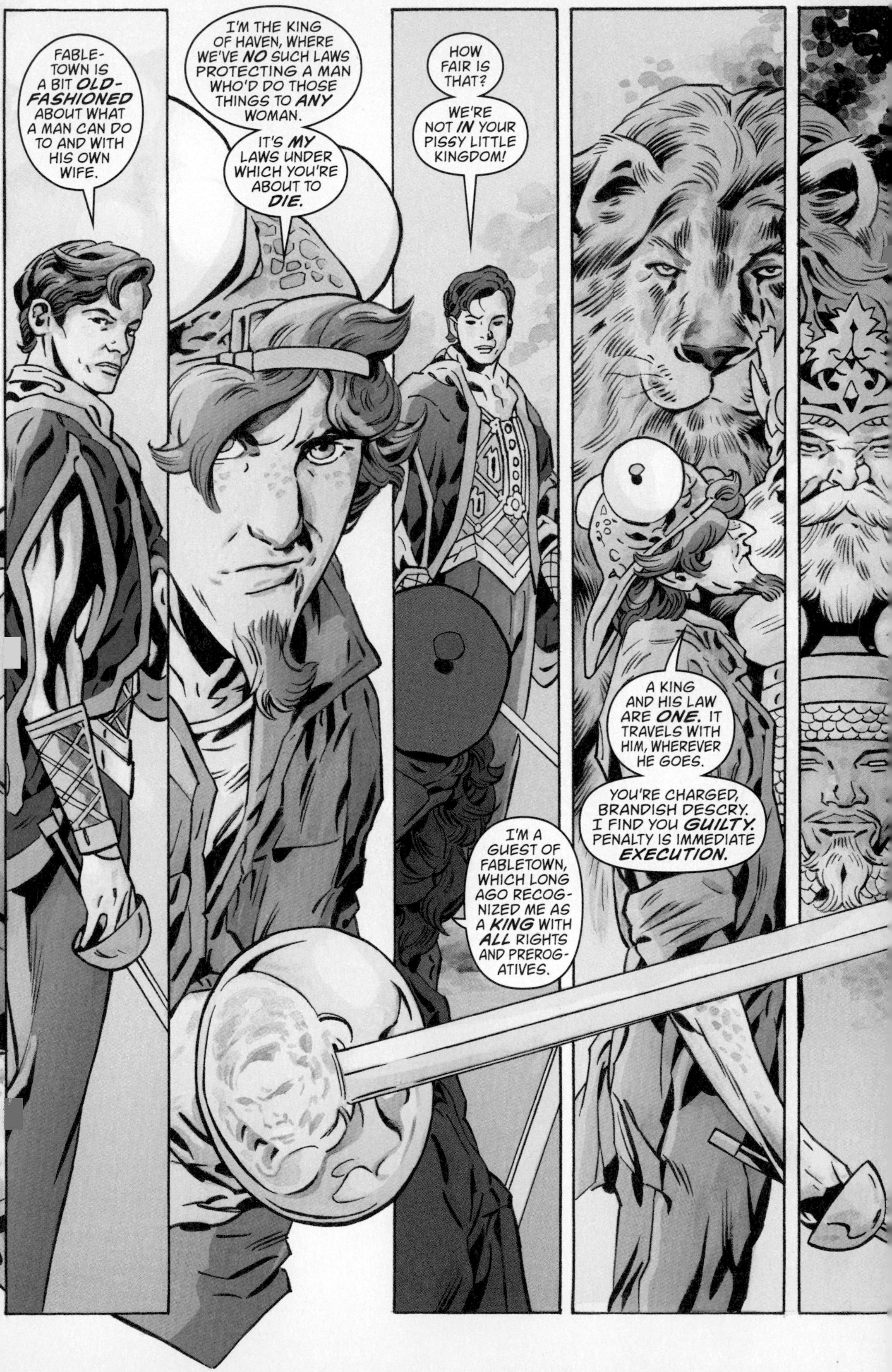
FABLE-TOWN IS A BIT OLD-FASHIONED ABOUT WHAT A MAN CAN DO TO AND WITH HIS OWN WIFE.
I'M THE KING OF HAVEN, WHERE WE'VE NO SUCH LAWS PROTECTING A MAN WHO'D DO THOSE THINGS TO ANY WOMAN.
IT'S MY LAWS UNDER WHICH YOU'RE ABOUT TO DIE.
HOW FAIR IS THAT?
WE'RE NOT IN YOUR PISSY LITTLE KINGDOM!
I'M A GUEST OF FABLETOWN, WHICH LONG AGO RECOG-NIZED ME AS A KING WITH ALL RIGHTS AND PREROG-ATIVES.
A KING AND HIS LAW ARE ONE. IT TRAVELS WITH HIM, WHEREVER HE GOES.
YOU'RE CHARGED, BRANDISH DESCRY. I FIND YOU GUILTY. PENALTY IS IMMEDIATE EXECUTION.

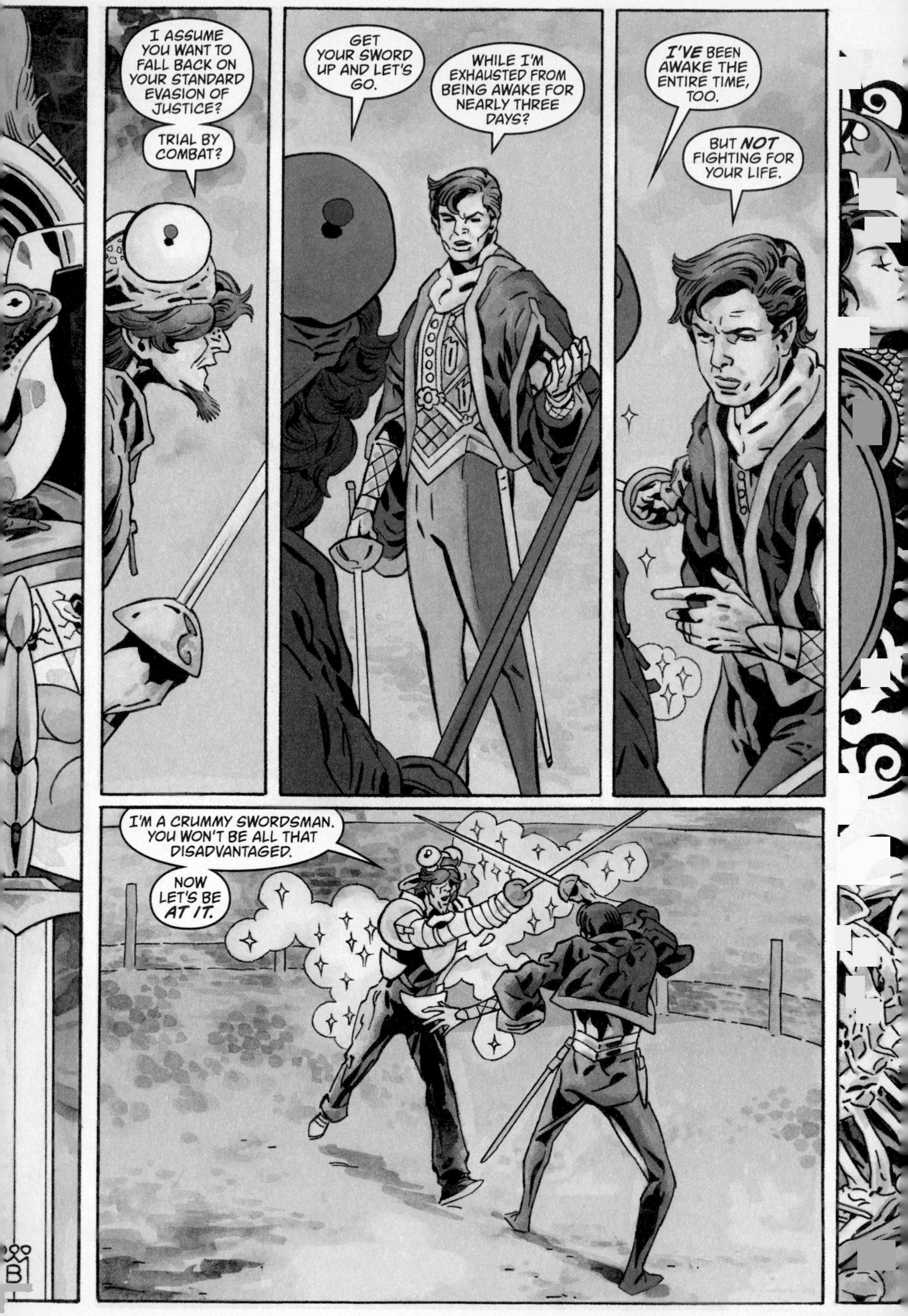
I ASSUME YOU WANT TO FALL BACK ON YOUR STANDARD EVASION OF JUSTICE?
TRIAL BY COMBAT?
GET YOUR SWORD UP AND LET'S GO.
WHILE I'M EXHAUSTED FROM BEING AWAKE FOR NEARLY THREE DAYS?
I'VE BEEN AWAKE THE ENTIRE TIME, TOO.
BUT NOT FIGHTING FOR YOUR LIFE.
I'M A CRUMMY SWORDSMAN. YOU WON'T BE ALL THAT DISADVANTAGED.
NOW LET'S BE AT IT.

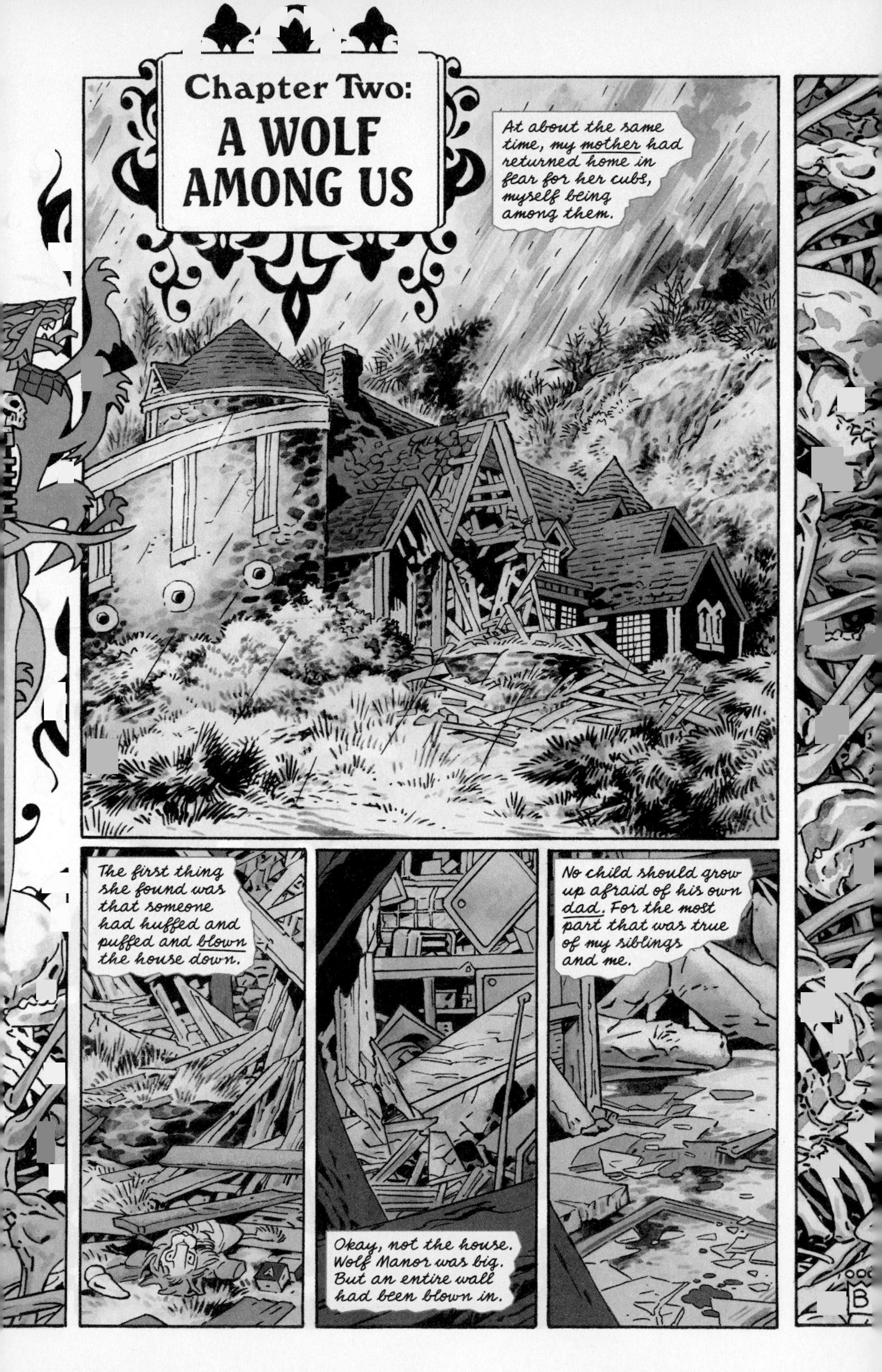
Chapter Two:
A WOLF AMONG US
At about the same time, my mother had returned home in fear for her cubs, myself being among them.
The first thing she found was that someone had huffed and puffed and blown the house down.
Okay, not the house. Wolf Manor was big. But an entire wall had been blown in.
No child should grow up afraid of his own dad. For the most part that was true of my siblings and me.

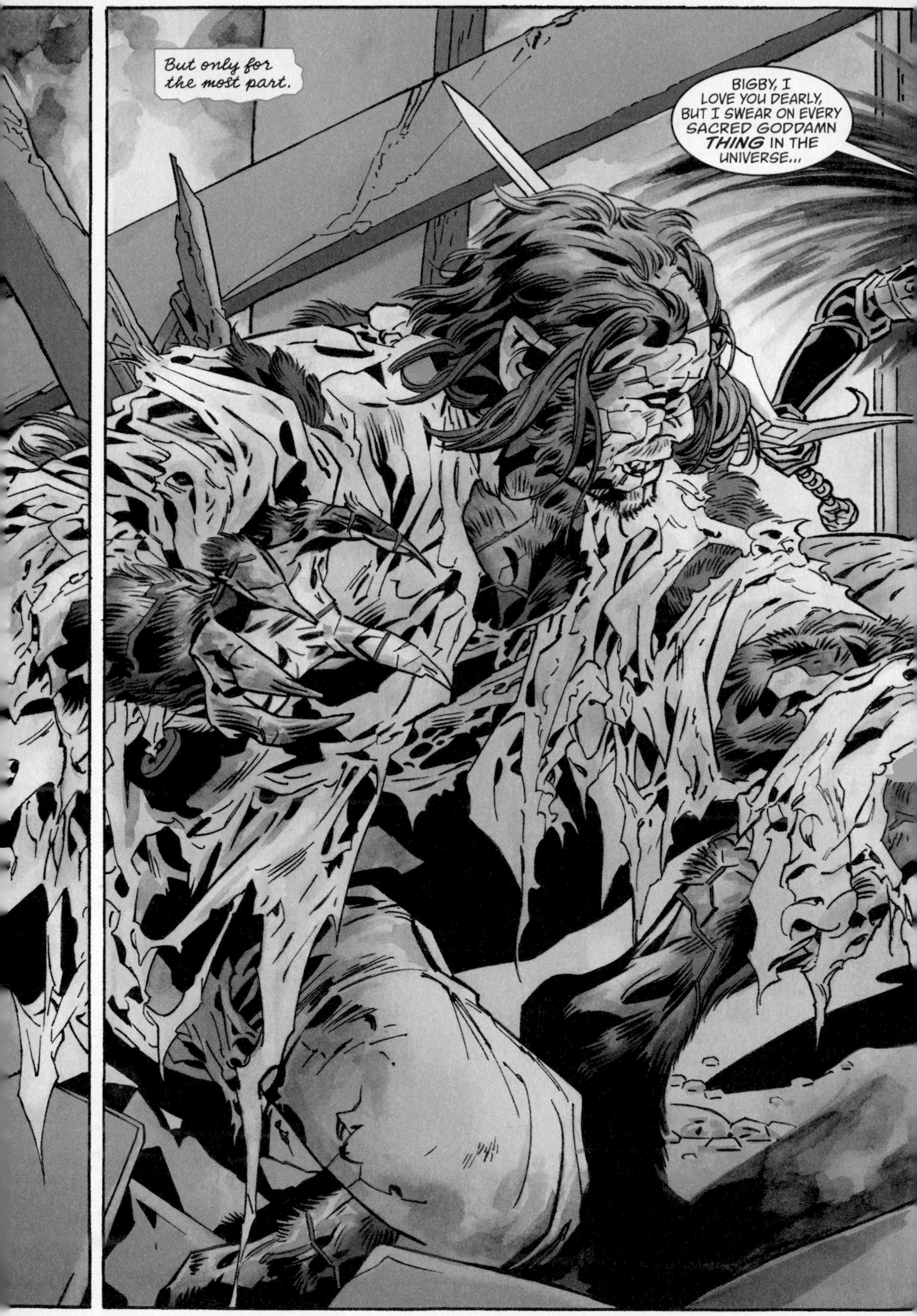
But only for the most part.
BIGBY, I LOVE YOU DEARLY, BUT I SWEAR ON EVERY SACRED GODDAMN THING IN THE UNIVERSE...

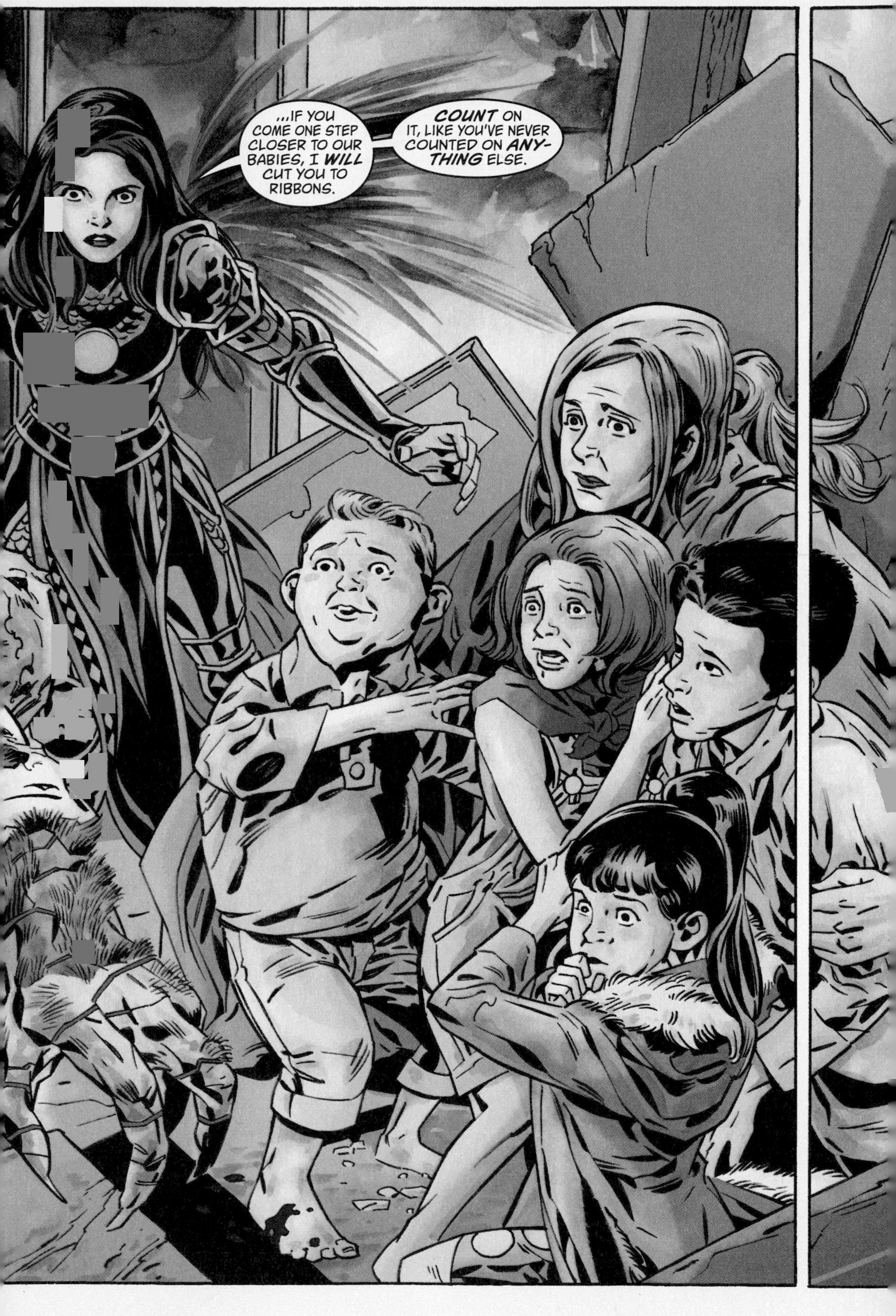
...IF YOU COME ONE STEP CLOSER TO OUR BABIES, I WILL CUT YOU TO RIBBONS.
COUNT ON IT, LIKE YOU'VE NEVER COUNTED ON ANYTHING ELSE.

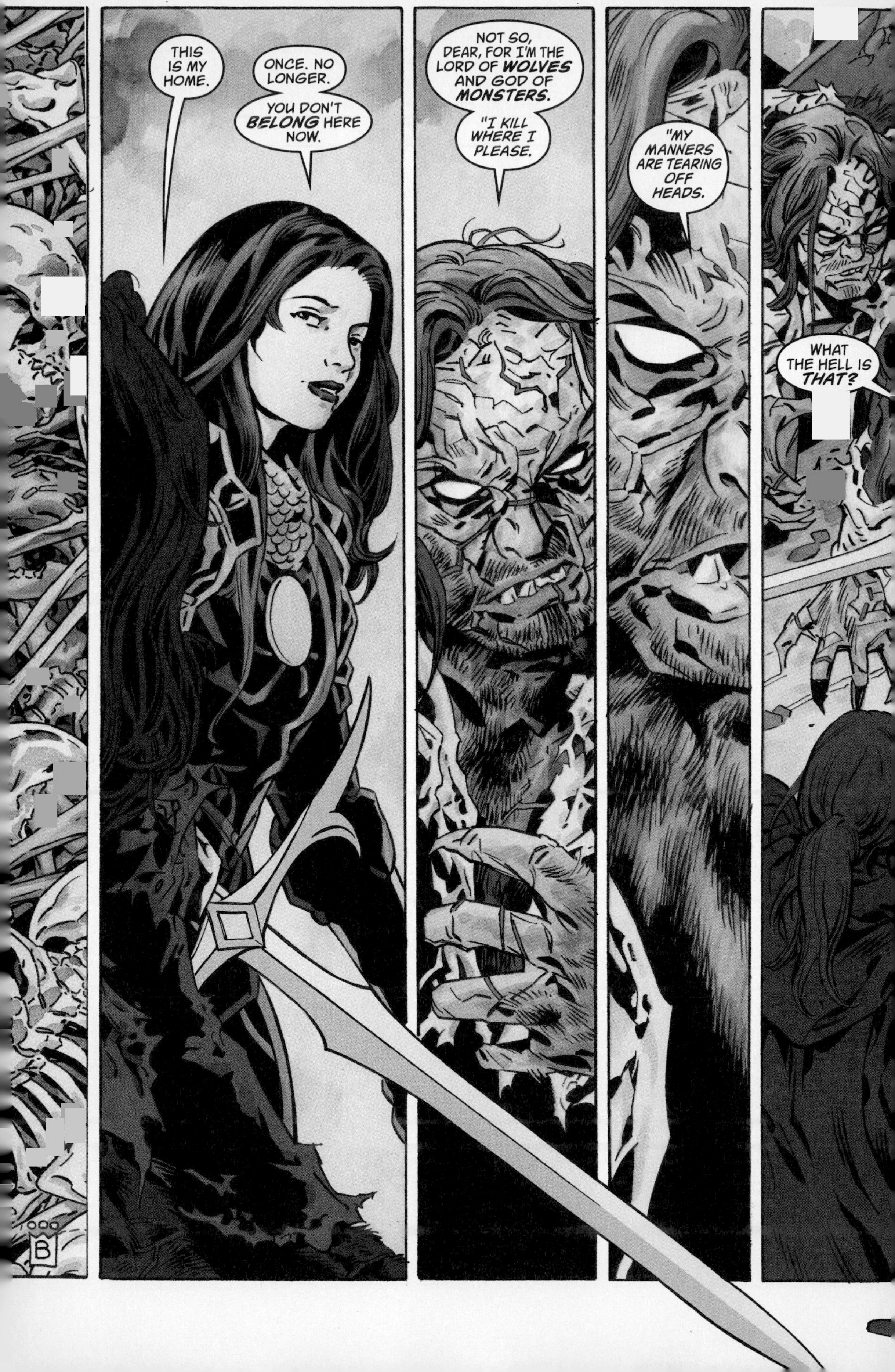
THIS IS MY HOME.
ONCE. NO LONGER.
YOU DON'T BELONG HERE NOW.
NOT SO, DEAR, FOR I'M THE LORD OF WOLVES AND GOD OF MONSTERS.
"I KILL WHERE I PLEASE.
"MY MANNERS ARE TEARING OFF HEADS.
WHAT THE HELL IS THAT?

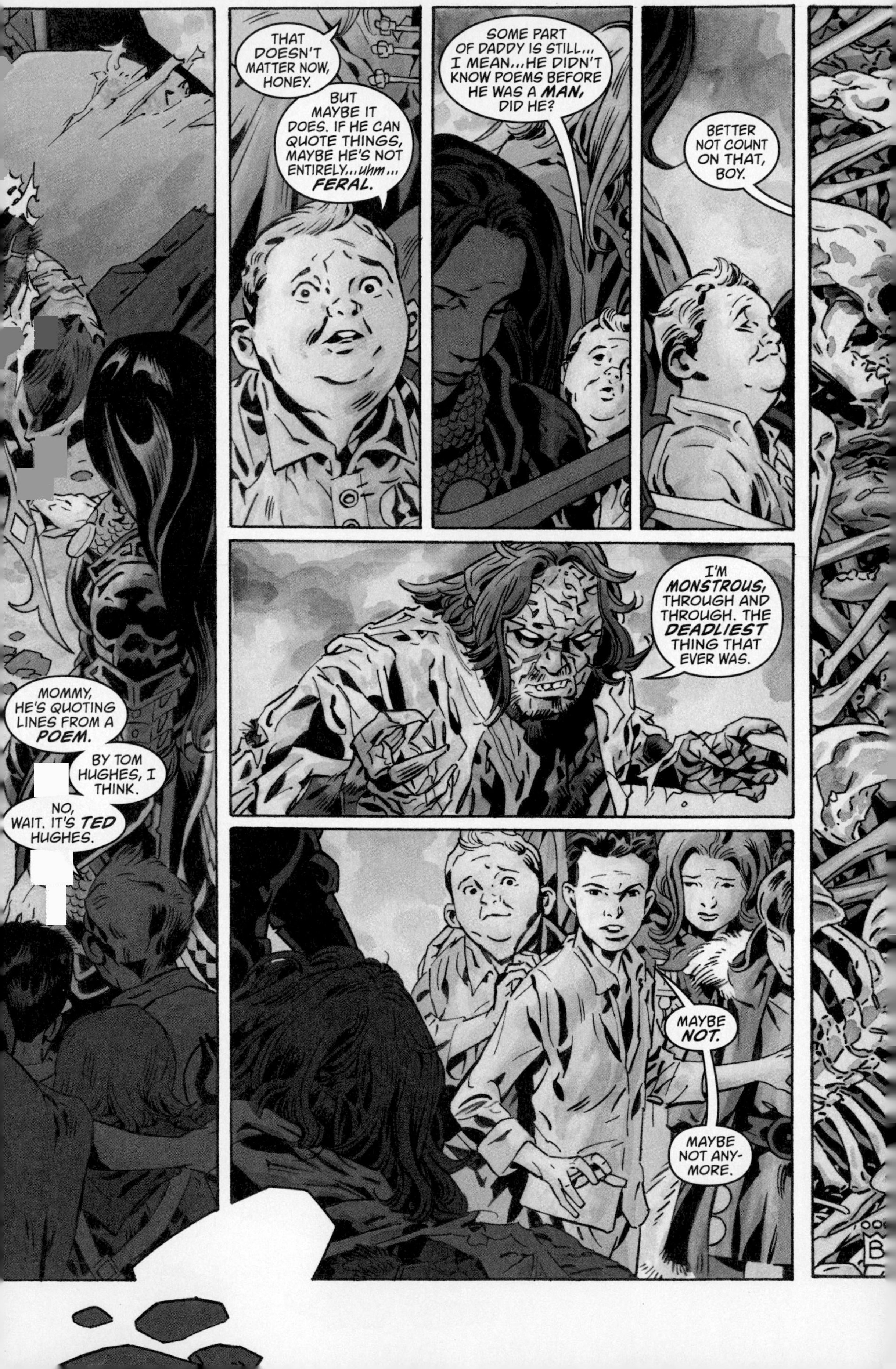
MOMMY, HE'S QUOTING LINES FROM A **POEM**.
BY TOM HUGHES, I THINK.
NO, WAIT. IT'S **TED** HUGHES.
THAT DOESN'T MATTER NOW, HONEY.
BUT MAYBE IT DOES. IF HE CAN QUOTE THINGS, MAYBE HE'S NOT ENTIRELY... *uhm*... **FERAL**.
SOME PART OF DADDY IS STILL... I MEAN... HE DIDN'T KNOW POEMS BEFORE HE WAS A **MAN**, DID HE?
BETTER NOT COUNT ON THAT, BOY.
I'M **MONSTROUS**, THROUGH AND THROUGH. THE **DEADLIEST** THING THAT EVER WAS.
MAYBE **NOT**.
MAYBE NOT ANY-MORE.

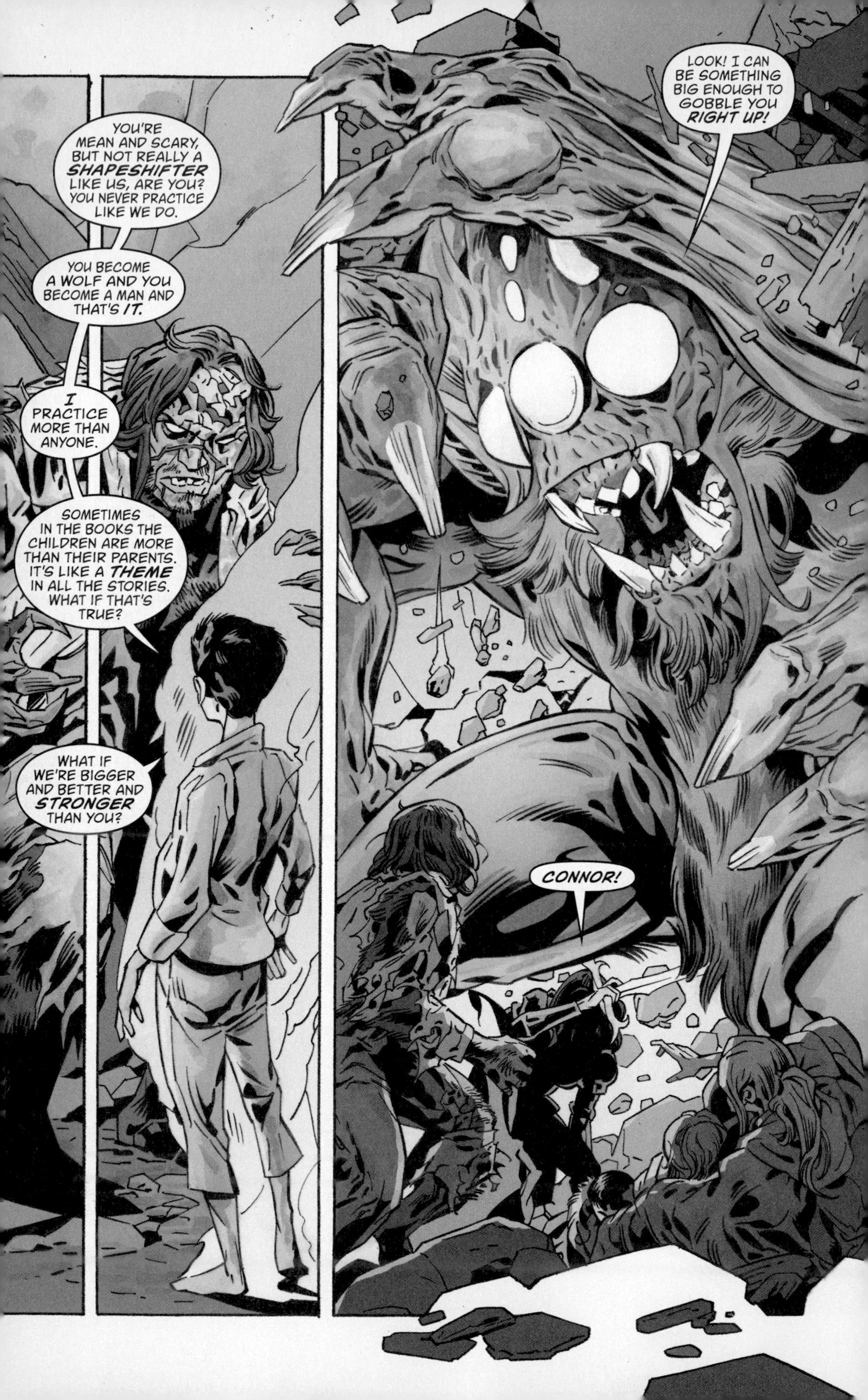
YOU'RE MEAN AND SCARY, BUT NOT REALLY A SHAPESHIFTER LIKE US, ARE YOU? YOU NEVER PRACTICE LIKE WE DO.
YOU BECOME A WOLF AND YOU BECOME A MAN AND THAT'S IT.
I PRACTICE MORE THAN ANYONE.
SOMETIMES IN THE BOOKS THE CHILDREN ARE MORE THAN THEIR PARENTS. IT'S LIKE A THEME IN ALL THE STORIES. WHAT IF THAT'S TRUE?
WHAT IF WE'RE BIGGER AND BETTER AND STRONGER THAN YOU?
LOOK! I CAN BE SOMETHING BIG ENOUGH TO GOBBLE YOU RIGHT UP!
CONNOR!

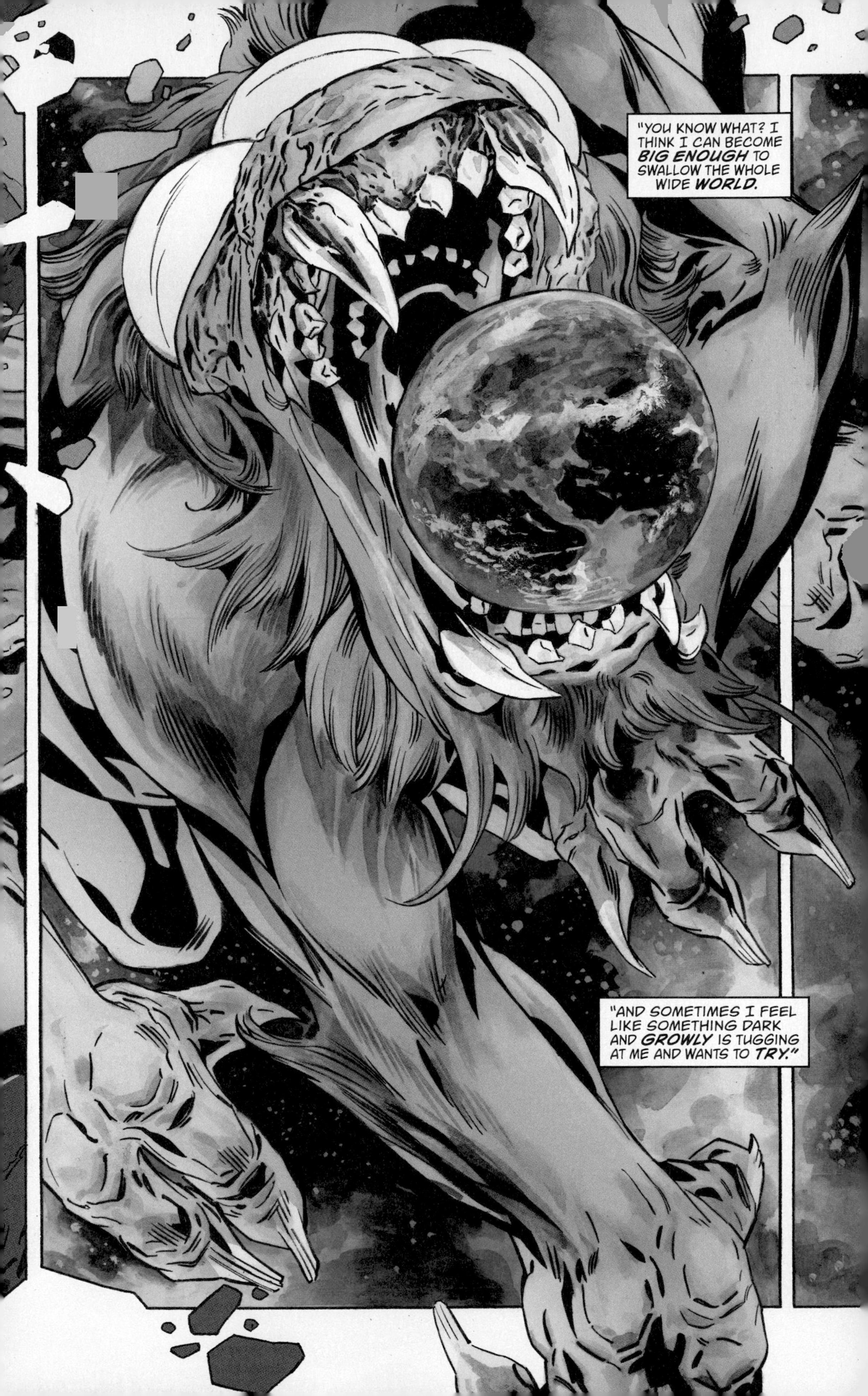
"YOU KNOW WHAT? I THINK I CAN BECOME BIG ENOUGH TO SWALLOW THE WHOLE WIDE WORLD.
"AND SOMETIMES I FEEL LIKE SOMETHING DARK AND GROWLY IS TUGGING AT ME AND WANTS TO TRY."

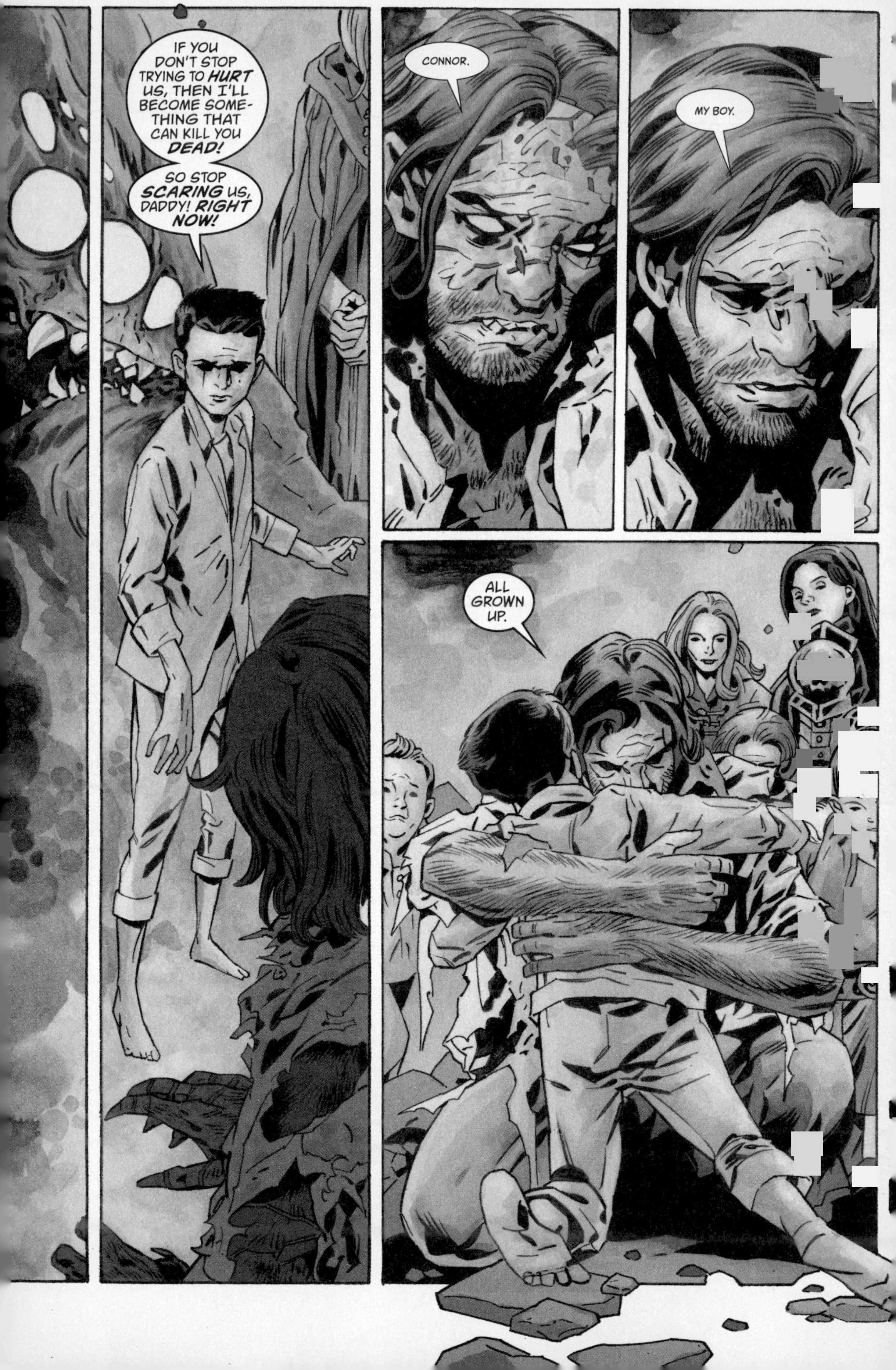
IF YOU DON'T STOP TRYING TO HURT US, THEN I'LL BECOME SOMETHING THAT CAN KILL YOU DEAD!
SO STOP SCARING US, DADDY! RIGHT NOW!
CONNOR.
MY BOY.
ALL GROWN UP.

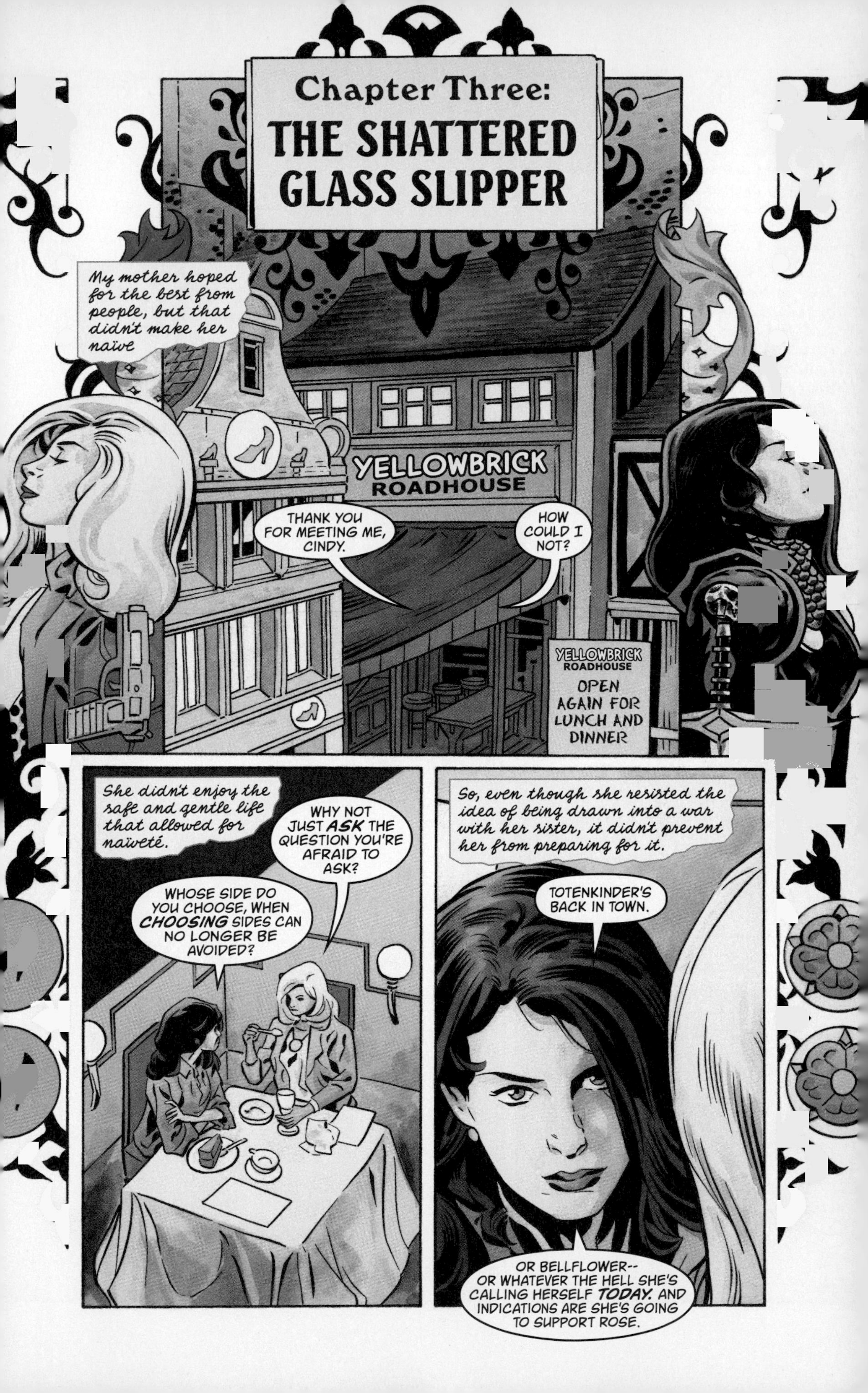
Chapter Three:
THE SHATTERED GLASS SLIPPER
My mother hoped for the best from people, but that didn't make her naïve
YELLOWBRICK ROADHOUSE
THANK YOU FOR MEETING ME, CINDY.
HOW COULD I NOT?
YELLOWBRICK ROADHOUSE OPEN AGAIN FOR LUNCH AND DINNER
She didn't enjoy the safe and gentle life that allowed for naïveté.
WHY NOT JUST ASK THE QUESTION YOU'RE AFRAID TO ASK?
WHOSE SIDE DO YOU CHOOSE, WHEN CHOOSING SIDES CAN NO LONGER BE AVOIDED?
So, even though she resisted the idea of being drawn into a war with her sister, it didn't prevent her from preparing for it.
TOTENKINDER'S BACK IN TOWN.
OR BELLFLOWER-- OR WHATEVER THE HELL SHE'S CALLING HERSELF TODAY. AND INDICATIONS ARE SHE'S GOING TO SUPPORT ROSE.

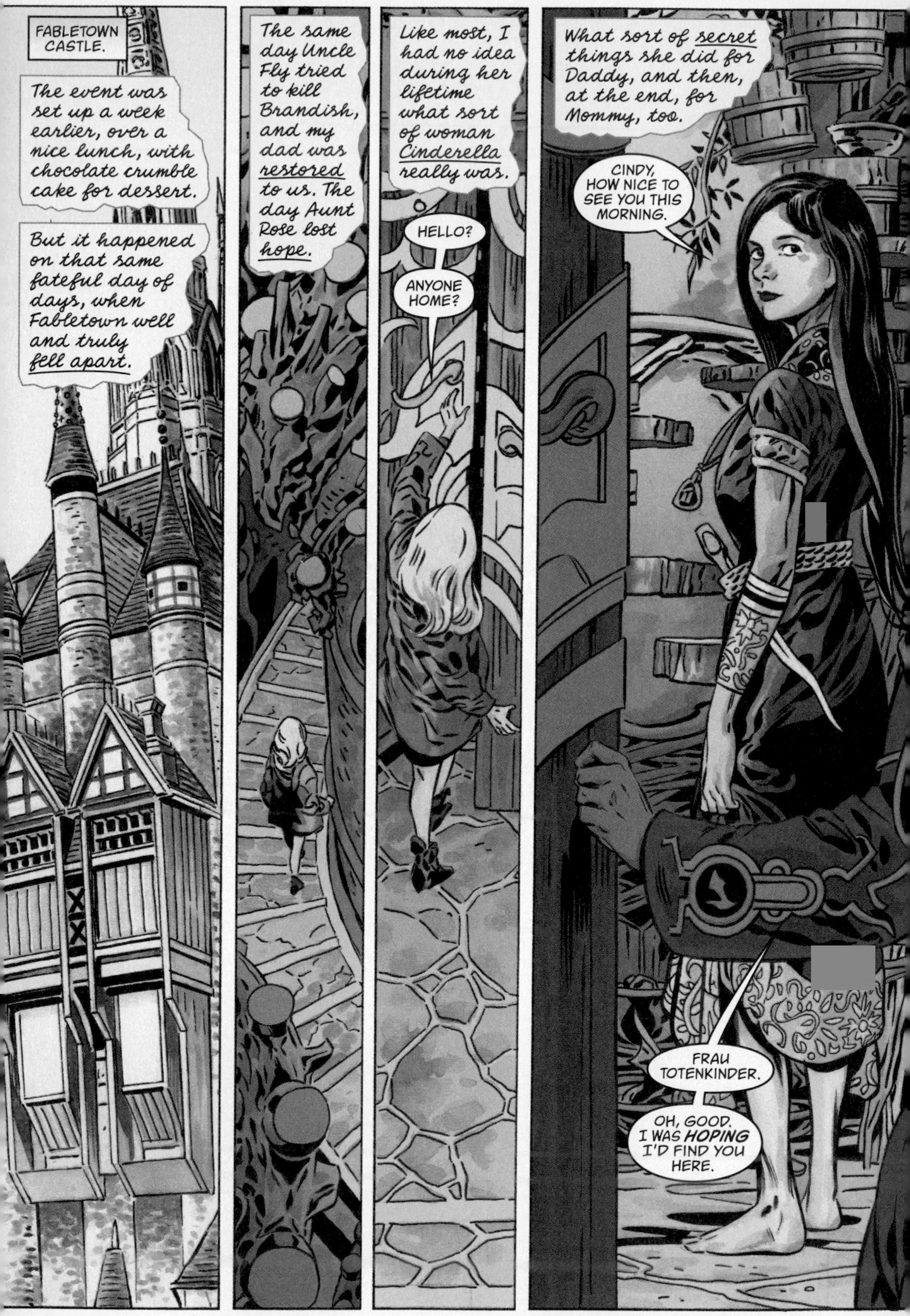

FABLETOWN CASTLE.
The event was set up a week earlier, over a nice lunch, with chocolate crumble cake for dessert.
But it happened on that same fateful day of days, when Fabletown well and truly fell apart.
The same day Uncle Fly tried to kill Brandish, and my dad was restored to us. The day Aunt Rose lost hope.
Like most, I had no idea during her lifetime what sort of woman Cinderella really was.
HELLO?
ANYONE HOME?
What sort of secret things she did for Daddy, and then, at the end, for Mommy, too.
CINDY, HOW NICE TO SEE YOU THIS MORNING.
FRAU TOTENKINDER.
OH, GOOD. I WAS HOPING I'D FIND YOU HERE.

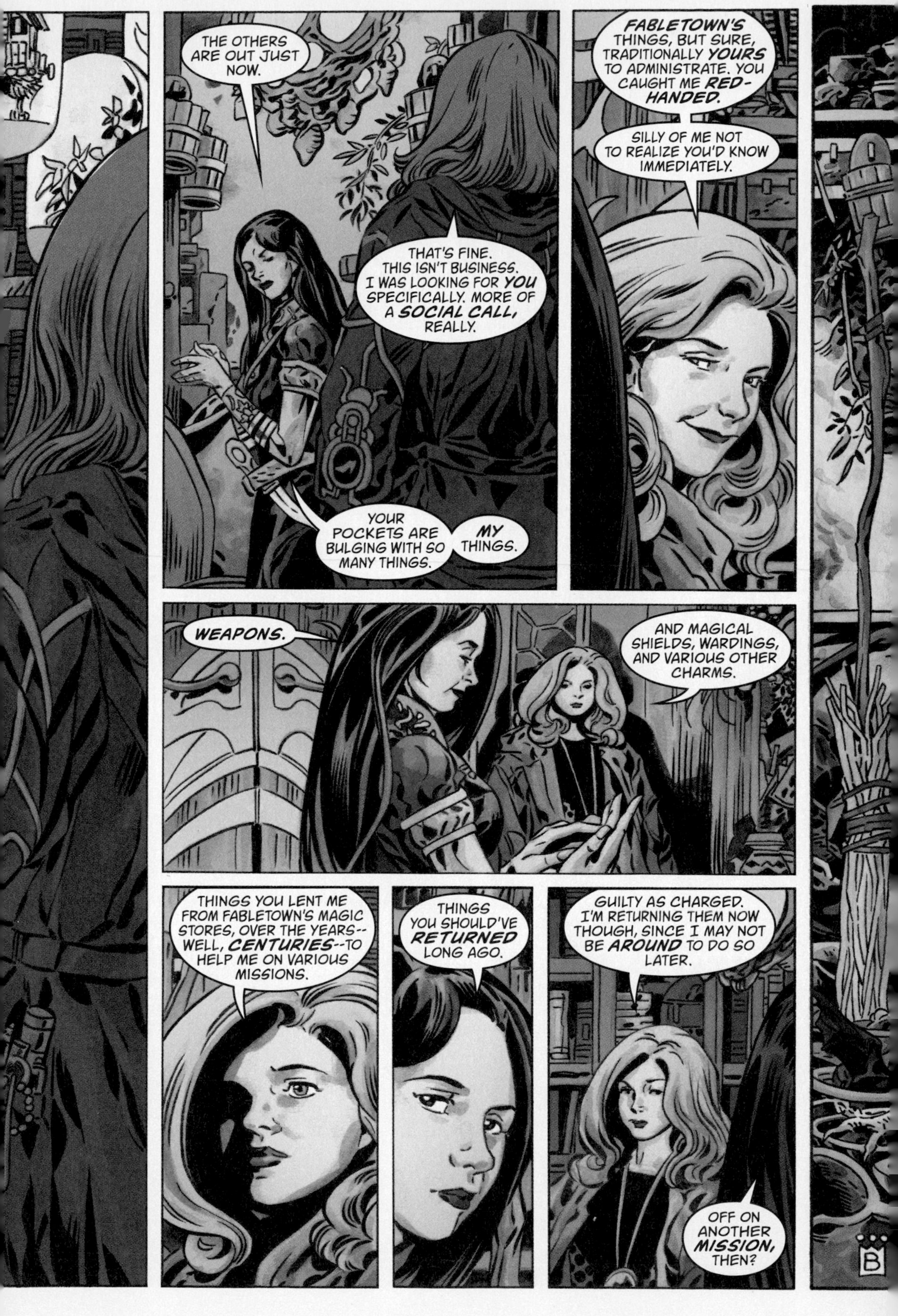

THE OTHERS ARE OUT JUST NOW.
THAT'S FINE. THIS ISN'T BUSINESS. I WAS LOOKING FOR YOU SPECIFICALLY. MORE OF A SOCIAL CALL, REALLY.
YOUR POCKETS ARE BULGING WITH SO MANY THINGS.
MY THINGS.
FABLETOWN'S THINGS, BUT SURE, TRADITIONALLY YOURS TO ADMINISTRATE. YOU CAUGHT ME RED-HANDED.
SILLY OF ME NOT TO REALIZE YOU'D KNOW IMMEDIATELY.
WEAPONS.
AND MAGICAL SHIELDS, WARDINGS, AND VARIOUS OTHER CHARMS.
THINGS YOU LENT ME FROM FABLETOWN'S MAGIC STORES, OVER THE YEARS--WELL, CENTURIES--TO HELP ME ON VARIOUS MISSIONS.
THINGS YOU SHOULD'VE RETURNED LONG AGO.
GUILTY AS CHARGED. I'M RETURNING THEM NOW THOUGH, SINCE I MAY NOT BE AROUND TO DO SO LATER.
OFF ON ANOTHER MISSION, THEN?

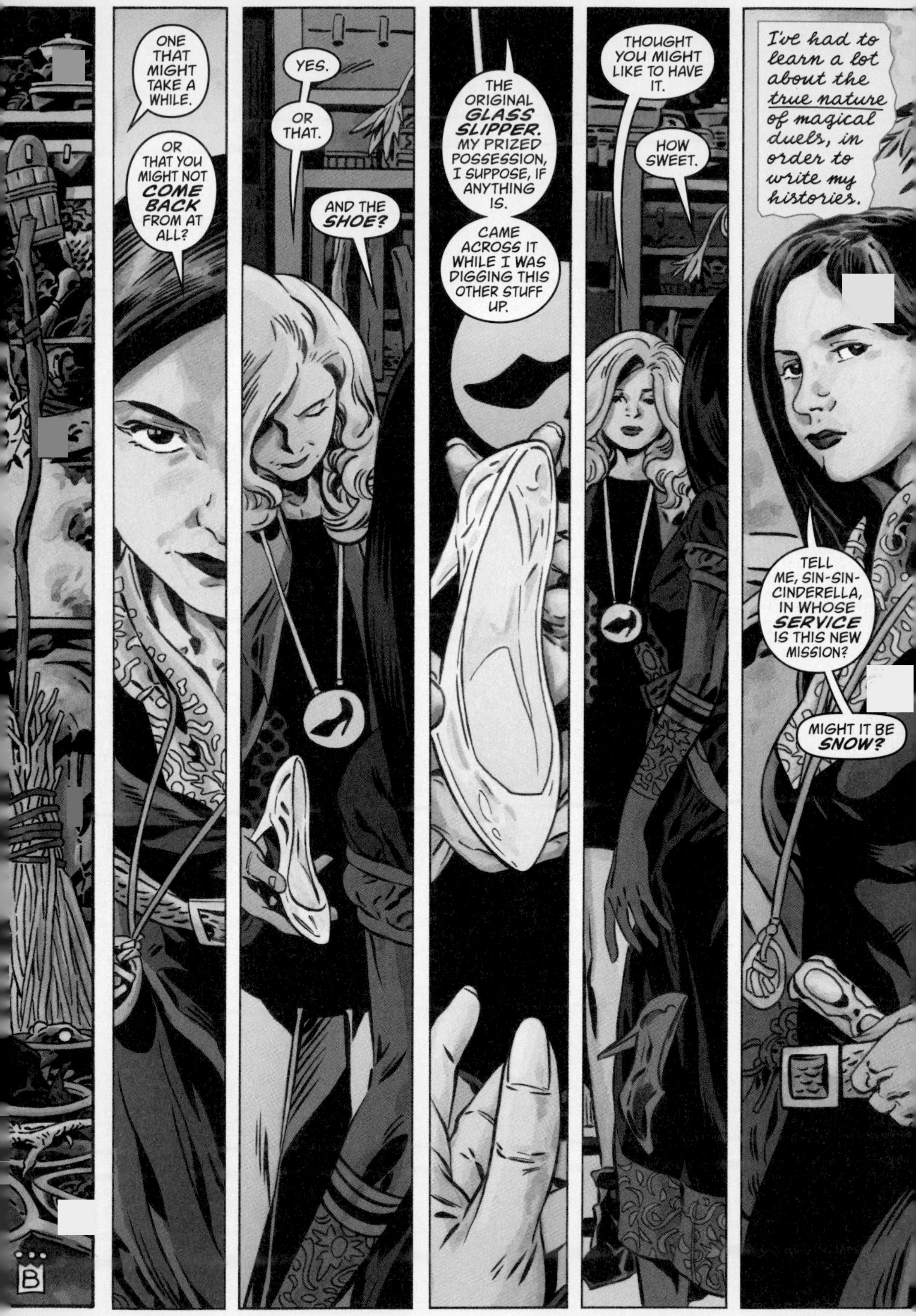
ONE THAT MIGHT TAKE A WHILE.
OR THAT YOU MIGHT NOT COME BACK FROM AT ALL?
YES.
OR THAT.
AND THE SHOE?
THE ORIGINAL GLASS SLIPPER. MY PRIZED POSSESSION, I SUPPOSE, IF ANYTHING IS.
CAME ACROSS IT WHILE I WAS DIGGING THIS OTHER STUFF UP.
THOUGHT YOU MIGHT LIKE TO HAVE IT.
HOW SWEET.
I've had to learn a lot about the true nature of magical duels, in order to write my histories.
TELL ME, SIN-SIN-CINDERELLA, IN WHOSE SERVICE IS THIS NEW MISSION?
MIGHT IT BE SNOW?

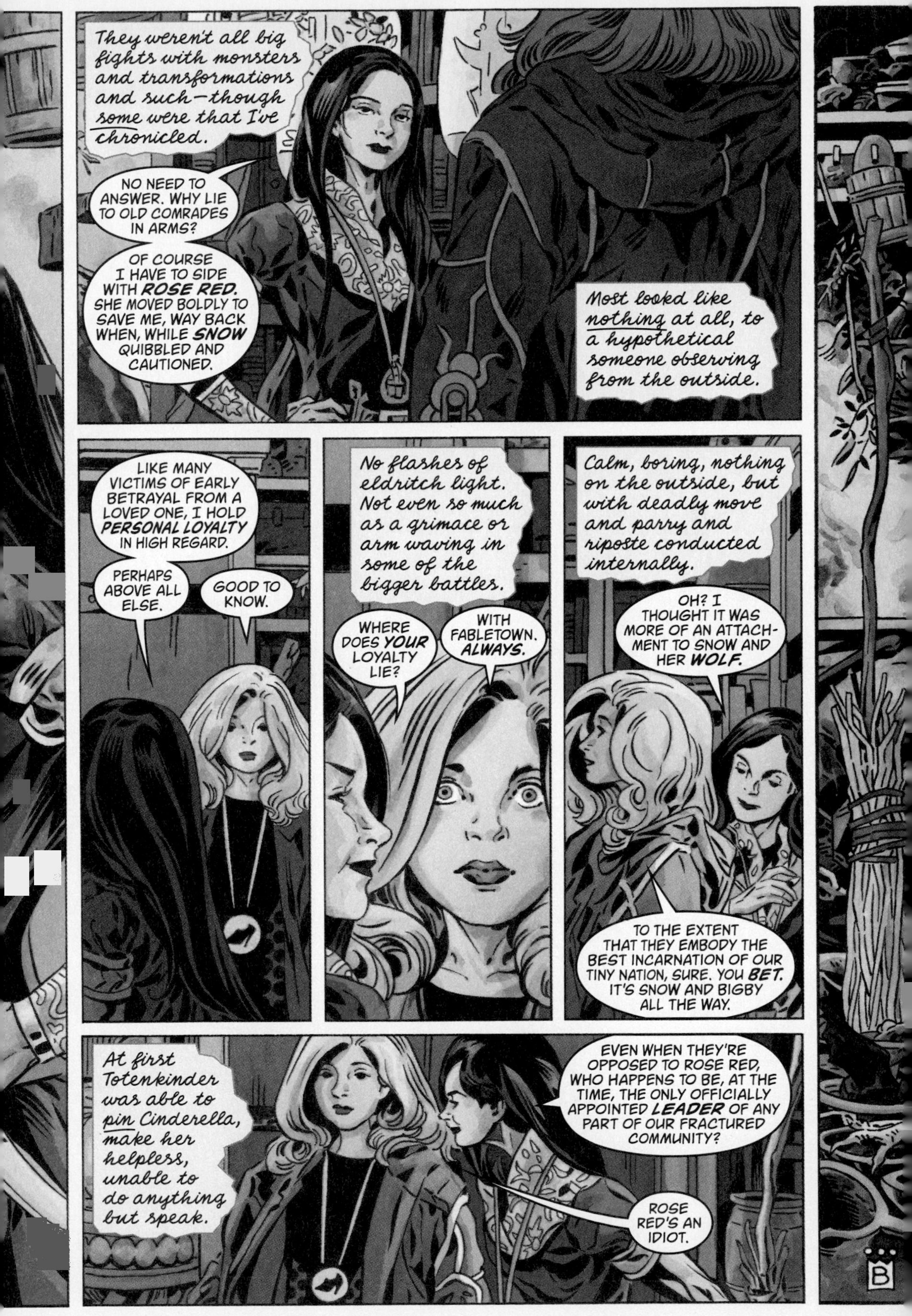
They weren't all big fights with monsters and transformations and such—though some were that I've chronicled.
NO NEED TO ANSWER. WHY LIE TO OLD COMRADES IN ARMS?
OF COURSE I HAVE TO SIDE WITH ROSE RED. SHE MOVED BOLDLY TO SAVE ME, WAY BACK WHEN, WHILE SNOW QUIBBLED AND CAUTIONED.
Most looked like nothing at all, to a hypothetical someone observing from the outside.
LIKE MANY VICTIMS OF EARLY BETRAYAL FROM A LOVED ONE, I HOLD PERSONAL LOYALTY IN HIGH REGARD.
PERHAPS ABOVE ALL ELSE.
GOOD TO KNOW.
No flashes of eldritch light. Not even so much as a grimace or arm waving in some of the bigger battles.
WHERE DOES YOUR LOYALTY LIE?
WITH FABLETOWN. ALWAYS.
Calm, boring, nothing on the outside, but with deadly move and parry and riposte conducted internally.
OH? I THOUGHT IT WAS MORE OF AN ATTACHMENT TO SNOW AND HER WOLF.
TO THE EXTENT THAT THEY EMBODY THE BEST INCARNATION OF OUR TINY NATION, SURE. YOU BET. IT'S SNOW AND BIGBY ALL THE WAY.
At first Totenkinder was able to pin Cinderella, make her helpless, unable to do anything but speak.
EVEN WHEN THEY'RE OPPOSED TO ROSE RED, WHO HAPPENS TO BE, AT THE TIME, THE ONLY OFFICIALLY APPOINTED LEADER OF ANY PART OF OUR FRACTURED COMMUNITY?
ROSE RED'S AN IDIOT.

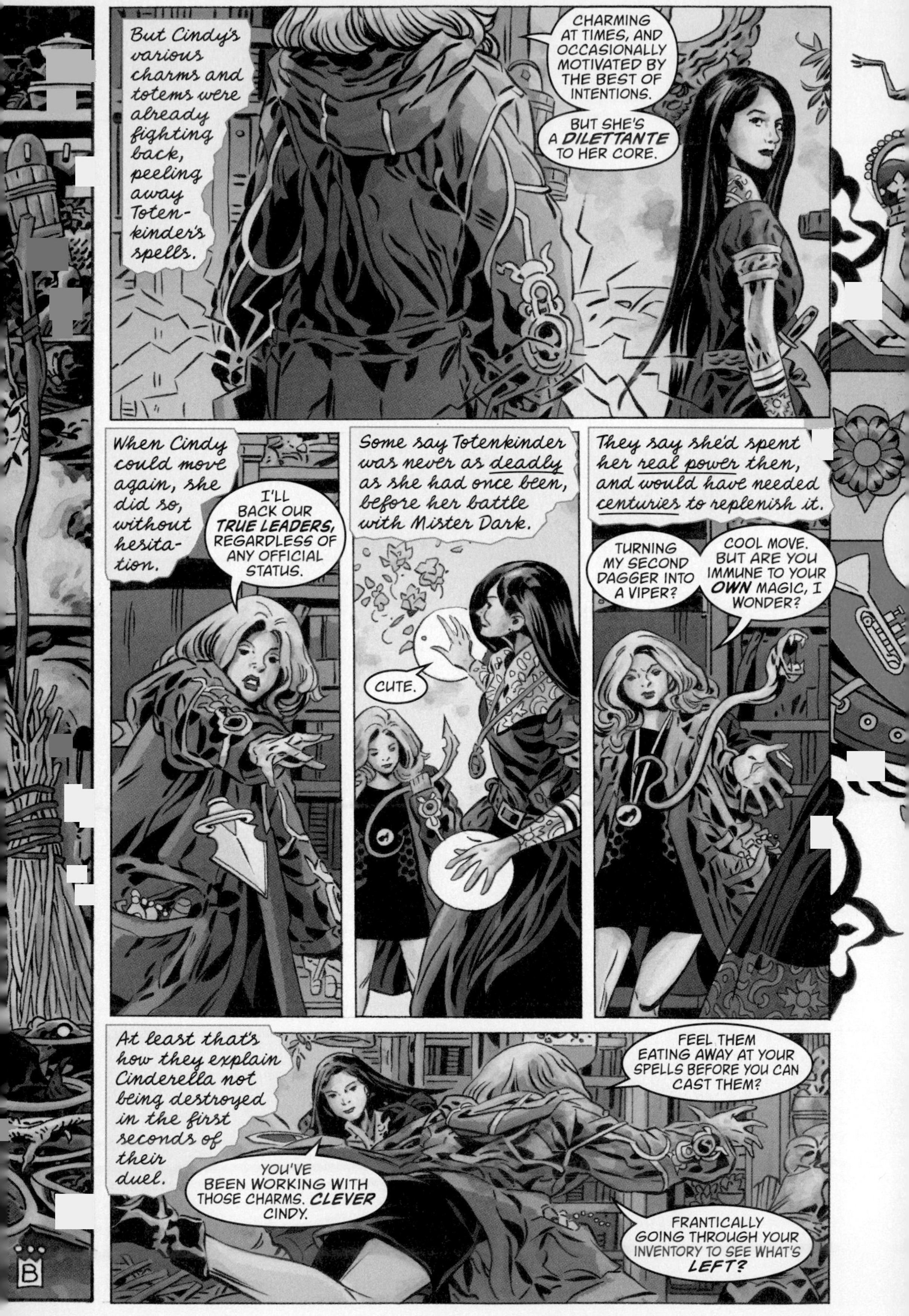
But Cindy's various charms and totems were already fighting back, peeling away Toten-kinder's spells.
CHARMING AT TIMES, AND OCCASIONALLY MOTIVATED BY THE BEST OF INTENTIONS.
BUT SHE'S A DILETTANTE TO HER CORE.
When Cindy could move again, she did so, without hesita-tion.
I'LL BACK OUR TRUE LEADERS, REGARDLESS OF ANY OFFICIAL STATUS.
Some say Totenkinder was never as deadly as she had once been, before her battle with Mister Dark.
CUTE.
They say she'd spent her real power then, and would have needed centuries to replenish it.
TURNING MY SECOND DAGGER INTO A VIPER?
COOL MOVE. BUT ARE YOU IMMUNE TO YOUR OWN MAGIC, I WONDER?
At least that's how they explain Cinderella not being destroyed in the first seconds of their duel.
FEEL THEM EATING AWAY AT YOUR SPELLS BEFORE YOU CAN CAST THEM?
YOU'VE BEEN WORKING WITH THOSE CHARMS. CLEVER CINDY.
FRANTICALLY GOING THROUGH YOUR INVENTORY TO SEE WHAT'S LEFT?

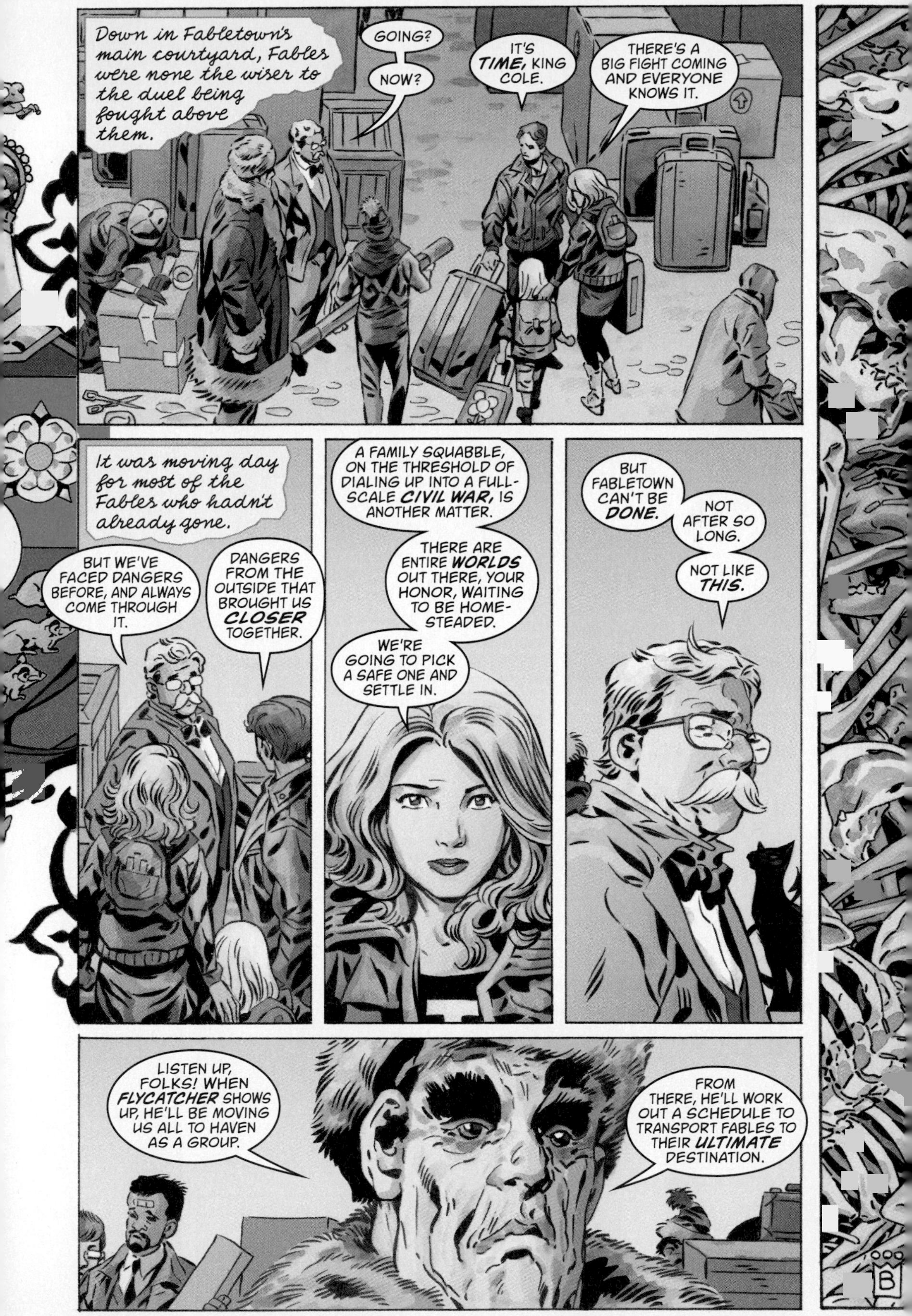

Down in Fabletown's main courtyard, Fables were none the wiser to the duel being fought above them.
GOING?
NOW?
IT'S TIME, KING COLE.
THERE'S A BIG FIGHT COMING AND EVERYONE KNOWS IT.
It was moving day for most of the Fables who hadn't already gone.
BUT WE'VE FACED DANGERS BEFORE, AND ALWAYS COME THROUGH IT.
DANGERS FROM THE OUTSIDE THAT BROUGHT US CLOSER TOGETHER.
A FAMILY SQUABBLE, ON THE THRESHOLD OF DIALING UP INTO A FULL-SCALE CIVIL WAR, IS ANOTHER MATTER.
THERE ARE ENTIRE WORLDS OUT THERE, YOUR HONOR, WAITING TO BE HOME-STEADED.
WE'RE GOING TO PICK A SAFE ONE AND SETTLE IN.
BUT FABLETOWN CAN'T BE DONE.
NOT AFTER SO LONG.
NOT LIKE THIS.
LISTEN UP, FOLKS! WHEN FLYCATCHER SHOWS UP, HE'LL BE MOVING US ALL TO HAVEN AS A GROUP.
FROM THERE, HE'LL WORK OUT A SCHEDULE TO TRANSPORT FABLES TO THEIR ULTIMATE DESTINATION.

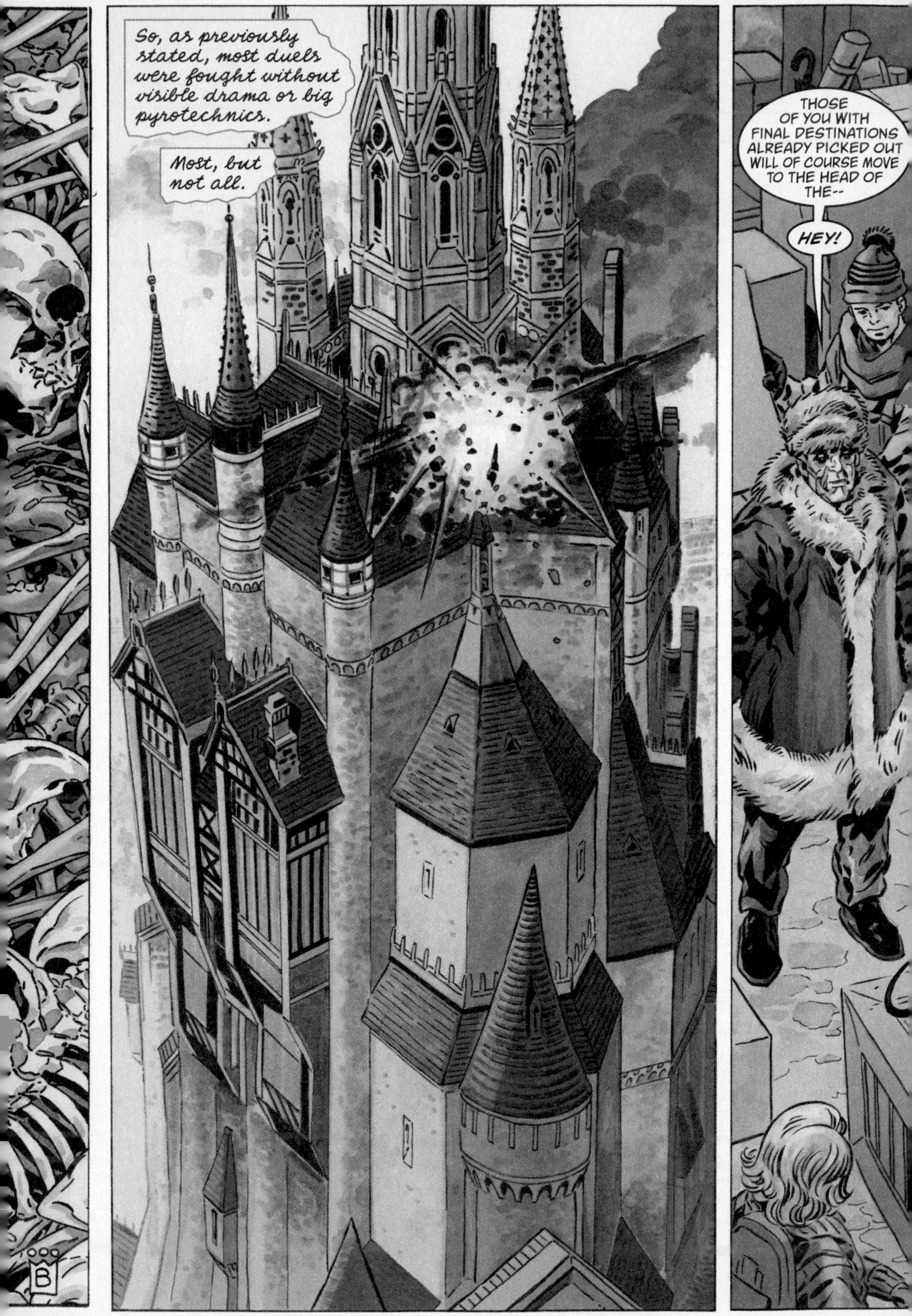
So, as previously stated, most duels were fought without visible drama or big pyrotechnics.
Most, but not all.
THOSE OF YOU WITH FINAL DESTINATIONS ALREADY PICKED OUT WILL OF COURSE MOVE TO THE HEAD OF THE--
HEY!

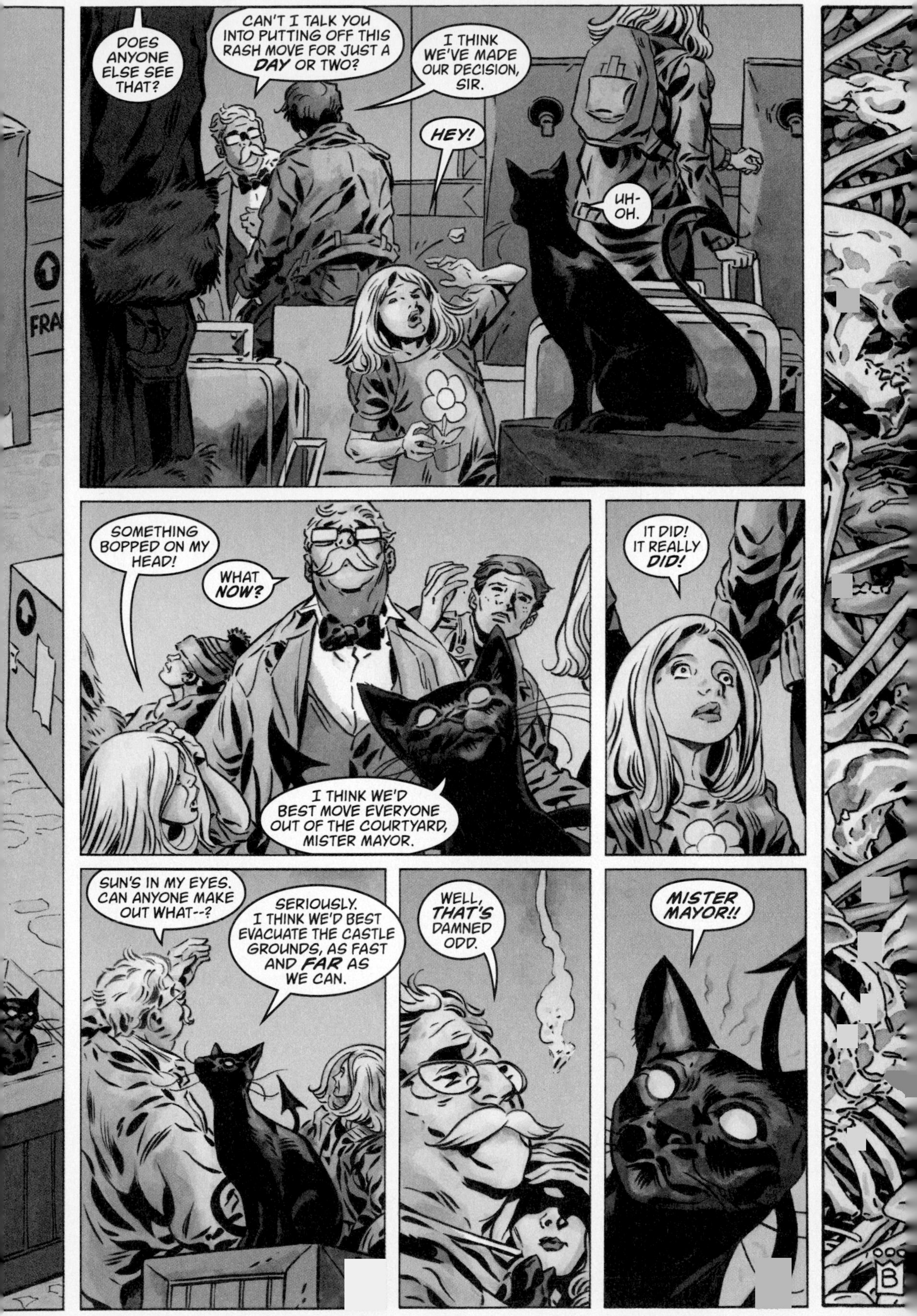

DOES ANYONE ELSE SEE THAT?
CAN'T I TALK YOU INTO PUTTING OFF THIS RASH MOVE FOR JUST A DAY OR TWO?
I THINK WE'VE MADE OUR DECISION, SIR.
HEY!
UH-OH.
FRA
SOMETHING BOPPED ON MY HEAD!
WHAT NOW?
I THINK WE'D BEST MOVE EVERYONE OUT OF THE COURTYARD, MISTER MAYOR.
IT DID! IT REALLY DID!
SUN'S IN MY EYES. CAN ANYONE MAKE OUT WHAT--?
SERIOUSLY. I THINK WE'D BEST EVACUATE THE CASTLE GROUNDS, AS FAST AND FAR AS WE CAN.
WELL, THAT'S DAMNED ODD.
MISTER MAYOR!!

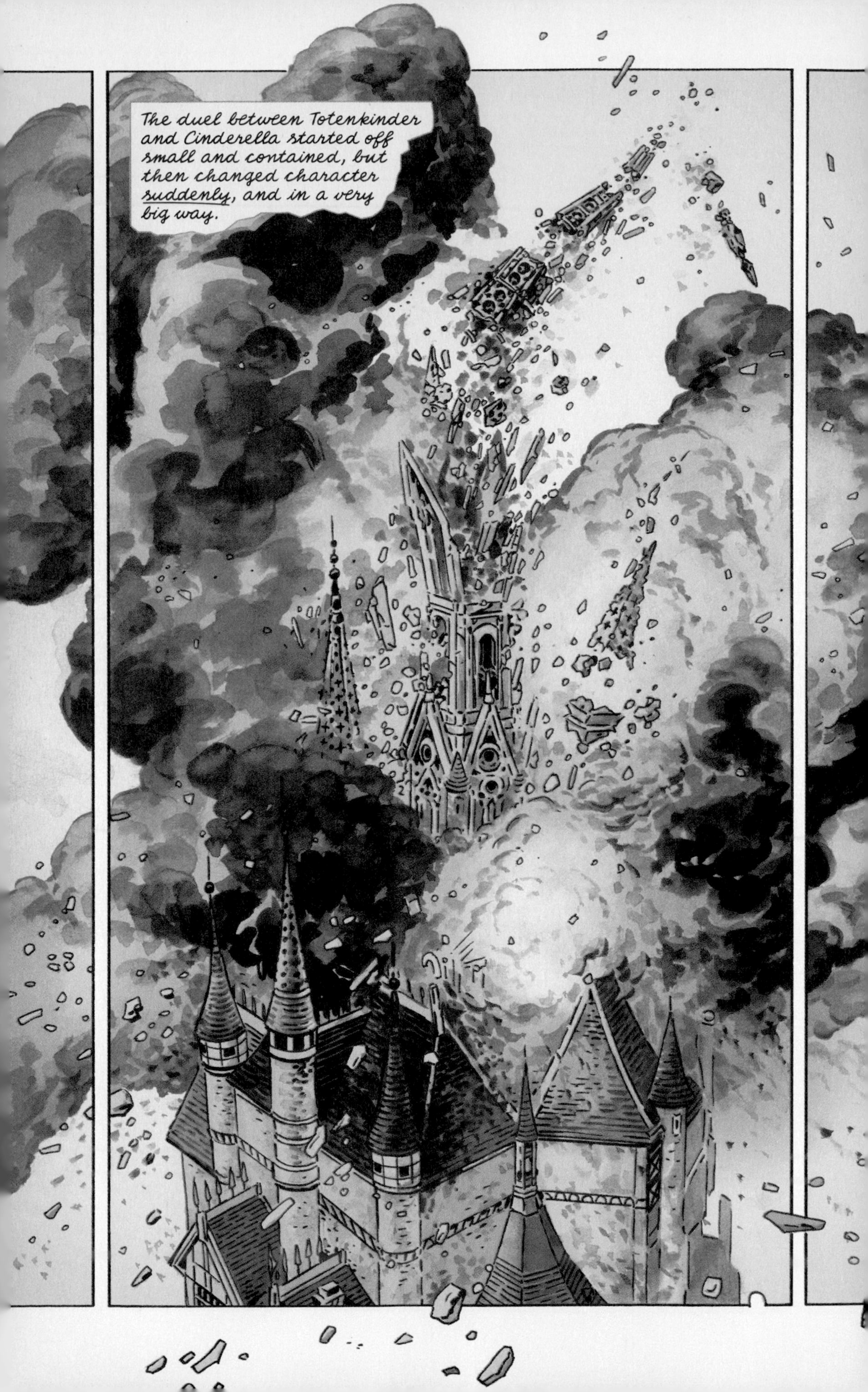
The duel between Totenkinder and Cinderella started off small and contained, but then changed character suddenly, and in a very big way.

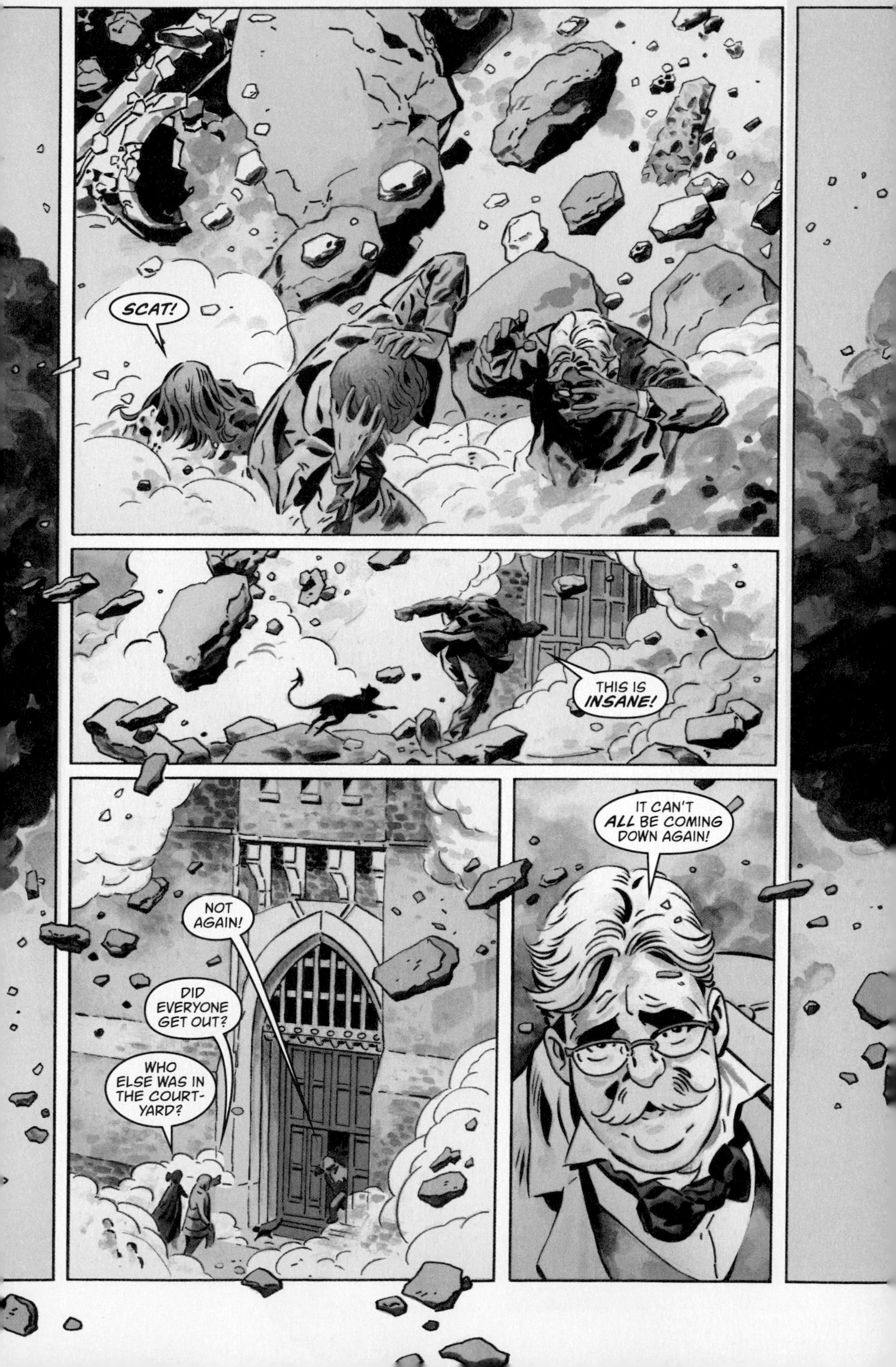
SCAT!
THIS IS INSANE!
NOT AGAIN!
DID EVERYONE GET OUT?
WHO ELSE WAS IN THE COURT-YARD?
IT CAN'T ALL BE COMING DOWN AGAIN!

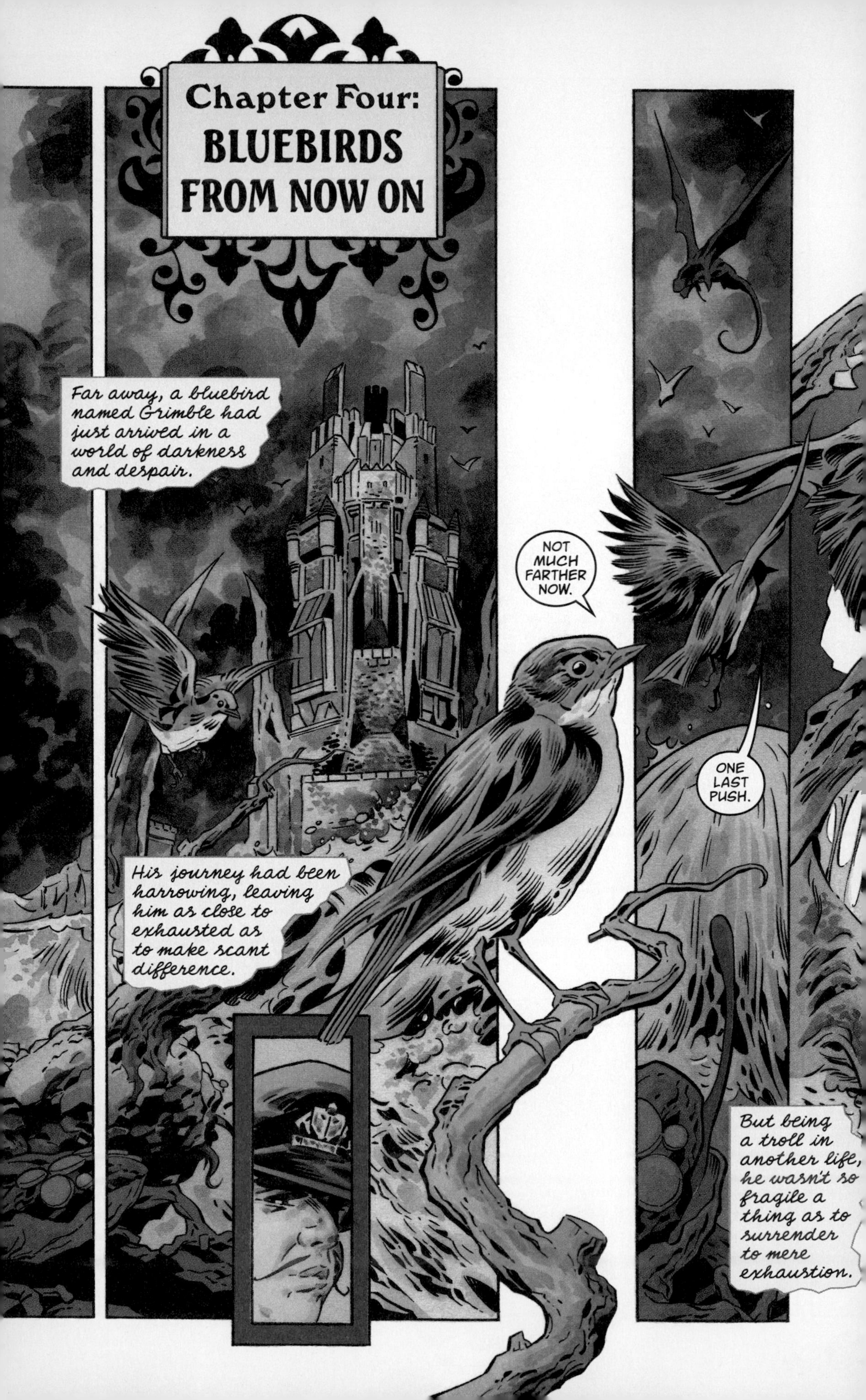
Chapter Four:
BLUEBIRDS FROM NOW ON
Far away, a bluebird named Grimble had just arrived in a world of darkness and despair.
His journey had been harrowing, leaving him as close to exhausted as to make scant difference.
NOT MUCH FARTHER NOW.
ONE LAST PUSH.
But being a troll in another life, he wasn't so fragile a thing as to surrender to mere exhaustion.

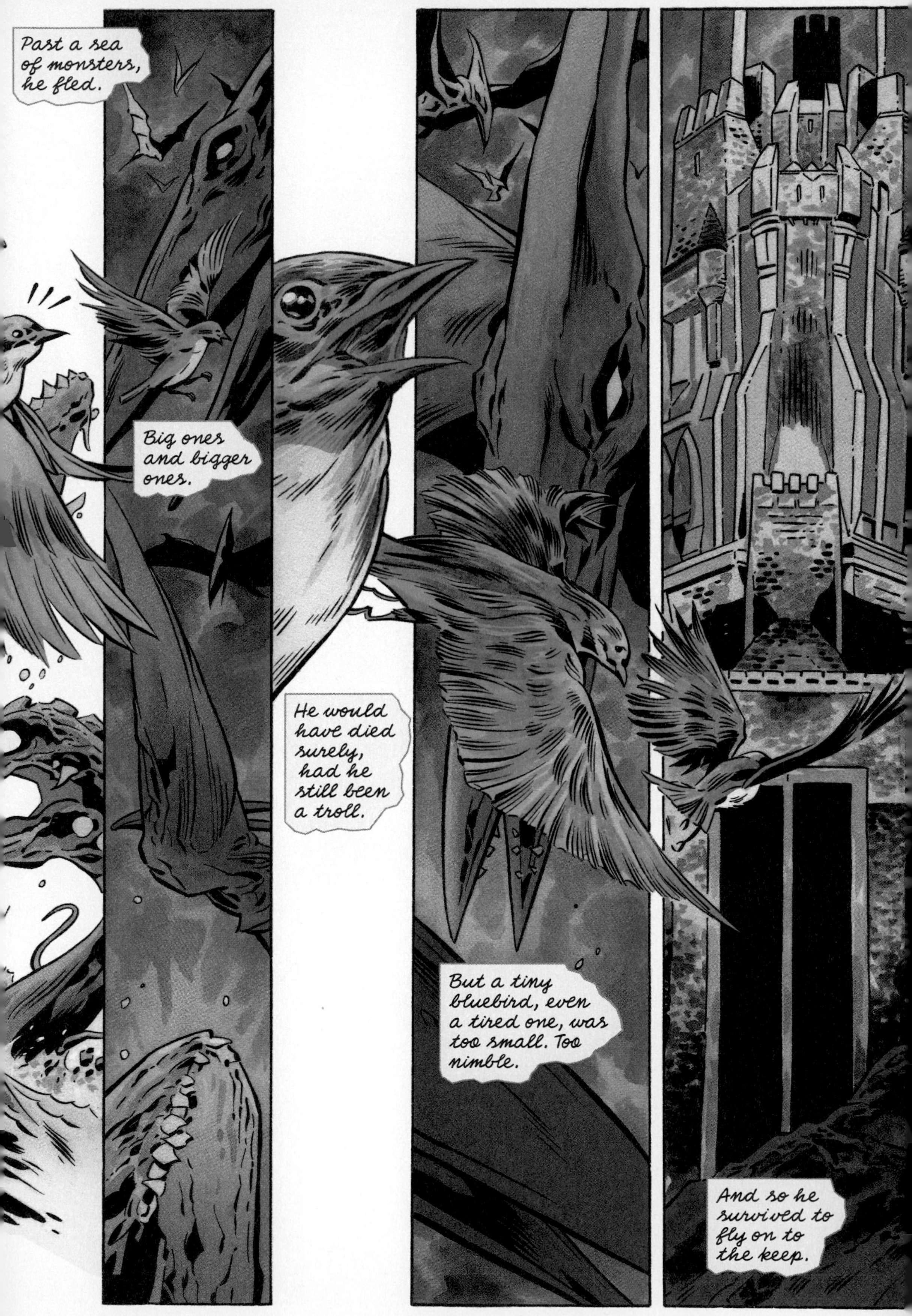

Past a sea of monsters, he fled.
Big ones and bigger ones.
He would have died surely, had he still been a troll.
But a tiny bluebird, even a tired one, was too small. Too nimble.
And so he survived to fly on to the keep.

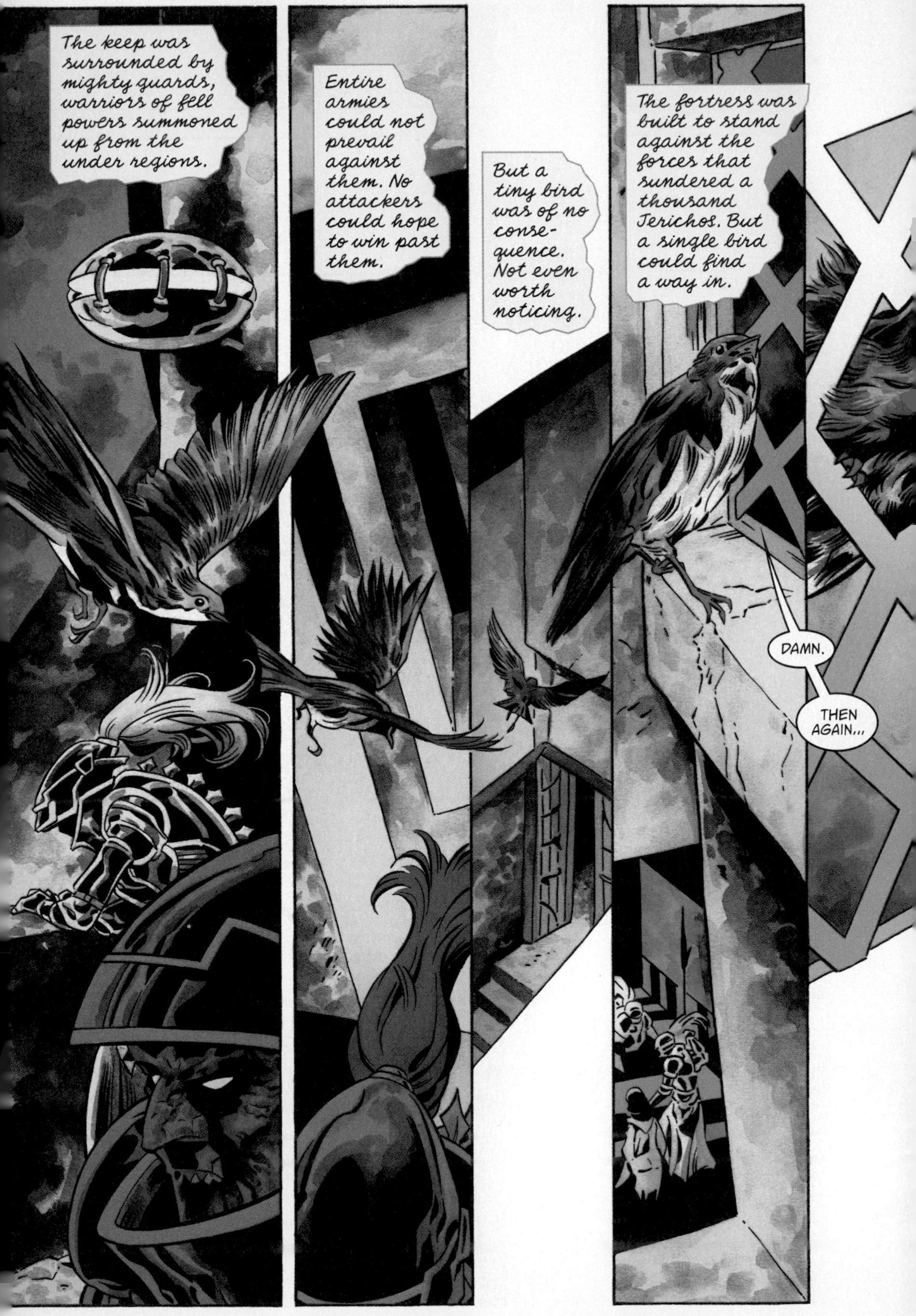
The keep was surrounded by mighty guards, warriors of fell powers summoned up from the under regions.
Entire armies could not prevail against them. No attackers could hope to win past them.
But a tiny bird was of no conse-quence. Not even worth noticing.
The fortress was built to stand against the forces that sundered a thousand Jerichos. But a single bird could find a way in.
DAMN.
THEN AGAIN...

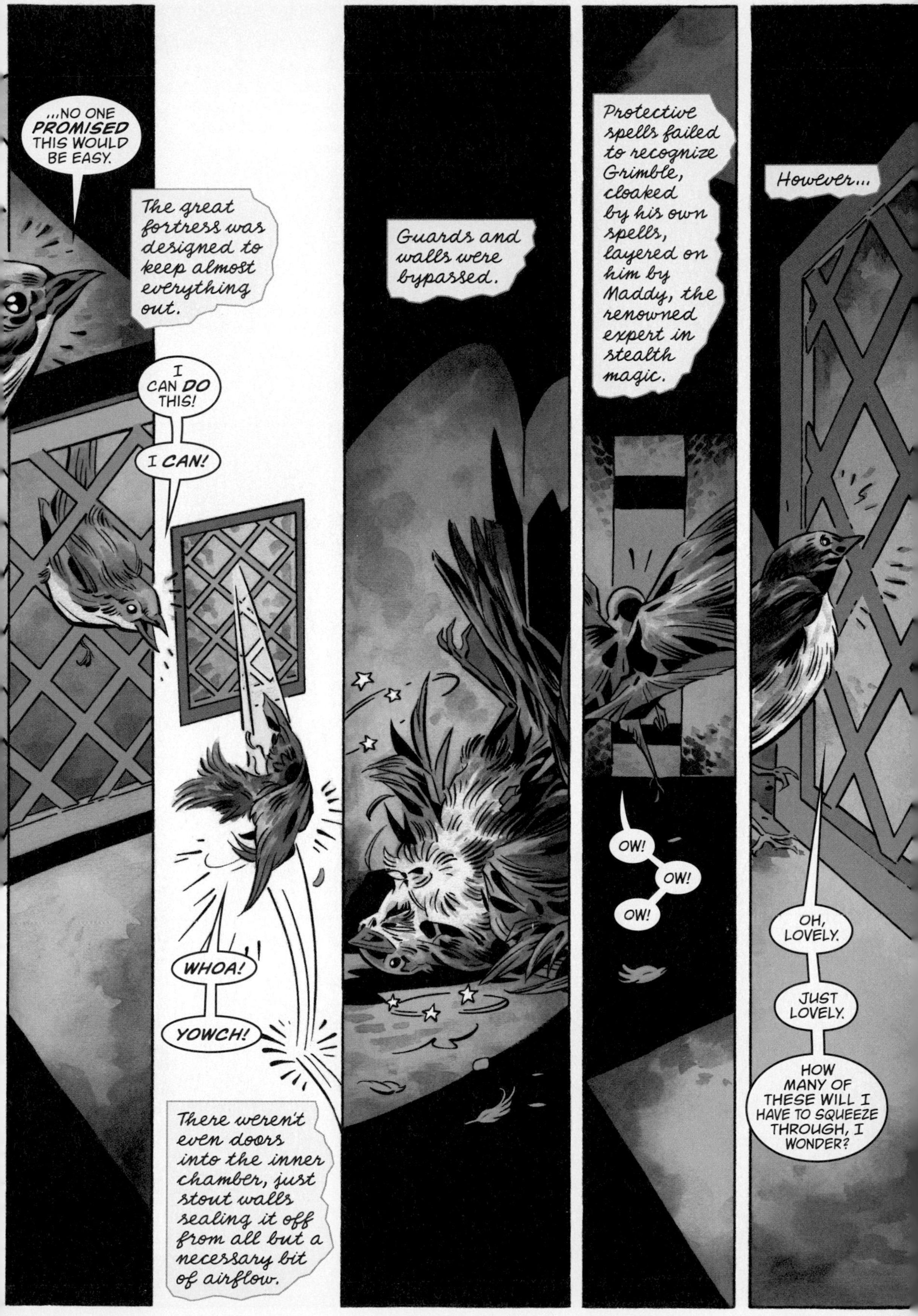

...NO ONE PROMISED THIS WOULD BE EASY.
The great fortress was designed to keep almost everything out.
I CAN DO THIS!
I CAN!
WHOA!
YOWCH!
There weren't even doors into the inner chamber, just stout walls sealing it off from all but a necessary bit of airflow.
Guards and walls were bypassed.
Protective spells failed to recognize Grimble, cloaked by his own spells, layered on him by Maddy, the renowned expert in stealth magic.
OW!
OW!
OW!
However...
OH, LOVELY.
JUST LOVELY.
HOW MANY OF THESE WILL I HAVE TO SQUEEZE THROUGH, I WONDER?

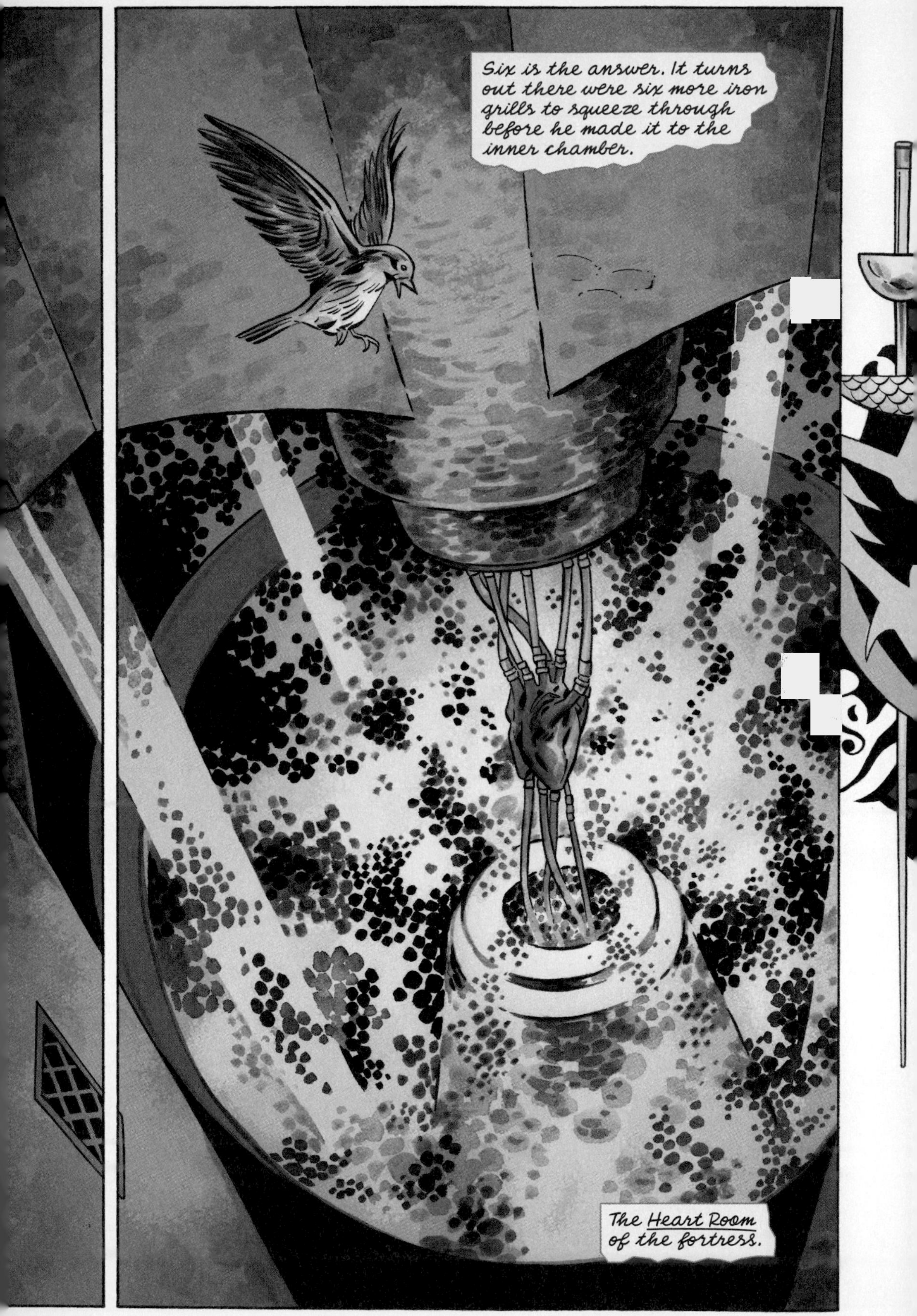
Six is the answer. It turns out there were six more iron grills to squeeze through before he made it to the inner chamber.
The Heart Room of the fortress.

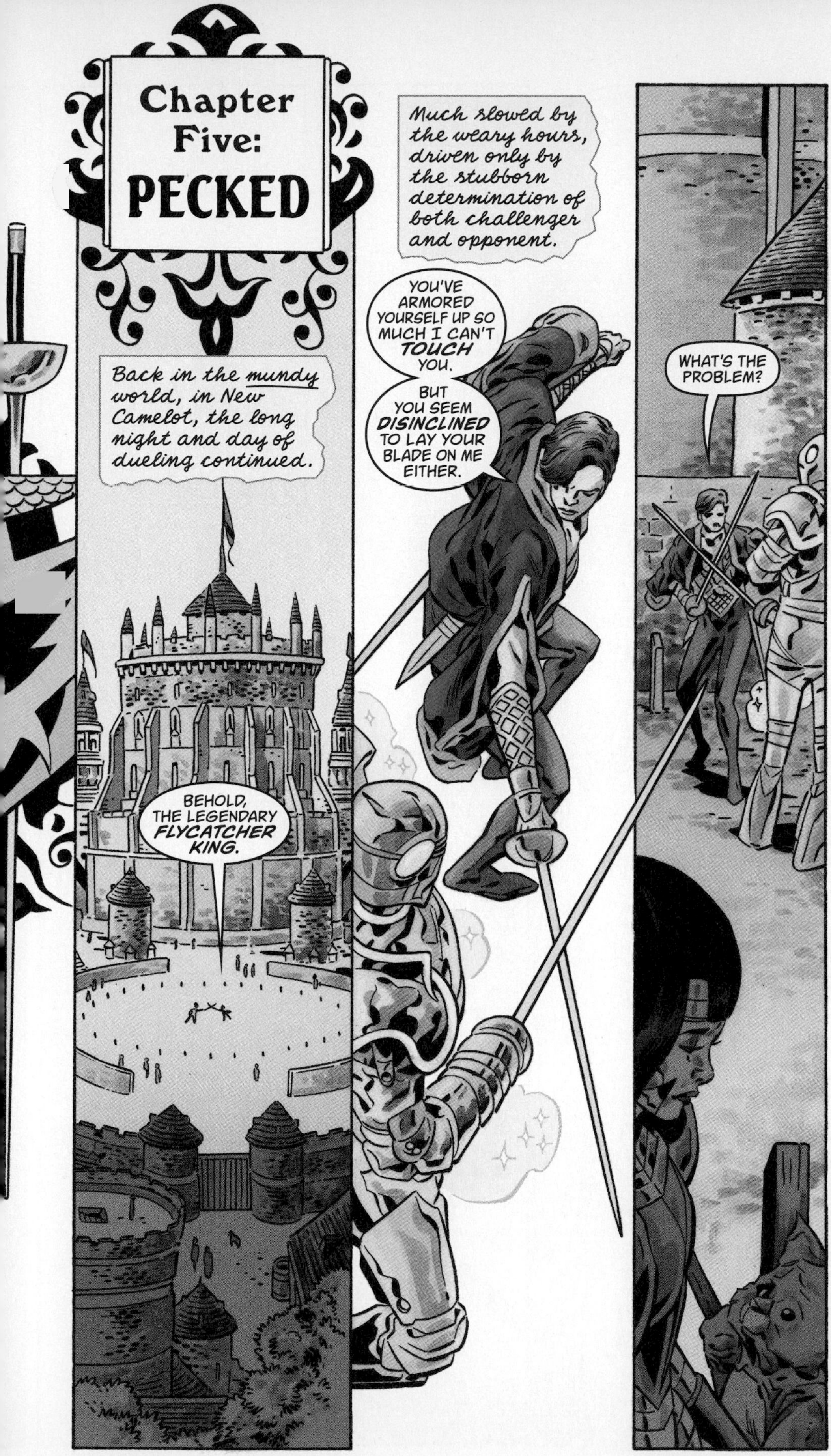

Chapter Five: PECKED
Back in the mundy world, in New Camelot, the long night and day of dueling continued.
BEHOLD, THE LEGENDARY FLYCATCHER KING.
Much slowed by the weary hours, driven only by the stubborn determination of both challenger and opponent.
YOU'VE ARMORED YOURSELF UP SO MUCH I CAN'T TOUCH YOU.
BUT YOU SEEM DISINCLINED TO LAY YOUR BLADE ON ME EITHER.
WHAT'S THE PROBLEM?

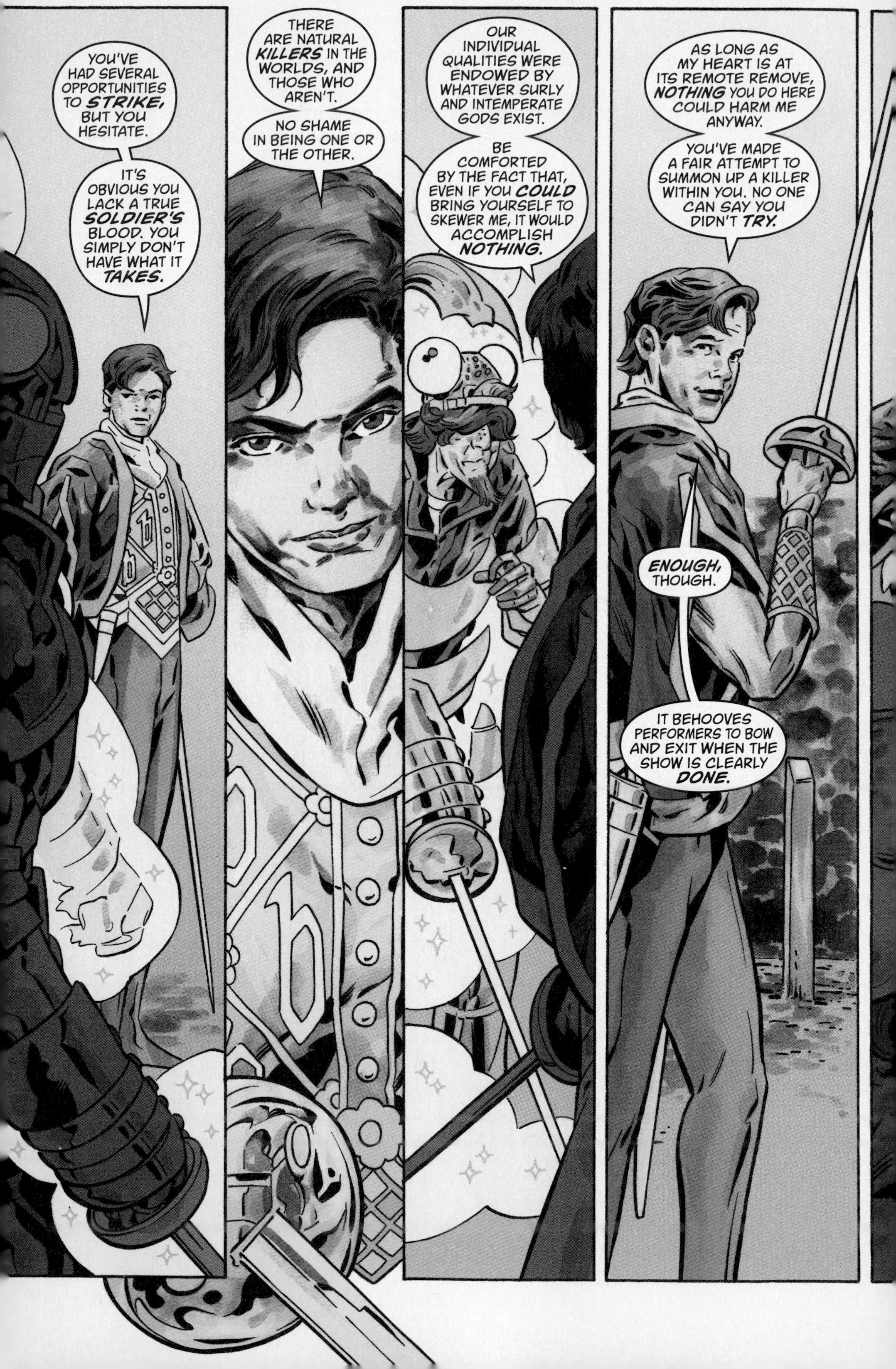
YOU'VE HAD SEVERAL OPPORTUNITIES TO STRIKE, BUT YOU HESITATE.
IT'S OBVIOUS YOU LACK A TRUE SOLDIER'S BLOOD. YOU SIMPLY DON'T HAVE WHAT IT TAKES.
THERE ARE NATURAL KILLERS IN THE WORLDS, AND THOSE WHO AREN'T.
NO SHAME IN BEING ONE OR THE OTHER.
OUR INDIVIDUAL QUALITIES WERE ENDOWED BY WHATEVER SURLY AND INTEMPERATE GODS EXIST.
BE COMFORTED BY THE FACT THAT, EVEN IF YOU COULD BRING YOURSELF TO SKEWER ME, IT WOULD ACCOMPLISH NOTHING.
AS LONG AS MY HEART IS AT ITS REMOTE REMOVE, NOTHING YOU DO HERE COULD HARM ME ANYWAY.
YOU'VE MADE A FAIR ATTEMPT TO SUMMON UP A KILLER WITHIN YOU. NO ONE CAN SAY YOU DIDN'T TRY.
ENOUGH, THOUGH.
IT BEHOOVES PERFORMERS TO BOW AND EXIT WHEN THE SHOW IS CLEARLY DONE.

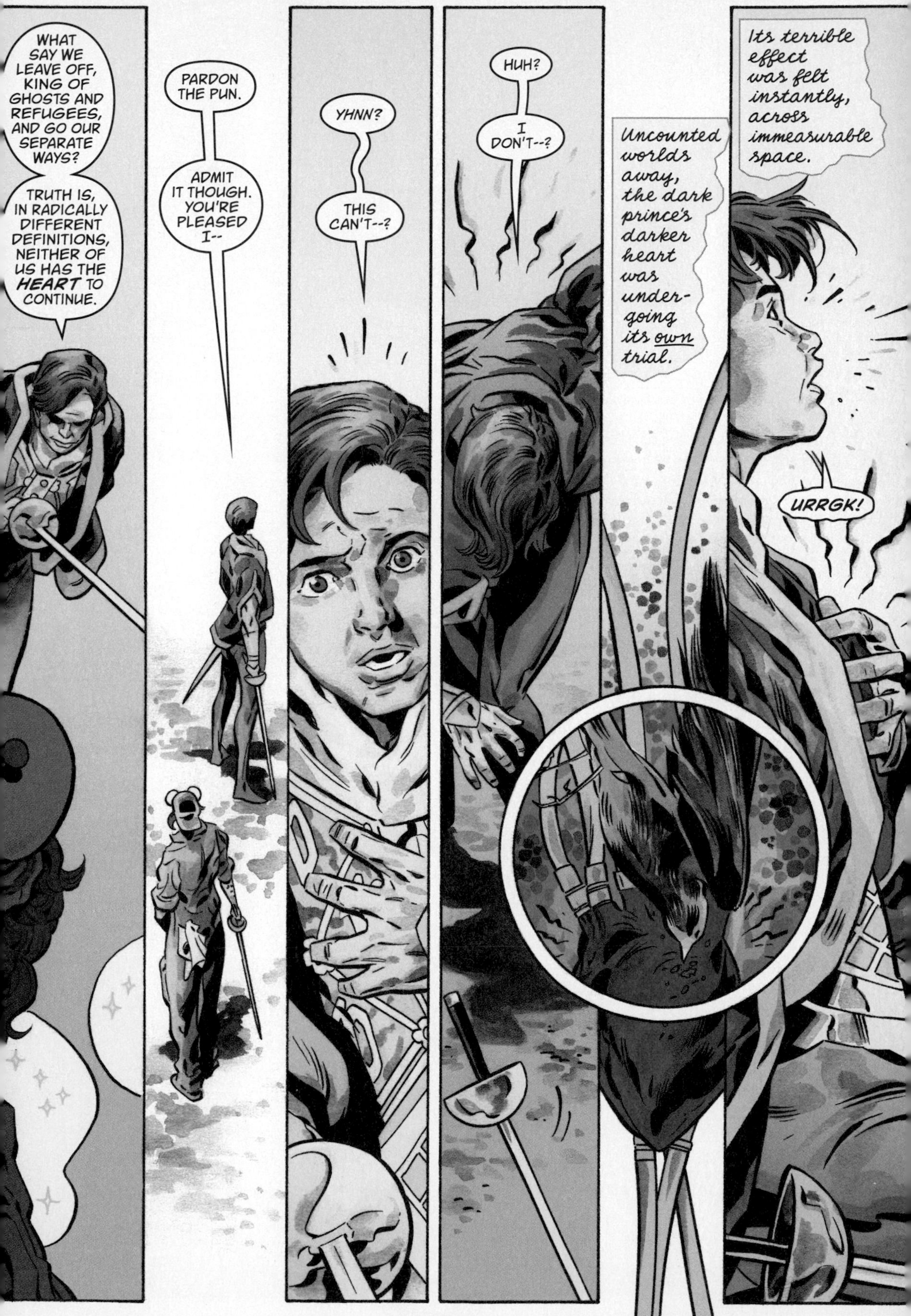
WHAT SAY WE LEAVE OFF, KING OF GHOSTS AND REFUGEES, AND GO OUR SEPARATE WAYS?
TRUTH IS, IN RADICALLY DIFFERENT DEFINITIONS, NEITHER OF US HAS THE HEART TO CONTINUE.
PARDON THE PUN.
ADMIT IT THOUGH. YOU'RE PLEASED I--
YHNN?
THIS CAN'T--?
HUH?
I DON'T--?
Uncounted worlds away, the dark prince's darker heart was undergoing its own trial.
Its terrible effect was felt instantly, across immeasurable space.
URRGK!

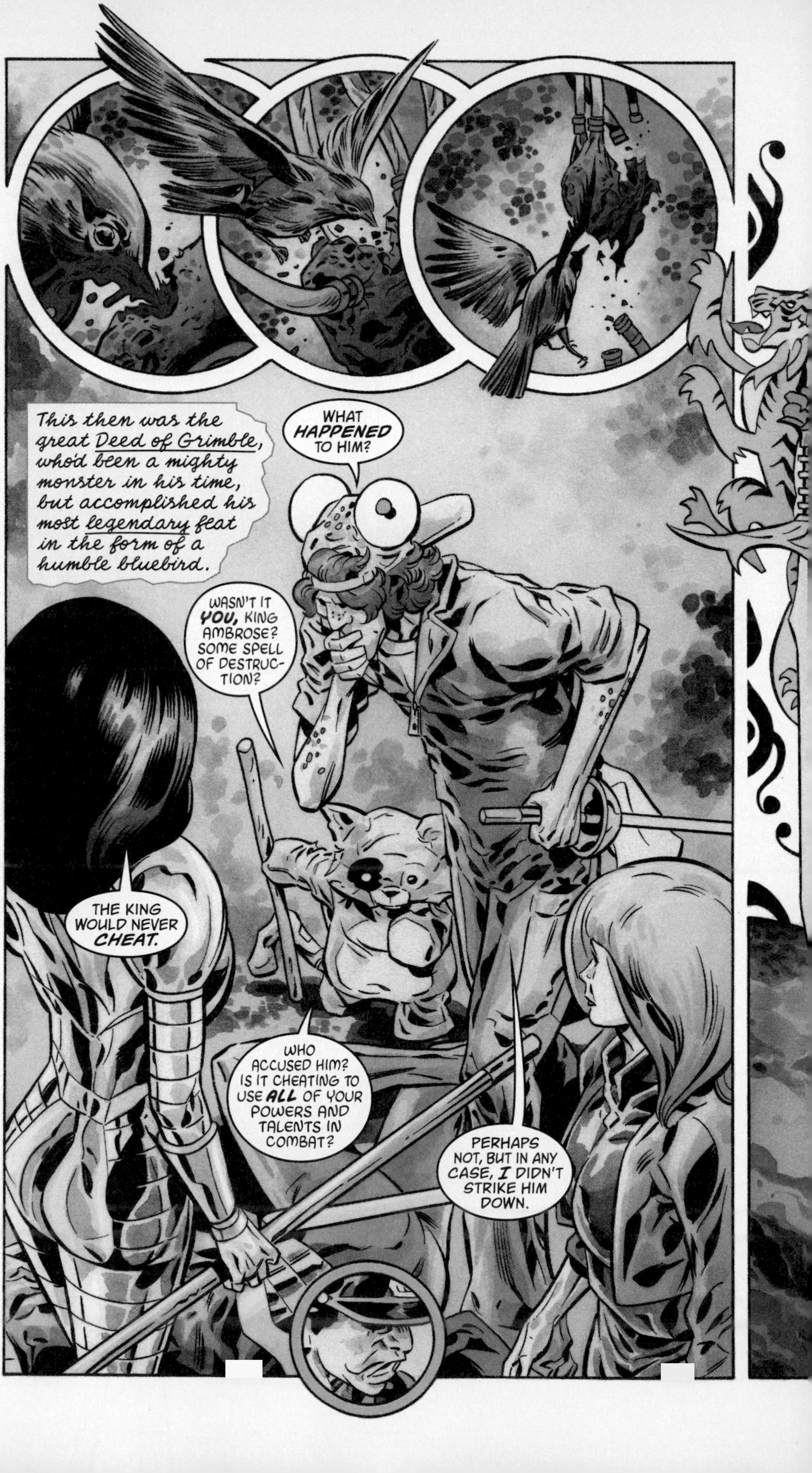
This then was the great Deed of Grimble, who'd been a mighty monster in his time, but accomplished his most legendary feat in the form of a humble bluebird.
WHAT HAPPENED TO HIM?
WASN'T IT YOU, KING AMBROSE? SOME SPELL OF DESTRUCTION?
THE KING WOULD NEVER CHEAT.
WHO ACCUSED HIM? IS IT CHEATING TO USE ALL OF YOUR POWERS AND TALENTS IN COMBAT?
PERHAPS NOT, BUT IN ANY CASE, I DIDN'T STRIKE HIM DOWN.

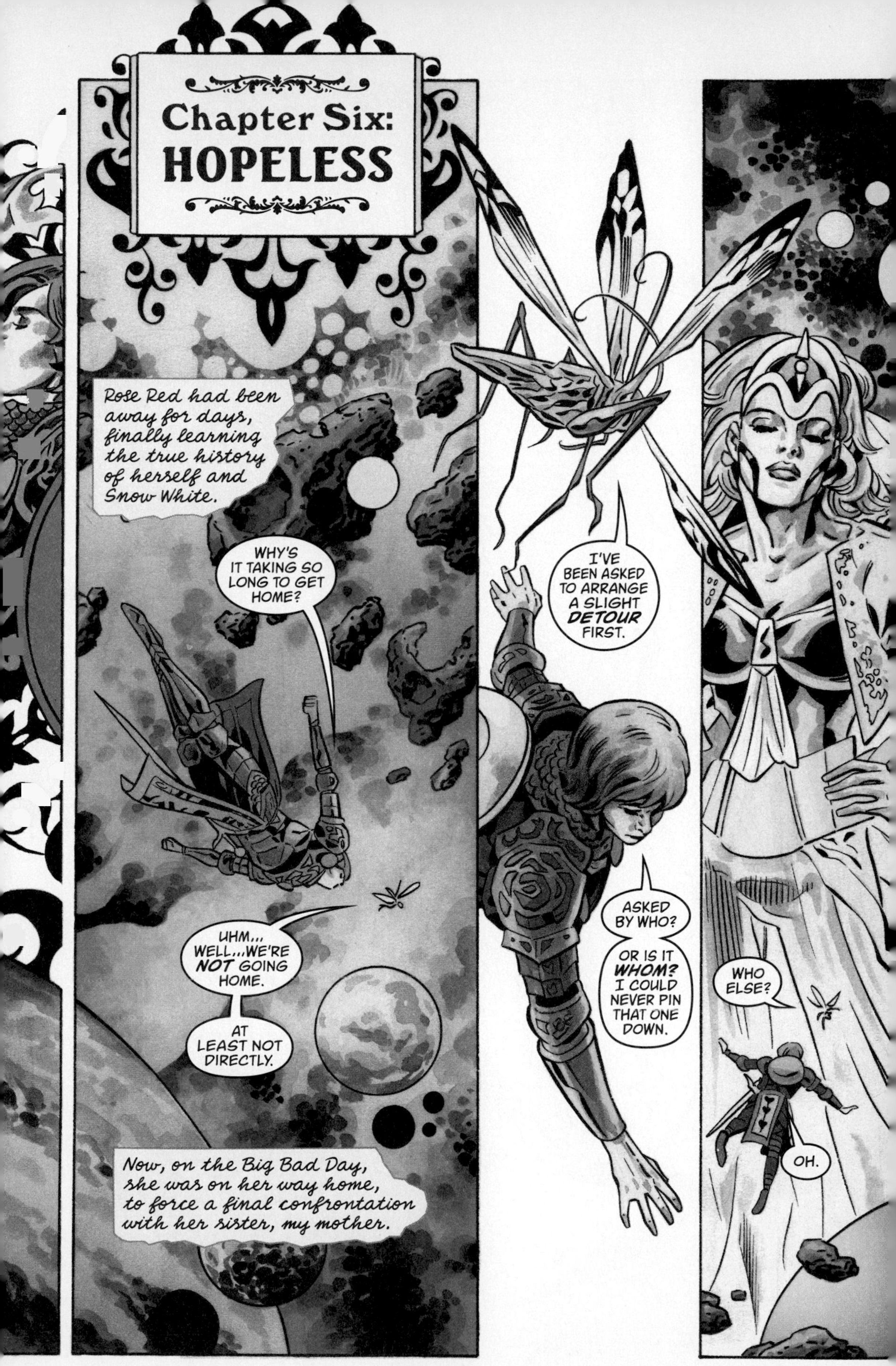
Chapter Six:
HOPELESS
Rose Red had been away for days, finally learning the true history of herself and Snow White.
WHY'S IT TAKING SO LONG TO GET HOME?
UHM... WELL...WE'RE NOT GOING HOME.
AT LEAST NOT DIRECTLY.
Now, on the Big Bad Day, she was on her way home, to force a final confrontation with her sister, my mother.
I'VE BEEN ASKED TO ARRANGE A SLIGHT DETOUR FIRST.
ASKED BY WHO?
OR IS IT WHOM? I COULD NEVER PIN THAT ONE DOWN.
WHO ELSE?
OH.

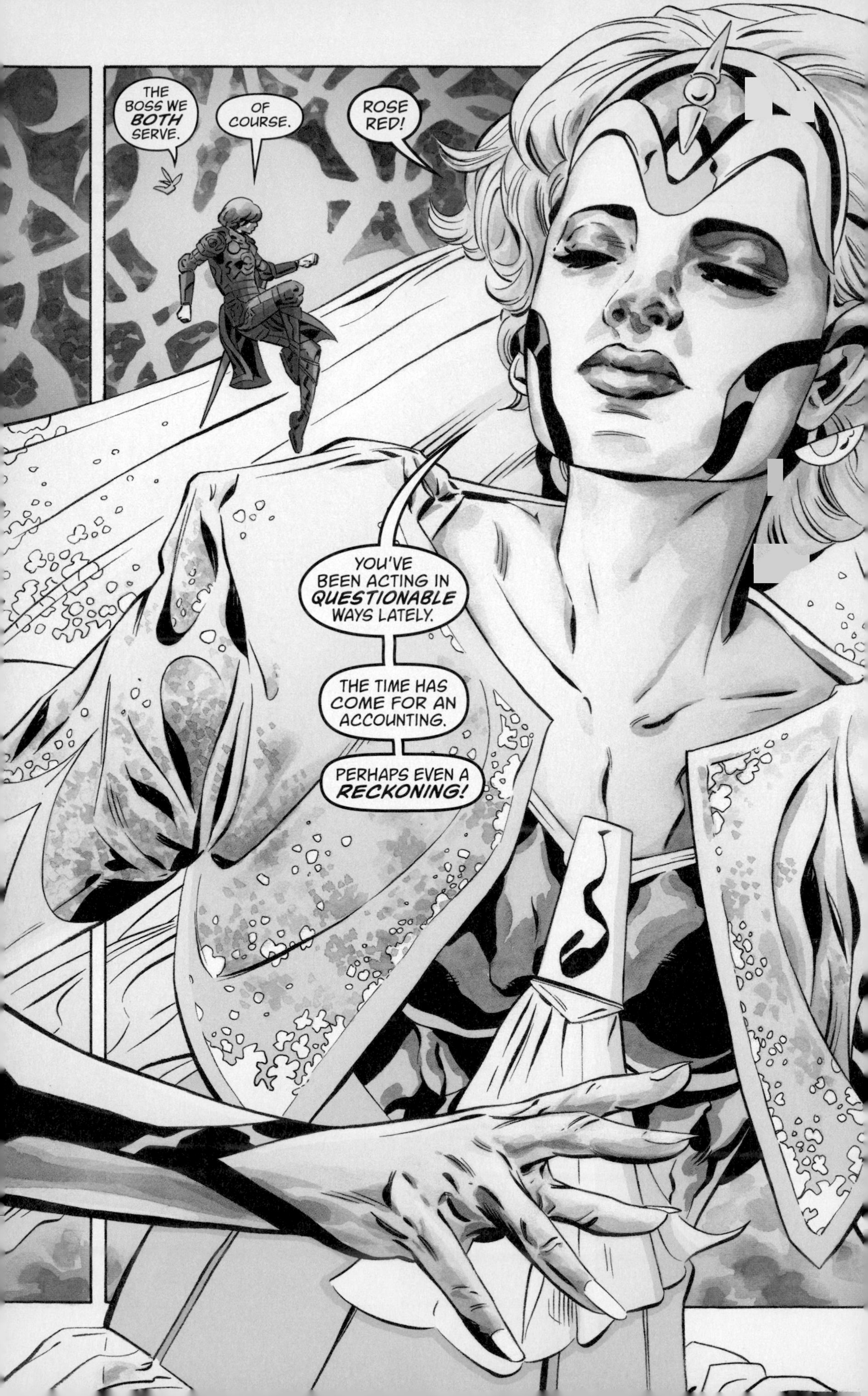
THE BOSS WE BOTH SERVE.
OF COURSE.
ROSE RED!
YOU'VE BEEN ACTING IN QUESTIONABLE WAYS LATELY.
THE TIME HAS COME FOR AN ACCOUNTING.
PERHAPS EVEN A RECKONING!

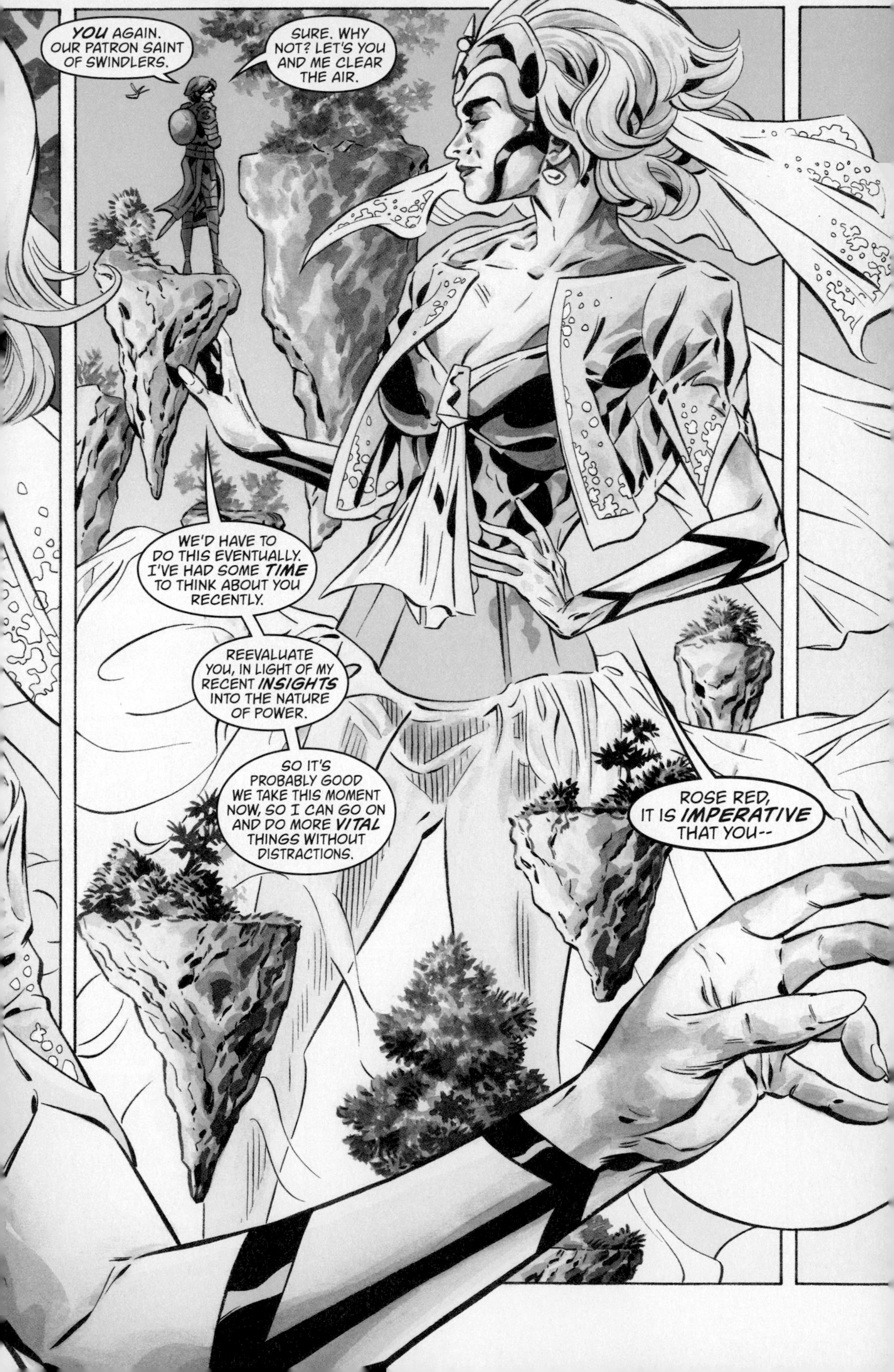
YOU AGAIN. OUR PATRON SAINT OF SWINDLERS.
SURE. WHY NOT? LET'S YOU AND ME CLEAR THE AIR.
WE'D HAVE TO DO THIS EVENTUALLY. I'VE HAD SOME TIME TO THINK ABOUT YOU RECENTLY.
REEVALUATE YOU, IN LIGHT OF MY RECENT INSIGHTS INTO THE NATURE OF POWER.
SO IT'S PROBABLY GOOD WE TAKE THIS MOMENT NOW, SO I CAN GO ON AND DO MORE VITAL THINGS WITHOUT DISTRACTIONS.
ROSE RED, IT IS IMPERATIVE THAT YOU--

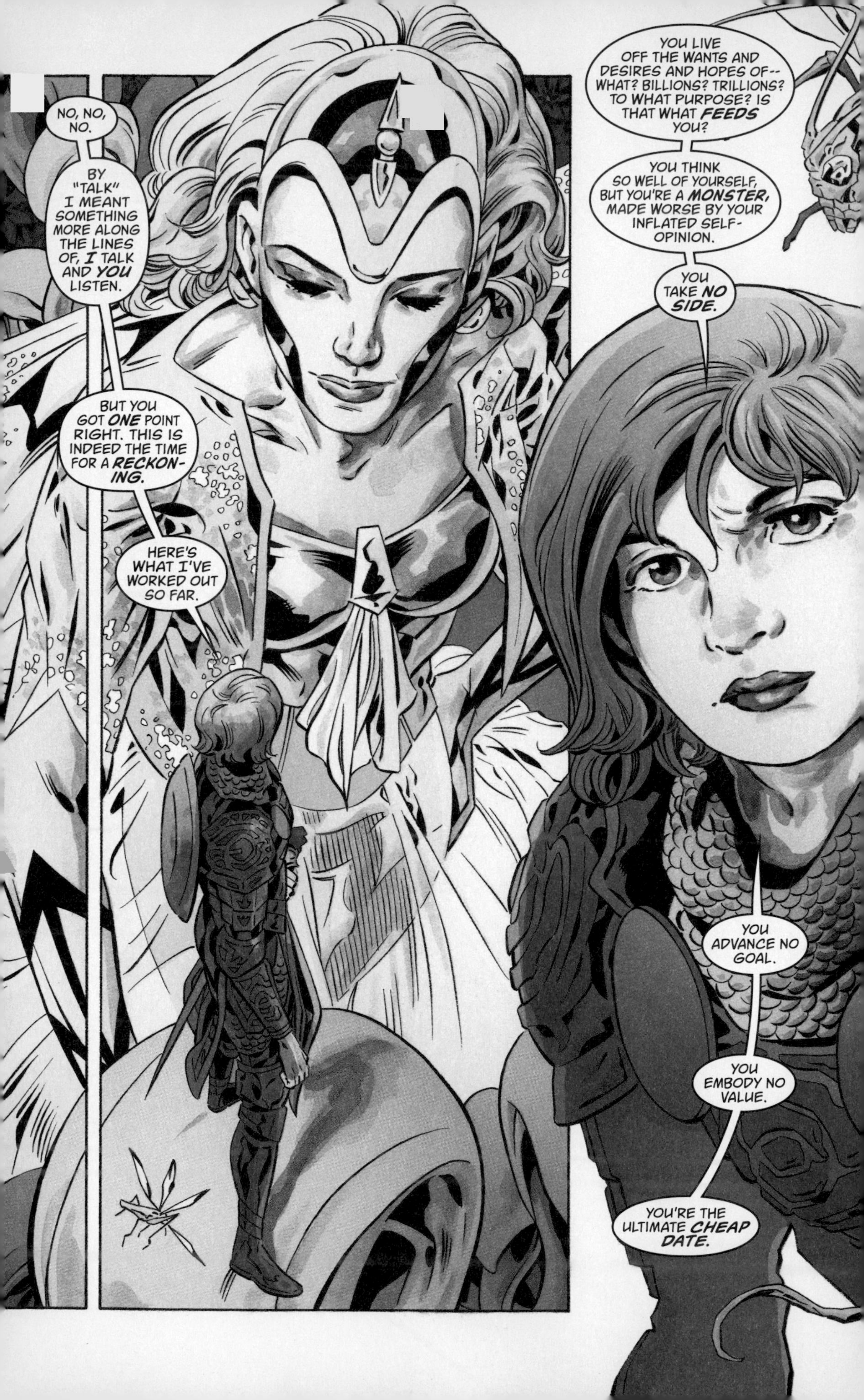
NO, NO, NO.
BY "TALK" I MEANT SOMETHING MORE ALONG THE LINES OF, I TALK AND YOU LISTEN.
BUT YOU GOT ONE POINT RIGHT. THIS IS INDEED THE TIME FOR A RECKONING.
HERE'S WHAT I'VE WORKED OUT SO FAR.
YOU LIVE OFF THE WANTS AND DESIRES AND HOPES OF-- WHAT? BILLIONS? TRILLIONS? TO WHAT PURPOSE? IS THAT WHAT FEEDS YOU?
YOU THINK SO WELL OF YOURSELF, BUT YOU'RE A MONSTER, MADE WORSE BY YOUR INFLATED SELF-OPINION.
YOU TAKE NO SIDE.
YOU ADVANCE NO GOAL.
YOU EMBODY NO VALUE.
YOU'RE THE ULTIMATE CHEAP DATE.

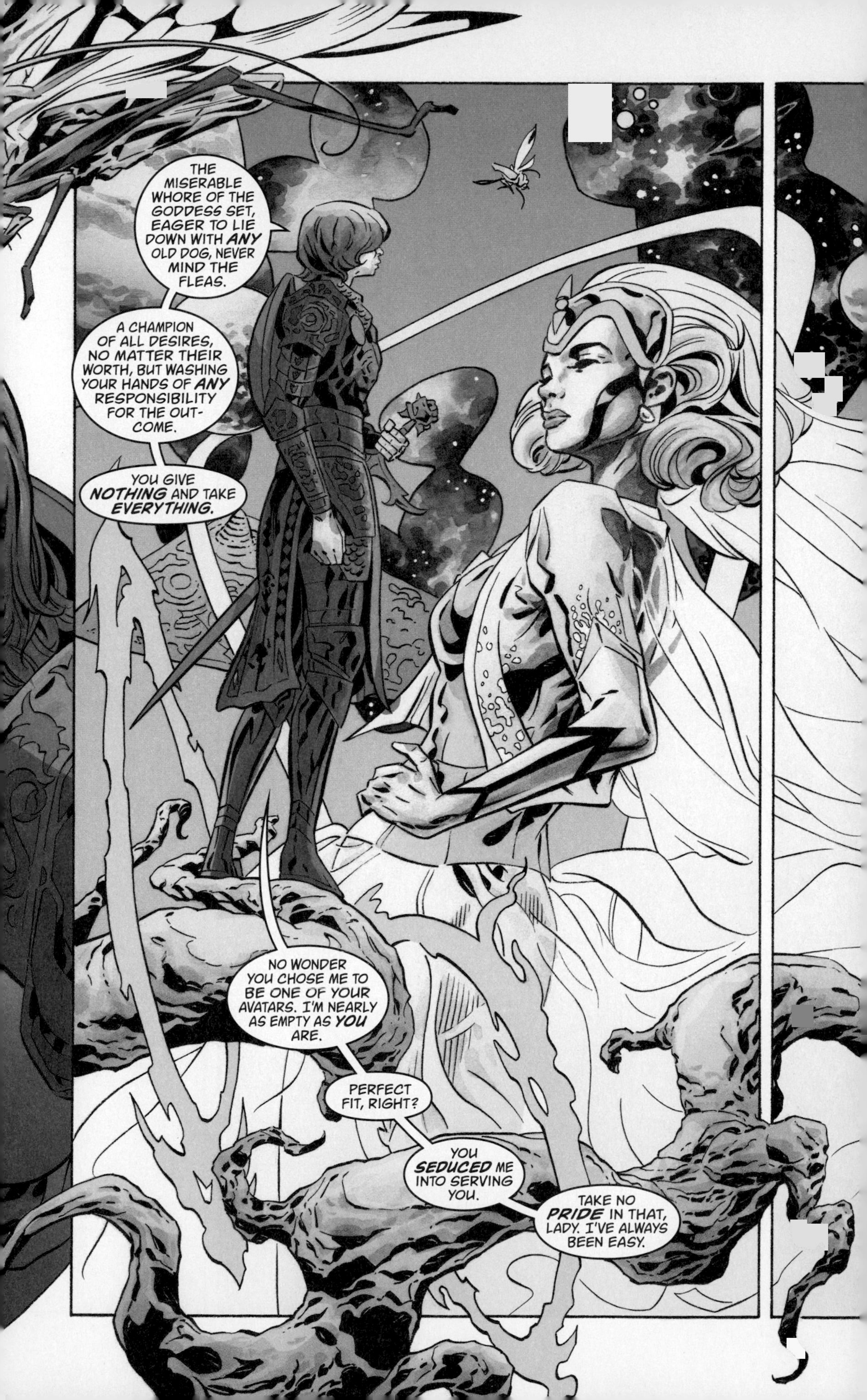
THE MISERABLE WHORE OF THE GODDESS SET, EAGER TO LIE DOWN WITH ANY OLD DOG, NEVER MIND THE FLEAS.
A CHAMPION OF ALL DESIRES, NO MATTER THEIR WORTH, BUT WASHING YOUR HANDS OF ANY RESPONSIBILITY FOR THE OUT-COME.
YOU GIVE NOTHING AND TAKE EVERYTHING.
NO WONDER YOU CHOSE ME TO BE ONE OF YOUR AVATARS. I'M NEARLY AS EMPTY AS YOU ARE.
PERFECT FIT, RIGHT?
YOU SEDUCED ME INTO SERVING YOU.
TAKE NO PRIDE IN THAT, LADY. I'VE ALWAYS BEEN EASY.

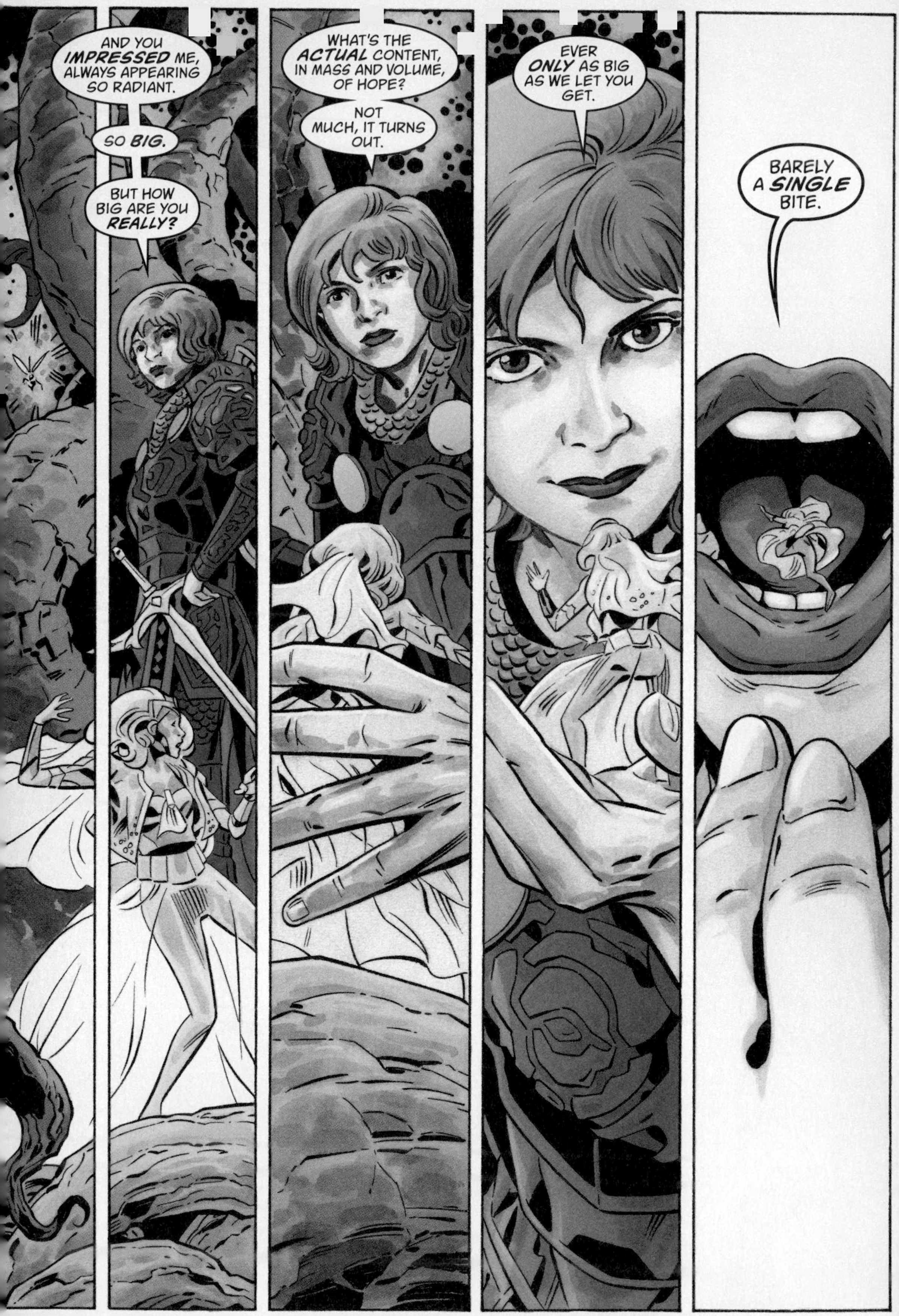

AND YOU IMPRESSED ME, ALWAYS APPEARING SO RADIANT.
SO BIG.
BUT HOW BIG ARE YOU REALLY?
WHAT'S THE ACTUAL CONTENT, IN MASS AND VOLUME, OF HOPE?
NOT MUCH, IT TURNS OUT.
EVER ONLY AS BIG AS WE LET YOU GET.
BARELY A SINGLE BITE.

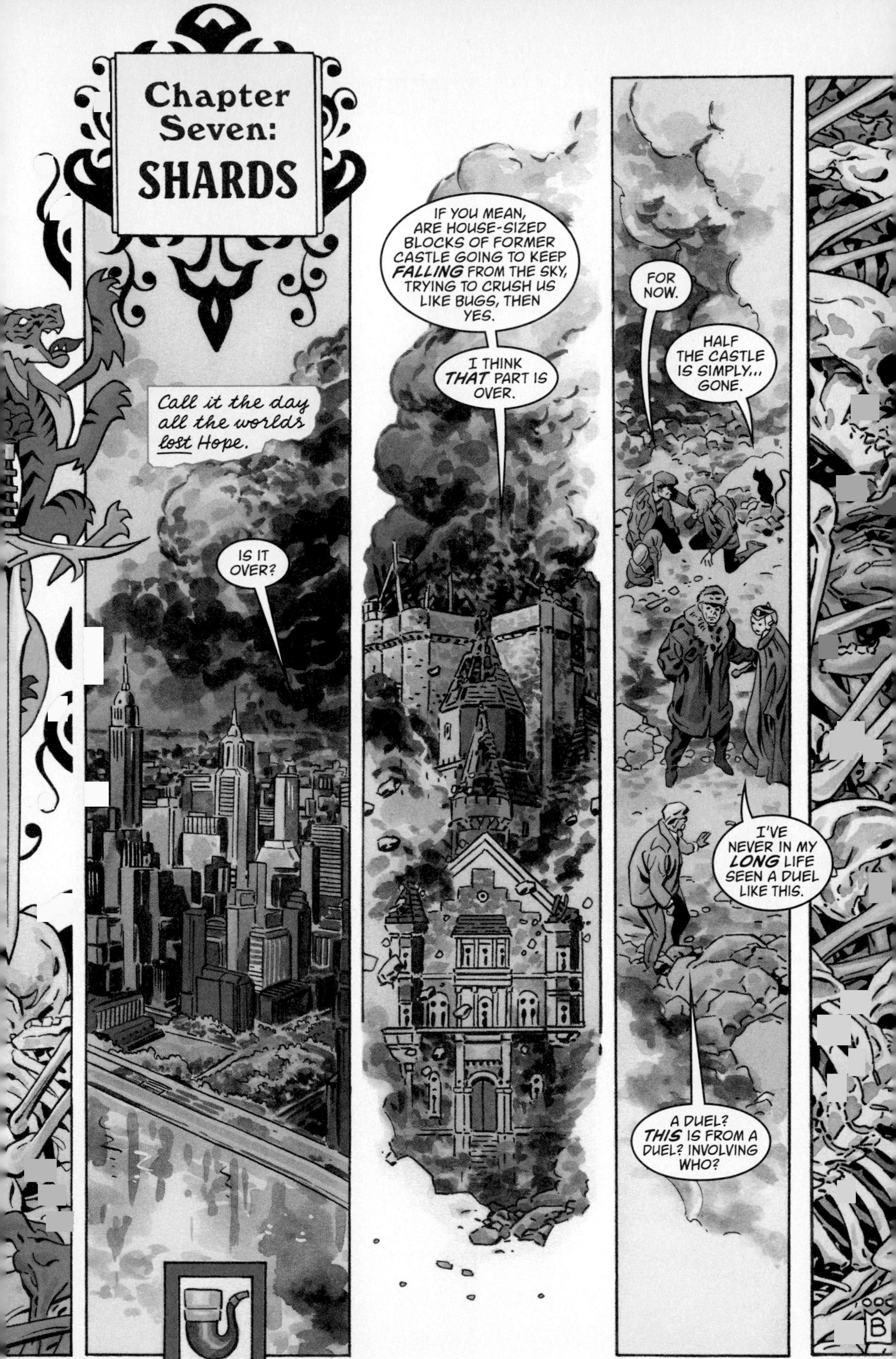
Chapter Seven:
SHARDS
Call it the day all the worlds lost Hope.
IS IT OVER?
IF YOU MEAN, ARE HOUSE-SIZED BLOCKS OF FORMER CASTLE GOING TO KEEP FALLING FROM THE SKY, TRYING TO CRUSH US LIKE BUGS, THEN YES.
I THINK THAT PART IS OVER.
FOR NOW.
HALF THE CASTLE IS SIMPLY... GONE.
I'VE NEVER IN MY LONG LIFE SEEN A DUEL LIKE THIS.
A DUEL? THIS IS FROM A DUEL? INVOLVING WHO?

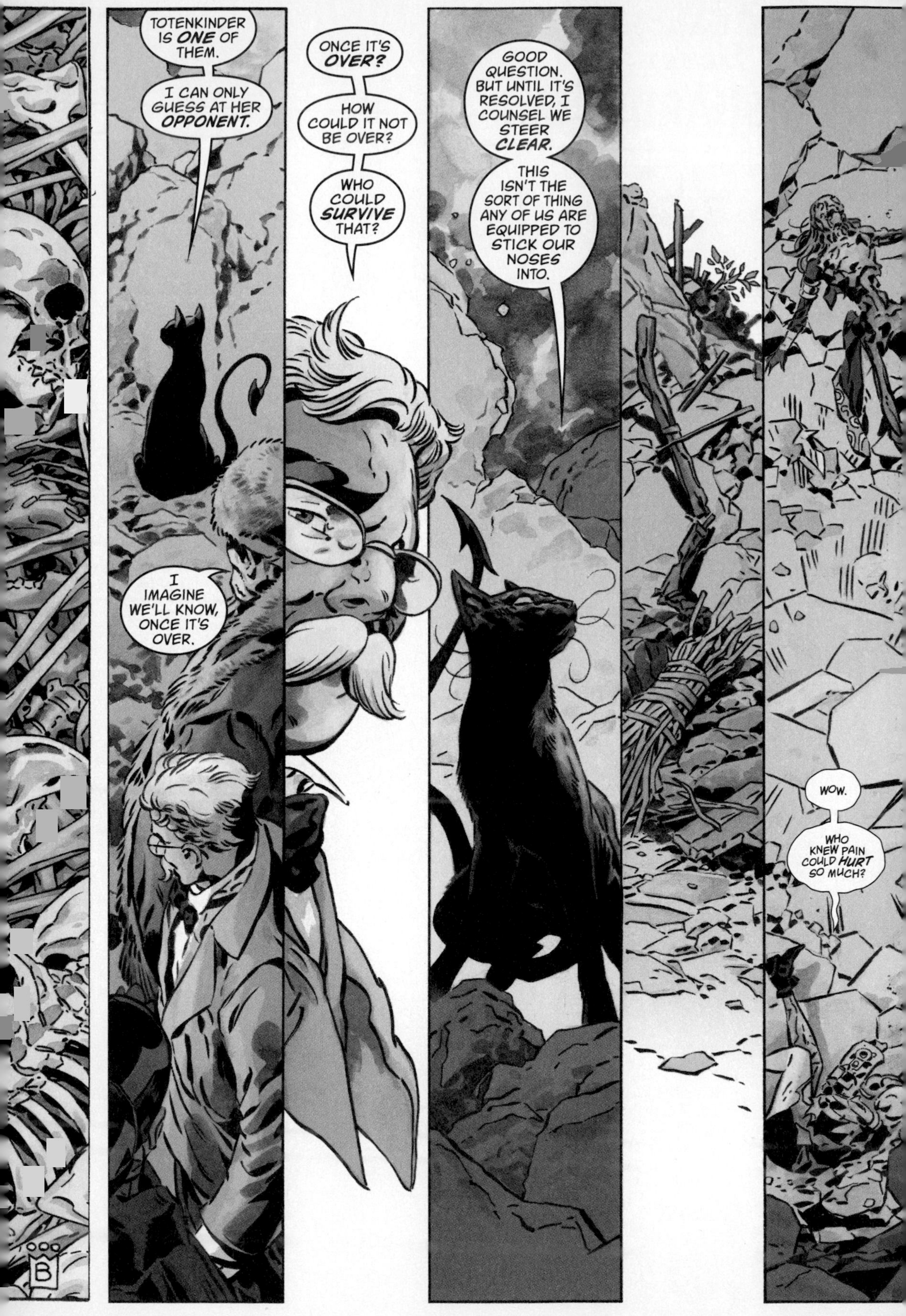

TOTENKINDER IS ONE OF THEM.
I CAN ONLY GUESS AT HER OPPONENT.
I IMAGINE WE'LL KNOW, ONCE IT'S OVER.
ONCE IT'S OVER?
HOW COULD IT NOT BE OVER?
WHO COULD SURVIVE THAT?
GOOD QUESTION. BUT UNTIL IT'S RESOLVED, I COUNSEL WE STEER CLEAR.
THIS ISN'T THE SORT OF THING ANY OF US ARE EQUIPPED TO STICK OUR NOSES INTO.
WOW.
WHO KNEW PAIN COULD HURT SO MUCH?

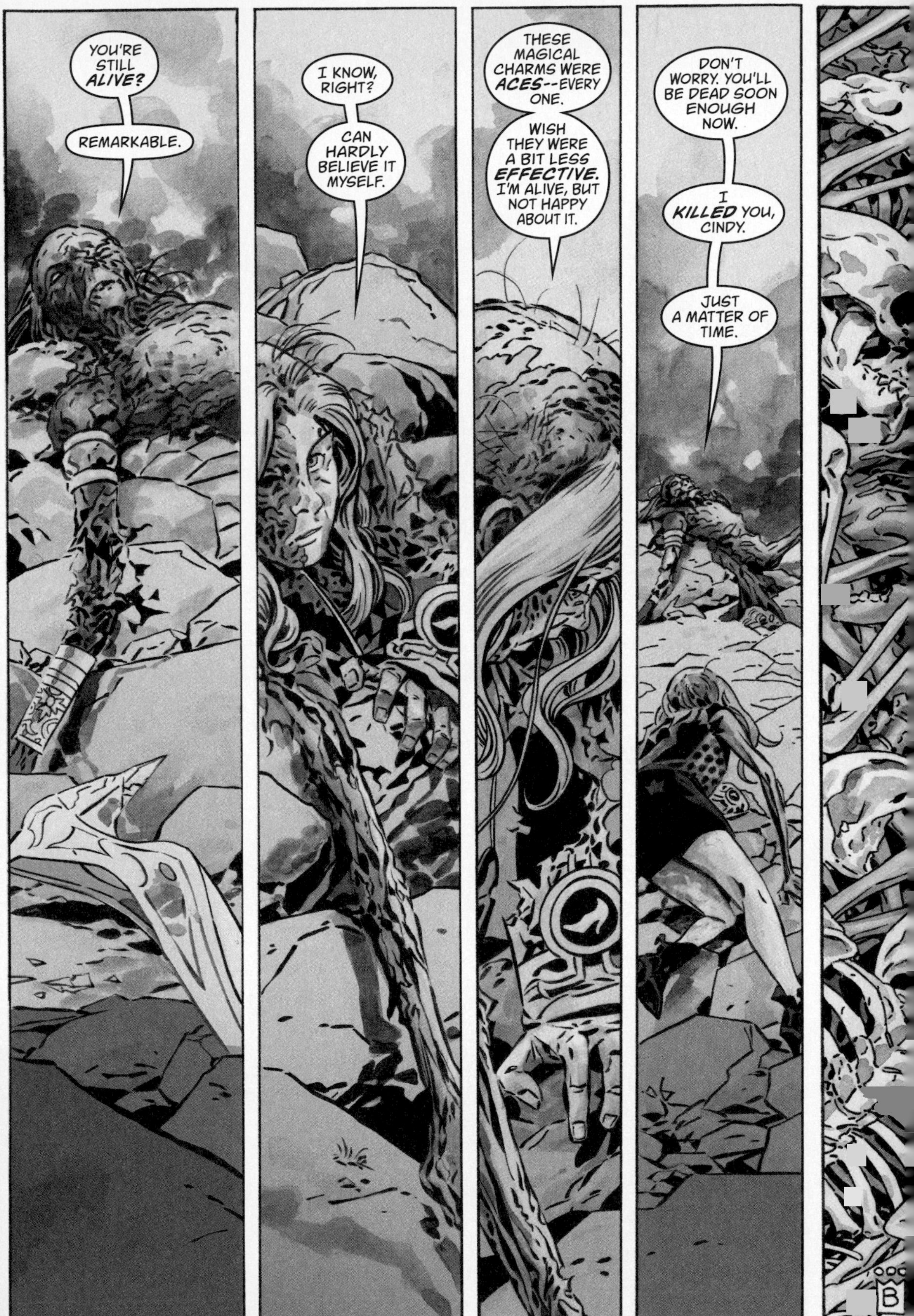
YOU'RE STILL ALIVE?
REMARKABLE.
I KNOW, RIGHT?
CAN HARDLY BELIEVE IT MYSELF.
THESE MAGICAL CHARMS WERE ACES--EVERY ONE.
WISH THEY WERE A BIT LESS EFFECTIVE. I'M ALIVE, BUT NOT HAPPY ABOUT IT.
DON'T WORRY. YOU'LL BE DEAD SOON ENOUGH NOW.
I KILLED YOU, CINDY.
JUST A MATTER OF TIME.

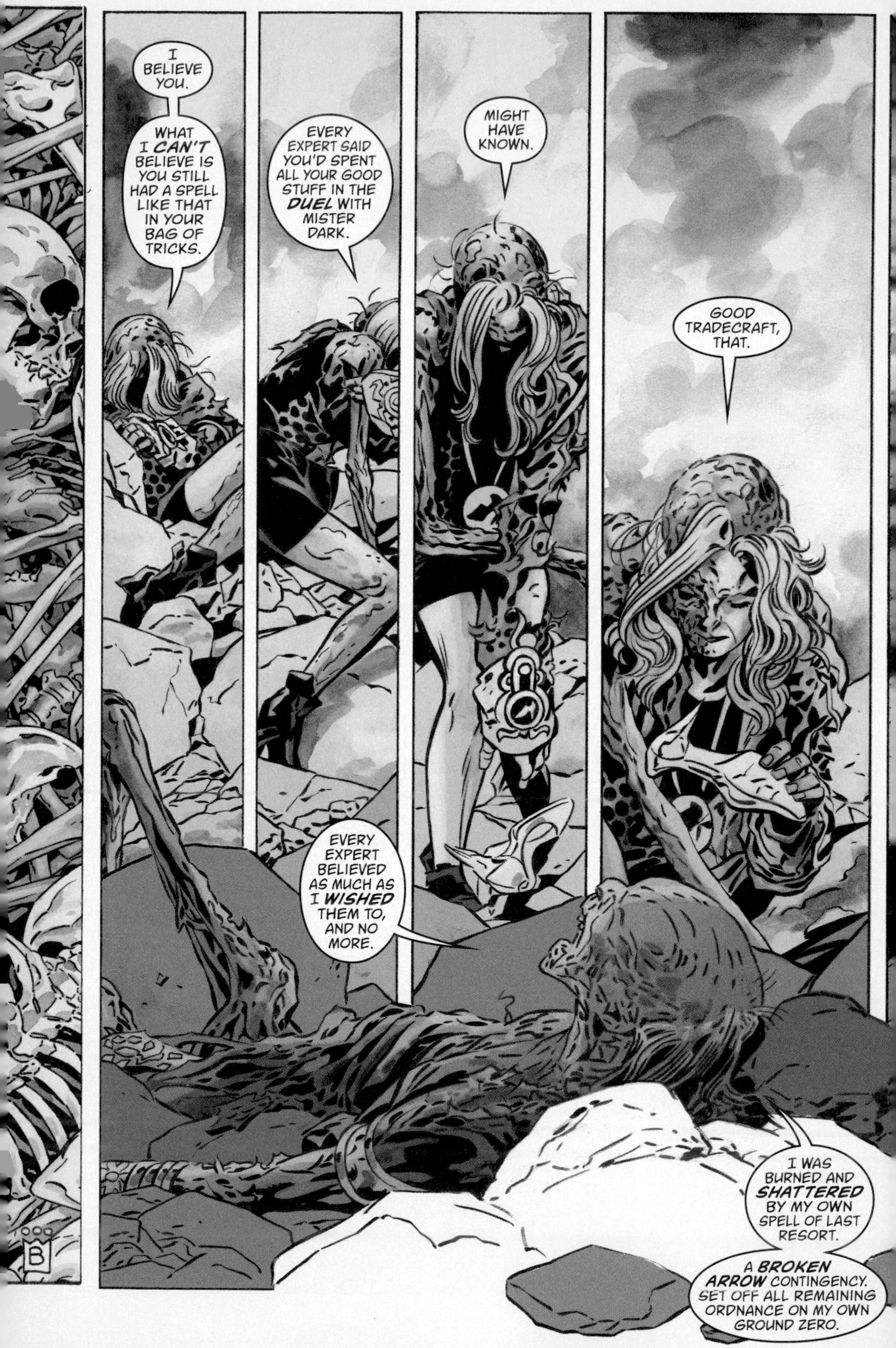
I BELIEVE YOU.
WHAT I CAN'T BELIEVE IS YOU STILL HAD A SPELL LIKE THAT IN YOUR BAG OF TRICKS.
EVERY EXPERT SAID YOU'D SPENT ALL YOUR GOOD STUFF IN THE DUEL WITH MISTER DARK.
MIGHT HAVE KNOWN.
GOOD TRADECRAFT, THAT.
EVERY EXPERT BELIEVED AS MUCH AS I WISHED THEM TO, AND NO MORE.
I WAS BURNED AND SHATTERED BY MY OWN SPELL OF LAST RESORT.
A BROKEN ARROW CONTINGENCY. SET OFF ALL REMAINING ORDNANCE ON MY OWN GROUND ZERO.

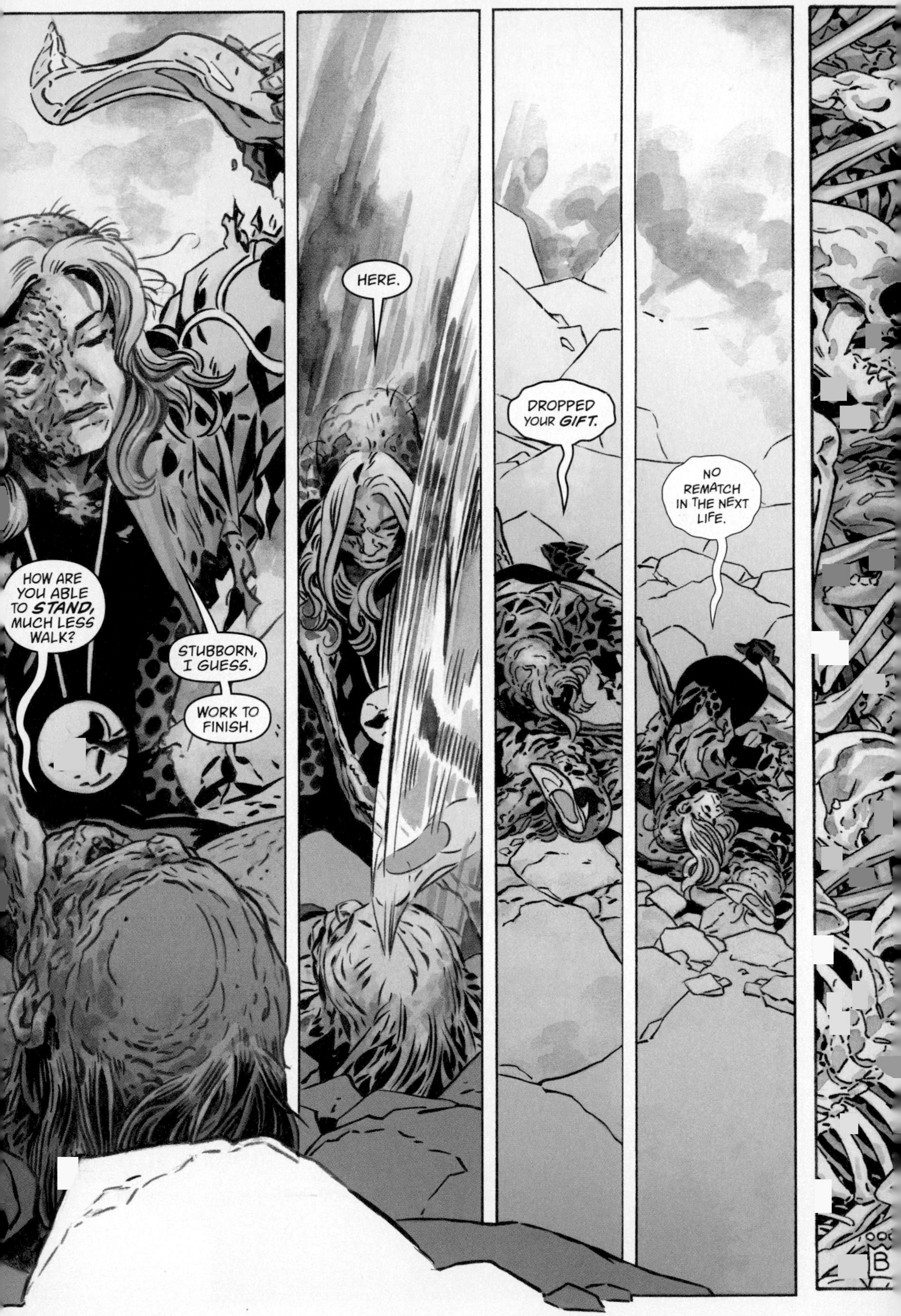
HOW ARE YOU ABLE TO STAND, MUCH LESS WALK?
STUBBORN, I GUESS.
WORK TO FINISH.
HERE.
DROPPED YOUR GIFT.
NO REMATCH IN THE NEXT LIFE.

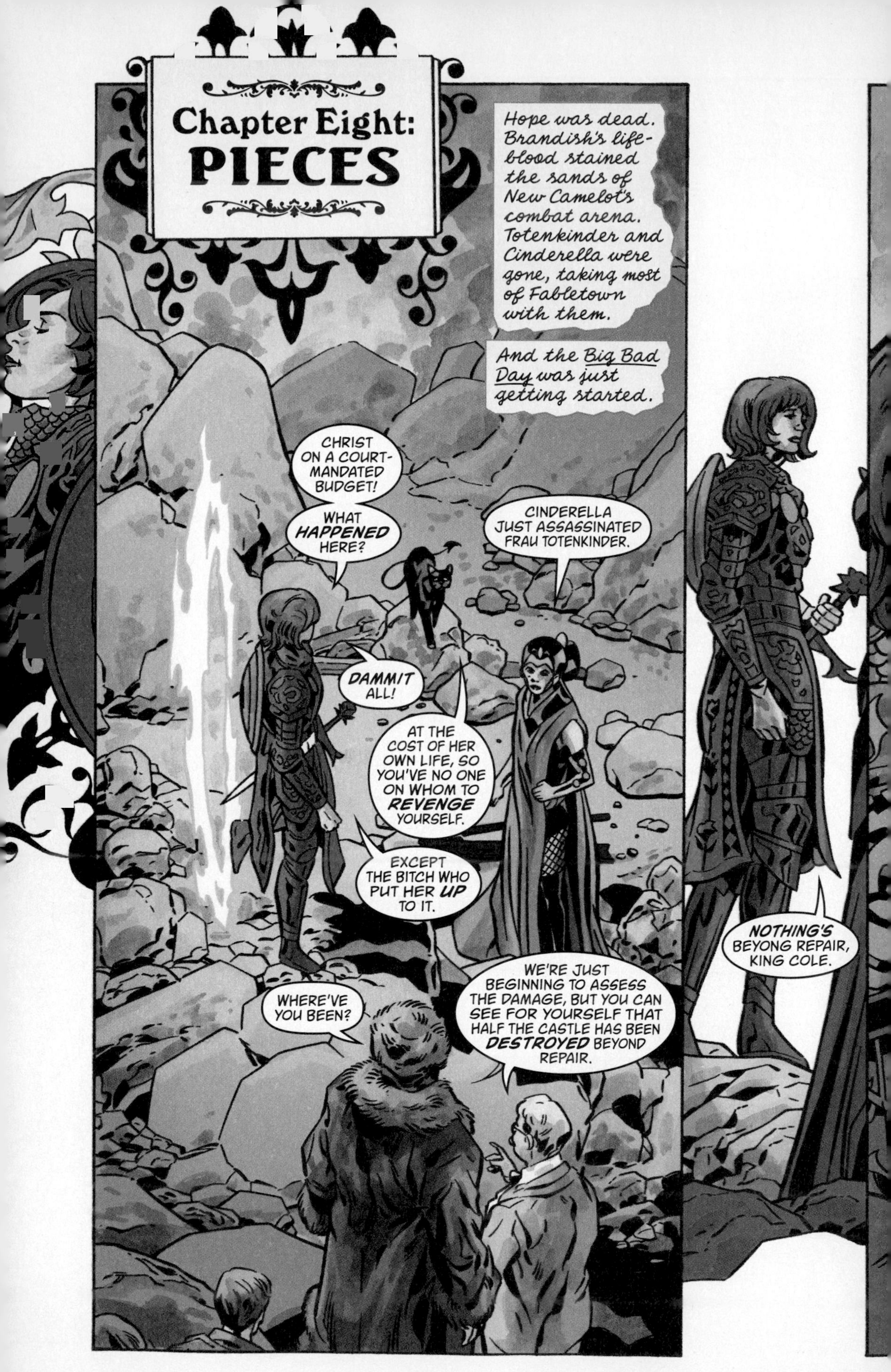
Chapter Eight:
PIECES
Hope was dead. Brandish's life-blood stained the sands of New Camelot's combat arena. Totenkinder and Cinderella were gone, taking most of Fabletown with them.
And the Big Bad Day was just getting started.
CHRIST ON A COURT-MANDATED BUDGET!
WHAT HAPPENED HERE?
CINDERELLA JUST ASSASSINATED FRAU TOTENKINDER.
DAMMIT ALL!
AT THE COST OF HER OWN LIFE, SO YOU'VE NO ONE ON WHOM TO REVENGE YOURSELF.
EXCEPT THE BITCH WHO PUT HER UP TO IT.
WHERE'VE YOU BEEN?
WE'RE JUST BEGINNING TO ASSESS THE DAMAGE, BUT YOU CAN SEE FOR YOURSELF THAT HALF THE CASTLE HAS BEEN DESTROYED BEYOND REPAIR.
NOTHING'S BEYONG REPAIR, KING COLE.

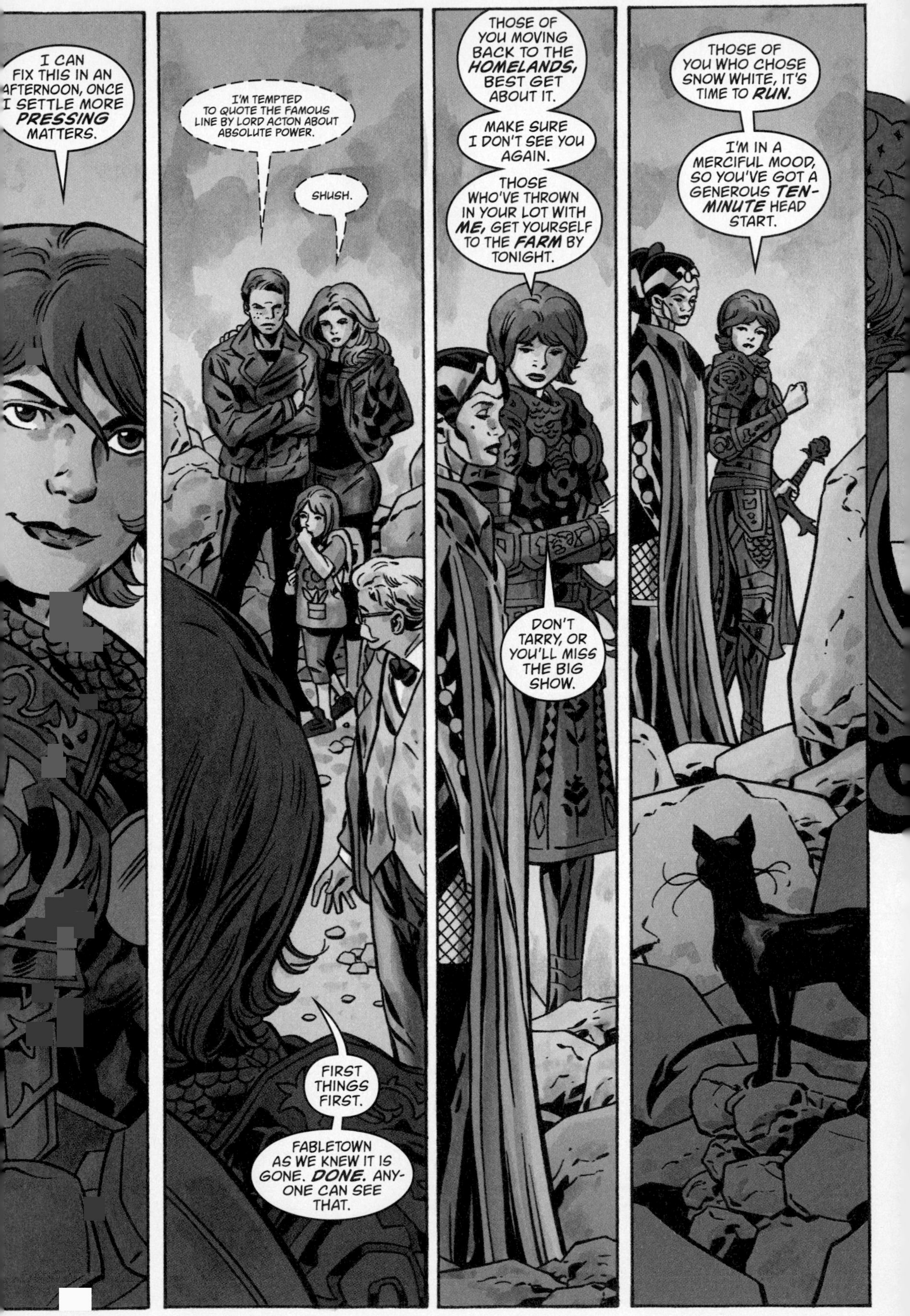
I CAN FIX THIS IN AN AFTERNOON, ONCE I SETTLE MORE PRESSING MATTERS.
I'M TEMPTED TO QUOTE THE FAMOUS LINE BY LORD ACTON ABOUT ABSOLUTE POWER.
SHUSH.
FIRST THINGS FIRST.
FABLETOWN AS WE KNEW IT IS GONE. DONE. ANY-ONE CAN SEE THAT.
THOSE OF YOU MOVING BACK TO THE HOMELANDS, BEST GET ABOUT IT.
MAKE SURE I DON'T SEE YOU AGAIN.
THOSE WHO'VE THROWN IN YOUR LOT WITH ME, GET YOURSELF TO THE FARM BY TONIGHT.
DON'T TARRY, OR YOU'LL MISS THE BIG SHOW.
THOSE OF YOU WHO CHOSE SNOW WHITE, IT'S TIME TO RUN.
I'M IN A MERCIFUL MOOD, SO YOU'VE GOT A GENEROUS TEN-MINUTE HEAD START.

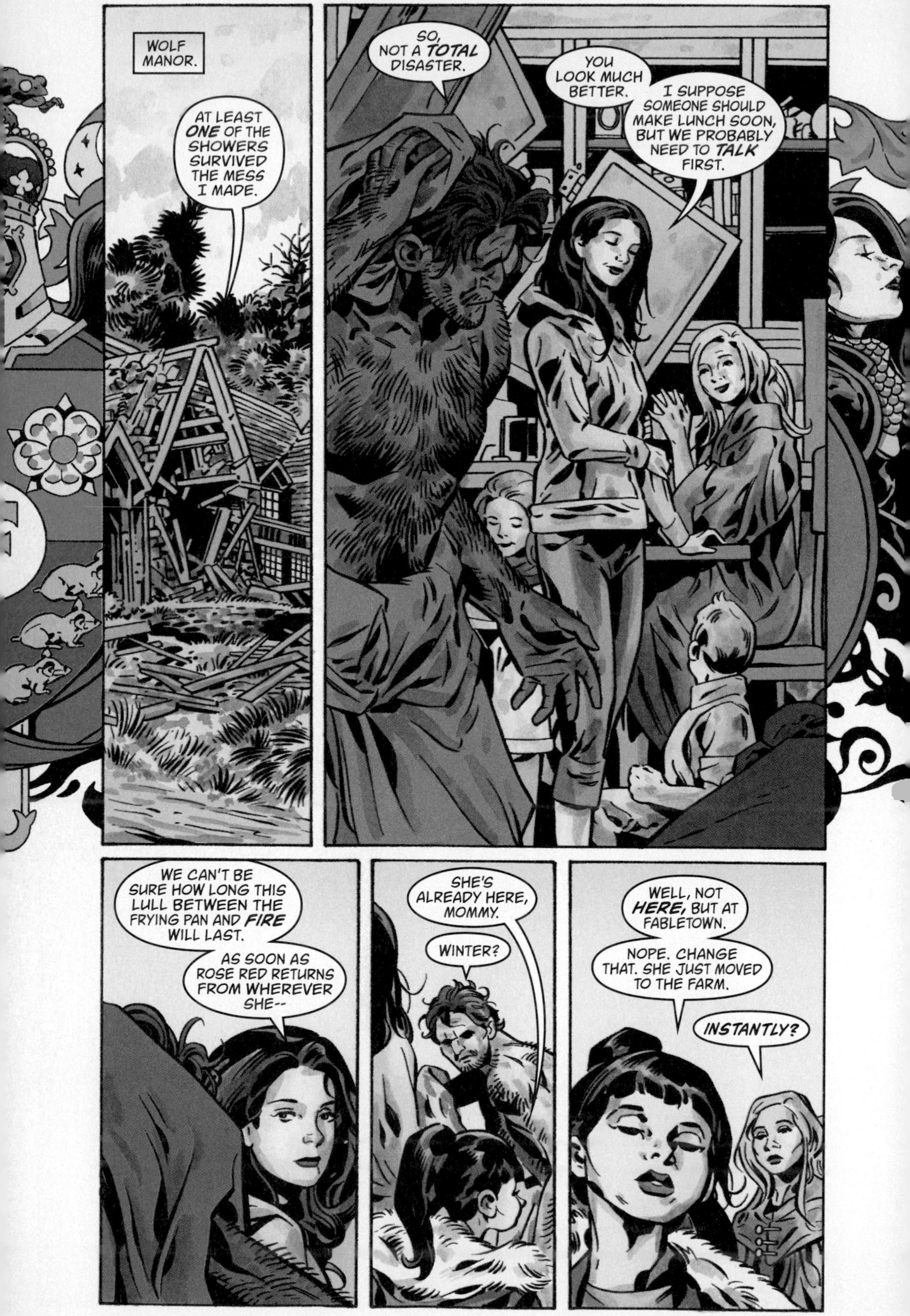
WOLF MANOR.
AT LEAST ONE OF THE SHOWERS SURVIVED THE MESS I MADE.
SO, NOT A TOTAL DISASTER.
YOU LOOK MUCH BETTER.
I SUPPOSE SOMEONE SHOULD MAKE LUNCH SOON, BUT WE PROBABLY NEED TO TALK FIRST.
WE CAN'T BE SURE HOW LONG THIS LULL BETWEEN THE FRYING PAN AND FIRE WILL LAST.
AS SOON AS ROSE RED RETURNS FROM WHEREVER SHE--
SHE'S ALREADY HERE, MOMMY.
WINTER?
WELL, NOT HERE, BUT AT FABLETOWN.
NOPE. CHANGE THAT. SHE JUST MOVED TO THE FARM.
INSTANTLY?

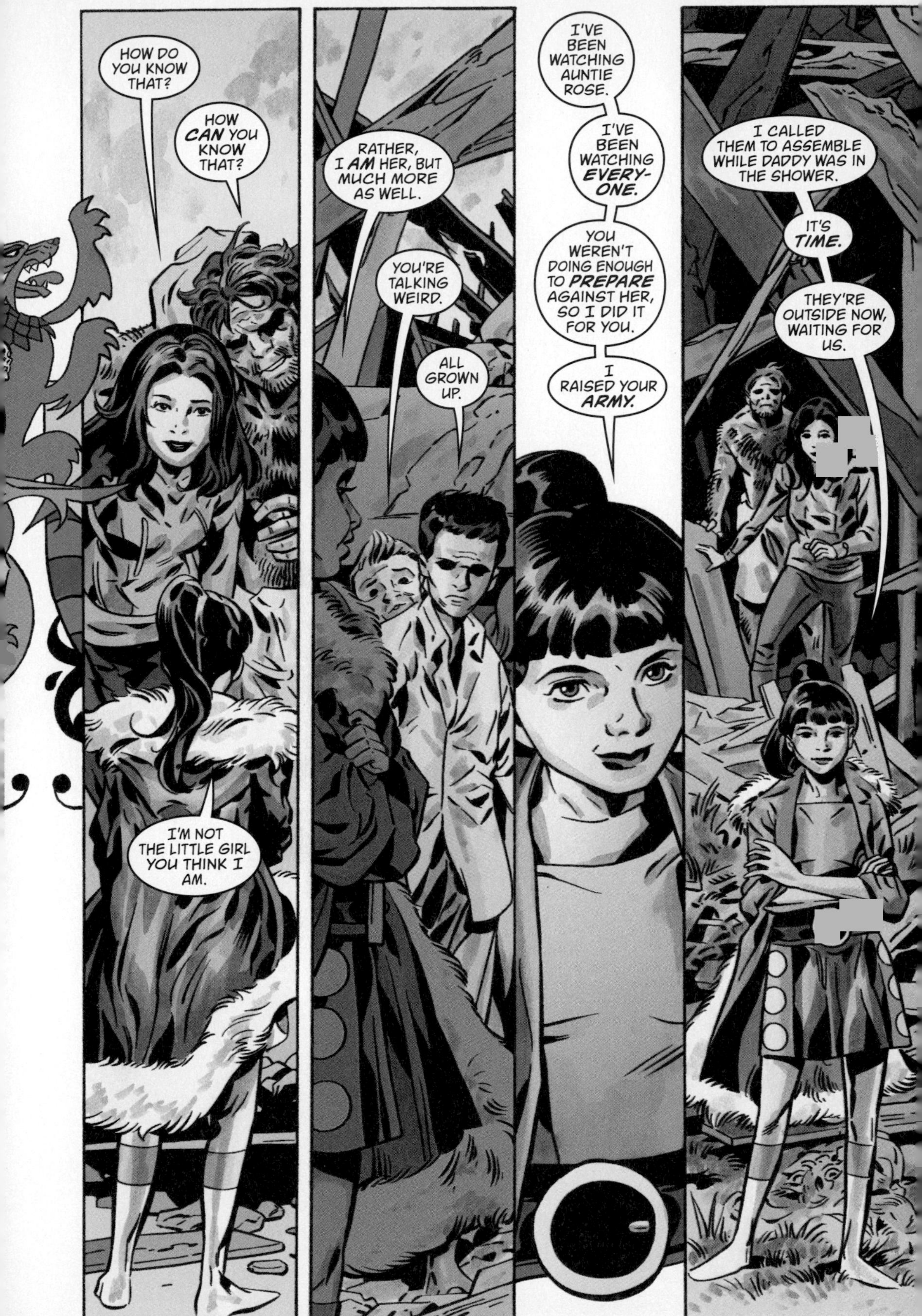
HOW DO YOU KNOW THAT?
HOW CAN YOU KNOW THAT?
I'M NOT THE LITTLE GIRL YOU THINK I AM.
RATHER, I AM HER, BUT MUCH MORE AS WELL.
YOU'RE TALKING WEIRD.
ALL GROWN UP.
I'VE BEEN WATCHING AUNTIE ROSE.
I'VE BEEN WATCHING EVERY-ONE.
YOU WEREN'T DOING ENOUGH TO PREPARE AGAINST HER, SO I DID IT FOR YOU.
I RAISED YOUR ARMY.
I CALLED THEM TO ASSEMBLE WHILE DADDY WAS IN THE SHOWER.
IT'S TIME.
THEY'RE OUTSIDE NOW, WAITING FOR US.

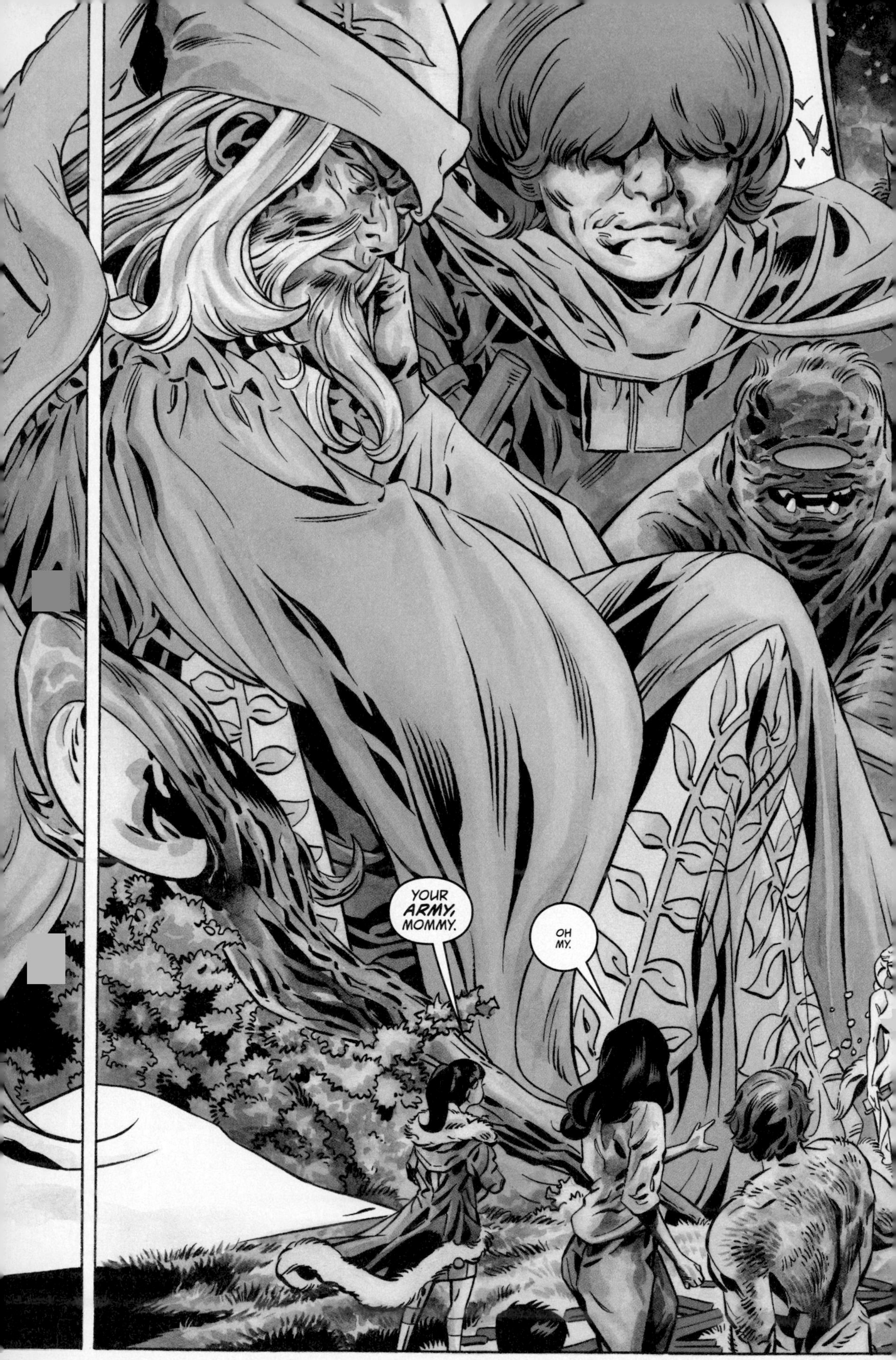
YOUR *ARMY,* MOMMY.
OH MY.

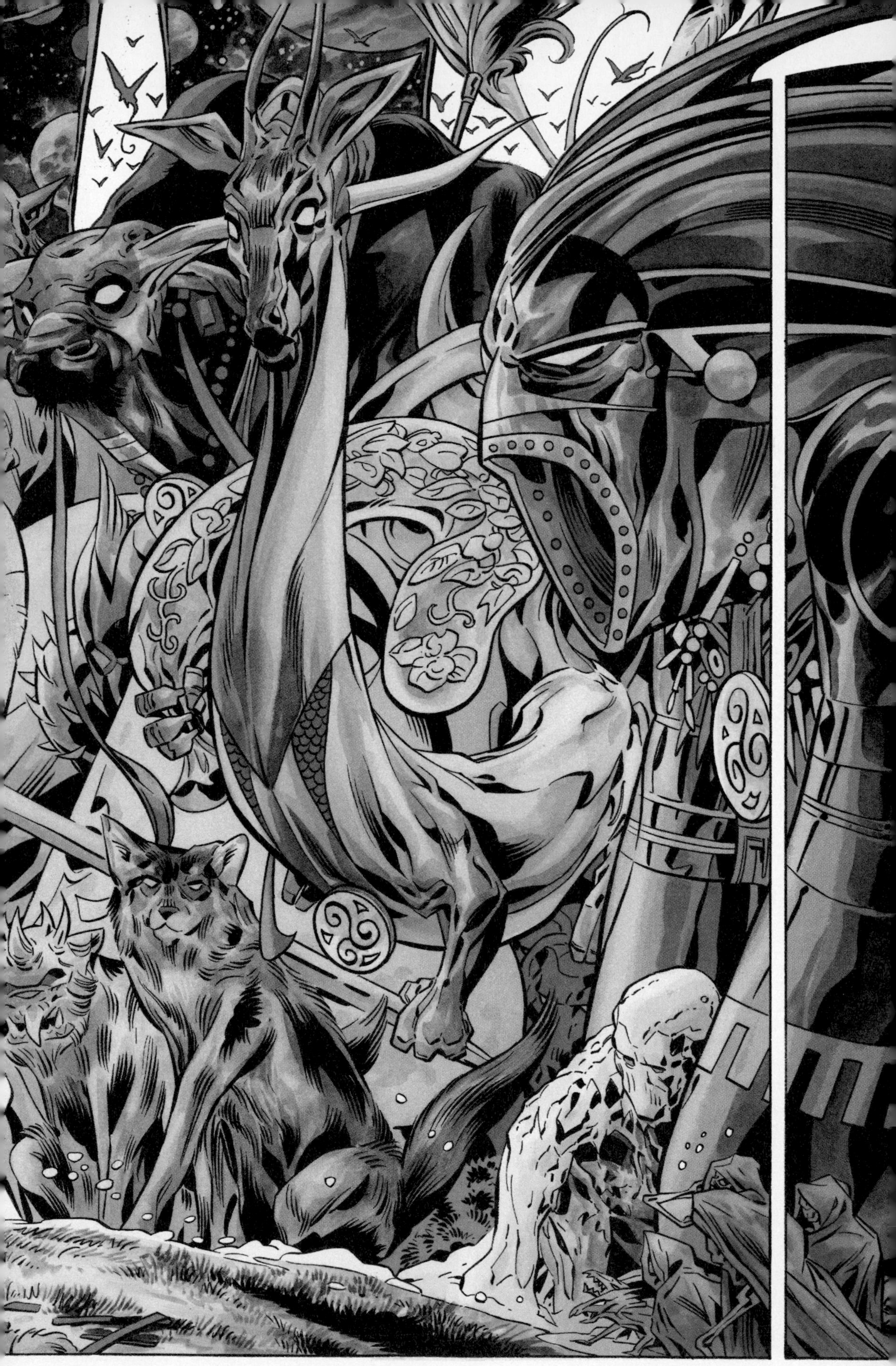

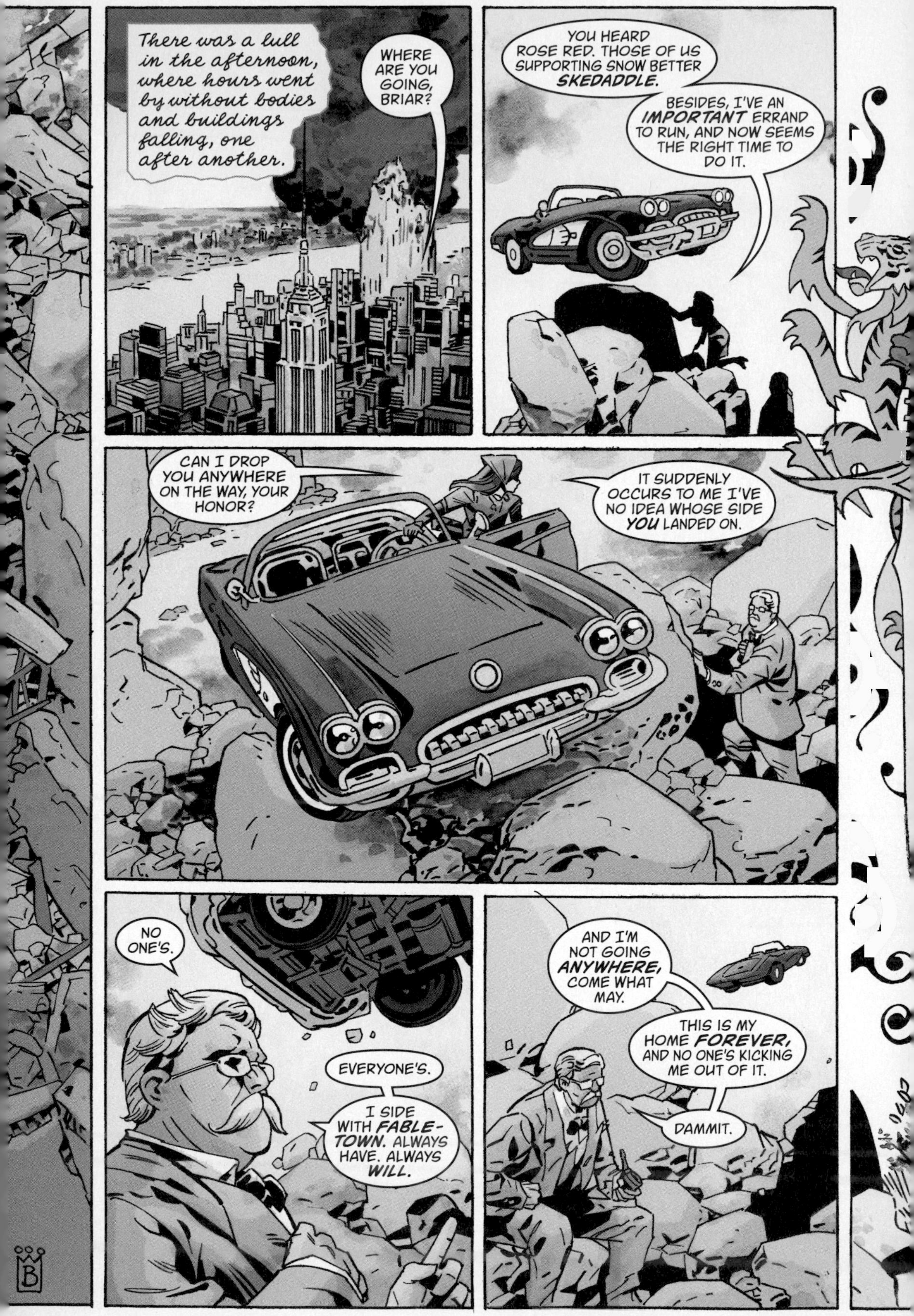
There was a lull in the afternoon, where hours went by without bodies and buildings falling, one after another.
WHERE ARE YOU GOING, BRIAR?
YOU HEARD ROSE RED. THOSE OF US SUPPORTING SNOW BETTER SKEDADDLE.
BESIDES, I'VE AN IMPORTANT ERRAND TO RUN, AND NOW SEEMS THE RIGHT TIME TO DO IT.
CAN I DROP YOU ANYWHERE ON THE WAY, YOUR HONOR?
IT SUDDENLY OCCURS TO ME I'VE NO IDEA WHOSE SIDE YOU LANDED ON.
NO ONE'S.
EVERYONE'S.
I SIDE WITH FABLE-TOWN. ALWAYS HAVE. ALWAYS WILL.
AND I'M NOT GOING ANYWHERE, COME WHAT MAY.
THIS IS MY HOME FOREVER, AND NO ONE'S KICKING ME OUT OF IT.
DAMMIT.

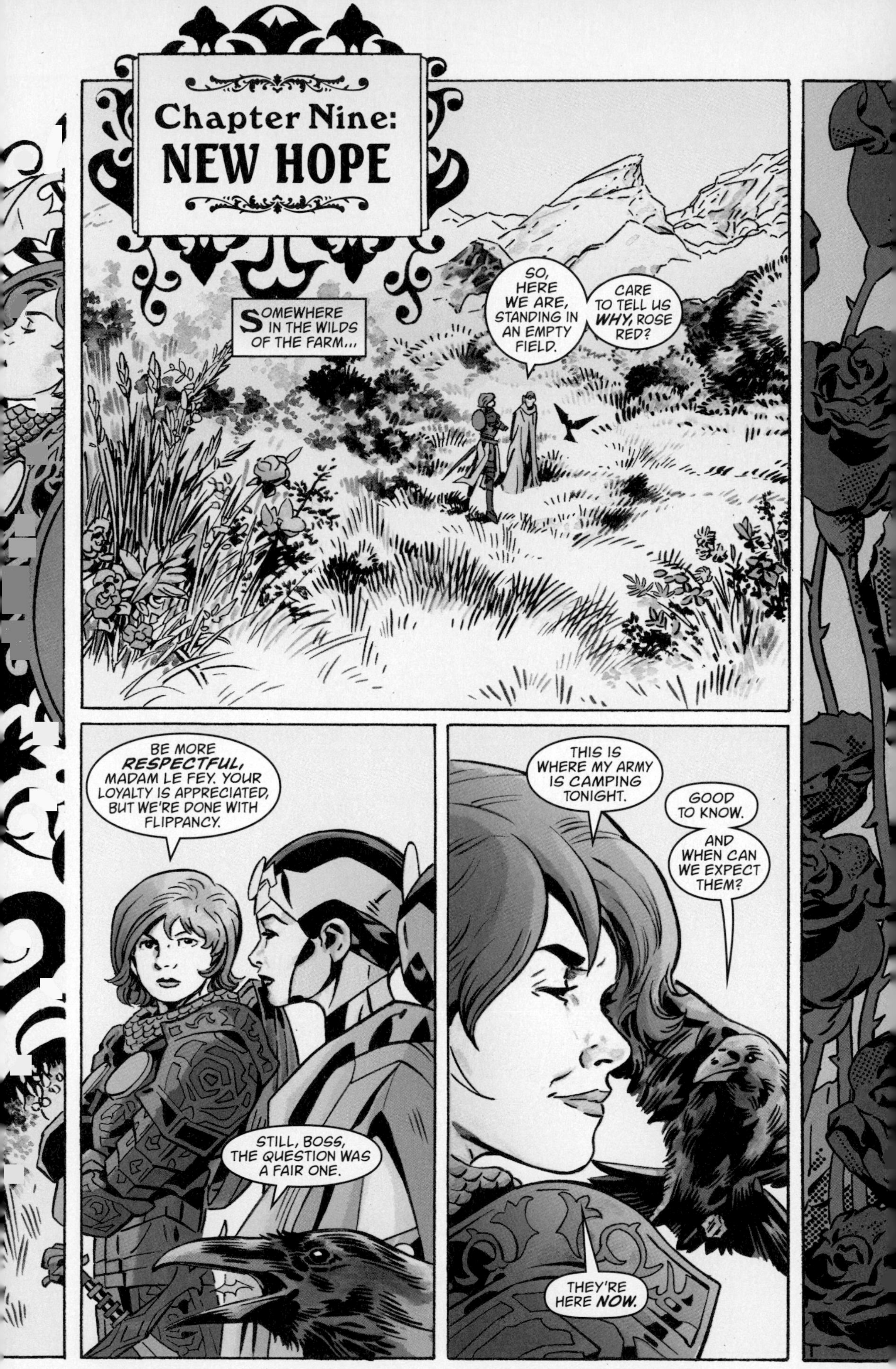
Chapter Nine:
NEW HOPE
SOMEWHERE IN THE WILDS OF THE FARM...
SO, HERE WE ARE, STANDING IN AN EMPTY FIELD.
CARE TO TELL US WHY, ROSE RED?
BE MORE RESPECTFUL, MADAM LE FEY. YOUR LOYALTY IS APPRECIATED, BUT WE'RE DONE WITH FLIPPANCY.
STILL, BOSS, THE QUESTION WAS A FAIR ONE.
THIS IS WHERE MY ARMY IS CAMPING TONIGHT.
GOOD TO KNOW.
AND WHEN CAN WE EXPECT THEM?
THEY'RE HERE NOW.

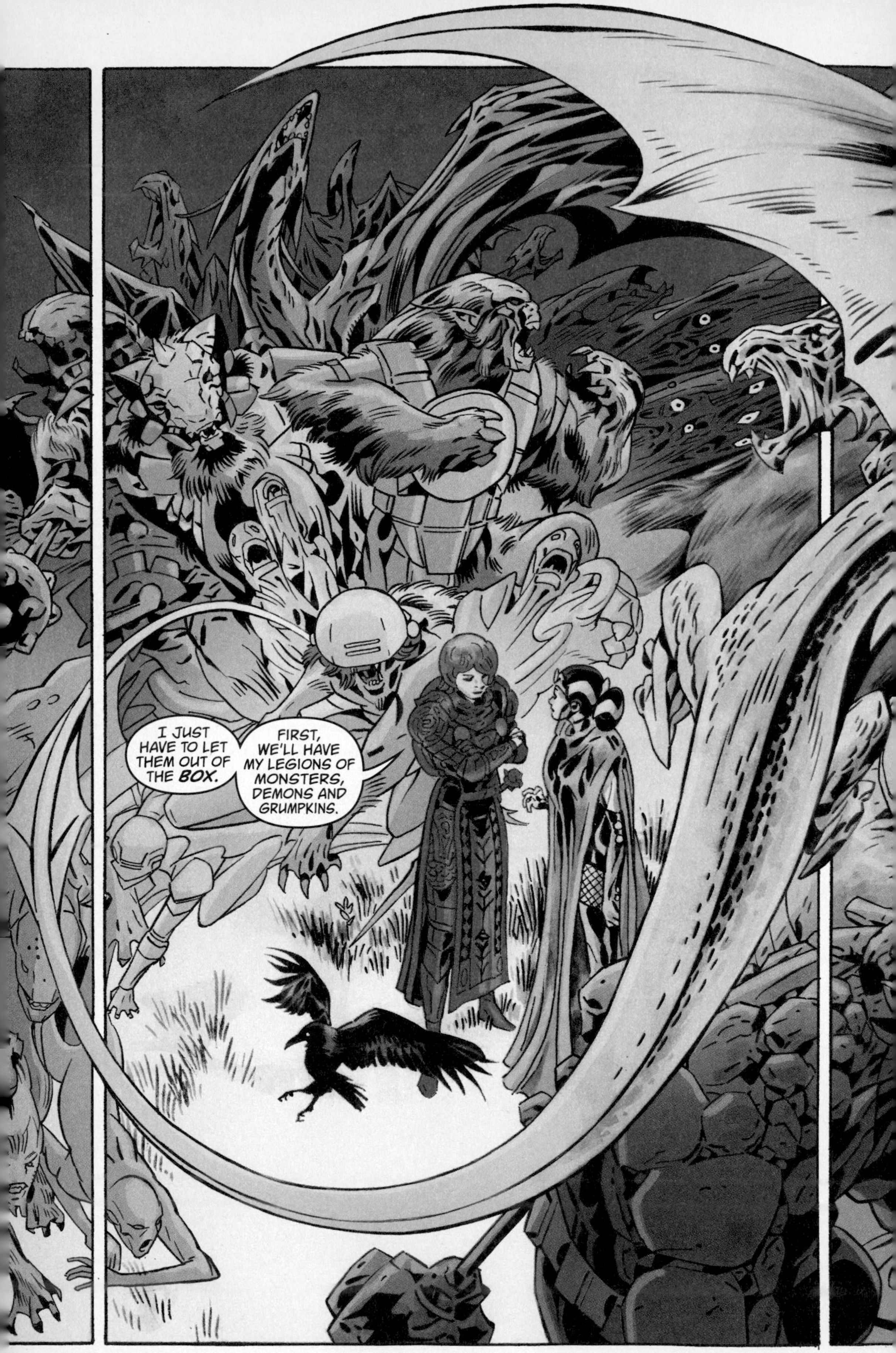
I JUST HAVE TO LET THEM OUT OF THE BOX.
FIRST, WE'LL HAVE MY LEGIONS OF MONSTERS, DEMONS AND GRUMPKINS.

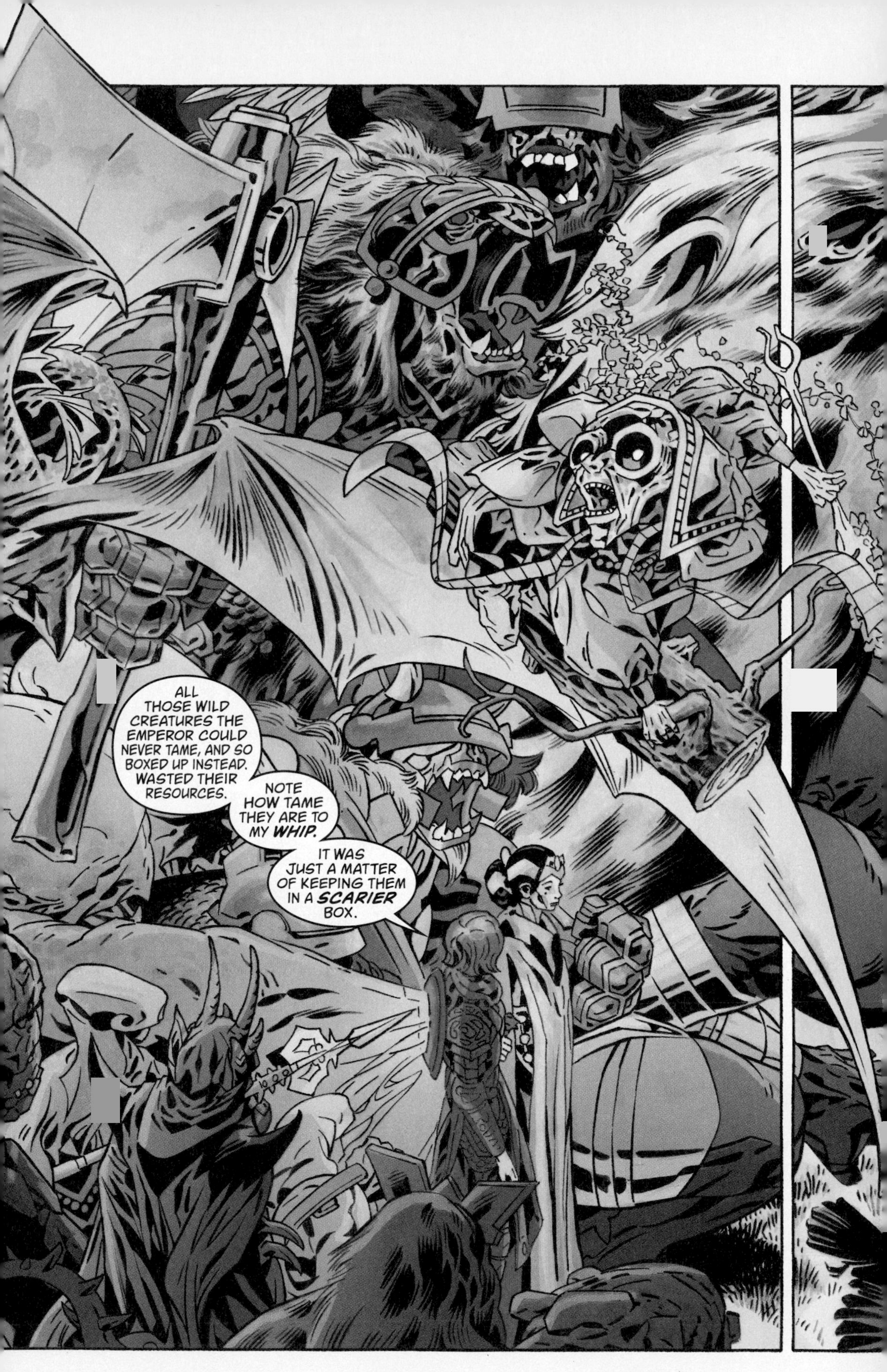
ALL THOSE WILD CREATURES THE EMPEROR COULD NEVER TAME, AND SO BOXED UP INSTEAD. WASTED THEIR RESOURCES.
NOTE HOW TAME THEY ARE TO MY WHIP.
IT WAS JUST A MATTER OF KEEPING THEM IN A SCARIER BOX.

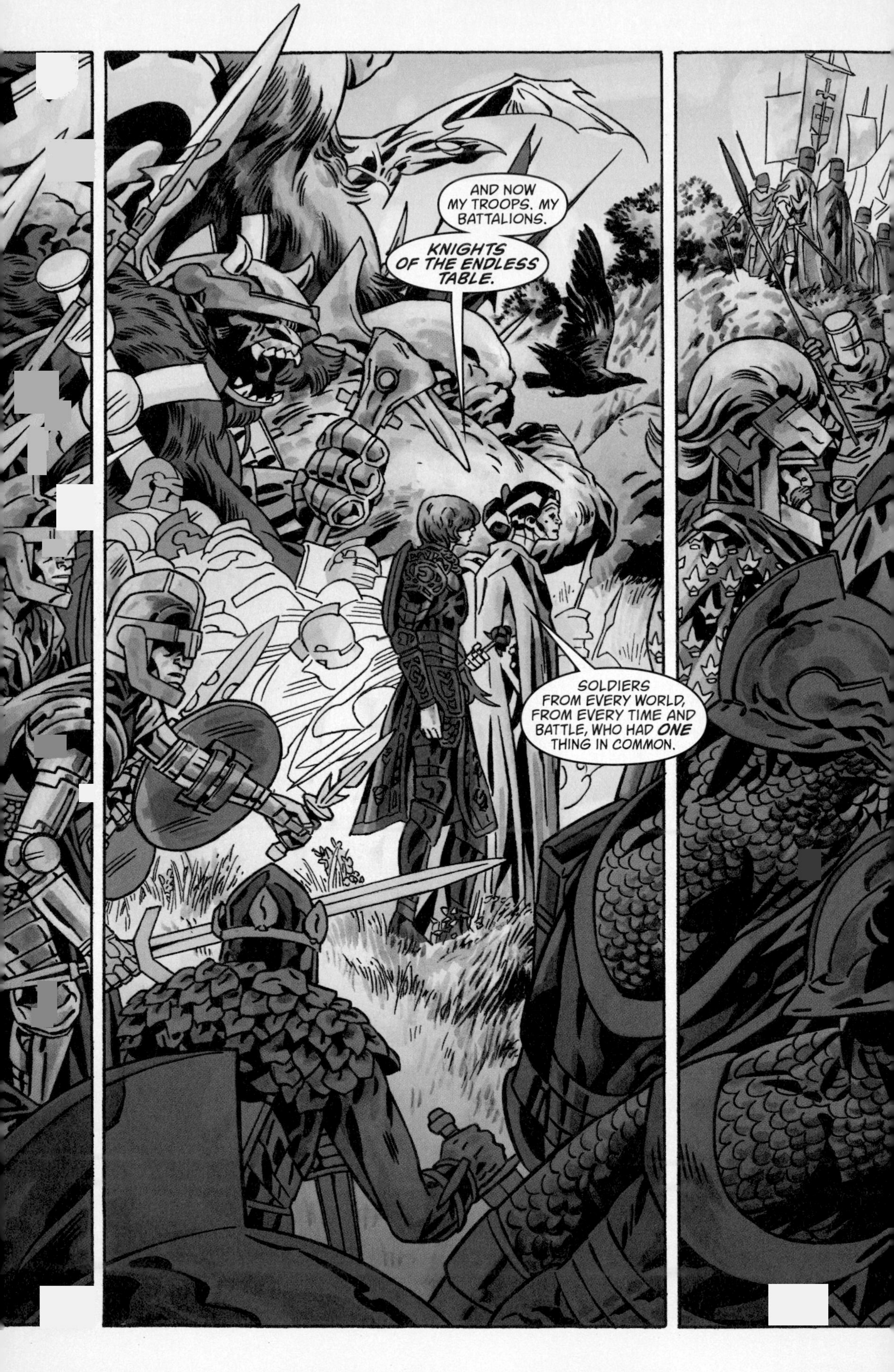
AND NOW MY TROOPS. MY BATTALIONS.
KNIGHTS OF THE ENDLESS TABLE.
SOLDIERS FROM EVERY WORLD, FROM EVERY TIME AND BATTLE, WHO HAD ONE THING IN COMMON.

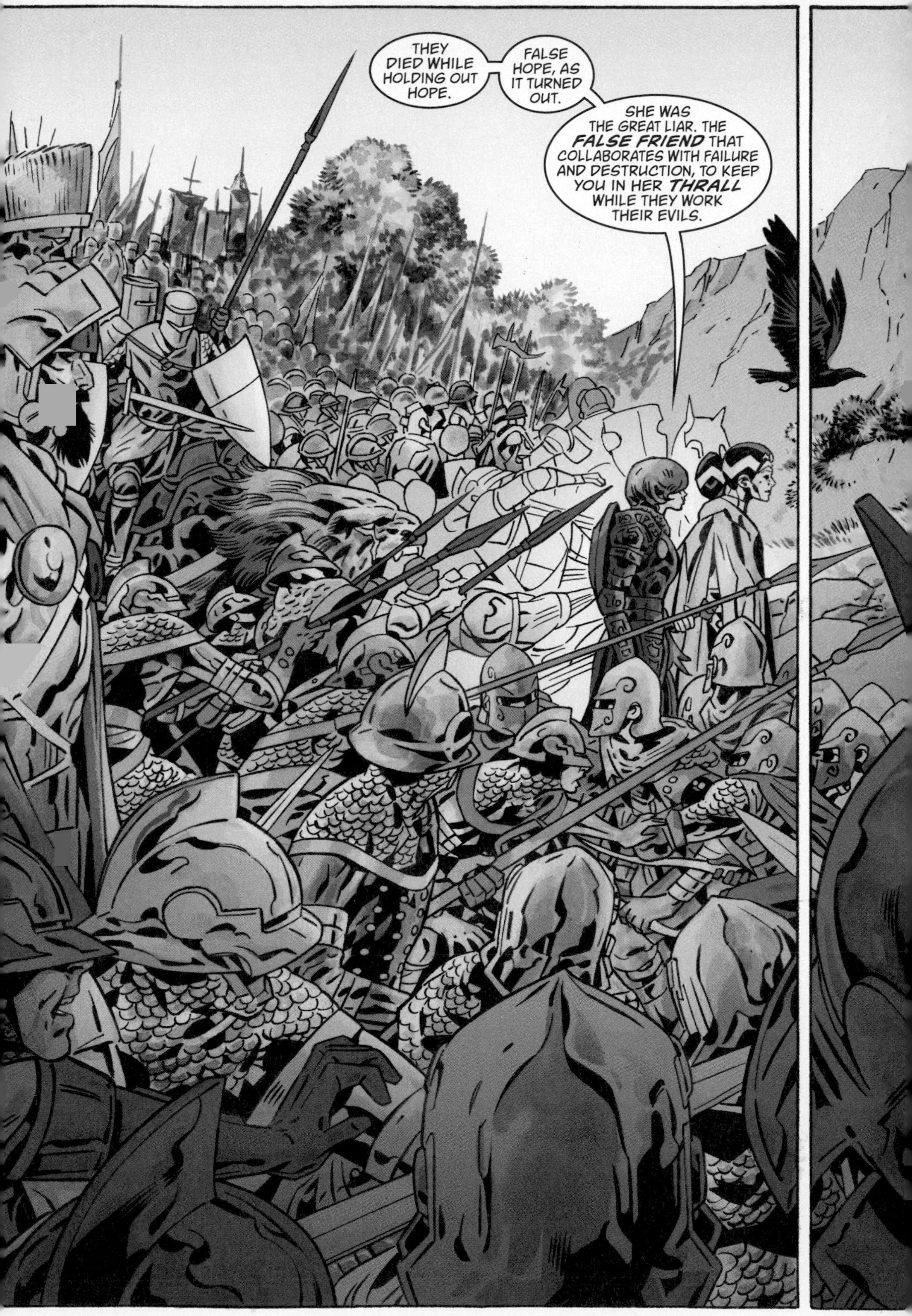
THEY DIED WHILE HOLDING OUT HOPE.
FALSE HOPE, AS IT TURNED OUT.
SHE WAS THE GREAT LIAR. THE ***FALSE FRIEND*** THAT COLLABORATES WITH FAILURE AND DESTRUCTION, TO KEEP YOU IN HER ***THRALL*** WHILE THEY WORK THEIR EVILS.

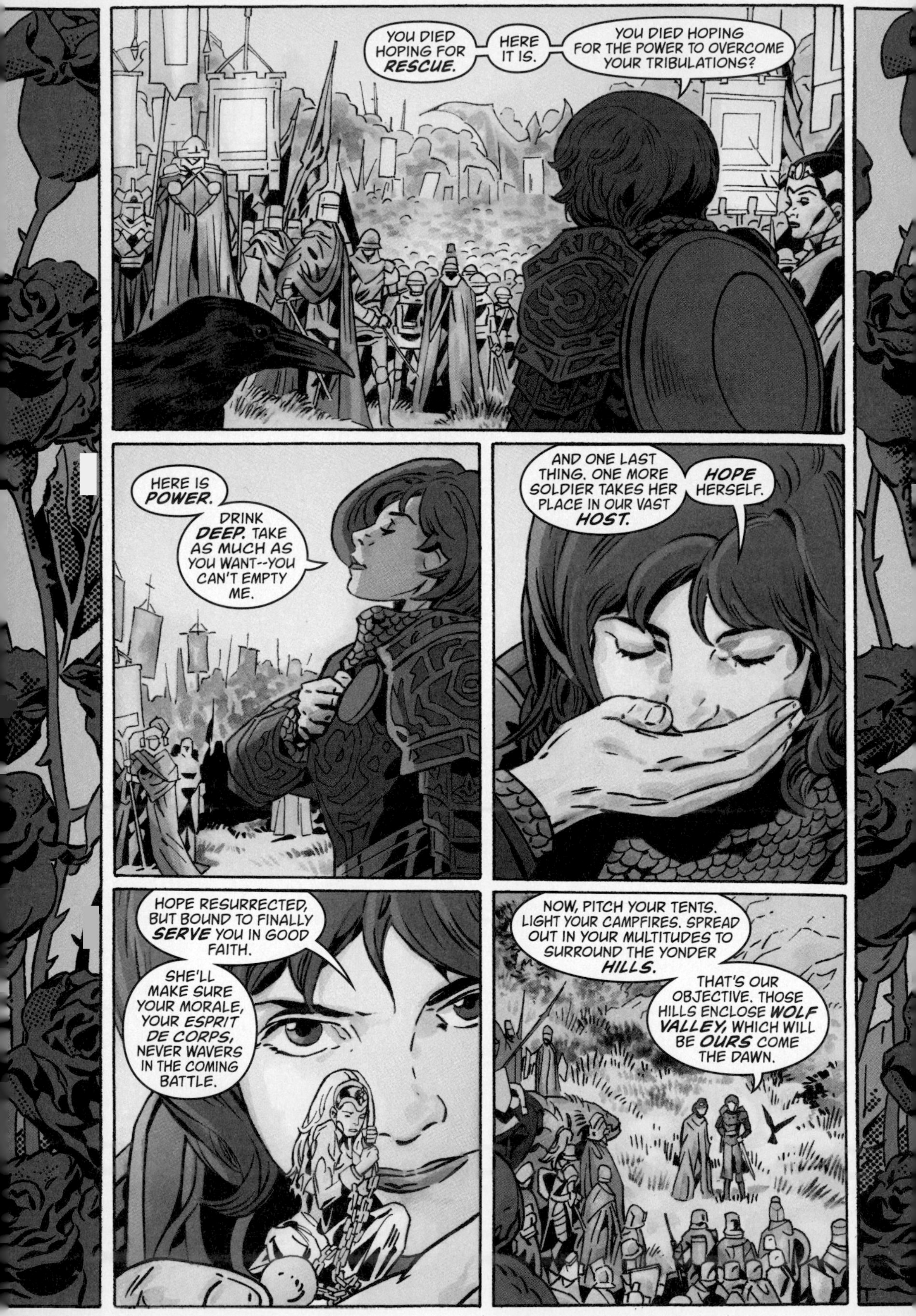
YOU DIED HOPING FOR RESCUE.
HERE IT IS.
YOU DIED HOPING FOR THE POWER TO OVERCOME YOUR TRIBULATIONS?
HERE IS POWER.
DRINK DEEP. TAKE AS MUCH AS YOU WANT--YOU CAN'T EMPTY ME.
AND ONE LAST THING. ONE MORE SOLDIER TAKES HER PLACE IN OUR VAST HOST.
HOPE HERSELF.
HOPE RESURRECTED, BUT BOUND TO FINALLY SERVE YOU IN GOOD FAITH.
SHE'LL MAKE SURE YOUR MORALE, YOUR ESPRIT DE CORPS, NEVER WAVERS IN THE COMING BATTLE.
NOW, PITCH YOUR TENTS. LIGHT YOUR CAMPFIRES. SPREAD OUT IN YOUR MULTITUDES TO SURROUND THE YONDER HILLS.
THAT'S OUR OBJECTIVE. THOSE HILLS ENCLOSE WOLF VALLEY, WHICH WILL BE OURS COME THE DAWN.

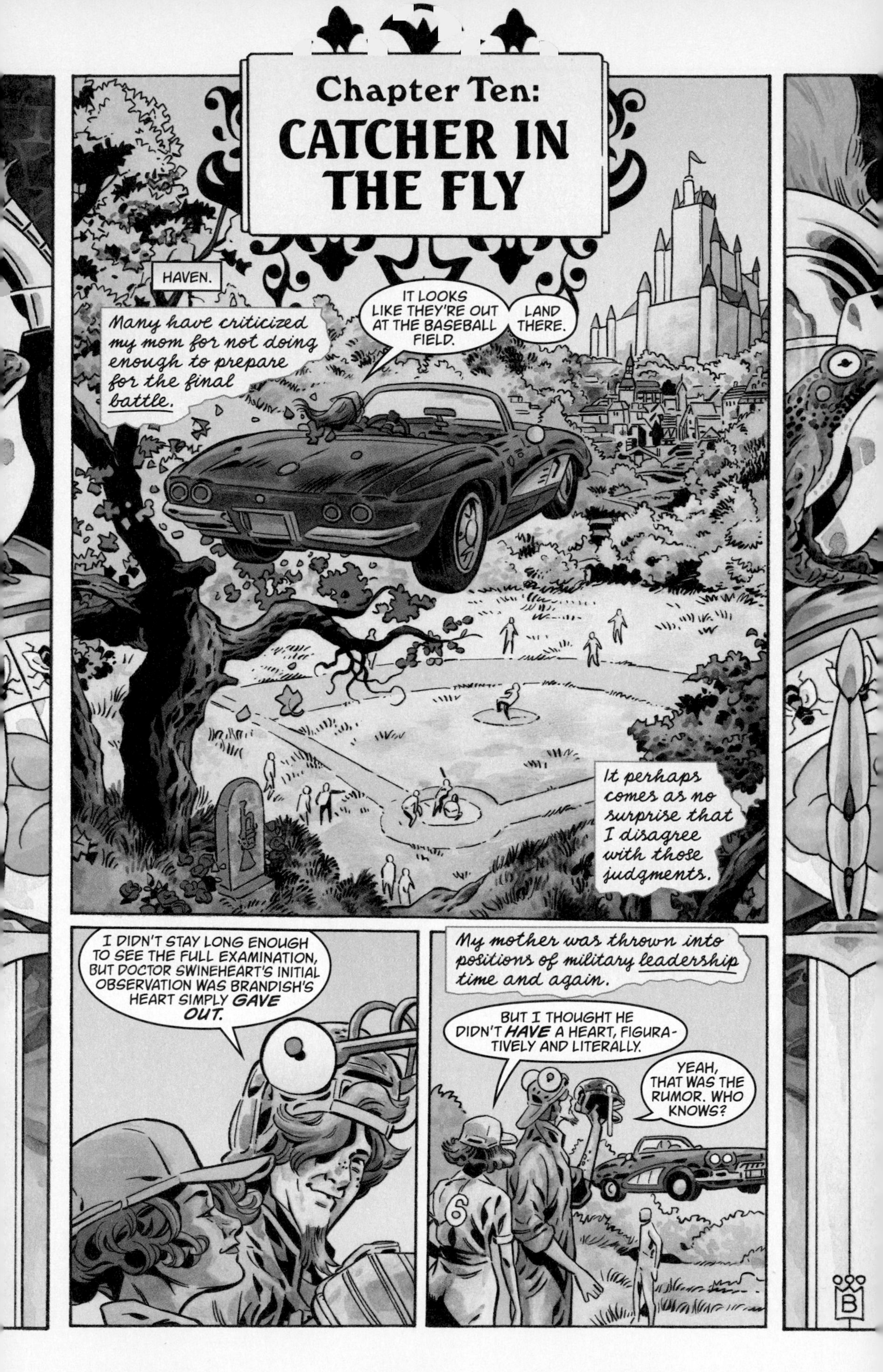
Chapter Ten:
CATCHER IN THE FLY
HAVEN.
Many have criticized my mom for not doing enough to prepare for the final battle.
IT LOOKS LIKE THEY'RE OUT AT THE BASEBALL FIELD.
LAND THERE.
It perhaps comes as no surprise that I disagree with those judgments.
I DIDN'T STAY LONG ENOUGH TO SEE THE FULL EXAMINATION, BUT DOCTOR SWINEHEART'S INITIAL OBSERVATION WAS BRANDISH'S HEART SIMPLY GAVE OUT.
My mother was thrown into positions of military leadership time and again.
BUT I THOUGHT HE DIDN'T HAVE A HEART, FIGURATIVELY AND LITERALLY.
YEAH, THAT WAS THE RUMOR. WHO KNOWS?

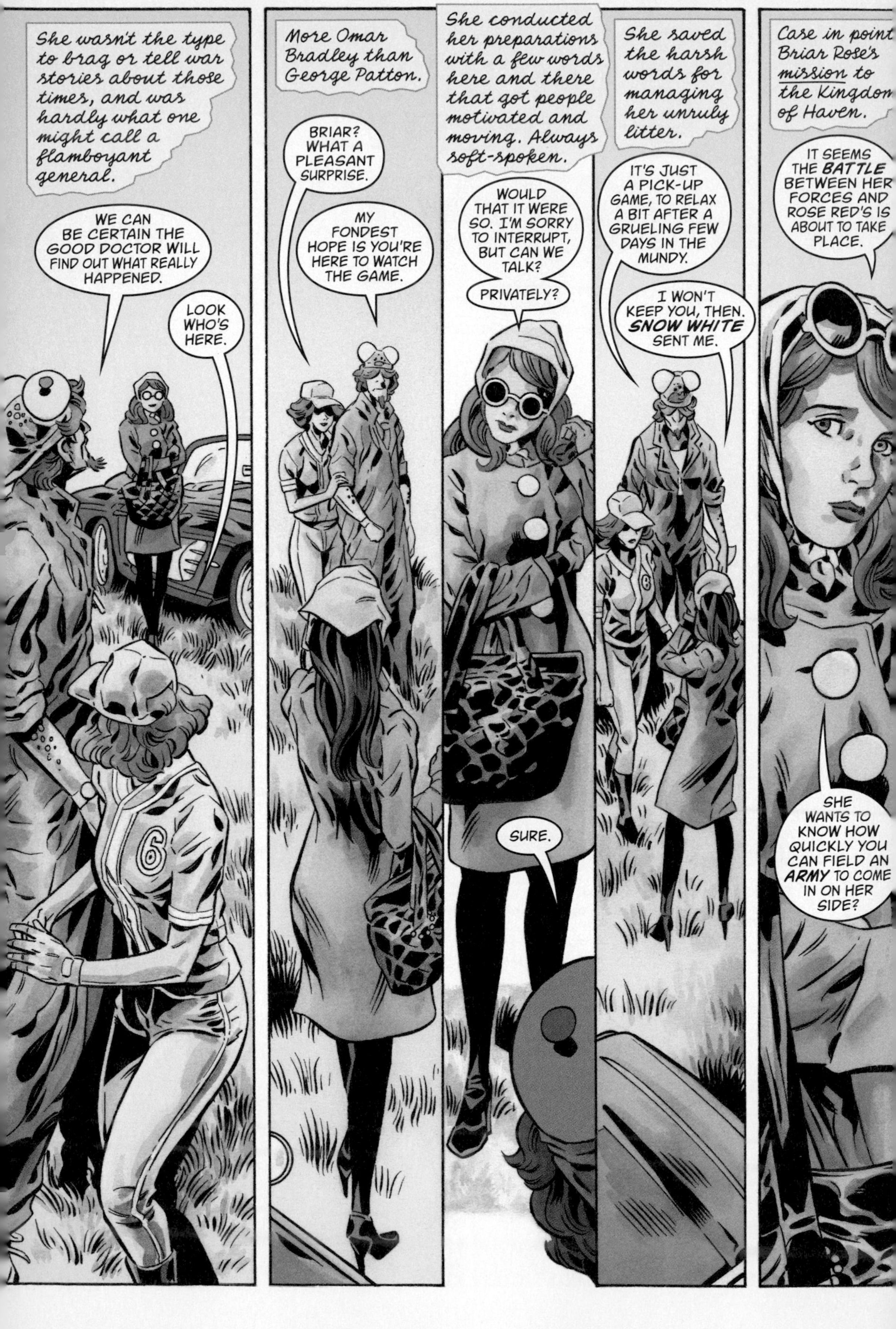
She wasn't the type to brag or tell war stories about those times, and was hardly what one might call a flamboyant general.
WE CAN BE CERTAIN THE GOOD DOCTOR WILL FIND OUT WHAT REALLY HAPPENED.
LOOK WHO'S HERE.
More Omar Bradley than George Patton.
BRIAR? WHAT A PLEASANT SURPRISE.
MY FONDEST HOPE IS YOU'RE HERE TO WATCH THE GAME.
She conducted her preparations with a few words here and there that got people motivated and moving. Always soft-spoken.
WOULD THAT IT WERE SO. I'M SORRY TO INTERRUPT, BUT CAN WE TALK?
PRIVATELY?
SURE.
She saved the harsh words for managing her unruly litter.
IT'S JUST A PICK-UP GAME, TO RELAX A BIT AFTER A GRUELING FEW DAYS IN THE MUNDY.
I WON'T KEEP YOU, THEN. SNOW WHITE SENT ME.
Case in point Briar Rose's mission to the Kingdom of Haven.
IT SEEMS THE BATTLE BETWEEN HER FORCES AND ROSE RED'S IS ABOUT TO TAKE PLACE.
SHE WANTS TO KNOW HOW QUICKLY YOU CAN FIELD AN ARMY TO COME IN ON HER SIDE?

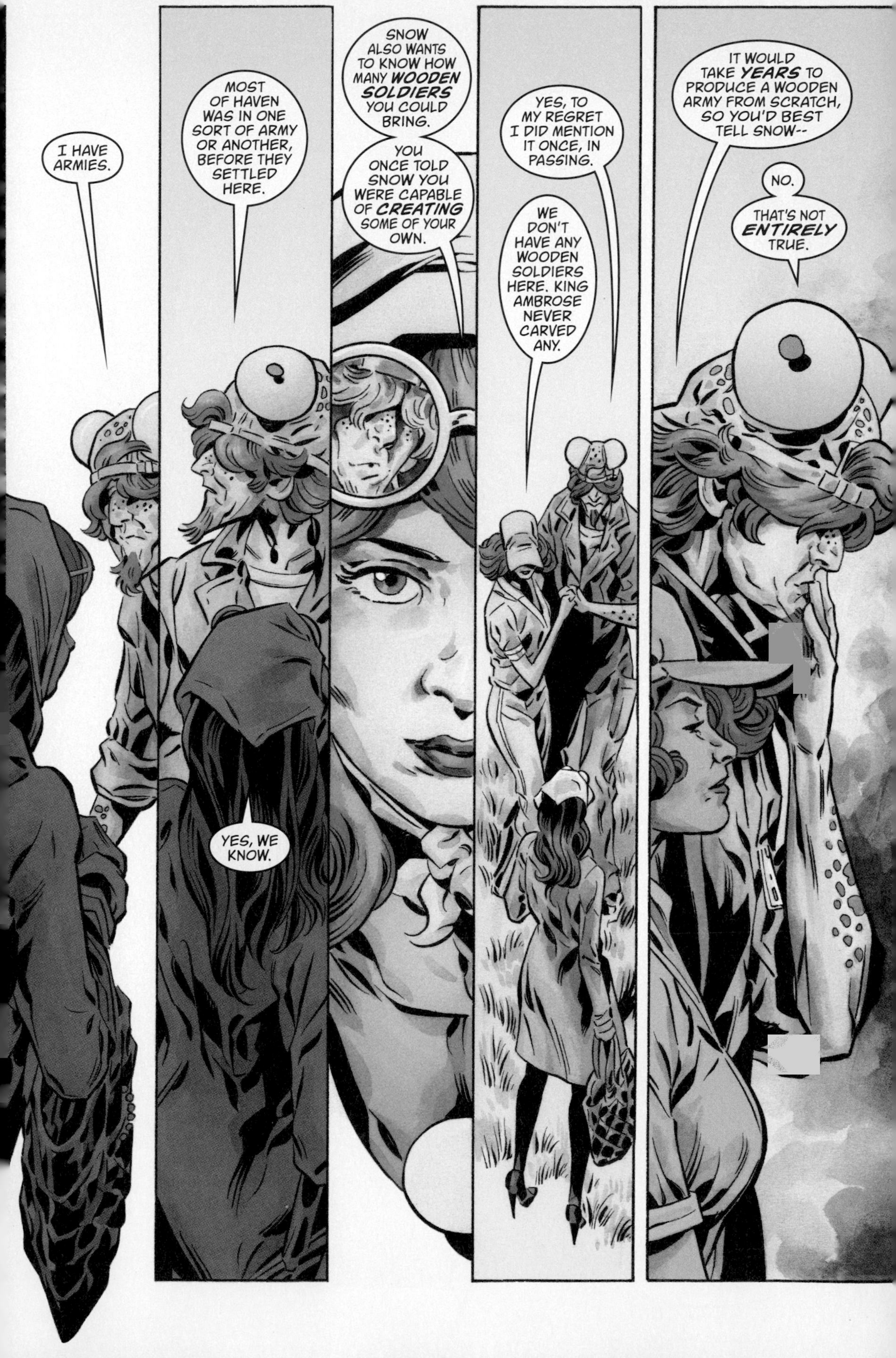
I HAVE ARMIES.
MOST OF HAVEN WAS IN ONE SORT OF ARMY OR ANOTHER, BEFORE THEY SETTLED HERE.
YES, WE KNOW.
SNOW ALSO WANTS TO KNOW HOW MANY WOODEN SOLDIERS YOU COULD BRING.
YOU ONCE TOLD SNOW YOU WERE CAPABLE OF CREATING SOME OF YOUR OWN.
YES, TO MY REGRET I DID MENTION IT ONCE, IN PASSING.
WE DON'T HAVE ANY WOODEN SOLDIERS HERE. KING AMBROSE NEVER CARVED ANY.
IT WOULD TAKE YEARS TO PRODUCE A WOODEN ARMY FROM SCRATCH, SO YOU'D BEST TELL SNOW--
NO.
THAT'S NOT ENTIRELY TRUE.

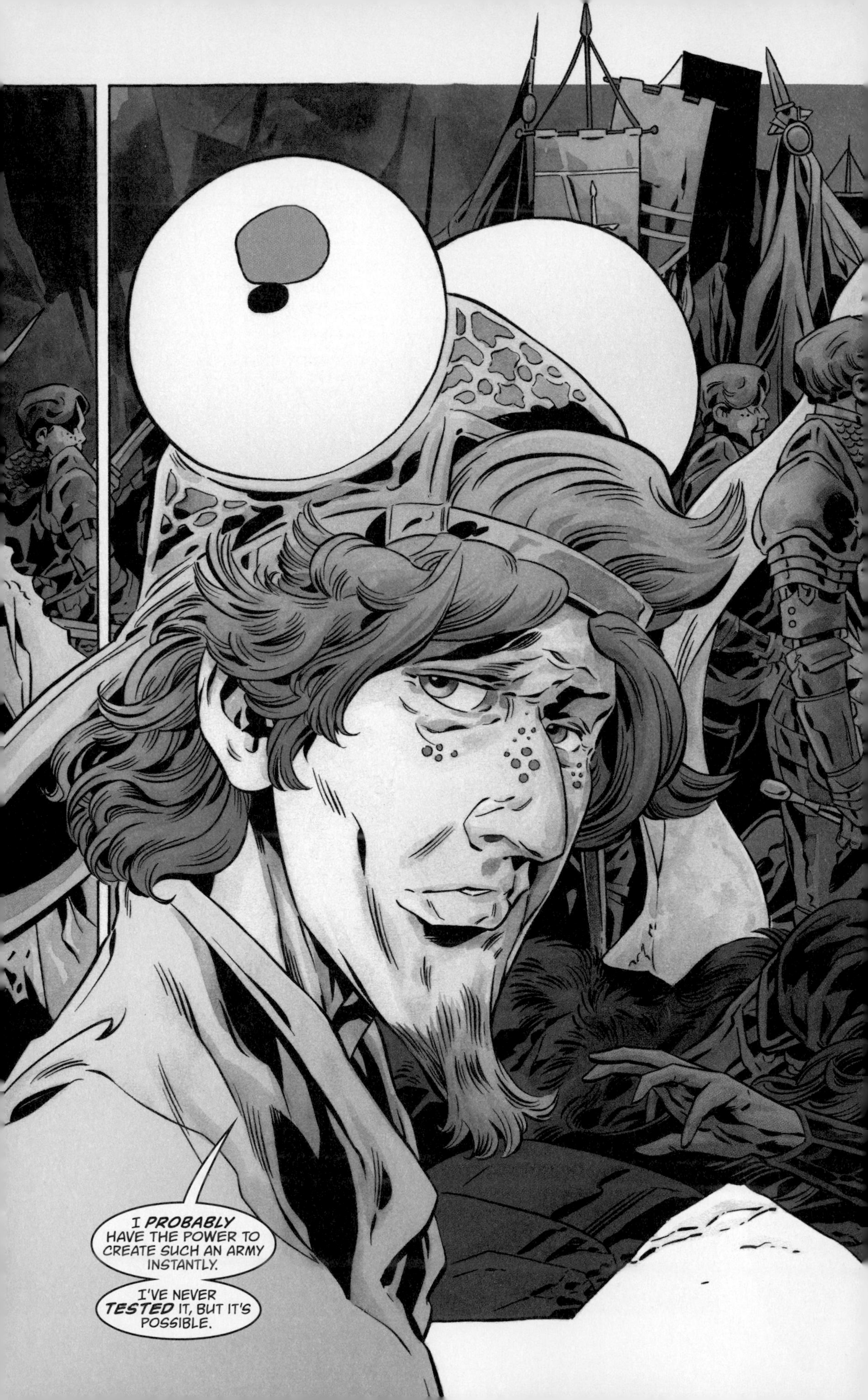
I *PROBABLY* HAVE THE POWER TO CREATE SUCH AN ARMY INSTANTLY.
I'VE NEVER *TESTED* IT, BUT IT'S POSSIBLE.

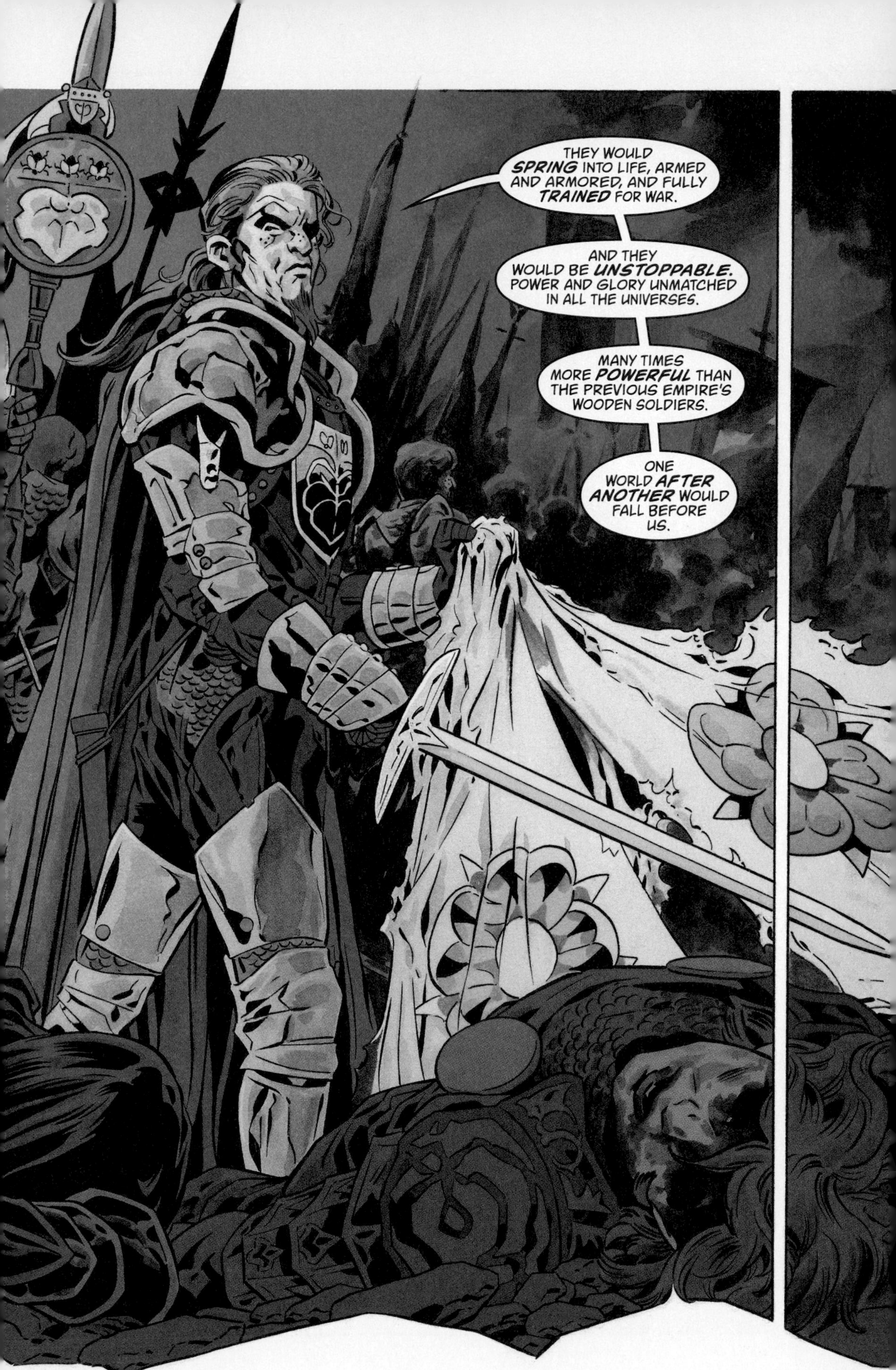
THEY WOULD SPRING INTO LIFE, ARMED AND ARMORED, AND FULLY TRAINED FOR WAR.
AND THEY WOULD BE UNSTOPPABLE. POWER AND GLORY UNMATCHED IN ALL THE UNIVERSES.
MANY TIMES MORE POWERFUL THAN THE PREVIOUS EMPIRE'S WOODEN SOLDIERS.
ONE WORLD AFTER ANOTHER WOULD FALL BEFORE US.

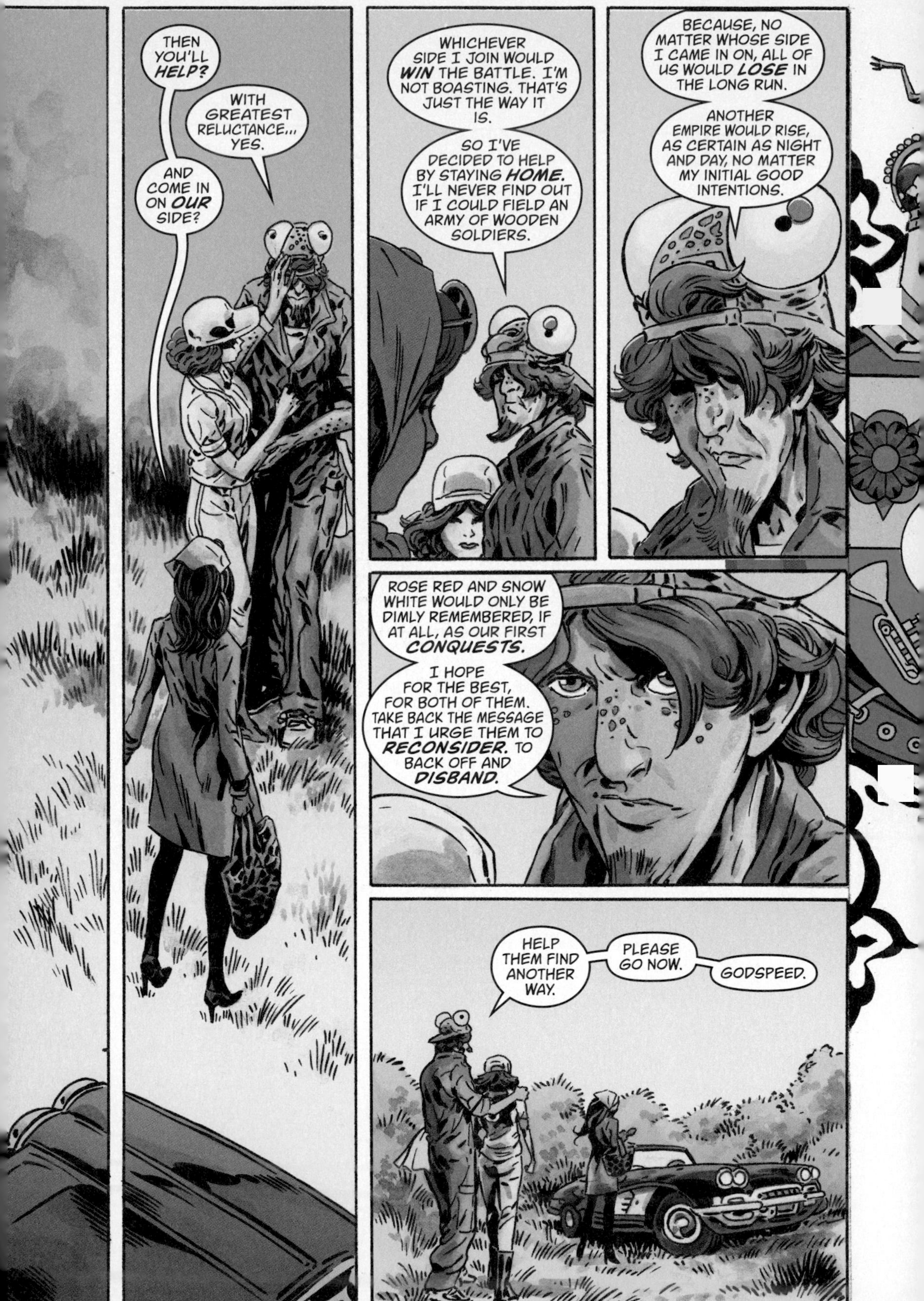

THEN YOU'LL HELP?
WITH GREATEST RELUCTANCE... YES.
AND COME IN ON OUR SIDE?
WHICHEVER SIDE I JOIN WOULD WIN THE BATTLE. I'M NOT BOASTING. THAT'S JUST THE WAY IT IS.
SO I'VE DECIDED TO HELP BY STAYING HOME. I'LL NEVER FIND OUT IF I COULD FIELD AN ARMY OF WOODEN SOLDIERS.
BECAUSE, NO MATTER WHOSE SIDE I CAME IN ON, ALL OF US WOULD LOSE IN THE LONG RUN.
ANOTHER EMPIRE WOULD RISE, AS CERTAIN AS NIGHT AND DAY, NO MATTER MY INITIAL GOOD INTENTIONS.
ROSE RED AND SNOW WHITE WOULD ONLY BE DIMLY REMEMBERED, IF AT ALL, AS OUR FIRST CONQUESTS.
I HOPE FOR THE BEST, FOR BOTH OF THEM. TAKE BACK THE MESSAGE THAT I URGE THEM TO RECONSIDER. TO BACK OFF AND DISBAND.
HELP THEM FIND ANOTHER WAY.
PLEASE GO NOW.
GODSPEED.

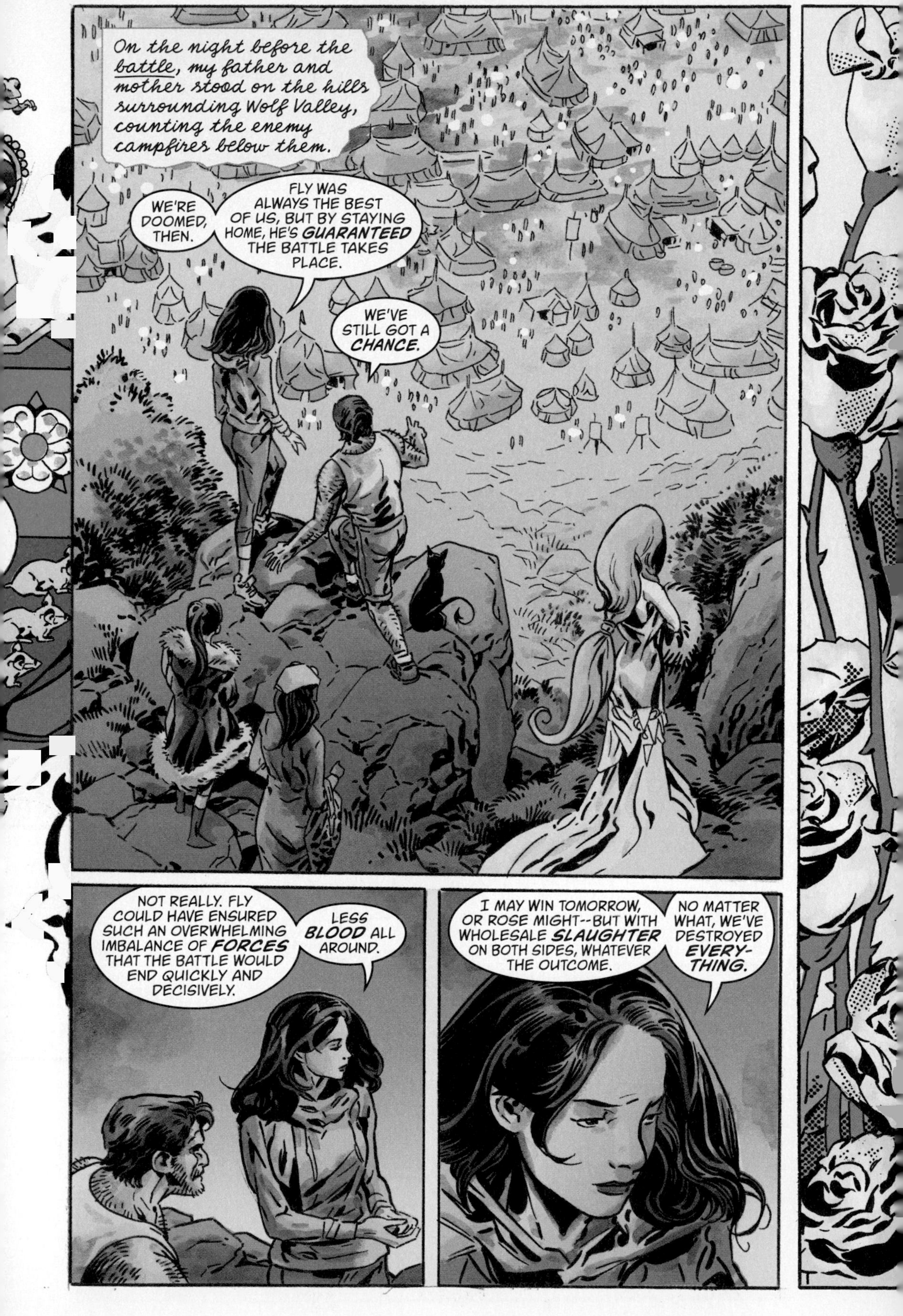
On the night before the battle, my father and mother stood on the hills surrounding Wolf Valley, counting the enemy campfires below them.
WE'RE DOOMED, THEN.
FLY WAS ALWAYS THE BEST OF US, BUT BY STAYING HOME, HE'S GUARANTEED THE BATTLE TAKES PLACE.
WE'VE STILL GOT A CHANCE.
NOT REALLY. FLY COULD HAVE ENSURED SUCH AN OVERWHELMING IMBALANCE OF FORCES THAT THE BATTLE WOULD END QUICKLY AND DECISIVELY.
LESS BLOOD ALL AROUND.
I MAY WIN TOMORROW, OR ROSE MIGHT--BUT WITH WHOLESALE SLAUGHTER ON BOTH SIDES, WHATEVER THE OUTCOME.
NO MATTER WHAT, WE'VE DESTROYED EVERYTHING.

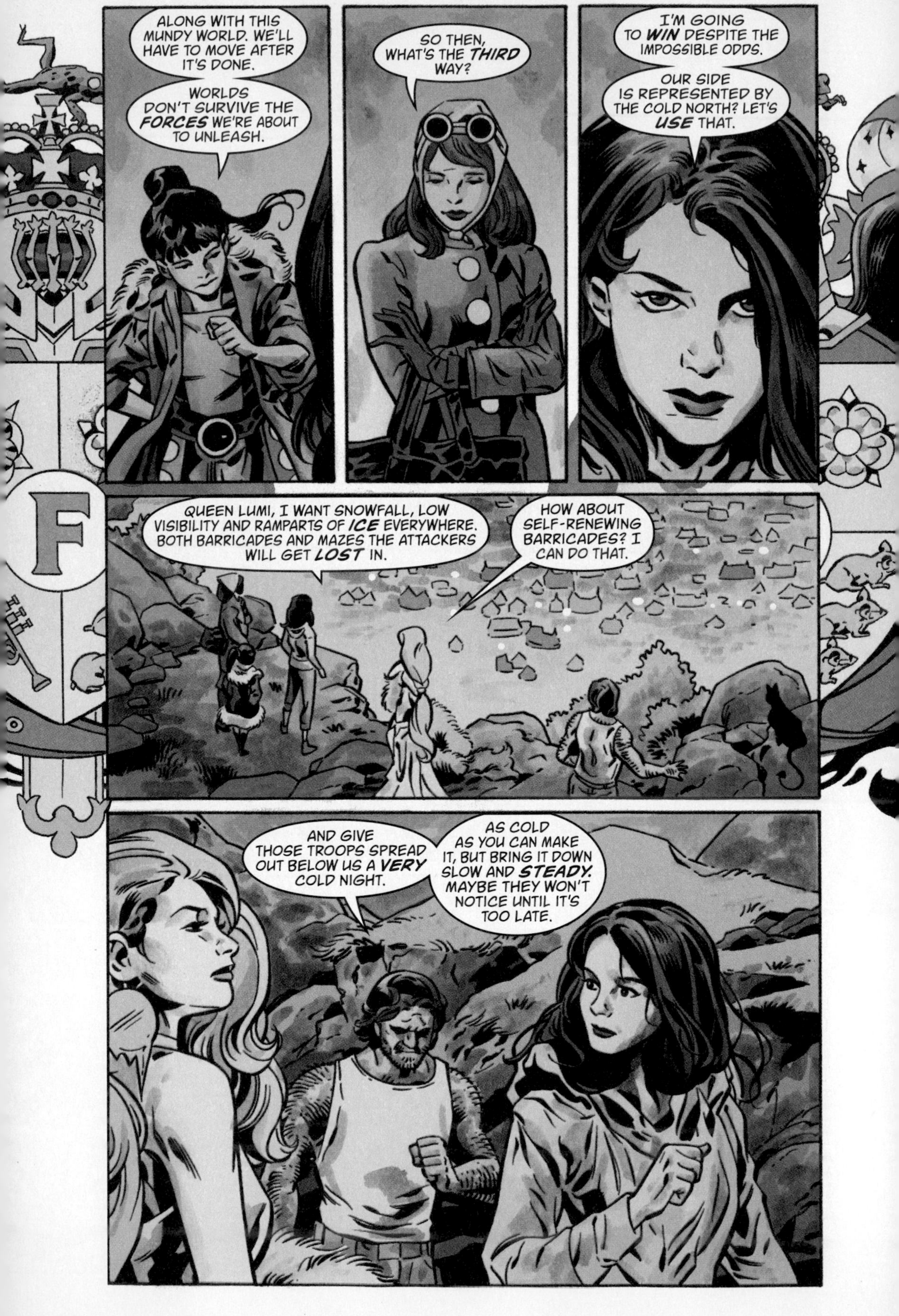
ALONG WITH THIS MUNDY WORLD. WE'LL HAVE TO MOVE AFTER IT'S DONE.
WORLDS DON'T SURVIVE THE FORCES WE'RE ABOUT TO UNLEASH.
SO THEN, WHAT'S THE THIRD WAY?
I'M GOING TO WIN DESPITE THE IMPOSSIBLE ODDS.
OUR SIDE IS REPRESENTED BY THE COLD NORTH? LET'S USE THAT.
QUEEN LUMI, I WANT SNOWFALL, LOW VISIBILITY AND RAMPARTS OF ICE EVERYWHERE. BOTH BARRICADES AND MAZES THE ATTACKERS WILL GET LOST IN.
HOW ABOUT SELF-RENEWING BARRICADES? I CAN DO THAT.
AND GIVE THOSE TROOPS SPREAD OUT BELOW US A VERY COLD NIGHT.
AS COLD AS YOU CAN MAKE IT, BUT BRING IT DOWN SLOW AND STEADY. MAYBE THEY WON'T NOTICE UNTIL IT'S TOO LATE.

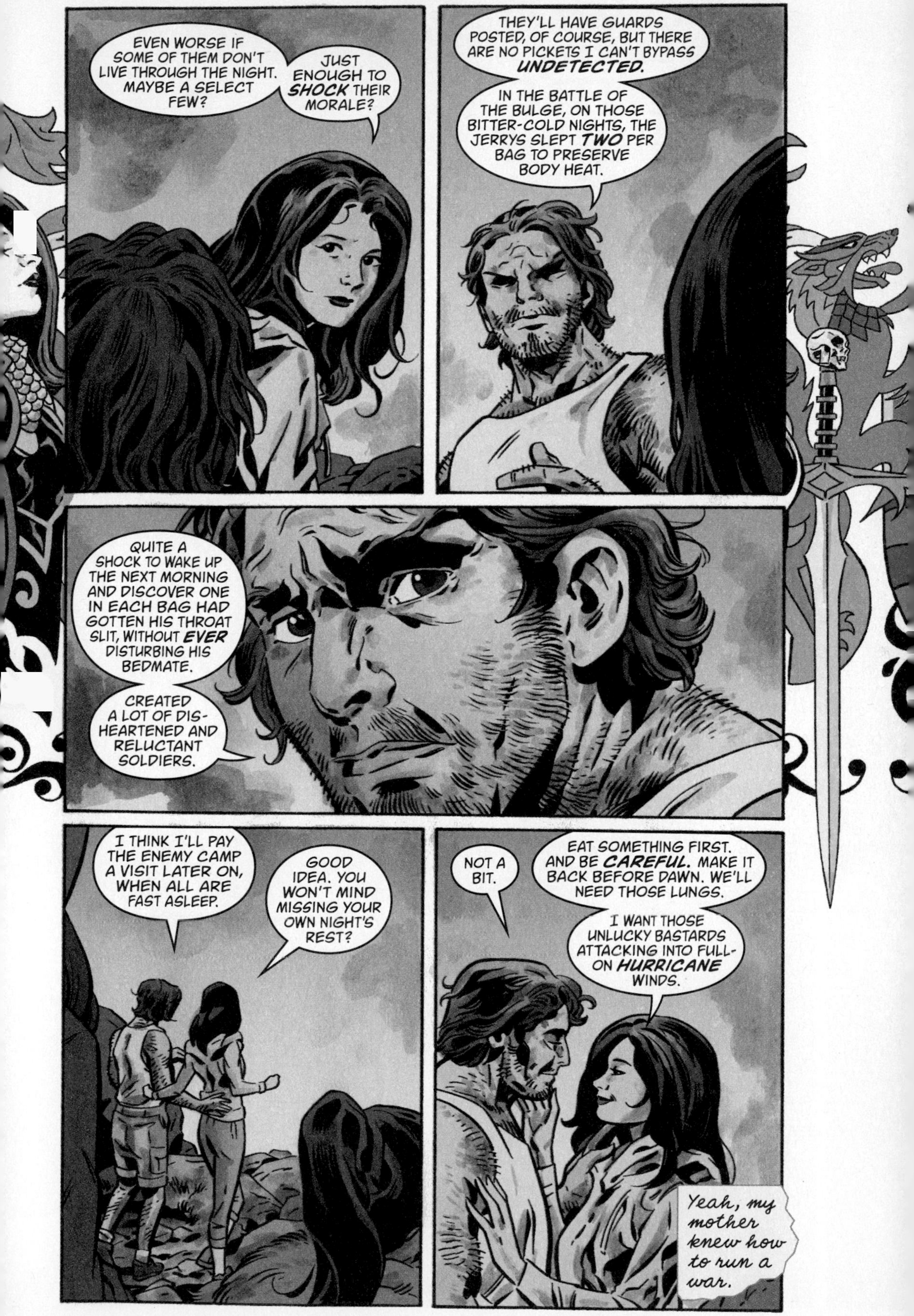
EVEN WORSE IF SOME OF THEM DON'T LIVE THROUGH THE NIGHT. MAYBE A SELECT FEW?
JUST ENOUGH TO SHOCK THEIR MORALE?
THEY'LL HAVE GUARDS POSTED, OF COURSE, BUT THERE ARE NO PICKETS I CAN'T BYPASS UNDETECTED.
IN THE BATTLE OF THE BULGE, ON THOSE BITTER-COLD NIGHTS, THE JERRYS SLEPT TWO PER BAG TO PRESERVE BODY HEAT.
QUITE A SHOCK TO WAKE UP THE NEXT MORNING AND DISCOVER ONE IN EACH BAG HAD GOTTEN HIS THROAT SLIT, WITHOUT EVER DISTURBING HIS BEDMATE.
CREATED A LOT OF DIS-HEARTENED AND RELUCTANT SOLDIERS.
I THINK I'LL PAY THE ENEMY CAMP A VISIT LATER ON, WHEN ALL ARE FAST ASLEEP.
GOOD IDEA. YOU WON'T MIND MISSING YOUR OWN NIGHT'S REST?
NOT A BIT.
EAT SOMETHING FIRST. AND BE CAREFUL. MAKE IT BACK BEFORE DAWN. WE'LL NEED THOSE LUNGS.
I WANT THOSE UNLUCKY BASTARDS ATTACKING INTO FULL-ON HURRICANE WINDS.
Yeah, my mother knew how to run a war.

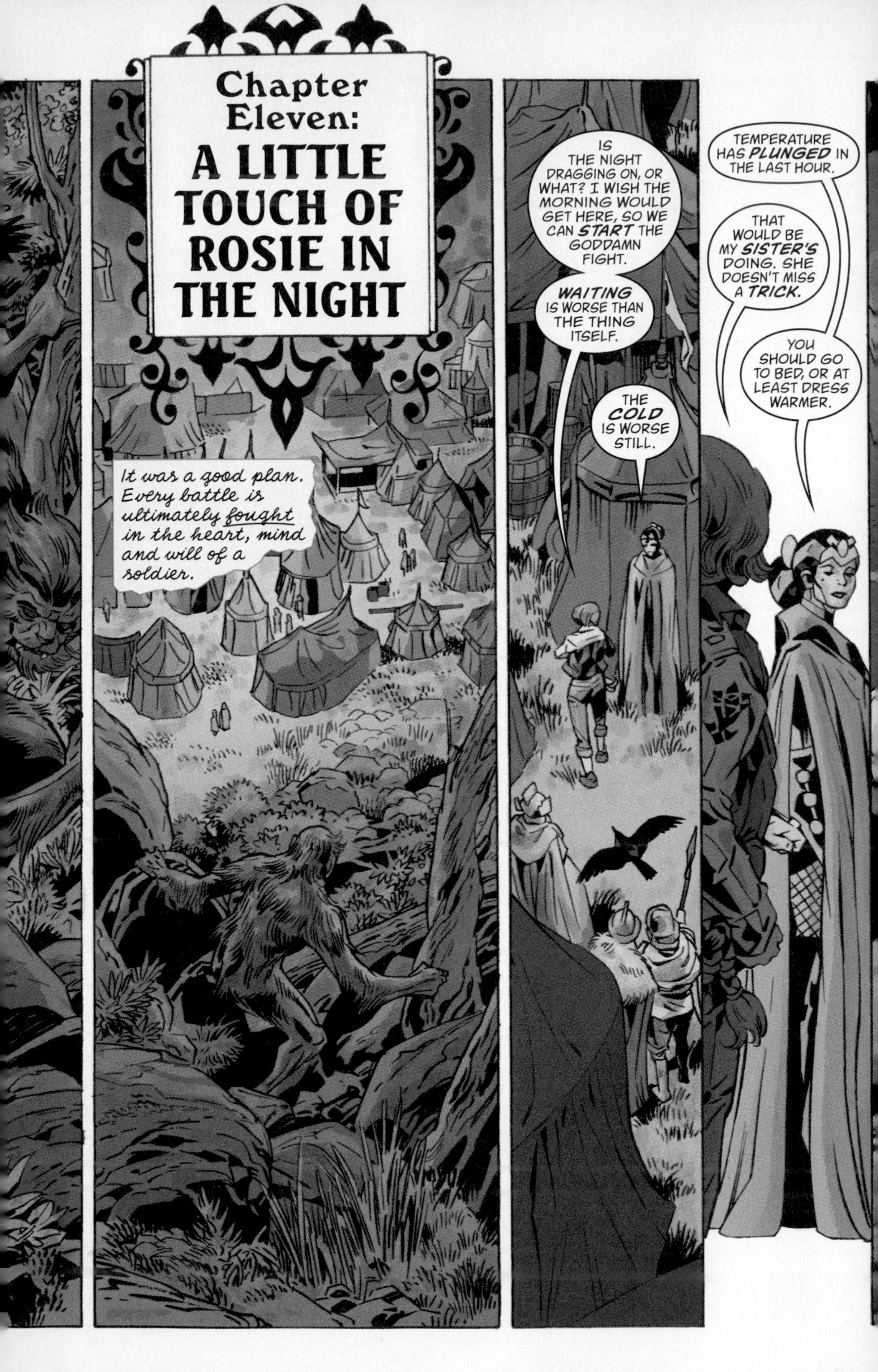
Chapter Eleven:
A LITTLE TOUCH OF ROSIE IN THE NIGHT
It was a good plan. Every battle is ultimately fought in the heart, mind and will of a soldier.
IS THE NIGHT DRAGGING ON, OR WHAT? I WISH THE MORNING WOULD GET HERE, SO WE CAN START THE GODDAMN FIGHT.
WAITING IS WORSE THAN THE THING ITSELF.
THE COLD IS WORSE STILL.
TEMPERATURE HAS PLUNGED IN THE LAST HOUR.
THAT WOULD BE MY SISTER'S DOING. SHE DOESN'T MISS A TRICK.
YOU SHOULD GO TO BED, OR AT LEAST DRESS WARMER.

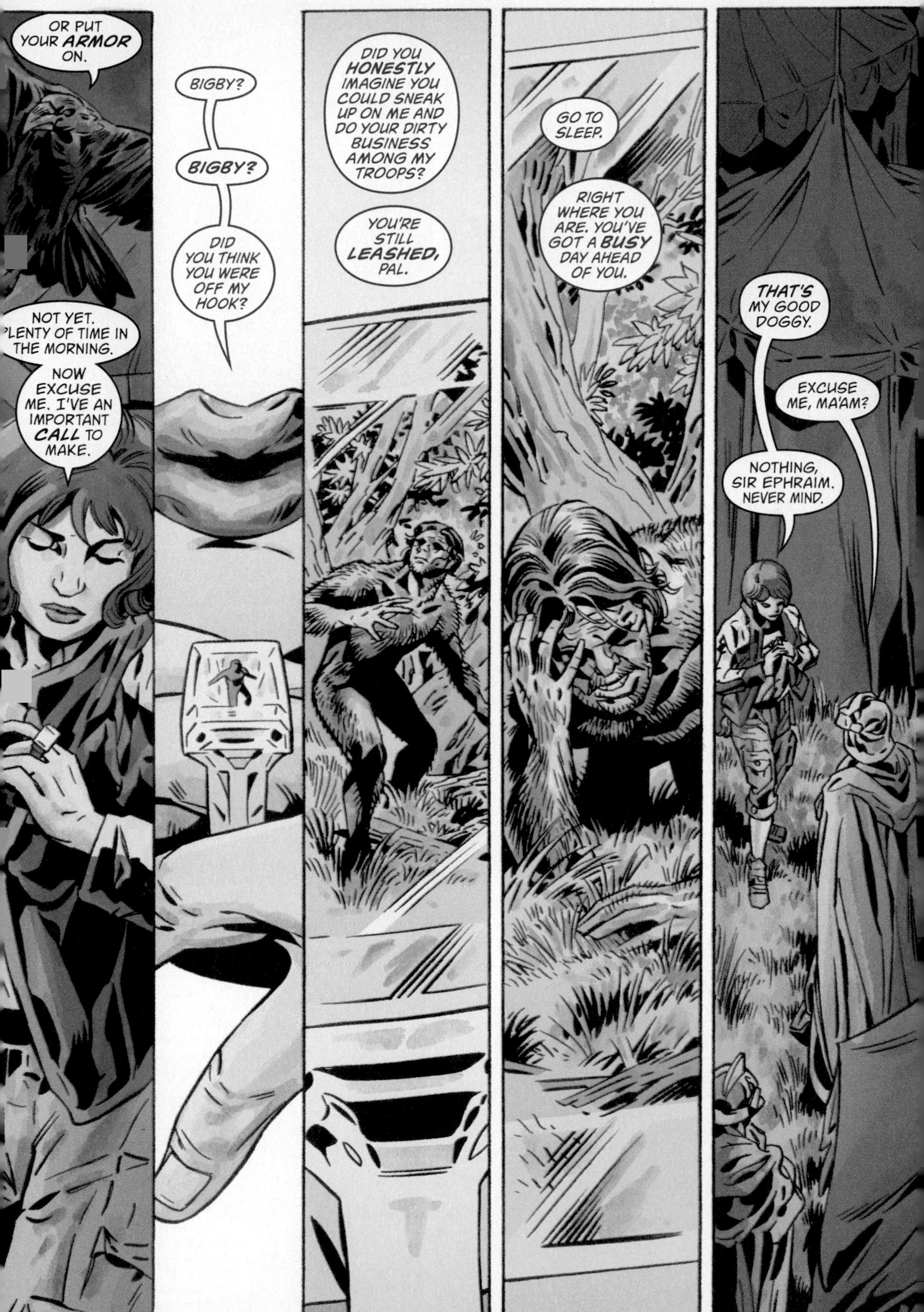
OR PUT YOUR ARMOR ON.
NOT YET. PLENTY OF TIME IN THE MORNING.
NOW EXCUSE ME. I'VE AN IMPORTANT CALL TO MAKE.
BIGBY?
BIGBY?
DID YOU THINK YOU WERE OFF MY HOOK?
DID YOU HONESTLY IMAGINE YOU COULD SNEAK UP ON ME AND DO YOUR DIRTY BUSINESS AMONG MY TROOPS?
YOU'RE STILL LEASHED, PAL.
GO TO SLEEP.
RIGHT WHERE YOU ARE. YOU'VE GOT A BUSY DAY AHEAD OF YOU.
THAT'S MY GOOD DOGGY.
EXCUSE ME, MA'AM?
NOTHING, SIR EPHRAIM. NEVER MIND.

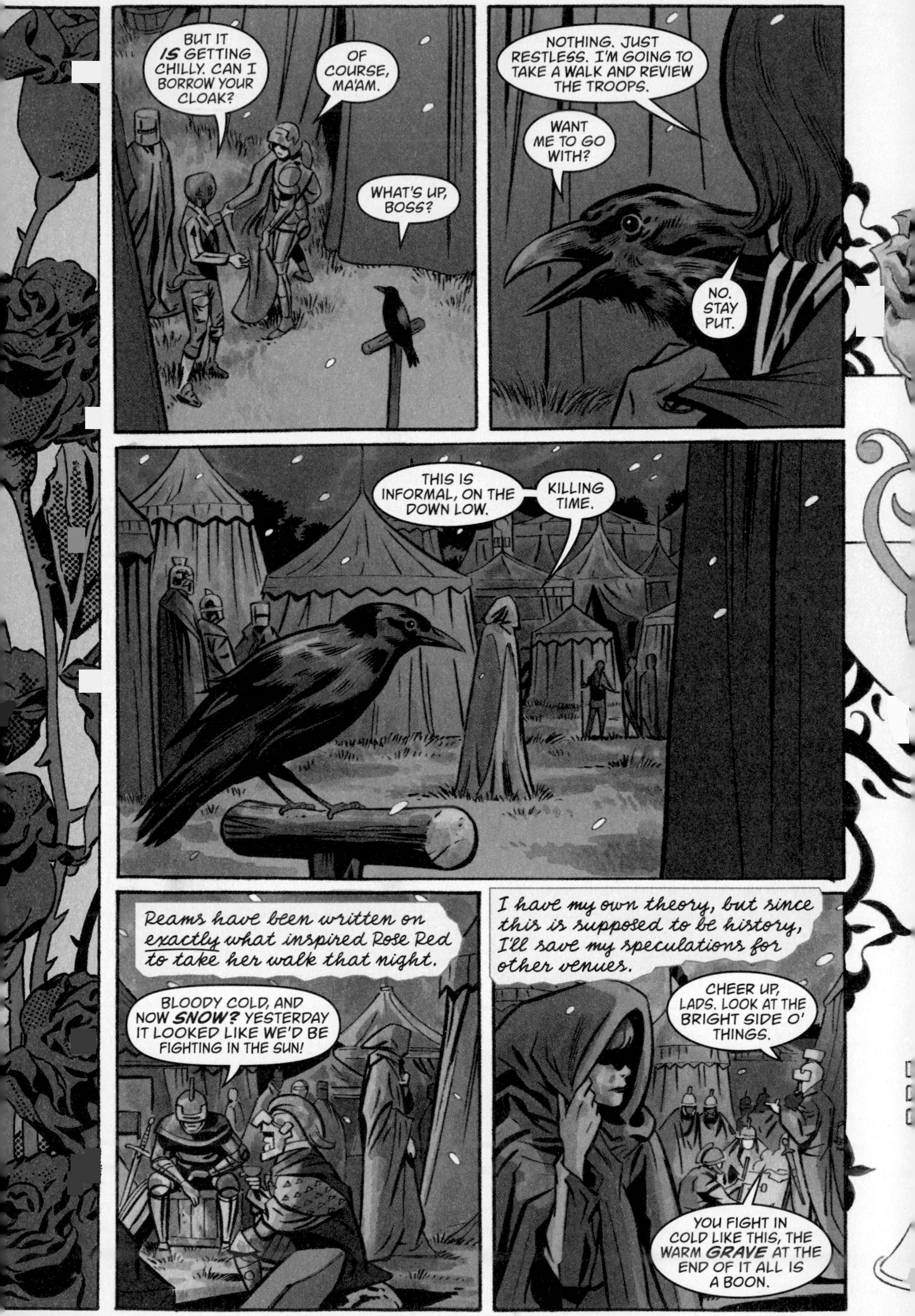
BUT IT *IS* GETTING CHILLY. CAN I BORROW YOUR CLOAK?
OF COURSE, MA'AM.
WHAT'S UP, BOSS?
NOTHING. JUST RESTLESS. I'M GOING TO TAKE A WALK AND REVIEW THE TROOPS.
WANT ME TO GO WITH?
NO. STAY PUT.
THIS IS INFORMAL, ON THE DOWN LOW.
KILLING TIME.
Reams have been written on exactly what inspired Rose Red to take her walk that night.
BLOODY COLD, AND NOW *SNOW?* YESTERDAY IT LOOKED LIKE WE'D BE FIGHTING IN THE SUN!
I have my own theory, but since this is supposed to be history, I'll save my speculations for other venues.
CHEER UP, LADS. LOOK AT THE BRIGHT SIDE O' THINGS.
YOU FIGHT IN COLD LIKE THIS, THE WARM *GRAVE* AT THE END OF IT ALL IS A BOON.

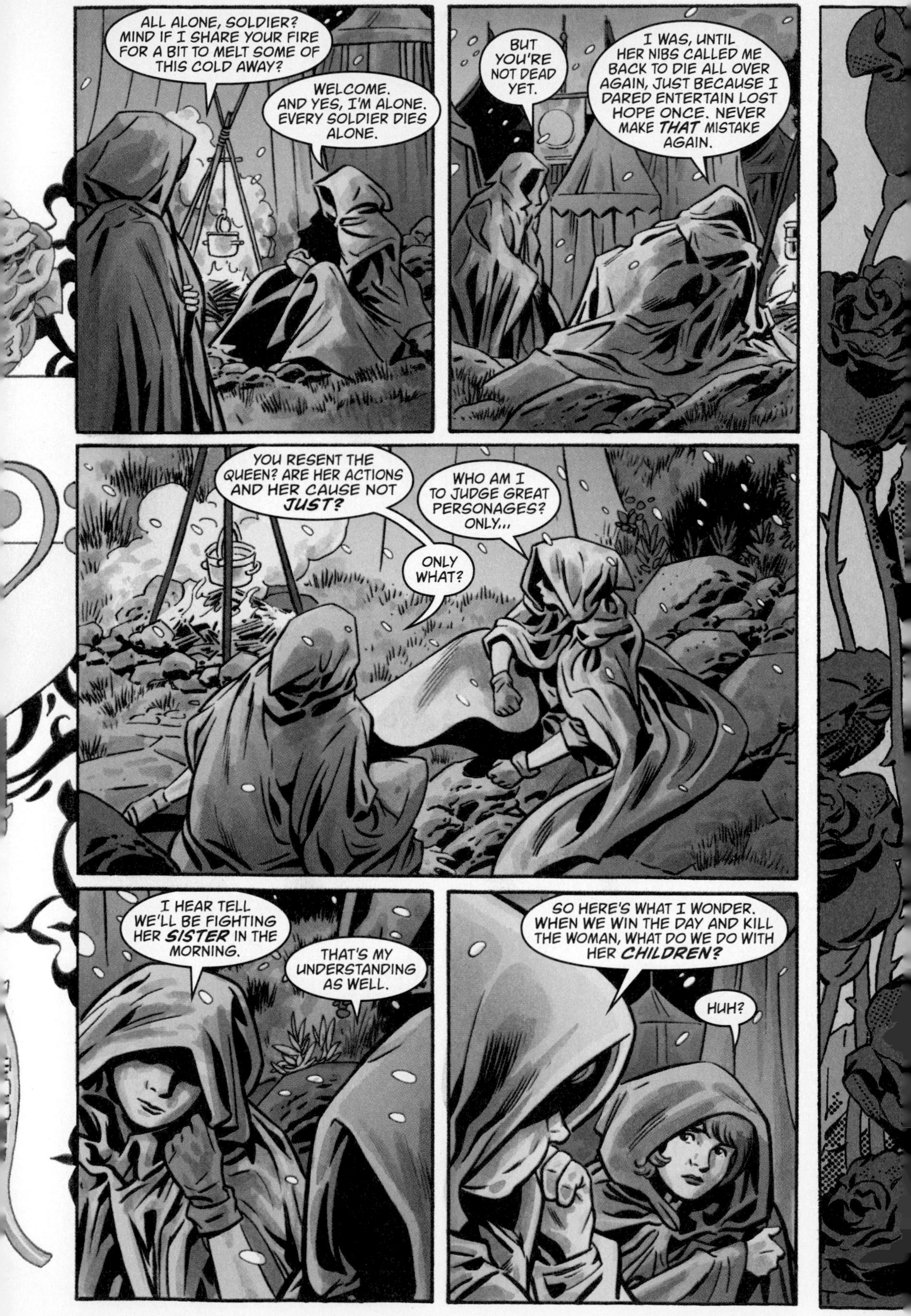
ALL ALONE, SOLDIER? MIND IF I SHARE YOUR FIRE FOR A BIT TO MELT SOME OF THIS COLD AWAY?
WELCOME. AND YES, I'M ALONE. EVERY SOLDIER DIES ALONE.
BUT YOU'RE NOT DEAD YET.
I WAS, UNTIL HER NIBS CALLED ME BACK TO DIE ALL OVER AGAIN, JUST BECAUSE I DARED ENTERTAIN LOST HOPE ONCE. NEVER MAKE THAT MISTAKE AGAIN.
YOU RESENT THE QUEEN? ARE HER ACTIONS AND HER CAUSE NOT JUST?
WHO AM I TO JUDGE GREAT PERSONAGES? ONLY...
ONLY WHAT?
I HEAR TELL WE'LL BE FIGHTING HER SISTER IN THE MORNING.
THAT'S MY UNDERSTANDING AS WELL.
SO HERE'S WHAT I WONDER. WHEN WE WIN THE DAY AND KILL THE WOMAN, WHAT DO WE DO WITH HER CHILDREN?
HUH?

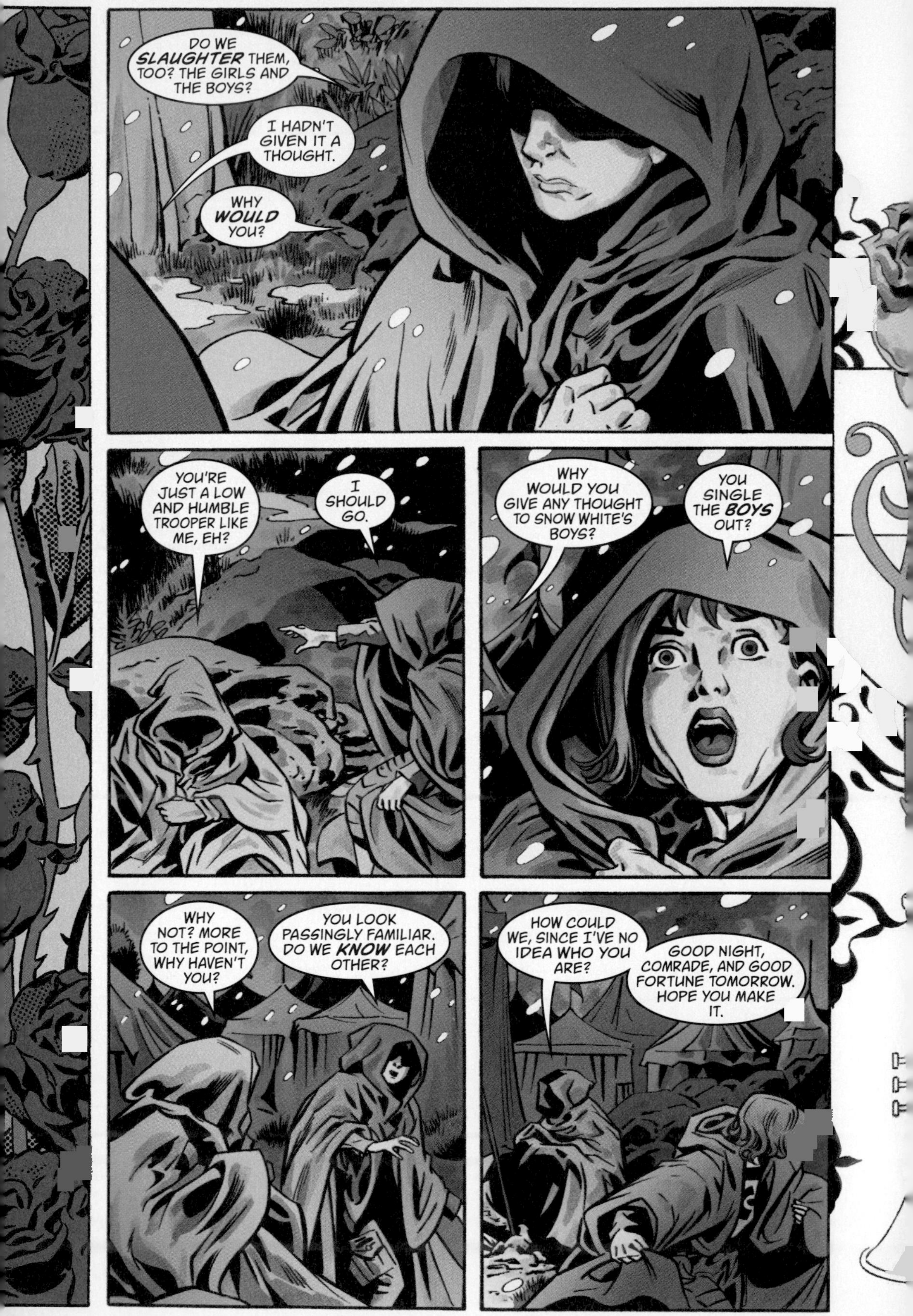
DO WE SLAUGHTER THEM, TOO? THE GIRLS AND THE BOYS?
I HADN'T GIVEN IT A THOUGHT.
WHY WOULD YOU?
YOU'RE JUST A LOW AND HUMBLE TROOPER LIKE ME, EH?
I SHOULD GO.
WHY WOULD YOU GIVE ANY THOUGHT TO SNOW WHITE'S BOYS?
YOU SINGLE THE BOYS OUT?
WHY NOT? MORE TO THE POINT, WHY HAVEN'T YOU?
YOU LOOK PASSINGLY FAMILIAR. DO WE KNOW EACH OTHER?
HOW COULD WE, SINCE I'VE NO IDEA WHO YOU ARE?
GOOD NIGHT, COMRADE, AND GOOD FORTUNE TOMORROW. HOPE YOU MAKE IT.

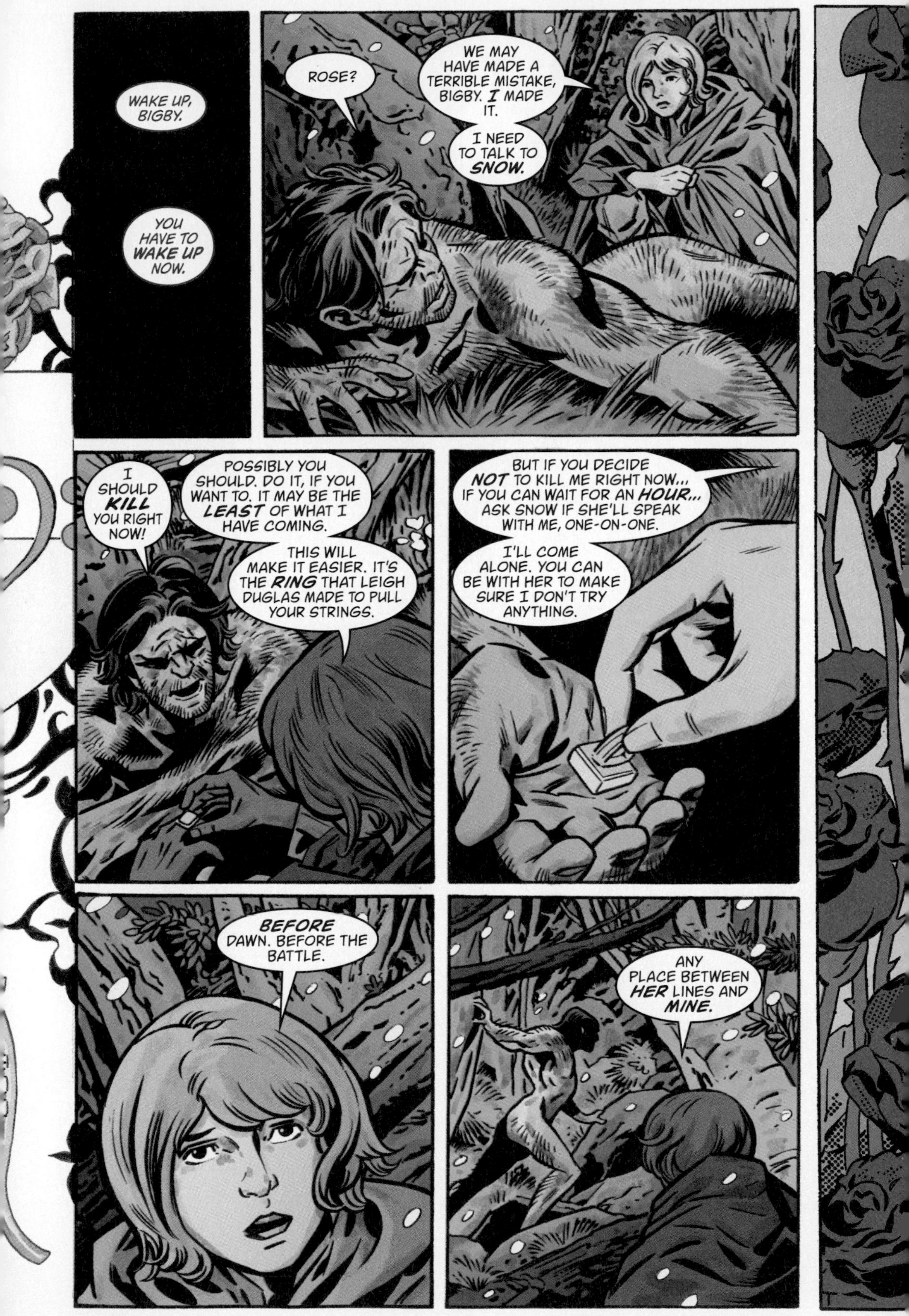
WAKE UP, BIGBY.
YOU HAVE TO WAKE UP NOW.
ROSE?
WE MAY HAVE MADE A TERRIBLE MISTAKE, BIGBY. I MADE IT.
I NEED TO TALK TO SNOW.
I SHOULD KILL YOU RIGHT NOW!
POSSIBLY YOU SHOULD. DO IT, IF YOU WANT TO. IT MAY BE THE LEAST OF WHAT I HAVE COMING.
THIS WILL MAKE IT EASIER. IT'S THE RING THAT LEIGH DUGLAS MADE TO PULL YOUR STRINGS.
BUT IF YOU DECIDE NOT TO KILL ME RIGHT NOW... IF YOU CAN WAIT FOR AN HOUR... ASK SNOW IF SHE'LL SPEAK WITH ME, ONE-ON-ONE.
I'LL COME ALONE. YOU CAN BE WITH HER TO MAKE SURE I DON'T TRY ANYTHING.
BEFORE DAWN. BEFORE THE BATTLE.
ANY PLACE BETWEEN HER LINES AND MINE.

Chapter Twelve: THE LAST BATTLE

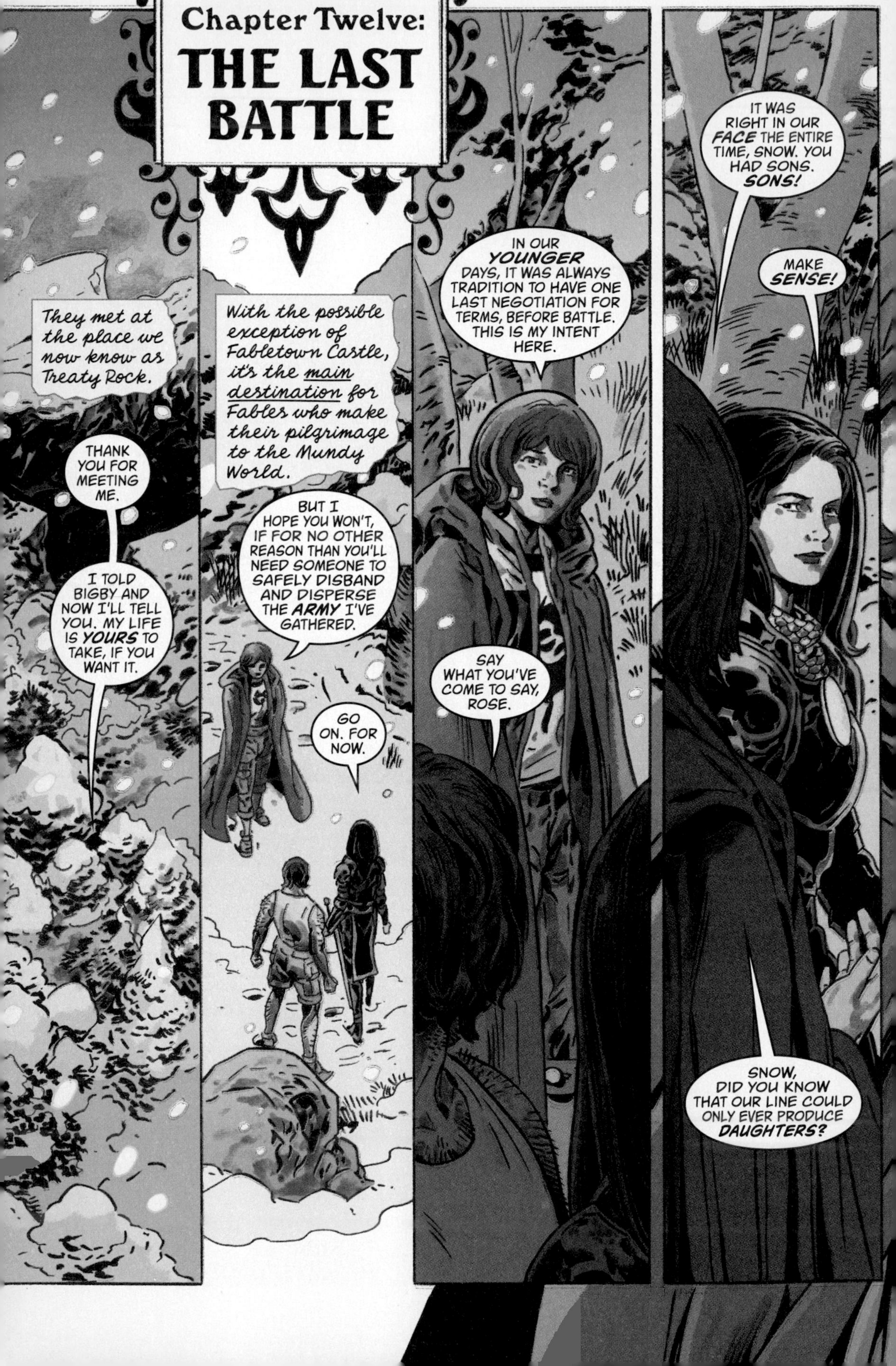
They met at the place we now know as Treaty Rock.
THANK YOU FOR MEETING ME.
I TOLD BIGBY AND NOW I'LL TELL YOU. MY LIFE IS YOURS TO TAKE, IF YOU WANT IT.
With the possible exception of Fabletown Castle, it's the main destination for Fables who make their pilgrimage to the Mundy World.
BUT I HOPE YOU WON'T, IF FOR NO OTHER REASON THAN YOU'LL NEED SOMEONE TO SAFELY DISBAND AND DISPERSE THE ARMY I'VE GATHERED.
GO ON. FOR NOW.
IN OUR YOUNGER DAYS, IT WAS ALWAYS TRADITION TO HAVE ONE LAST NEGOTIATION FOR TERMS, BEFORE BATTLE. THIS IS MY INTENT HERE.
SAY WHAT YOU'VE COME TO SAY, ROSE.
IT WAS RIGHT IN OUR FACE THE ENTIRE TIME, SNOW. YOU HAD SONS. SONS!
MAKE SENSE!
SNOW, DID YOU KNOW THAT OUR LINE COULD ONLY EVER PRODUCE DAUGHTERS?

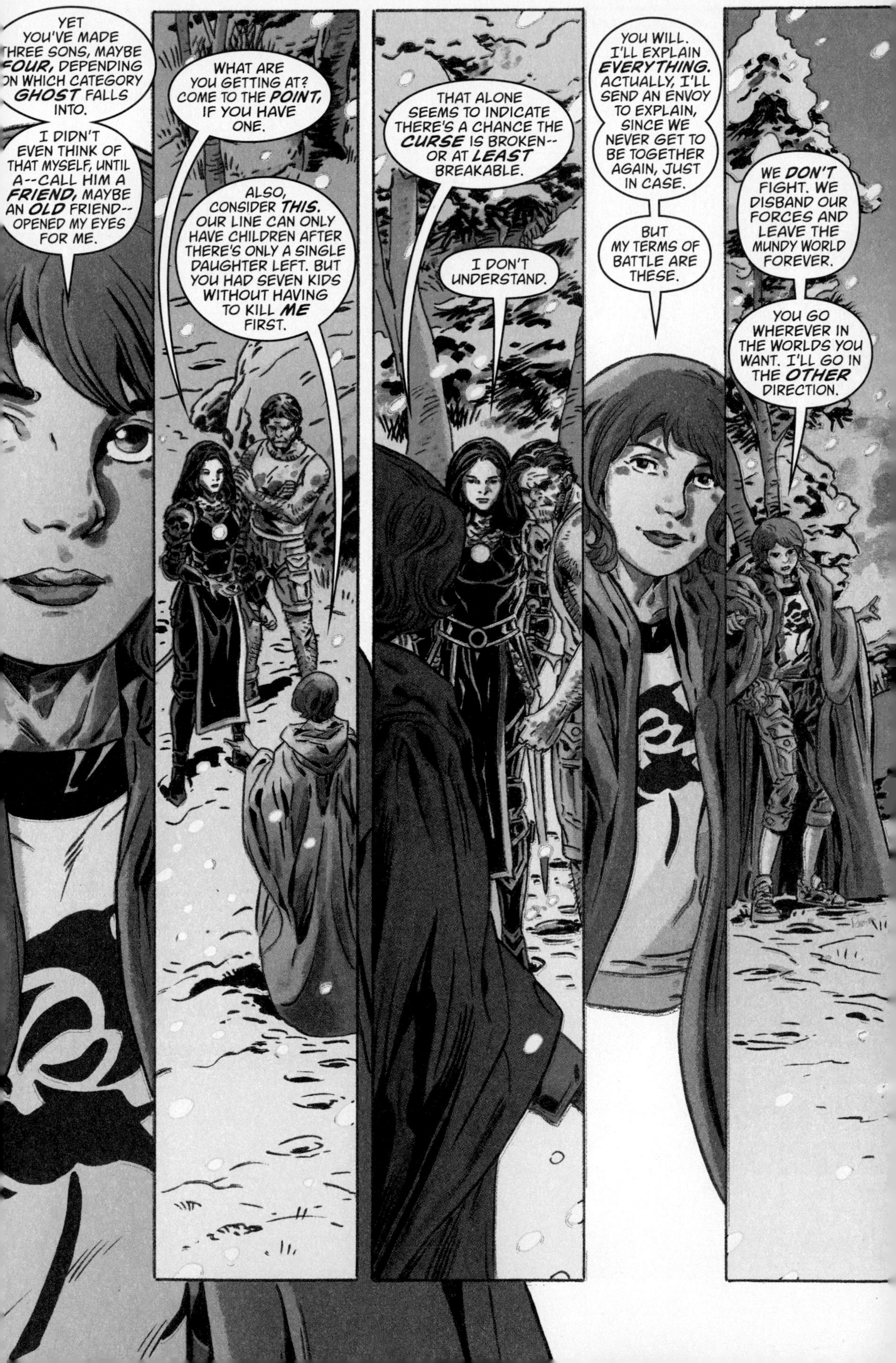

YET YOU'VE MADE THREE SONS, MAYBE FOUR, DEPENDING ON WHICH CATEGORY GHOST FALLS INTO.
I DIDN'T EVEN THINK OF THAT MYSELF, UNTIL A--CALL HIM A FRIEND, MAYBE AN OLD FRIEND--OPENED MY EYES FOR ME.
WHAT ARE YOU GETTING AT? COME TO THE POINT, IF YOU HAVE ONE.
ALSO, CONSIDER THIS. OUR LINE CAN ONLY HAVE CHILDREN AFTER THERE'S ONLY A SINGLE DAUGHTER LEFT. BUT YOU HAD SEVEN KIDS WITHOUT HAVING TO KILL ME FIRST.
THAT ALONE SEEMS TO INDICATE THERE'S A CHANCE THE CURSE IS BROKEN--OR AT LEAST BREAKABLE.
I DON'T UNDERSTAND.
YOU WILL. I'LL EXPLAIN EVERYTHING. ACTUALLY, I'LL SEND AN ENVOY TO EXPLAIN, SINCE WE NEVER GET TO BE TOGETHER AGAIN, JUST IN CASE.
BUT MY TERMS OF BATTLE ARE THESE.
WE DON'T FIGHT. WE DISBAND OUR FORCES AND LEAVE THE MUNDY WORLD FOREVER.
YOU GO WHEREVER IN THE WORLDS YOU WANT. I'LL GO IN THE OTHER DIRECTION.

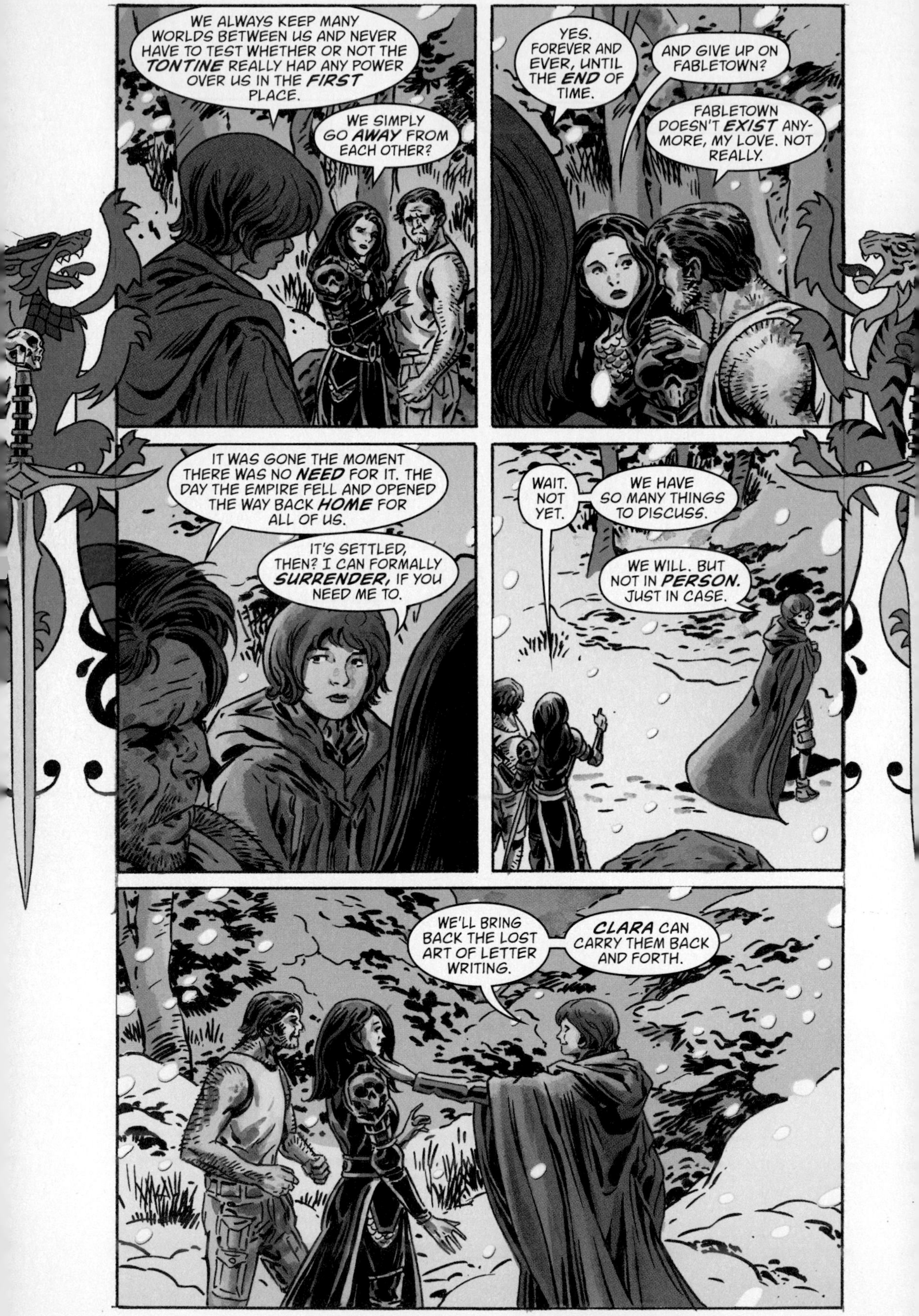
WE ALWAYS KEEP MANY WORLDS BETWEEN US AND NEVER HAVE TO TEST WHETHER OR NOT THE TONTINE REALLY HAD ANY POWER OVER US IN THE FIRST PLACE.
WE SIMPLY GO AWAY FROM EACH OTHER?
YES. FOREVER AND EVER, UNTIL THE END OF TIME.
AND GIVE UP ON FABLETOWN?
FABLETOWN DOESN'T EXIST ANY-MORE, MY LOVE. NOT REALLY.
IT WAS GONE THE MOMENT THERE WAS NO NEED FOR IT. THE DAY THE EMPIRE FELL AND OPENED THE WAY BACK HOME FOR ALL OF US.
IT'S SETTLED, THEN? I CAN FORMALLY SURRENDER, IF YOU NEED ME TO.
WAIT. NOT YET.
WE HAVE SO MANY THINGS TO DISCUSS.
WE WILL. BUT NOT IN PERSON. JUST IN CASE.
WE'LL BRING BACK THE LOST ART OF LETTER WRITING.
CLARA CAN CARRY THEM BACK AND FORTH.

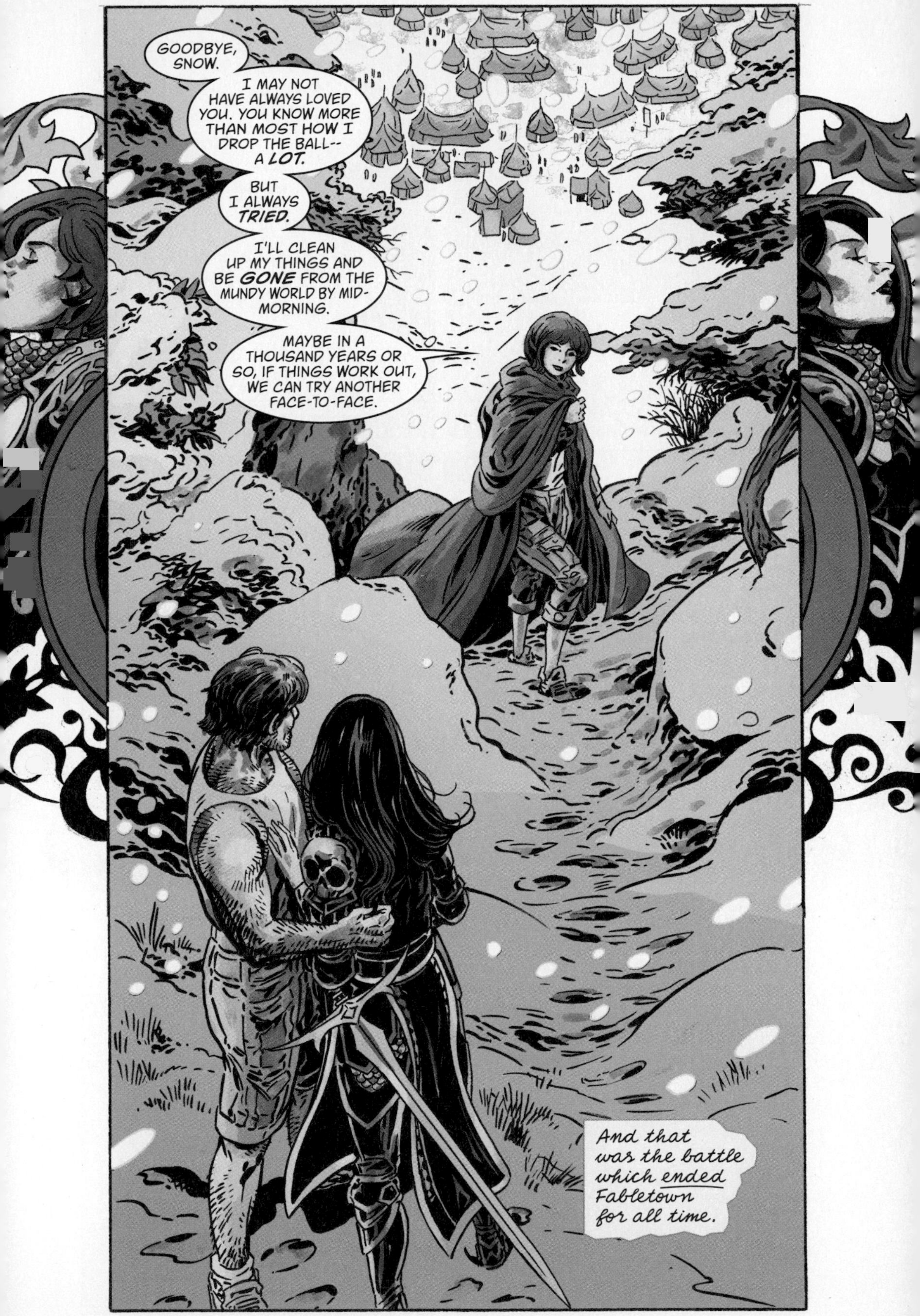
GOODBYE, SNOW.
I MAY NOT HAVE ALWAYS LOVED YOU. YOU KNOW MORE THAN MOST HOW I DROP THE BALL-- A LOT.
BUT I ALWAYS TRIED.
I'LL CLEAN UP MY THINGS AND BE GONE FROM THE MUNDY WORLD BY MID-MORNING.
MAYBE IN A THOUSAND YEARS OR SO, IF THINGS WORK OUT, WE CAN TRY ANOTHER FACE-TO-FACE.
And that was the battle which ended Fabletown for all time.

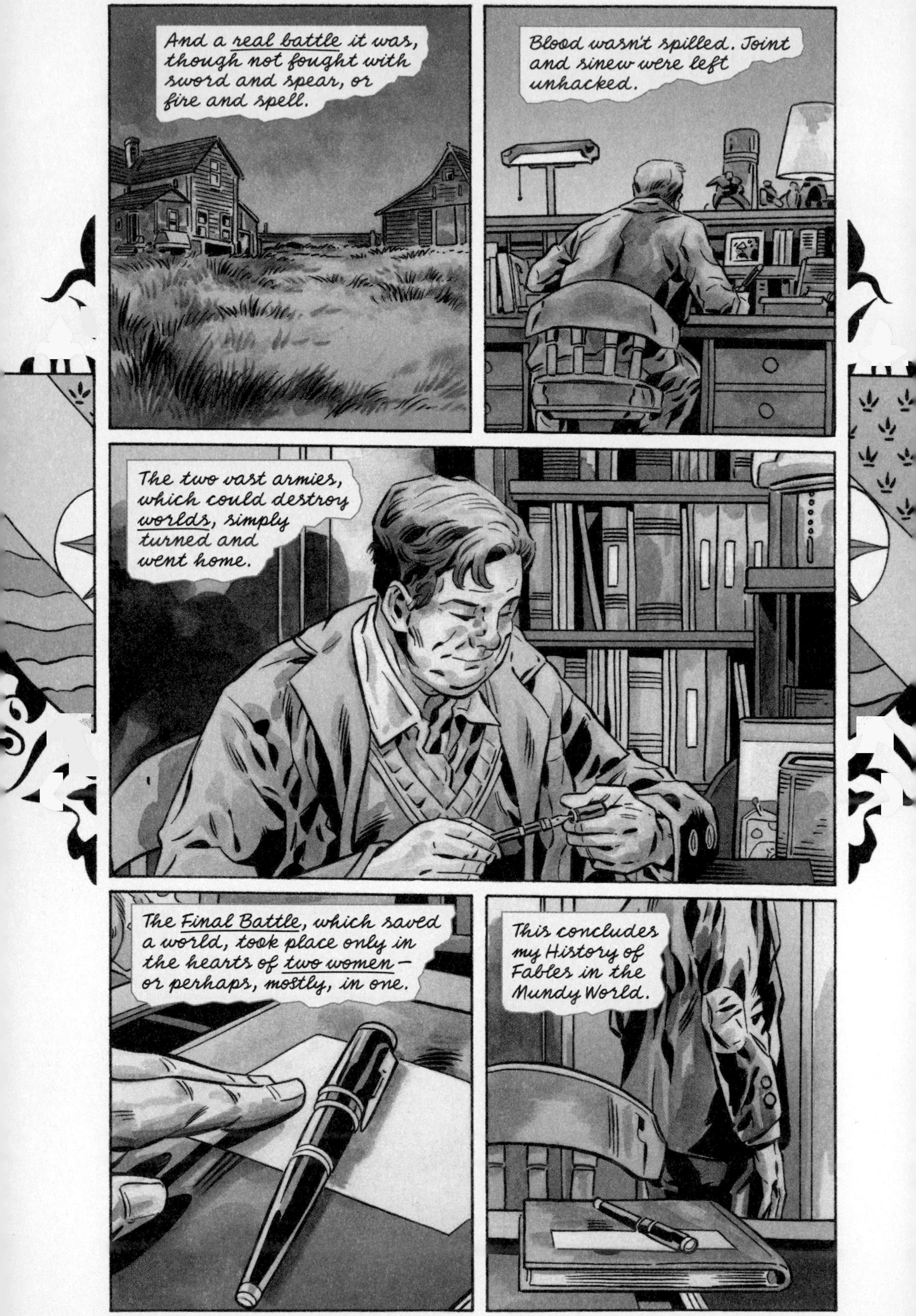
And a real battle it was, though not fought with sword and spear, or fire and spell.
Blood wasn't spilled. Joint and sinew were left unhacked.
The two vast armies, which could destroy worlds, simply turned and went home.
The Final Battle, which saved a world, took place only in the hearts of two women—or perhaps, mostly, in one.
This concludes my History of Fables in the Mundy World.

THE LAST CLARA STORY

Bill Willingham writer - creator
David Petersen artist
Andrew Dalhouse colors
Todd Klein letters
Rowena Yow assoc. editor
Shelly Bond editor

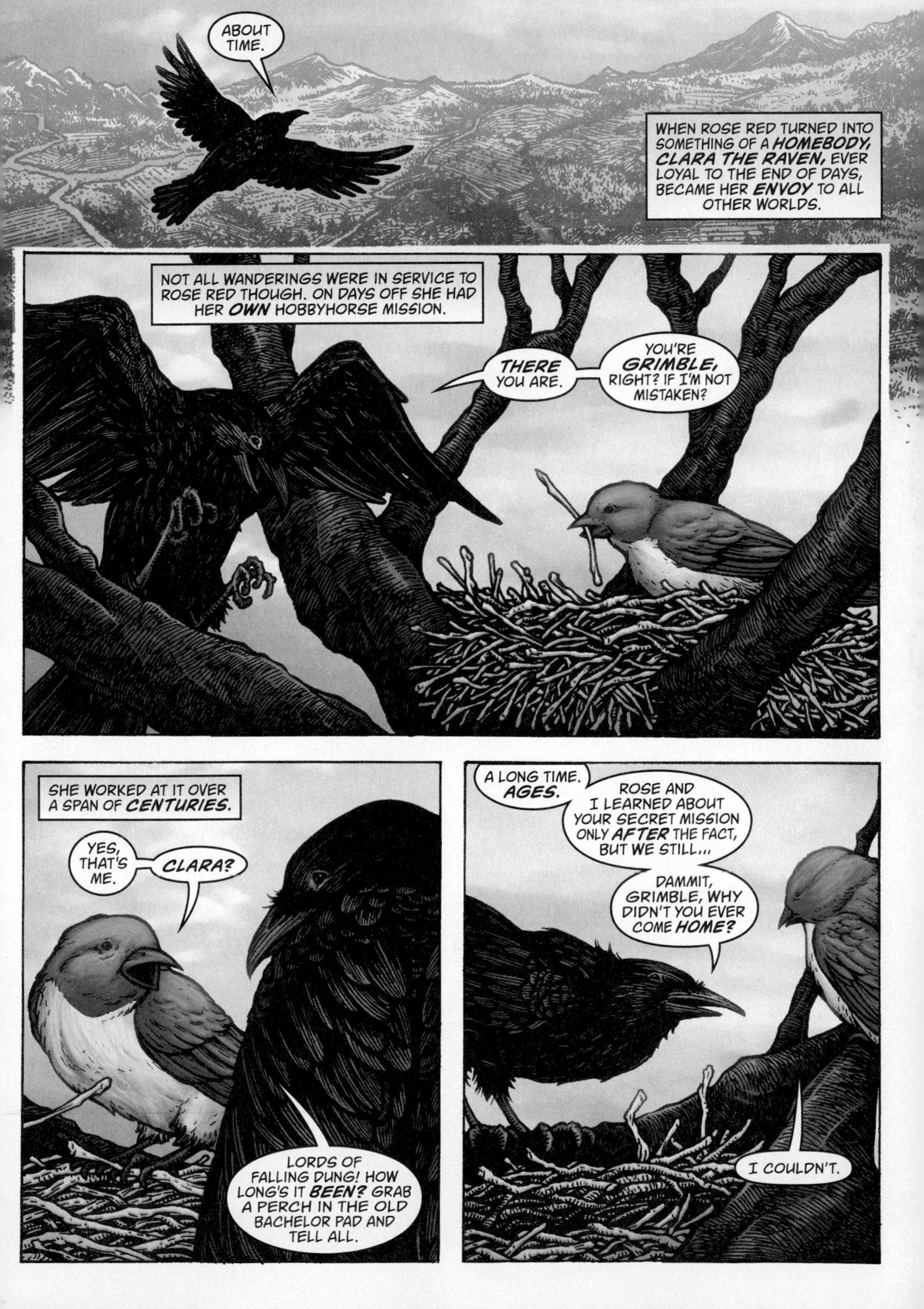
ABOUT TIME.
WHEN ROSE RED TURNED INTO SOMETHING OF A HOMEBODY, CLARA THE RAVEN, EVER LOYAL TO THE END OF DAYS, BECAME HER ENVOY TO ALL OTHER WORLDS.
NOT ALL WANDERINGS WERE IN SERVICE TO ROSE RED THOUGH. ON DAYS OFF SHE HAD HER OWN HOBBYHORSE MISSION.
THERE YOU ARE.
YOU'RE GRIMBLE, RIGHT? IF I'M NOT MISTAKEN?
SHE WORKED AT IT OVER A SPAN OF CENTURIES.
YES, THAT'S ME.
CLARA?
LORDS OF FALLING DUNG! HOW LONG'S IT BEEN? GRAB A PERCH IN THE OLD BACHELOR PAD AND TELL ALL.
A LONG TIME. AGES.
ROSE AND I LEARNED ABOUT YOUR SECRET MISSION ONLY AFTER THE FACT, BUT WE STILL...
DAMMIT, GRIMBLE, WHY DIDN'T YOU EVER COME HOME?
I COULDN'T.

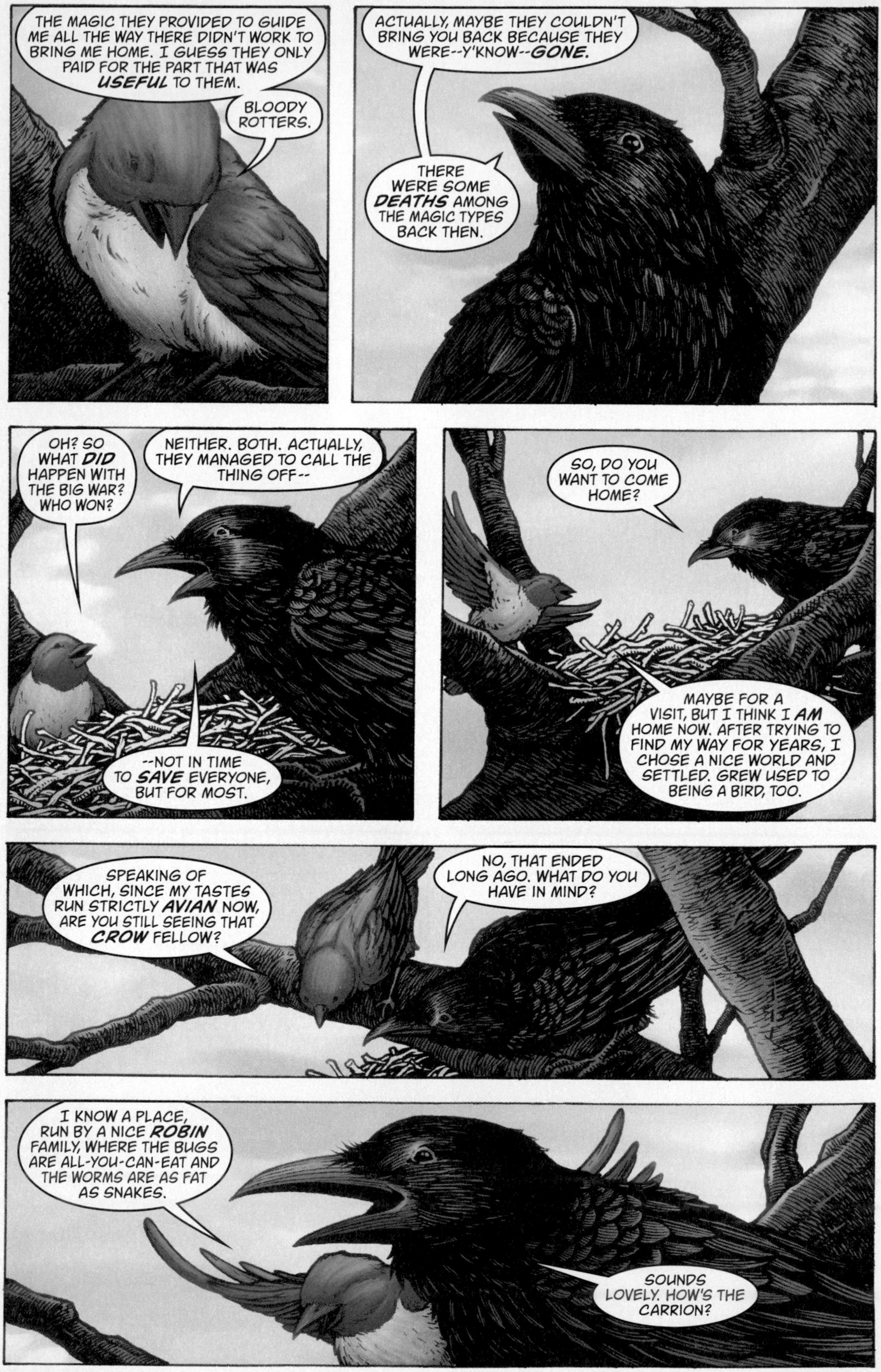
THE MAGIC THEY PROVIDED TO GUIDE ME ALL THE WAY THERE DIDN'T WORK TO BRING ME HOME. I GUESS THEY ONLY PAID FOR THE PART THAT WAS USEFUL TO THEM.
BLOODY ROTTERS.
ACTUALLY, MAYBE THEY COULDN'T BRING YOU BACK BECAUSE THEY WERE--Y'KNOW--GONE.
THERE WERE SOME DEATHS AMONG THE MAGIC TYPES BACK THEN.
OH? SO WHAT DID HAPPEN WITH THE BIG WAR? WHO WON?
NEITHER. BOTH. ACTUALLY, THEY MANAGED TO CALL THE THING OFF--
--NOT IN TIME TO SAVE EVERYONE, BUT FOR MOST.
SO, DO YOU WANT TO COME HOME?
MAYBE FOR A VISIT, BUT I THINK I AM HOME NOW. AFTER TRYING TO FIND MY WAY FOR YEARS, I CHOSE A NICE WORLD AND SETTLED. GREW USED TO BEING A BIRD, TOO.
SPEAKING OF WHICH, SINCE MY TASTES RUN STRICTLY AVIAN NOW, ARE YOU STILL SEEING THAT CROW FELLOW?
NO, THAT ENDED LONG AGO. WHAT DO YOU HAVE IN MIND?
I KNOW A PLACE, RUN BY A NICE ROBIN FAMILY, WHERE THE BUGS ARE ALL-YOU-CAN-EAT AND THE WORMS ARE AS FAT AS SNAKES.
SOUNDS LOVELY. HOW'S THE CARRION?

The Last Snow Queen Story

Bill Willingham writer - creator · Russ Braun artist · Andrew Dalhouse colors · Todd Klein letters · Rowena Yow associate ed. · Shelly Bond editor

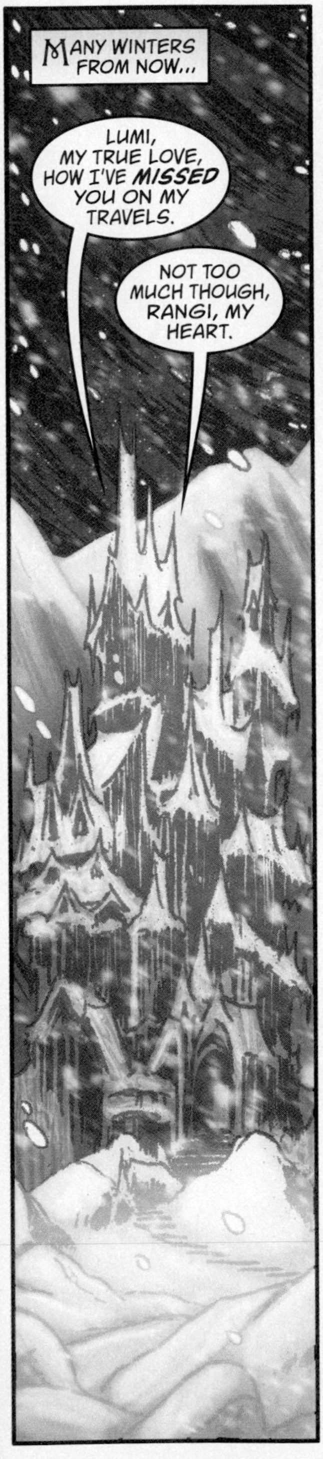

MANY WINTERS FROM NOW...
LUMI, MY TRUE LOVE, HOW I'VE MISSED YOU ON MY TRAVELS.
NOT TOO MUCH THOUGH, RANGI, MY HEART.

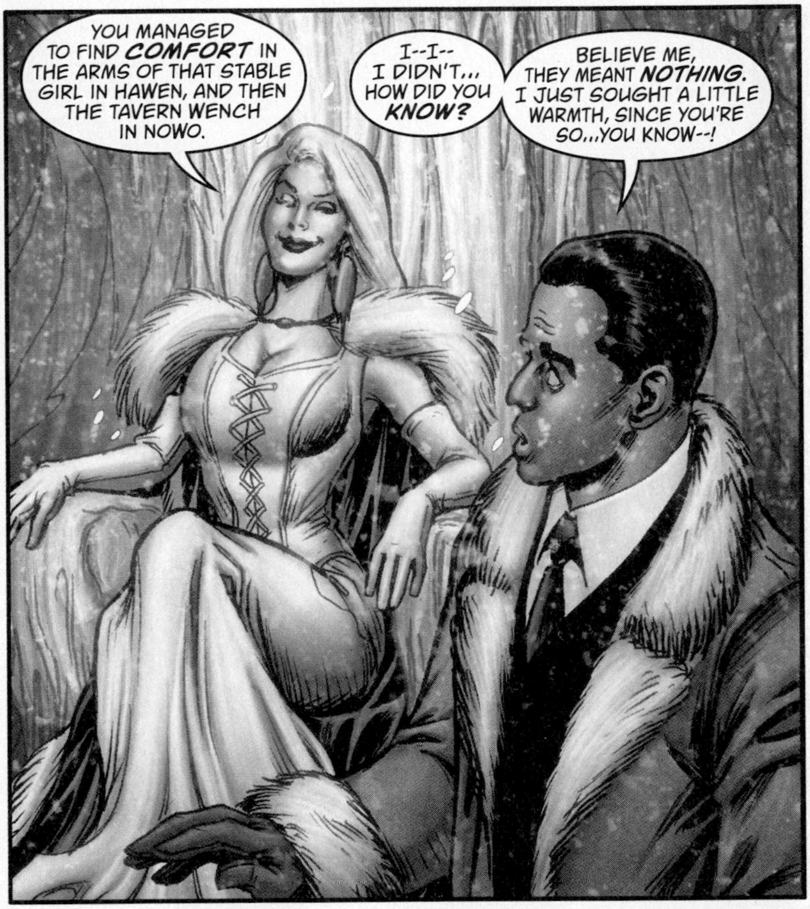

YOU MANAGED TO FIND COMFORT IN THE ARMS OF THAT STABLE GIRL IN HAWEN, AND THEN THE TAVERN WENCH IN NOWO.
I--I-- I DIDN'T... HOW DID YOU KNOW?
BELIEVE ME, THEY MEANT NOTHING. I JUST SOUGHT A LITTLE WARMTH, SINCE YOU'RE SO...YOU KNOW--!

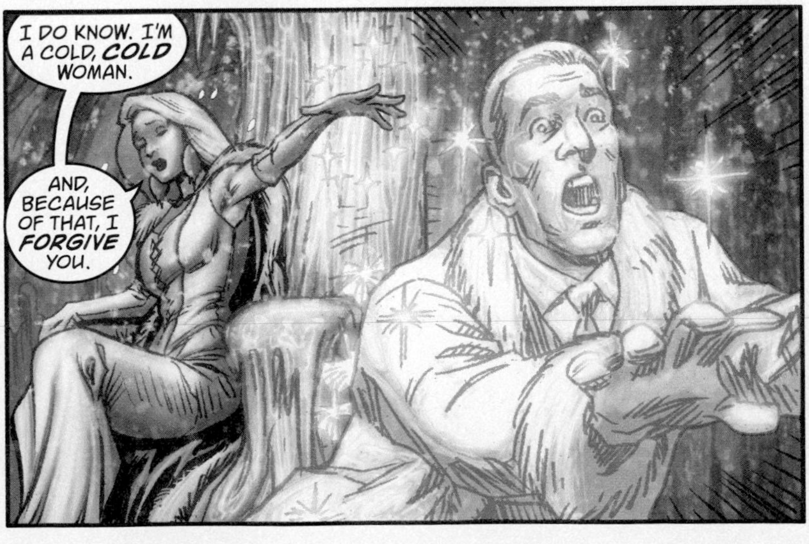

I DO KNOW. I'M A COLD, COLD WOMAN.
AND, BECAUSE OF THAT, I FORGIVE YOU.

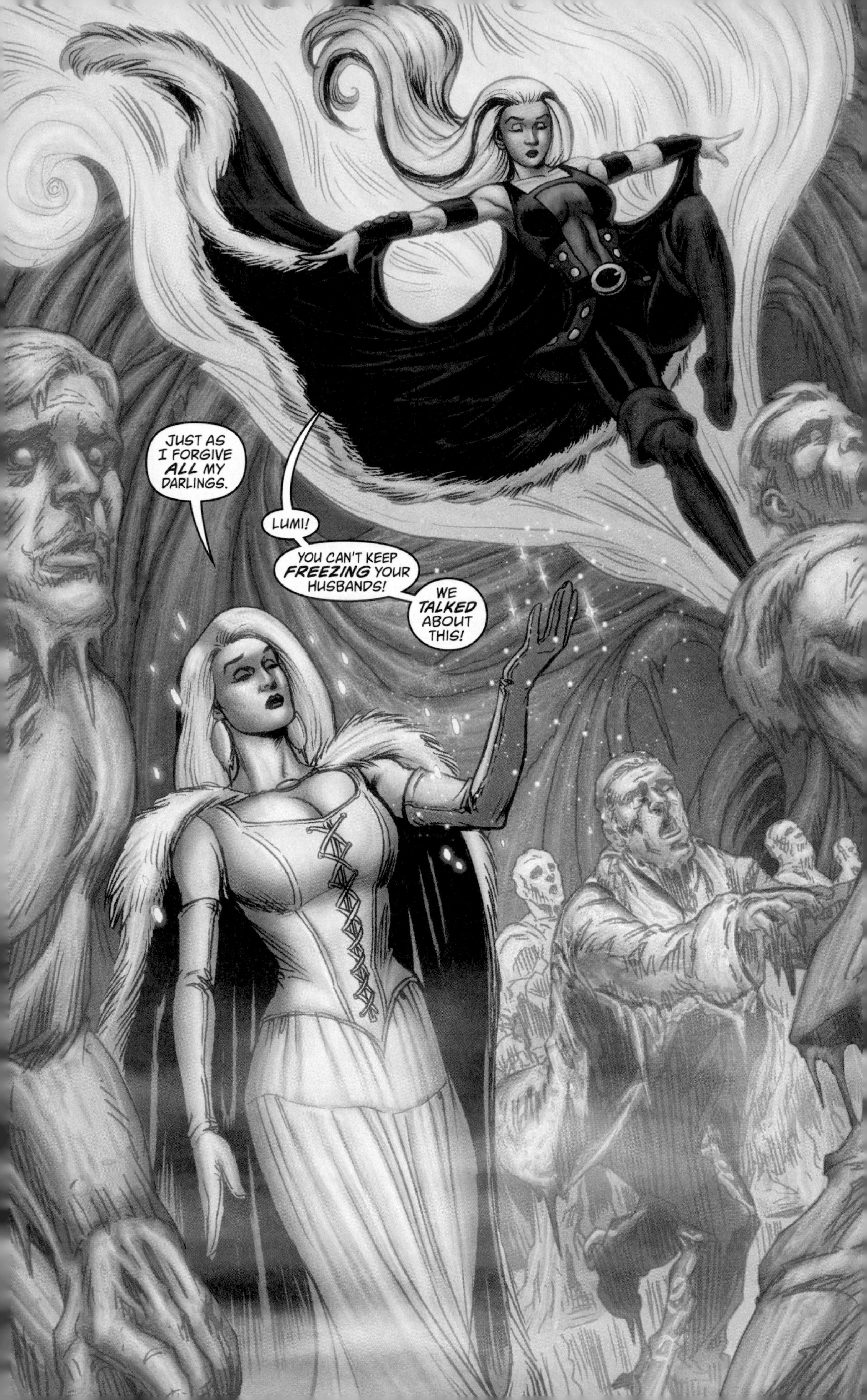
JUST AS I FORGIVE ALL MY DARLINGS.
LUMI!
YOU CAN'T KEEP FREEZING YOUR HUSBANDS!
WE TALKED ABOUT THIS!

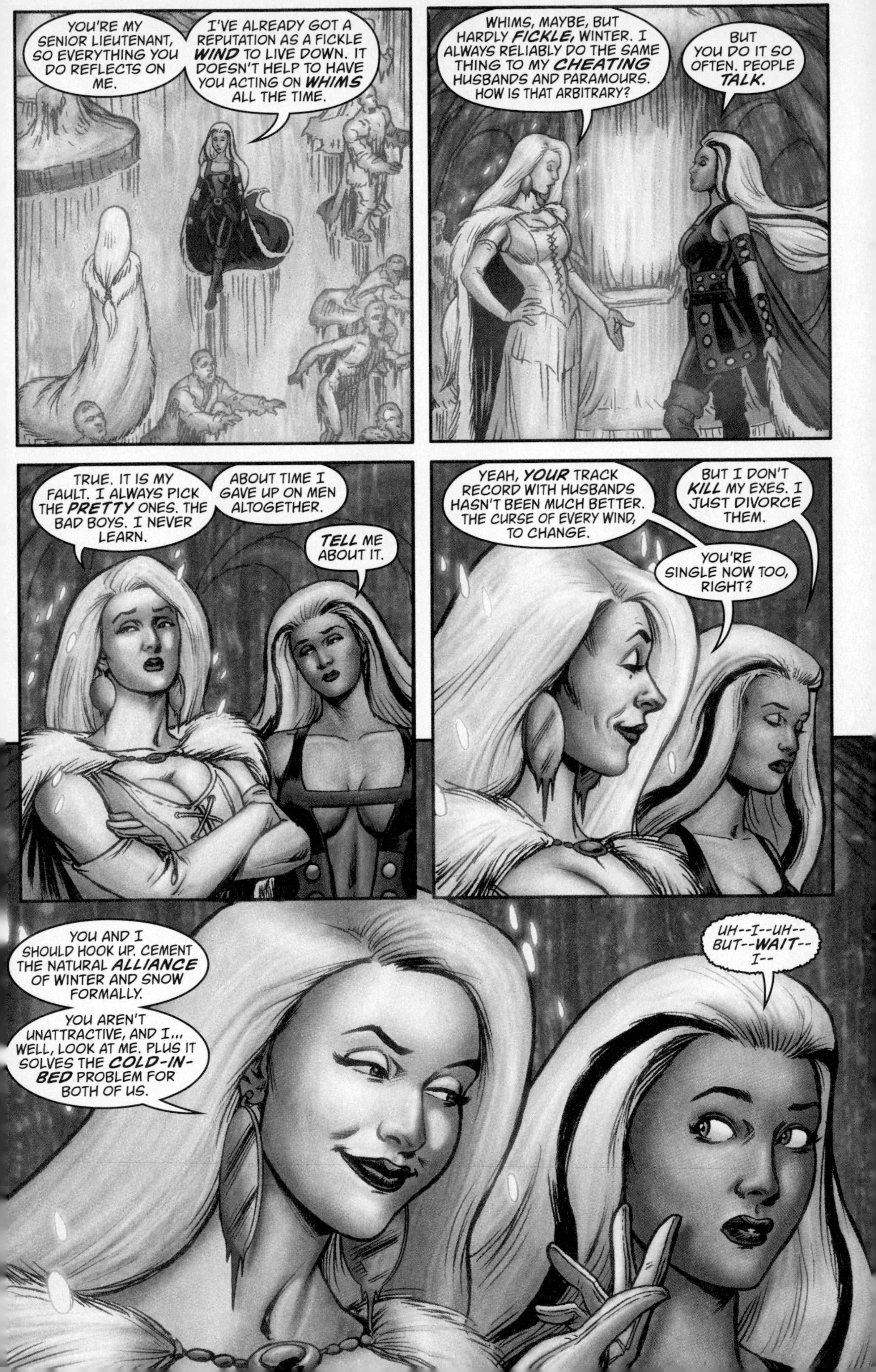
YOU'RE MY SENIOR LIEUTENANT, SO EVERYTHING YOU DO REFLECTS ON ME.
I'VE ALREADY GOT A REPUTATION AS A FICKLE WIND TO LIVE DOWN. IT DOESN'T HELP TO HAVE YOU ACTING ON WHIMS ALL THE TIME.
WHIMS, MAYBE, BUT HARDLY FICKLE, WINTER. I ALWAYS RELIABLY DO THE SAME THING TO MY CHEATING HUSBANDS AND PARAMOURS. HOW IS THAT ARBITRARY?
BUT YOU DO IT SO OFTEN. PEOPLE TALK.
TRUE. IT IS MY FAULT. I ALWAYS PICK THE PRETTY ONES. THE BAD BOYS. I NEVER LEARN.
ABOUT TIME I GAVE UP ON MEN ALTOGETHER.
TELL ME ABOUT IT.
YEAH, YOUR TRACK RECORD WITH HUSBANDS HASN'T BEEN MUCH BETTER. THE CURSE OF EVERY WIND, TO CHANGE.
BUT I DON'T KILL MY EXES. I JUST DIVORCE THEM.
YOU'RE SINGLE NOW TOO, RIGHT?
YOU AND I SHOULD HOOK UP. CEMENT THE NATURAL ALLIANCE OF WINTER AND SNOW FORMALLY.
YOU AREN'T UNATTRACTIVE, AND I... WELL, LOOK AT ME. PLUS IT SOLVES THE COLD-IN-BED PROBLEM FOR BOTH OF US.
UH--I--UH-- BUT--WAIT-- I--

THE LAST BLOSSOM STORY

In which we spend what might be a typical day with a grown demigoddess of nature and the hunt.

Bill Willingham
writer - creator

Mark Schultz
illustrator

Todd Klein
design

Rowena Yow
assoc. editor

Shelly Bond
editor

THERE is an owl in the anxious night, hooting loudly to summon the change in season. His name is Bringer of the Dying, because he knows the language of sleeping winter and commands the leaves to turn. Geese among the bulrushes hear his song and taste the chill in the new air. Sluggishly at first, waking from the nesting dream, they recall the exquisite urgency of the chevron, and begin to trumpet their intentions for long flights to come. Some insist they will lead this time, at the spear point of one of the hundred thousand formations. Others contest, or bluster, or surrender, each according to her strengths and will.

Chill winds carried the claxon honking south, to shaggy elk, in their regal battalions, and to gray bears that began to search out their winter's den, and badgers in their sett and, more distantly, to Bloss, who was out early, hunting.

She was lithe and untiring, moving swiftly across rolling plains of yellow-brown grass that had been green only weeks earlier. It would be misleading to say she didn't feel the cold, for she felt it to an extent matchless by the dull senses of mortals. But the cold air was a delight rather than a hardship to her. What clothing she wore was for reasons other than protection from the elements. It was decoration and statement, tribal, symbolic, a story told in a collection of carefully selected talismans.

From the waist down she told the tale of the army of conquest, who'd boldly marched across the golden plains and through river valleys last summer, with their overflying drones and portable missile batteries. They had rifles and side arms, terrible in their wonder, that shot beams of disdainful light, which left nothing behind of their targets. They'd come looking for war, but were frustrated in their efforts to find it.

Instead Bloss followed them in the day and killed them in the dark, silent and untraceable. She was patient and resolute. Three or four were slain in the night, every night, for weeks that became months, until the invaders' desire for this world was poisoned beyond recovery. In time the entire bunch packed up one day and fled back through the gate from which they'd appeared.

Now she wore some of the trappings of their officers, belt and boots of fine black leather, and finely woven wine-dark slacks that clung to her like an embrace. She took special delight in the bold gold stripe that ran down each leg, as if to say, "I am someone who walks with more import of purpose than you."

One of the disintegration pistols rode on her belt, too light, it seemed, for the gravity of its power. She'd never used it, because it seemed a wasteful thing to remove an object or body entirely from this existence, leaving naught to scavenge or bury. But she'd taken it from a man who'd also failed to use it in time, and that had amused her in a trophy-taking way. For those reasons, and perhaps a bit of just-in-case, she enjoyed having it.

Her dress from the waist up told a different story. Her vest was fashioned from the magically impenetrable skin of Manaha Wendigo, whom she'd tracked for years, as it slaughtered its way across two continents. The filigreed shirt underneath was the last surviving treasure from an old lover, who lavished her with gifts of fine silk and linen on each visit to her world. He'd stopped coming years ago, after it was clear he would continue to age, while it seemed she never would.

She carried a bow and other weapons she'd made herself, fine things of subtle, painstaking artifice and elegant design.

"Bel! Kai! Catch up!" she called to the twins behind her. Bellerophon and Kaimera, were Aniwye Panthers, startlingly quick in the short sprint, but lacking in long chase endurance.

"Or maybe you can slow down a bit," Kai shouted back to her between labored breaths. "Better yet, a rest."

"Slackers," Bloss said. "You don't see Jakro whining for rest."

A giant pewter-colored cave bear ran beside her. Jakro was fat and powerful, covered in many old scars of battle. He huffed clouds of vapor into the night air, as it teased its way into morning.

"Actually, I could use a breather," Jakro said, "if for no other reason than kindness towards fellow travelers."

"Fine," Bloss said, and slowed from run, to lope, to walk.

By the time the panthers had caught up, they had paused on a rocky escarpment overlooking a river valley. A branch of the Bone River meandered below them, still a dark

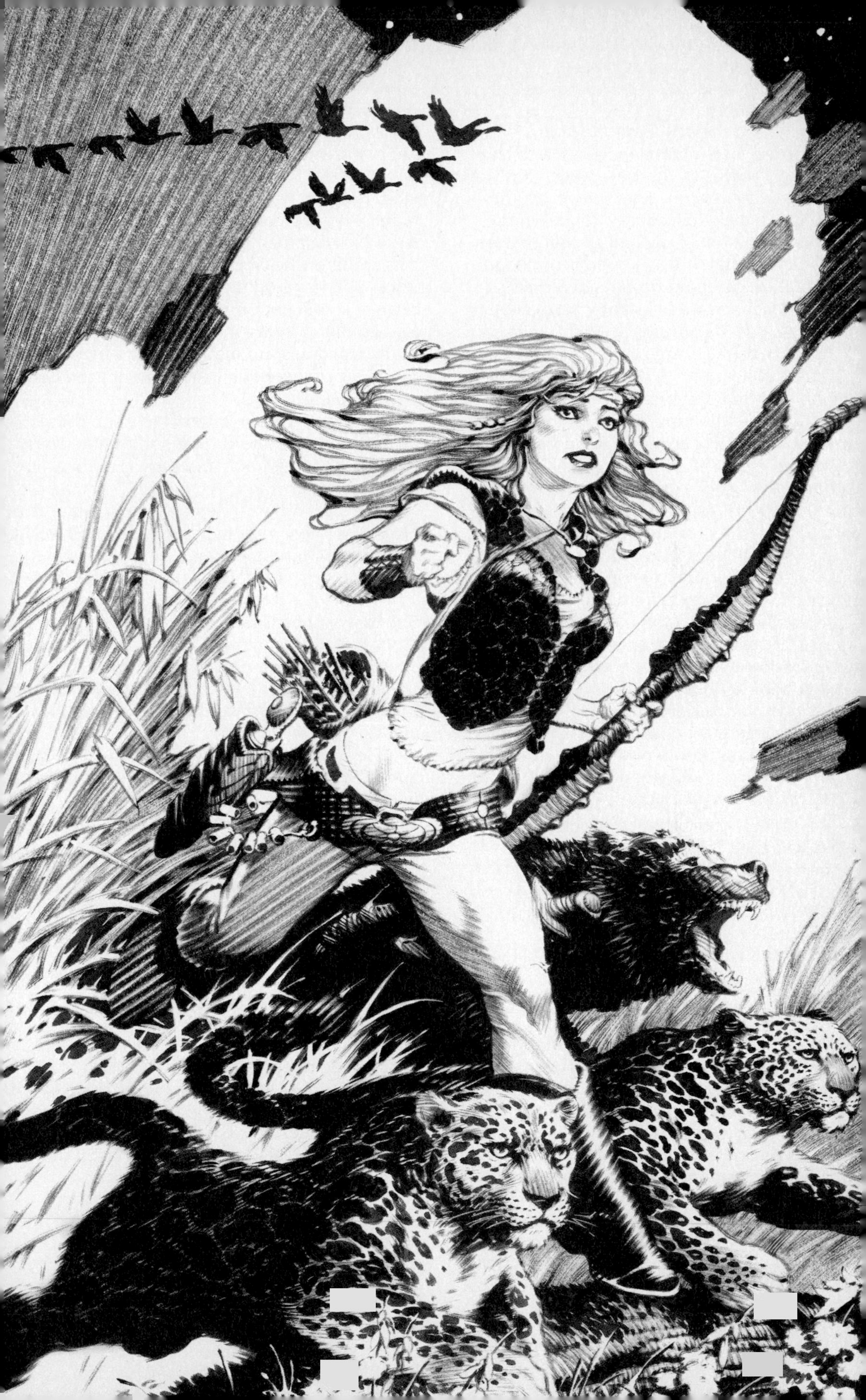

ribbon in the waxing light, that wouldn't find the valley for an hour to come.

"Bloss has a scent," Jakro said, as the twins joined them.

Descended directly from the North Wind, she'd forged a special relationship with the gusts and breezes of this new, unspoiled world she'd made her home. She always got the scent first, which sometimes frustrated the animals, who knew they had keener senses than low humans. It was a matter of debate, though, if Bloss could be considered strictly human. If so, she was certainly an exception to the rule – to most rules, in fact.

"Breakfast?" Bel said.

"Hunters, not prey," Bloss said. "New arrivals."

She had that scrunch of the skin above her eyes that indicated annoyance, a mental thorn that would bother her until she addressed it. From past experience Bel realized (and immediately resigned himself to the knowledge) the important business of securing their next meal would be delayed.

"Let's go have a look at them," she said, and started off again in a loping run she could maintain, without rest, for days on end. Jakro could easily keep up with her, for most of a day. The twin panthers could only do the same, perhaps for as much as an hour, before lagging behind again.

Bloss could have left them all far behind, had she chosen to do so. She was, in truth, a creature of remarkable power. She could take on any number of different forms that could run with unbelievable speed. Or she could simply launch herself into swift flight, merely by demanding the sky accept her. But there were strict courtesies of the hunt to observe. She'd set off in the night with her three companions, proven friends, and wouldn't abandon them lightly.

So instead they ran together, the twins growling and grumbling all the way.

******

The bulrushes were still green along the riverbank, where the changing seasons hadn't touched them yet. Three men and one woman walked through the rushes by the river. Cautiously they moved, in single file, alert and wary. They carried heavy packs on their backs and held high-powered hunting rifles, ready to use them in an instant. The sun had finally reached the low valley an hour ago and the day was warming.

They wore khaki and camouflage, smelled of powerful chemical repellants, and kept the rising sun at bay under wide-brimmed hats.

"We should establish our first camp soon," Pierce said. He tried to hide the fact that he was struggling under the weight of his gear,

but couldn't quite keep the strain out of his voice. Pack your own load was one of the agreed-upon rules of their outing. They styled themselves veterans of hardship and bravado, the Alphas, adventurous true heirs of Clovis People in a world gone irretrievably soft.

"Not yet," Olembe, their elected leader, said. His skin was as black as the darkest night, in sharp contrast to the others, who were Nordic pale. "Not down here by the main river, where who-knows-what will come to drink. What we want — what we're doing here now — is to locate a smaller creek or rivulet joining this, flowing into it. We'll follow that out of the tall grass, up into the hills. Make camp there, where we have water, but not the main body of water."

"We have the sonic fence to keep things away," Anna Bily said. She had freckles over every inch of her face and bare forearms like the stars in the sky.

"We do, and we'll deploy it to be sure. But I'm not familiar with the animals of this world. Are you?" Olembe asked.

"Of course not. That's why we're all here."

"Then let's start out taking every reasonable precaution and not simply rely on a few electronic trinkets that have yet to be proved."

"But they have been proved, time and again," she said. "I've camped amongst polar bears and slept undisturbed. Trust me, they work."

"Good to know. But what if there's something bigger and meaner here, with no evolutionary aversion to high-pitched frequencies? Better we camp higher up, where we can see everything coming."

In the aftermath of the magical revolution that had transformed what had previously been known to some as the Mundy World, they'd learned about the gateways connecting uncounted new worlds, ripe for exploitation. In time they'd heard whispered rumors of the Hunting World, where the great creatures of old still thrived.

"Megafauna and more," Pierce had said, putting together his dream expedition of the best of the best, by invitation only. He'd spent a fortune to do it, but eventually gained acceptance into the company of the finest sports hunters alive. "Hell, even dinosaurs, or dragons. I heard all sorts of stories."

Olembe's will prevailed and they constructed their base camp high, just below the scree field of a looming mountain giant, and above any vegetation tall enough to conceal anything larger than an approaching mouse. There was, after all, a good reason they unanimously chose him to lead. Even among the finest on Earth, his deeds stood out.

"We should name it," Pierce said. "Do you

think we should name it?"

"What's that?"

"The mountain," he said. "It's as big as any I've seen, outside of Everest." Pierce had never actually seen Everest, but didn't consider that relevant to his larger point. "Hell, we should probably name the river too, and everything else. We've earned that much just by showing up."

"Maybe they already have names," Lawrence said. He seemed a bit too bookish to be a hunter of renown, but had often proved himself more than capable. He worked without wasted movement to pitch his small tent. Personal tents were the closest things to luxury they'd agreed to allow themselves. Other than that, weight, bulk and portability ruled every decision. Dehydrated food pouches would be reconstituted in collapsible pots and heated over individual chemical stoves. They would endure privations of comfort and abundance in order to keep the expedition down to the five principals. No porters. No cooks or camp managers. Only pack what you can personally carry was the new gospel. Old-style safaris were permanently out of vogue.

"Not likely. Do you see any signs of even primitive habitation? There are no people here and never were. Besides, even if this place were crawling with locals, history has shown us time and again that nothing counts until an educated white man shows up with the ability to write it down."

"No offense, Olembe," Pierce added as an afterthought.

"None taken, white devil," Olembe said without inflection, or even a hint of a forgiving smile. "Name it, if you want to. You spent enough getting us here. At the least, that should also buy you naming rights."

"It does make sense," Lawrence said. "If we publish an account of this excursion, and I intend to do so, we can't just say we found a valley with a river, near a mountain, where we shot a big critter. Fiction or history, one needs proper names to give a story life. *'And out of the ground the Lord God formed every beast of the field, and every fowl of the air; and brought them unto Adam to see what he would call them: and whatsoever Adam called every living creature, that was the name thereof.'* There's significance to the fact that assigning names was the very first job God gave to man."

They slept restless in the first night, awaking often to unfamiliar sounds.

******

In the morning they awoke to find Bloss and her companions within the heart of their camp. The chemical deterrents of the outer perimeter had been moved and buried. The small plastic pylons forming the inner sonic fence had been smashed, exposing the ruins of their battery packs and solid-state circuits.

She crouched by the stone ring of the campfire they'd made to mark the center of the camp, after painstakingly hauling armfuls of wood up from below. She had rekindled the dead fire and sipped some of their coffee out of Anna Bily's metal cup.

"I miss coffee," Bloss said to Olembe, as he was the first to emerge from his tent. "Mom and Dad always have coffee when I visit."

Olembe took in the improbable scene in a silence that masked his fluster. There was a giant bear sitting placidly near the strange woman, a bear bigger than any species ever recorded on Earth. Two mature panthers, with alien markings on their dark coats, prowled around them, coughing their feline restlessness. The woman seemed completely relaxed in their company. One by one, the other hunters emerged. Lawrence and Bily, sensing something amiss, both had the presence of mind to bring their rifles with them.

"Don't try to use those against my friends," Bloss said, "or me, for that matter. If I had to take them from you, I might not be able to do it gently enough to keep them in good working order.

"Who are you?" Anna Bily said.

"What do you want?" Olembe said.

"You're from the Mundy World, aren't you?" Bloss said. She smiled, not so much in welcome, but in the way a scientist might marvel at an interesting find. "Earth, I mean. Probably not very mundy at all anymore. Lots of big changes about the time I moved away. Just a child back then. Hard to remember much."

"Yes," Lawrence said. "Earth. Some do still call it Mundy, but in a nostalgic way, I think, or maybe ironically."

"Amazing. And you finally found your way here. I suppose it had to happen sooner or later. You'll have to pack up and go home though. Right now."

"Why?" Olembe said.

"According to whose laws?" Pierce said. One panther and then the other growled low growls his way.

"Don't be rude," Bloss said to the cats. Then to Pierce, "Mine, I suppose. Not really formal laws, since I'm alone in making them. You have to go because I just told you so."

"The reason we're here in the first place," Pierce said, "is that none of us do well under those who like to tell folks what to do. We don't much hold ourselves accountable to any man – or woman – and whatever laws or whims they try to impose."

The giant bear rose to his four legs, and all at once there seemed to be a dark heat emanating from it. Olembe measured the distance to his tent, and his own rifle within. He silently cursed himself for breaking his own rule about carrying his weapon at all times, especially when there was no chance he might need it.

"I don't like that one," Jakro said, looking at Pierce.

There weren't quite gasps of astonishment, to hear a bear talk. Expressions of surprise, at most. Talking animals weren't entirely unknown in their world since the change, which had occurred long before any of these were born. They were a rarity still, but not unheard of.

"Quiet, Jak," Bloss said. "This is my business. Mind your own."

She threw the dregs of her borrowed coffee into the fire and stood to her full height, stretching a bit as she did so.

"Good for you," Bloss said, singling Pierce out with her unsettling gaze. "A man who stands his ground. I like those with an independent mind and a practiced stubbornness against those who can't live and let live. Reminds me of my dad. But this is a different matter altogether. This isn't your ground to stand on. It's mine."

"This valley?" Bily said.

"A bit more than that. I can't put off the boys' breakfast too much longer, so let's wrap this up. I'll give it to you formally."

Bloss took a moment to compose herself. She brushed dirt off her knees and carefully placed an errant strand of hair behind one ear.

"I am Blossom," she said, "daughter of the Wolf God; daughter of Snow White, who gave both the dying and the renewal into my care. This is my world. You're trespassing."

"Some sort of self-elected nature goddess?" Bily said.

"My pedigree might suggest as much."

"The entire world is yours?" Lawrence said. "How is that so?"

Pierce said, "What right have you to take all of it and leave none for others?"

"No right to deprive others," Bloss said. "But the others are already here. You imagine a wasteland in which I'm alone and greedy for every empty hill and valley. In fact it's fat with population. Every nook and cranny is filled with homesteaders, each of which has prior claim. My ownership then is more a matter of a caretaker's authority, rather than possession. But to answer your real question, anyone who owns this world does so by the only law that pertains – the ability to keep it."

"Implying you've done violence against those like us, from the outside, who've stumbled onto it," Pierce said.

"No one stumbles through a world gate. One look at your gear and I know you're here by intention. But yes, I've killed to discourage intruders."

"You're Cerberus," Lawrence said. "A guard at the gate to paradise."

"Among other things. I wear a lot of hats. In the spring I call up the growing and birthing. In the fall I hunt, to cull the weak, prior to the trials of winter."

"You encourage and protect life in one season," Bily said, "but turn around and kill it in another?"

"Every coin has two sides. What true hunter isn't also a devoted naturalist? It's getting late and I'm beginning to suspect you're trying to keep me talking. Gather up your things and I'll escort you back to the gate. We'll want to move fast, so only bring what you can easily carry."

"But this world," Olembe said. He used her invitation as leave to walk back to his tent, within quick reach of his rifle now.

"Yes?"

"Are you aware it's referred to as The Hunting World?"

"Very much so, in the myriad languages of man and beast, that's what we call it too."

"But we're hunters," he said. "And yet we're not welcome here?"

"Ah, that's where you got confused," Bloss said. "I'll have to figure out some way to get the word out about that. Yes, this is a world dedicated to the hunt. But whatever made you think you could show up and be the hunters?"

In his dark nidifice at the summit of Sky Reaching Mountain, Arok the Thunderhawk stirred and tasted the cloying flavor of exotic prey on the wind.

Horraru the Terror rose up from his buried lair under the Bone River, letting the clean cold water of the surface wash the bottom mud from his scales. He felt the remote internal sizzle as supercharged adrenaline flooded his sprinting sacks.

"What if we refuse to leave?" Pierce said.

"Do you think I offered you my escort to protect them from you?" Bloss said. "If you refuse to go, then I wash my hands of you, withdraw my protection, and let the Hunting World hunt."

In the sky, lusty and raucous formations of geese flew south, honking their deeds and intentions to all who would listen. In mountain and valley, lake and forest, for leagues in every direction, things rustled and stirred, tasting the air, which carried the news that sacred Blossom of the Sky and Earth had moved on, leaving four unguarded things behind. The message was clear. The hunt could now begin.

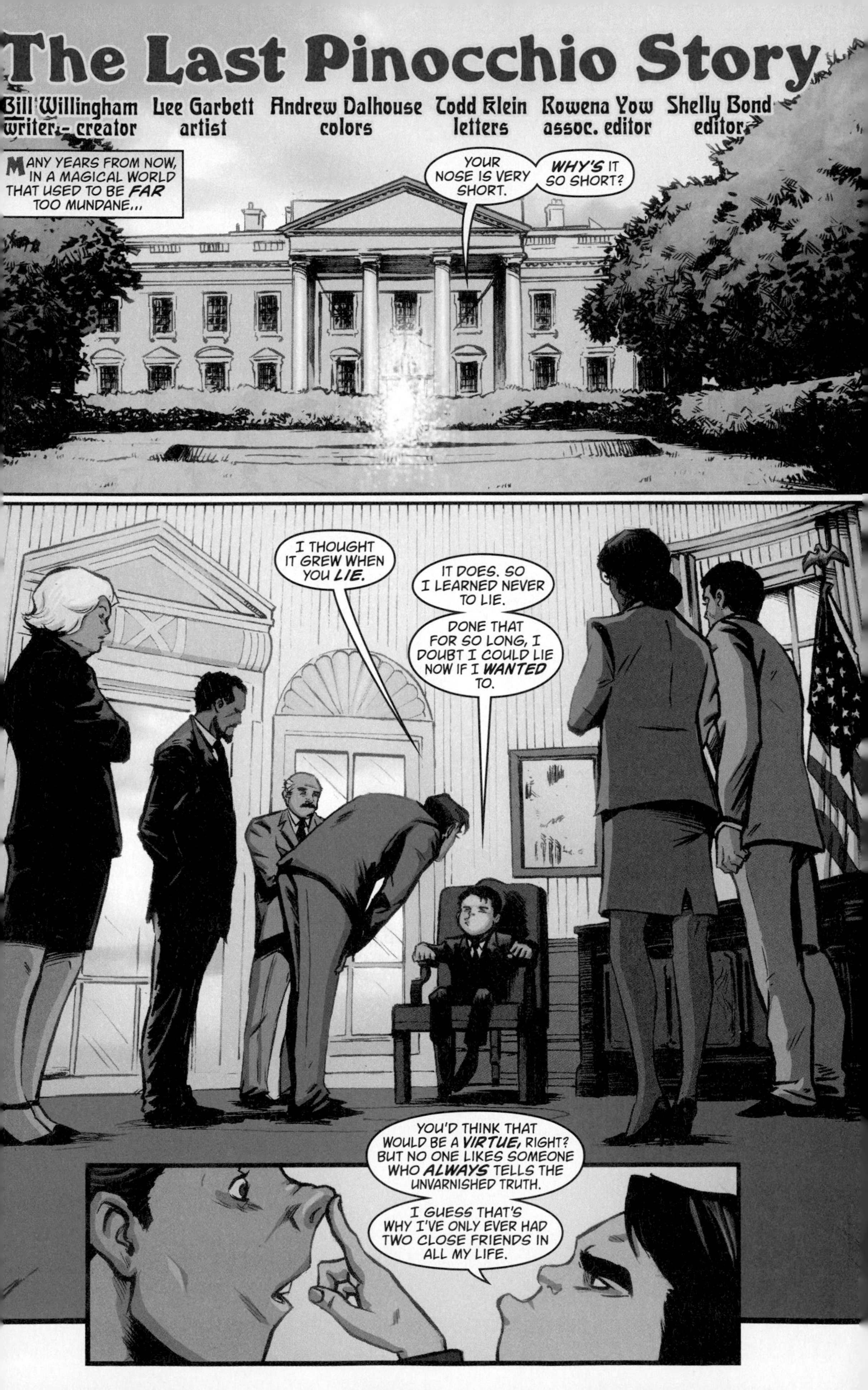
The Last Pinocchio Story
Bill Willingham writer - creator
Lee Garbett artist
Andrew Dalhouse colors
Todd Klein letters
Rowena Yow assoc. editor
Shelly Bond editor
MANY YEARS FROM NOW, IN A MAGICAL WORLD THAT USED TO BE FAR TOO MUNDANE...
YOUR NOSE IS VERY SHORT.
WHY'S IT SO SHORT?
I THOUGHT IT GREW WHEN YOU LIE.
IT DOES. SO I LEARNED NEVER TO LIE.
DONE THAT FOR SO LONG, I DOUBT I COULD LIE NOW IF I WANTED TO.
YOU'D THINK THAT WOULD BE A VIRTUE, RIGHT? BUT NO ONE LIKES SOMEONE WHO ALWAYS TELLS THE UNVARNISHED TRUTH.
I GUESS THAT'S WHY I'VE ONLY EVER HAD TWO CLOSE FRIENDS IN ALL MY LIFE.

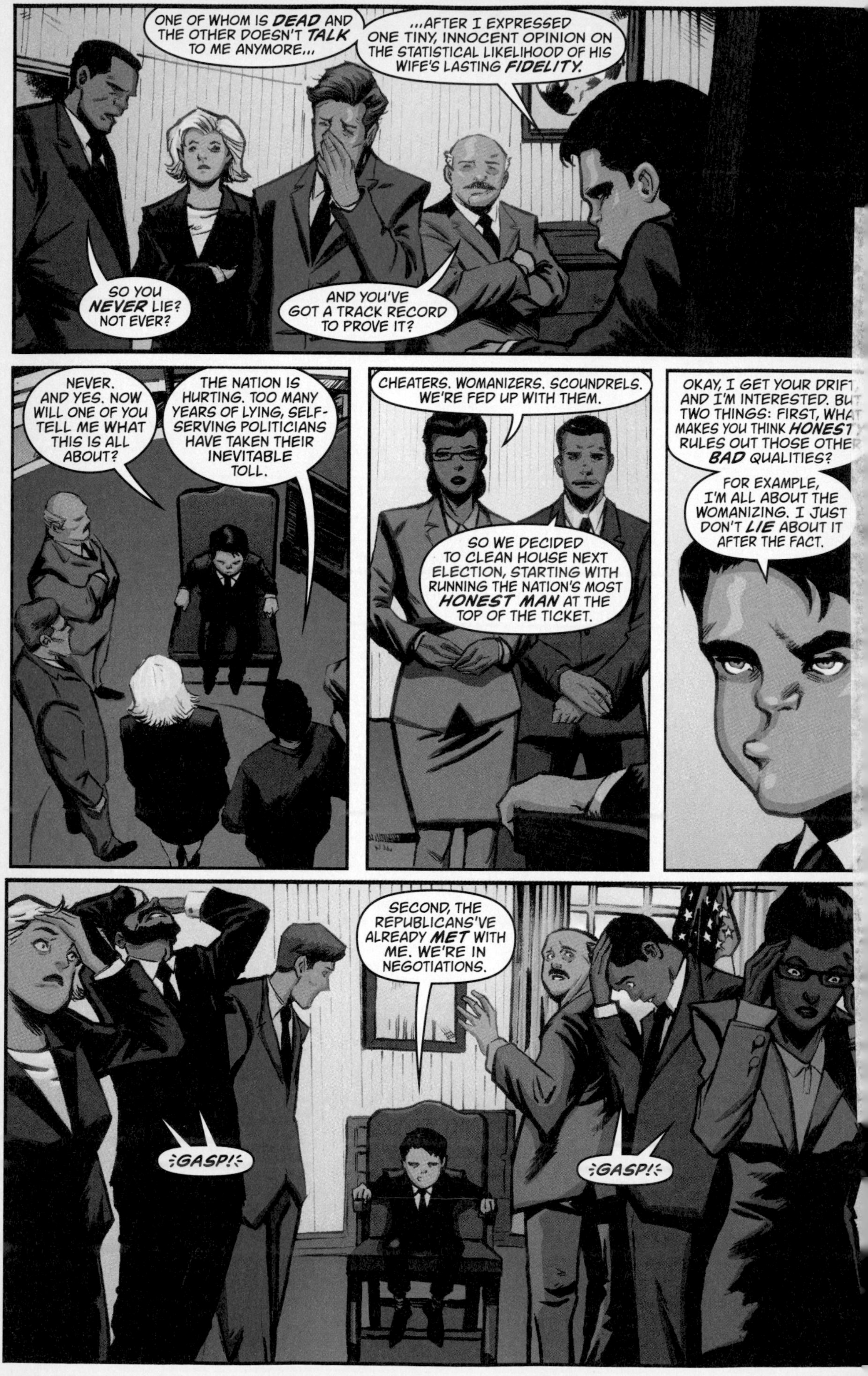
ONE OF WHOM IS DEAD AND THE OTHER DOESN'T TALK TO ME ANYMORE...
...AFTER I EXPRESSED ONE TINY, INNOCENT OPINION ON THE STATISTICAL LIKELIHOOD OF HIS WIFE'S LASTING FIDELITY.
SO YOU NEVER LIE? NOT EVER?
AND YOU'VE GOT A TRACK RECORD TO PROVE IT?
NEVER. AND YES. NOW WILL ONE OF YOU TELL ME WHAT THIS IS ALL ABOUT?
THE NATION IS HURTING. TOO MANY YEARS OF LYING, SELF-SERVING POLITICIANS HAVE TAKEN THEIR INEVITABLE TOLL.
CHEATERS. WOMANIZERS. SCOUNDRELS. WE'RE FED UP WITH THEM.
SO WE DECIDED TO CLEAN HOUSE NEXT ELECTION, STARTING WITH RUNNING THE NATION'S MOST HONEST MAN AT THE TOP OF THE TICKET.
OKAY, I GET YOUR DRIFT, AND I'M INTERESTED. BUT TWO THINGS: FIRST, WHAT MAKES YOU THINK HONESTY RULES OUT THOSE OTHER BAD QUALITIES?
FOR EXAMPLE, I'M ALL ABOUT THE WOMANIZING. I JUST DON'T LIE ABOUT IT AFTER THE FACT.
SECOND, THE REPUBLICANS'VE ALREADY MET WITH ME. WE'RE IN NEGOTIATIONS.
GASP!
GASP!

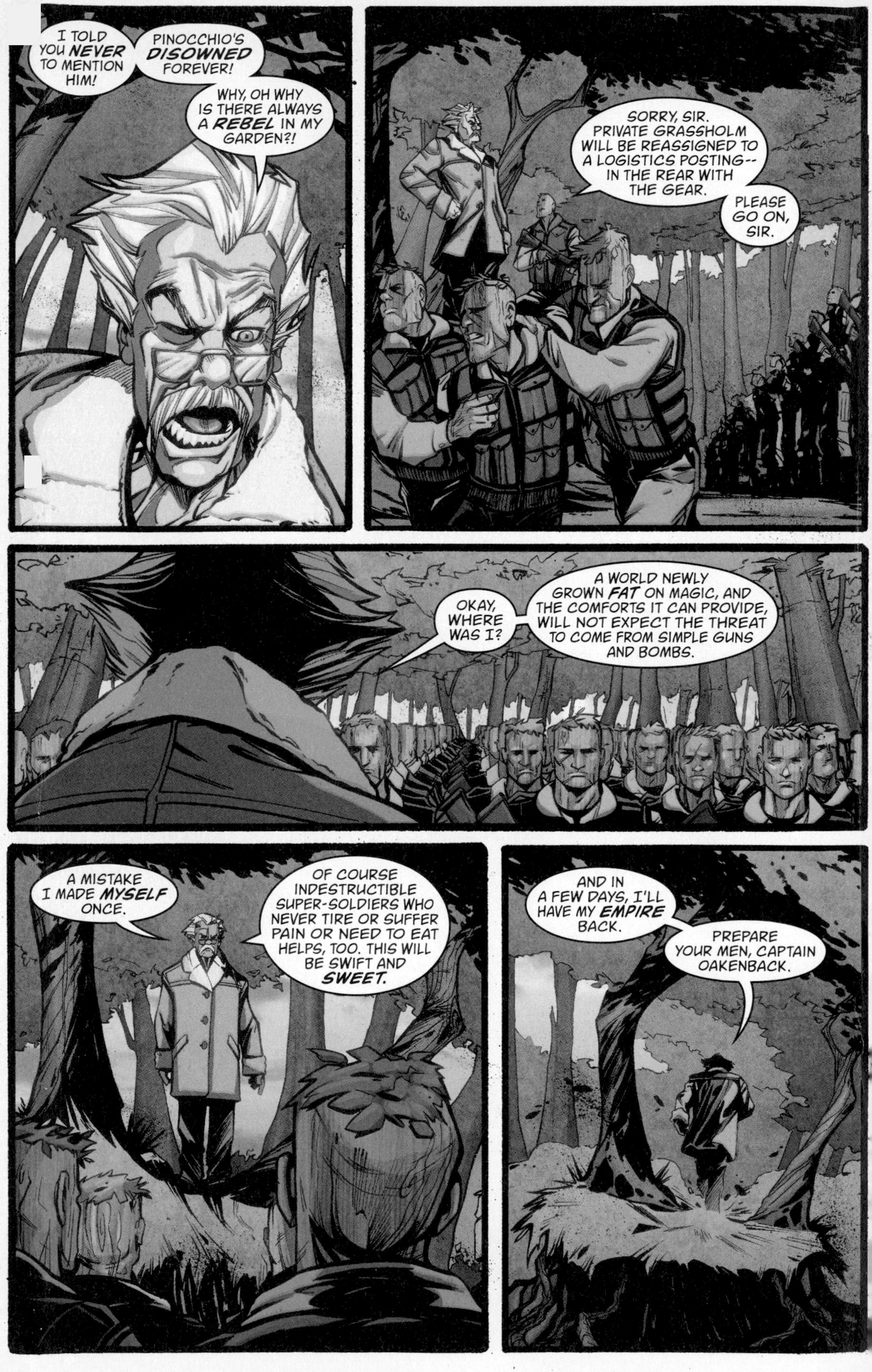
I TOLD YOU NEVER TO MENTION HIM!
PINOCCHIO'S DISOWNED FOREVER!
WHY, OH WHY IS THERE ALWAYS A REBEL IN MY GARDEN?!
SORRY, SIR. PRIVATE GRASSHOLM WILL BE REASSIGNED TO A LOGISTICS POSTING-- IN THE REAR WITH THE GEAR.
PLEASE GO ON, SIR.
OKAY, WHERE WAS I?
A WORLD NEWLY GROWN FAT ON MAGIC, AND THE COMFORTS IT CAN PROVIDE, WILL NOT EXPECT THE THREAT TO COME FROM SIMPLE GUNS AND BOMBS.
A MISTAKE I MADE MYSELF ONCE.
OF COURSE INDESTRUCTIBLE SUPER-SOLDIERS WHO NEVER TIRE OR SUFFER PAIN OR NEED TO EAT HELPS, TOO. THIS WILL BE SWIFT AND SWEET.
AND IN A FEW DAYS, I'LL HAVE MY EMPIRE BACK.
PREPARE YOUR MEN, CAPTAIN OAKENBACK.

The Last Geppetto Story

Bill Willingham writer - creator
Joëlle Jones artist
Andrew Dalhouse colors
Todd Klein letters
Rowena Yow assoc. editor
Shelly Bond editor

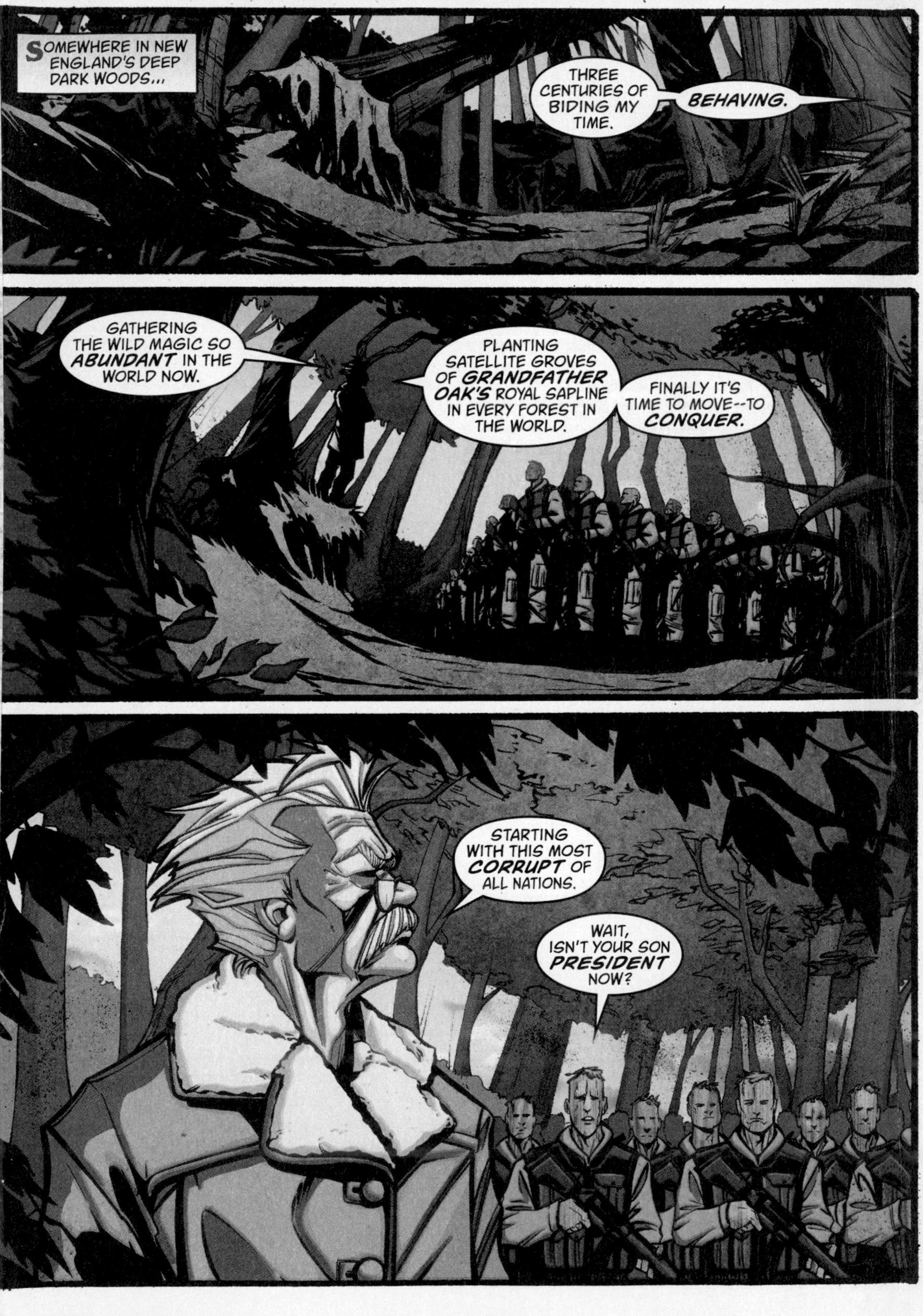
SOMEWHERE IN NEW ENGLAND'S DEEP DARK WOODS...
THREE CENTURIES OF BIDING MY TIME.
BEHAVING.
GATHERING THE WILD MAGIC SO ABUNDANT IN THE WORLD NOW.
PLANTING SATELLITE GROVES OF GRANDFATHER OAK'S ROYAL SAPLINE IN EVERY FOREST IN THE WORLD.
FINALLY IT'S TIME TO MOVE--TO CONQUER.
STARTING WITH THIS MOST CORRUPT OF ALL NATIONS.
WAIT, ISN'T YOUR SON PRESIDENT NOW?

THE LAST LAKE STORY

Bill Willingham writer - creator
Gene Ha artist
Peter Gross layouts
Andrew Dalhouse colors
Todd Klein letters
Rowena Yow assoc. editor
Shelly Bond editor

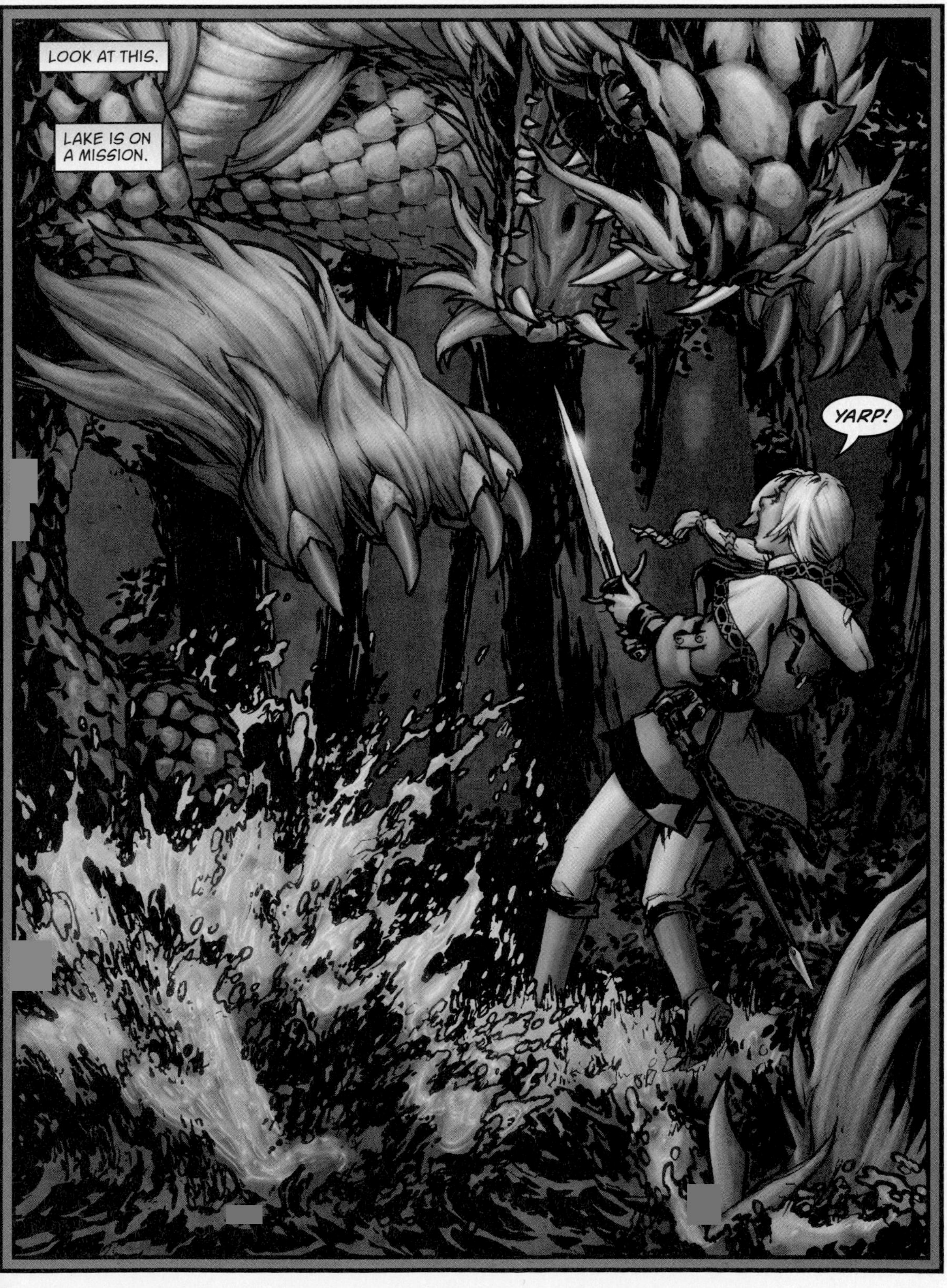
LOOK AT THIS.
LAKE IS ON A MISSION.
YARP!

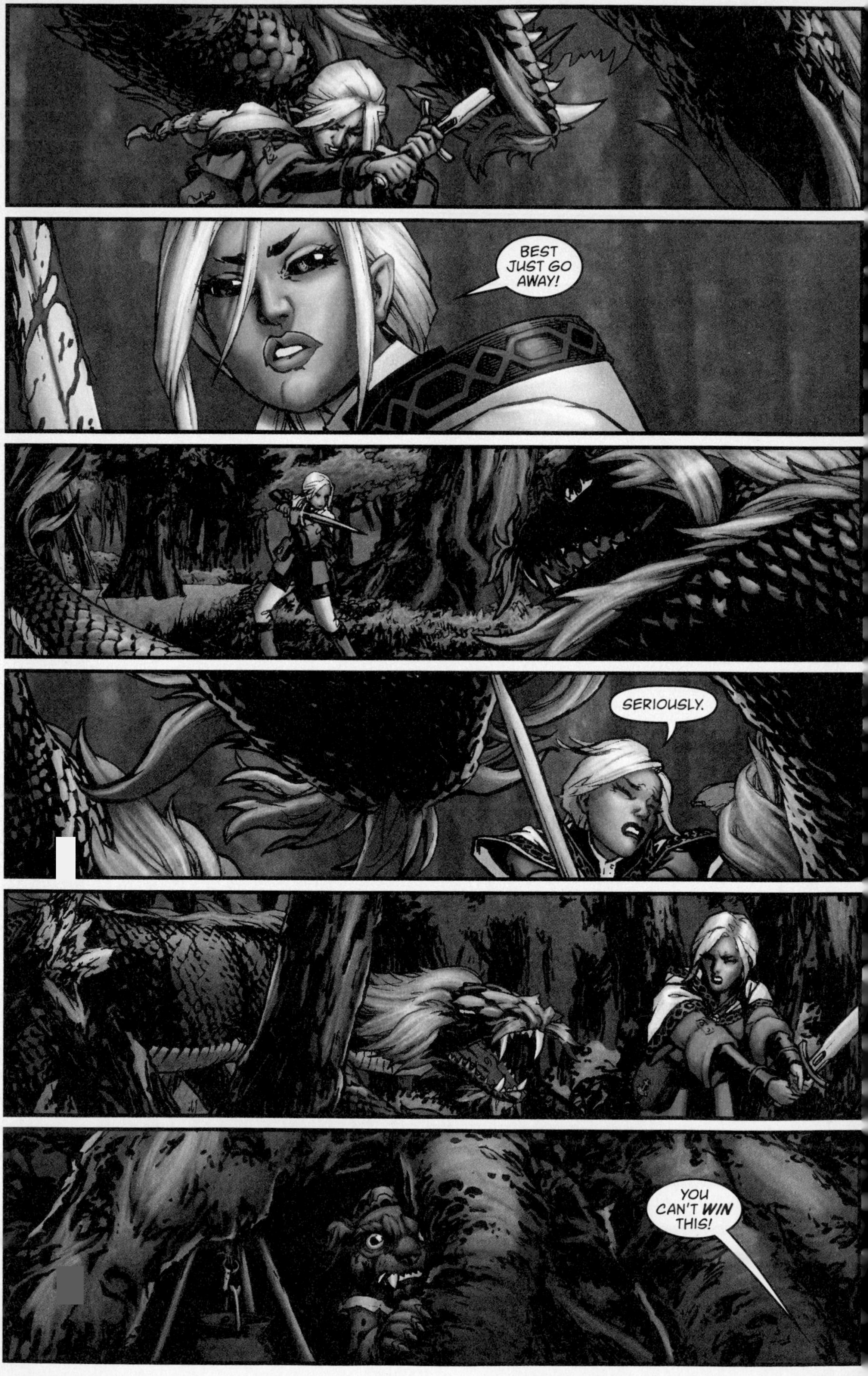
BEST JUST GO AWAY!
SERIOUSLY.
YOU CAN'T WIN THIS!

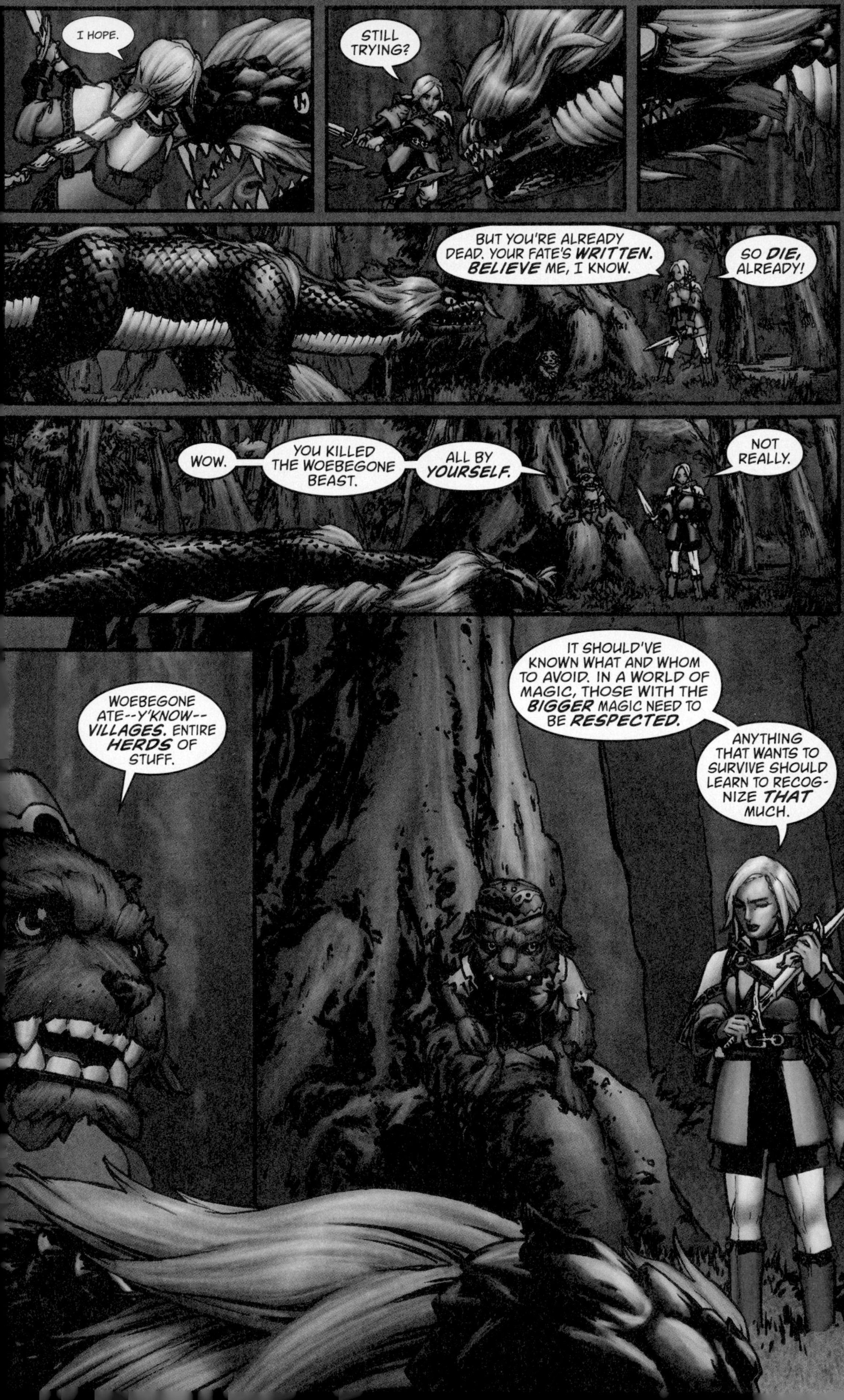
I HOPE.
STILL TRYING?
BUT YOU'RE ALREADY DEAD. YOUR FATE'S WRITTEN. BELIEVE ME, I KNOW.
SO DIE, ALREADY!
WOW.
YOU KILLED THE WOEBEGONE BEAST.
ALL BY YOURSELF.
NOT REALLY.
WOEBEGONE ATE--Y'KNOW--VILLAGES. ENTIRE HERDS OF STUFF.
IT SHOULD'VE KNOWN WHAT AND WHOM TO AVOID. IN A WORLD OF MAGIC, THOSE WITH THE BIGGER MAGIC NEED TO BE RESPECTED.
ANYTHING THAT WANTS TO SURVIVE SHOULD LEARN TO RECOG-NIZE THAT MUCH.

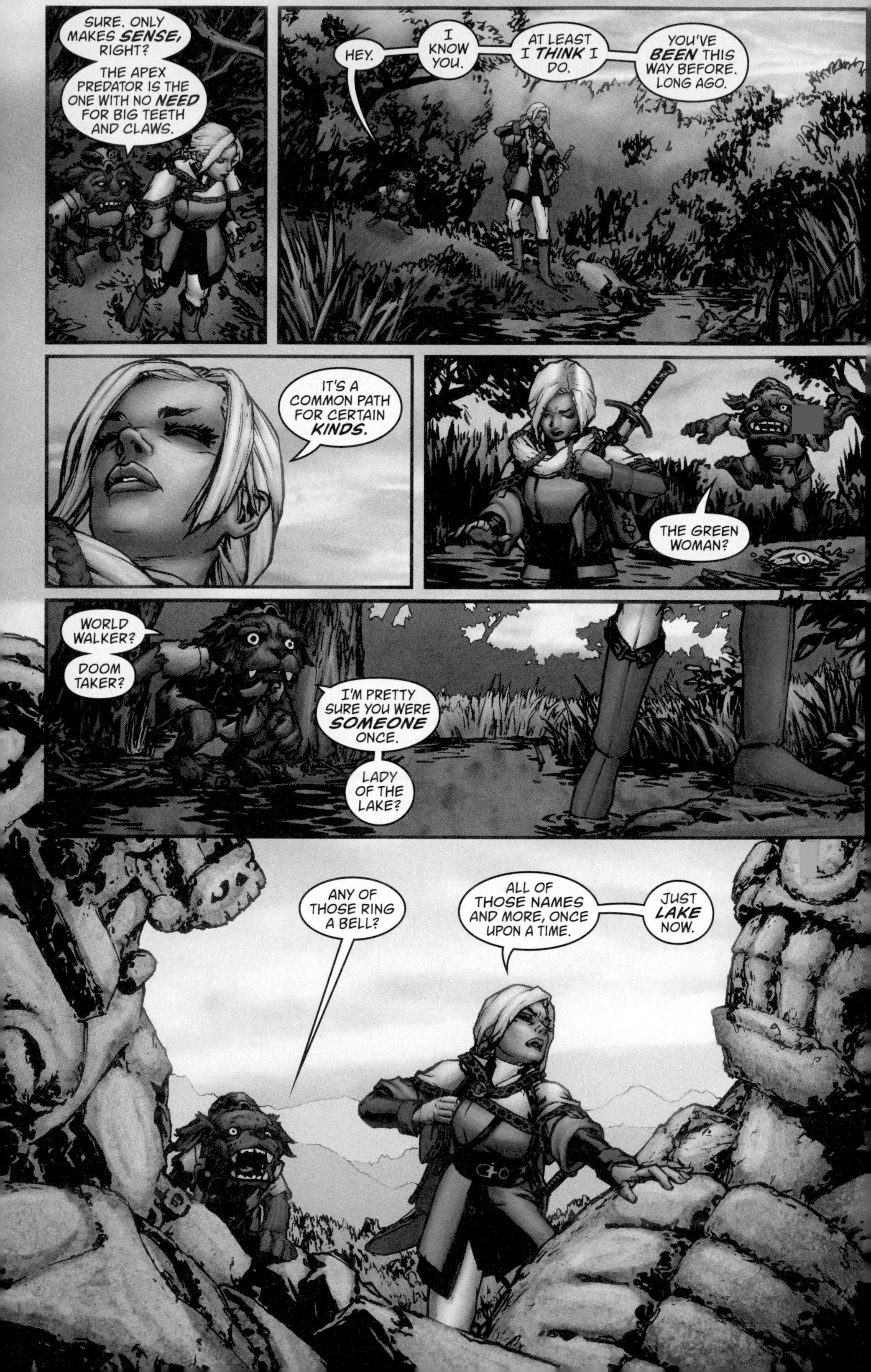
SURE. ONLY MAKES SENSE, RIGHT?
THE APEX PREDATOR IS THE ONE WITH NO NEED FOR BIG TEETH AND CLAWS.
HEY.
I KNOW YOU.
AT LEAST I THINK I DO.
YOU'VE BEEN THIS WAY BEFORE. LONG AGO.
IT'S A COMMON PATH FOR CERTAIN KINDS.
THE GREEN WOMAN?
WORLD WALKER?
DOOM TAKER?
I'M PRETTY SURE YOU WERE SOMEONE ONCE.
LADY OF THE LAKE?
ANY OF THOSE RING A BELL?
ALL OF THOSE NAMES AND MORE, ONCE UPON A TIME.
JUST LAKE NOW.

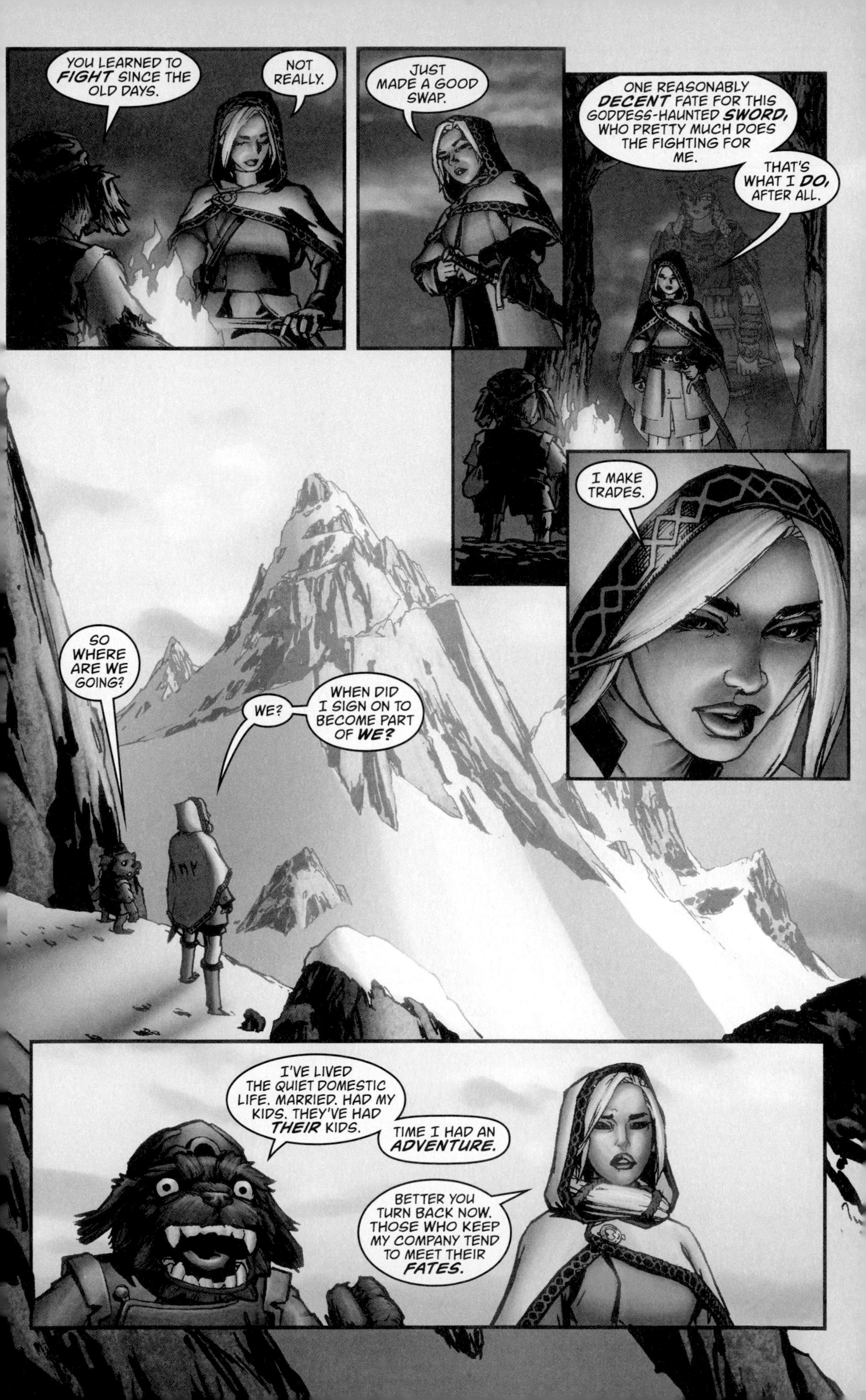

YOU LEARNED TO FIGHT SINCE THE OLD DAYS.
NOT REALLY.
JUST MADE A GOOD SWAP.
ONE REASONABLY DECENT FATE FOR THIS GODDESS-HAUNTED SWORD, WHO PRETTY MUCH DOES THE FIGHTING FOR ME.
THAT'S WHAT I DO, AFTER ALL.
I MAKE TRADES.
SO WHERE ARE WE GOING?
WE?
WHEN DID I SIGN ON TO BECOME PART OF WE?
I'VE LIVED THE QUIET DOMESTIC LIFE. MARRIED. HAD MY KIDS. THEY'VE HAD THEIR KIDS.
TIME I HAD AN ADVENTURE.
BETTER YOU TURN BACK NOW. THOSE WHO KEEP MY COMPANY TEND TO MEET THEIR FATES.

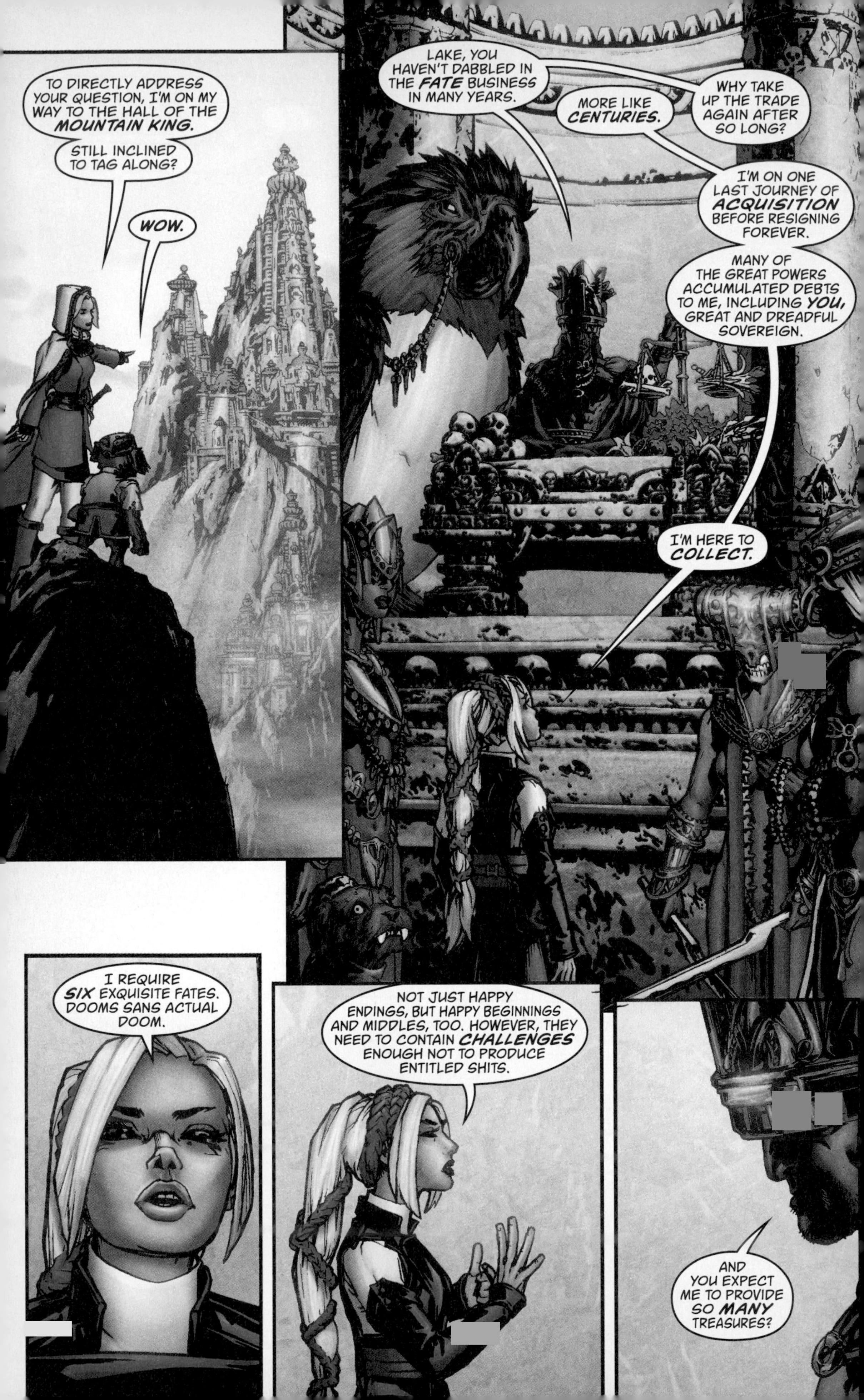
TO DIRECTLY ADDRESS YOUR QUESTION, I'M ON MY WAY TO THE HALL OF THE MOUNTAIN KING.
STILL INCLINED TO TAG ALONG?
WOW.
LAKE, YOU HAVEN'T DABBLED IN THE FATE BUSINESS IN MANY YEARS.
WHY TAKE UP THE TRADE AGAIN AFTER SO LONG?
MORE LIKE CENTURIES.
I'M ON ONE LAST JOURNEY OF ACQUISITION BEFORE RESIGNING FOREVER.
MANY OF THE GREAT POWERS ACCUMULATED DEBTS TO ME, INCLUDING YOU, GREAT AND DREADFUL SOVEREIGN.
I'M HERE TO COLLECT.
I REQUIRE SIX EXQUISITE FATES. DOOMS SANS ACTUAL DOOM.
NOT JUST HAPPY ENDINGS, BUT HAPPY BEGINNINGS AND MIDDLES, TOO. HOWEVER, THEY NEED TO CONTAIN CHALLENGES ENOUGH NOT TO PRODUCE ENTITLED SHITS.
AND YOU EXPECT ME TO PROVIDE SO MANY TREASURES?

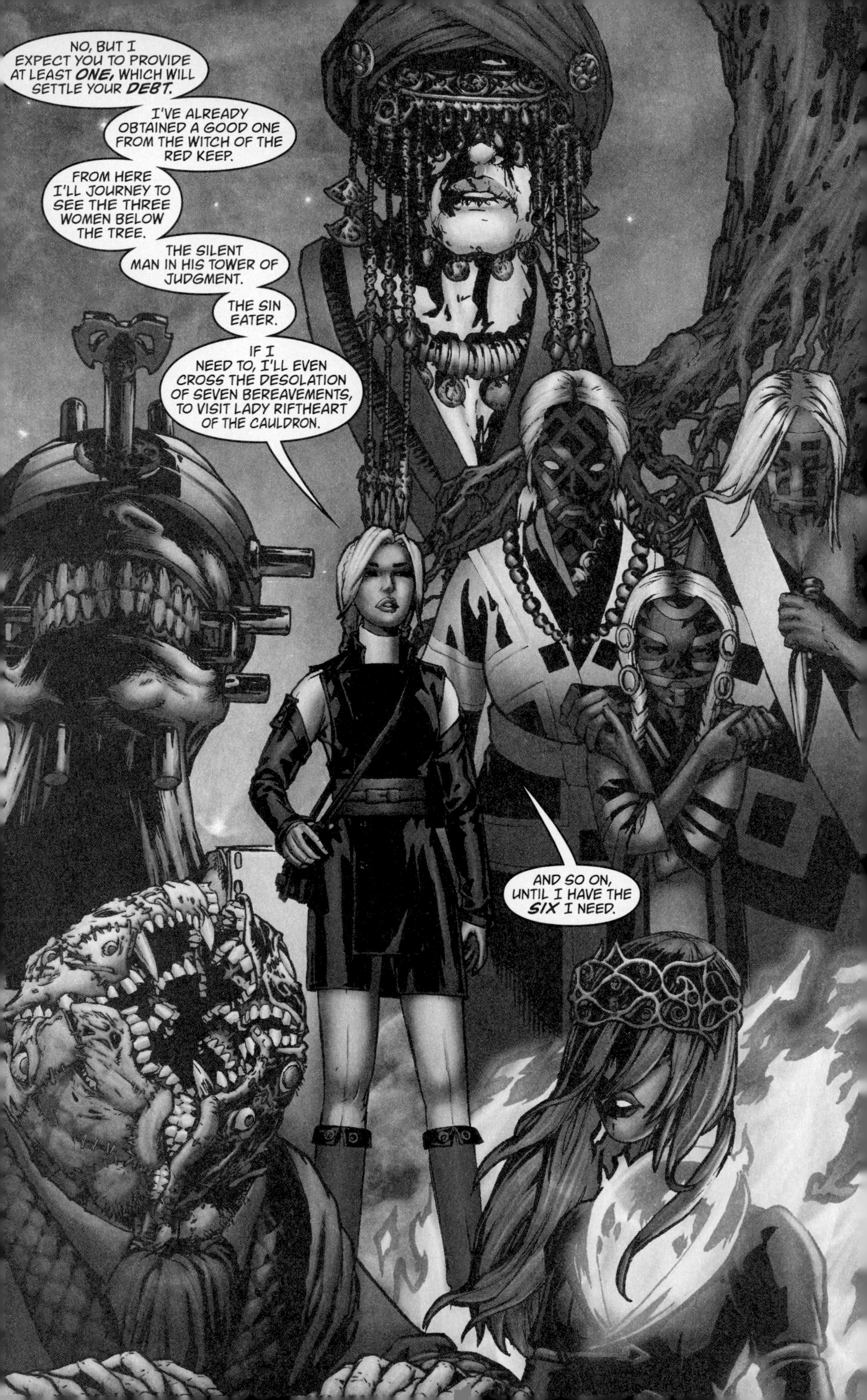
NO, BUT I EXPECT YOU TO PROVIDE AT LEAST ONE, WHICH WILL SETTLE YOUR DEBT.
I'VE ALREADY OBTAINED A GOOD ONE FROM THE WITCH OF THE RED KEEP.
FROM HERE I'LL JOURNEY TO SEE THE THREE WOMEN BELOW THE TREE.
THE SILENT MAN IN HIS TOWER OF JUDGMENT.
THE SIN EATER.
IF I NEED TO, I'LL EVEN CROSS THE DESOLATION OF SEVEN BEREAVEMENTS, TO VISIT LADY RIFTHEART OF THE CAULDRON.
AND SO ON, UNTIL I HAVE THE SIX I NEED.

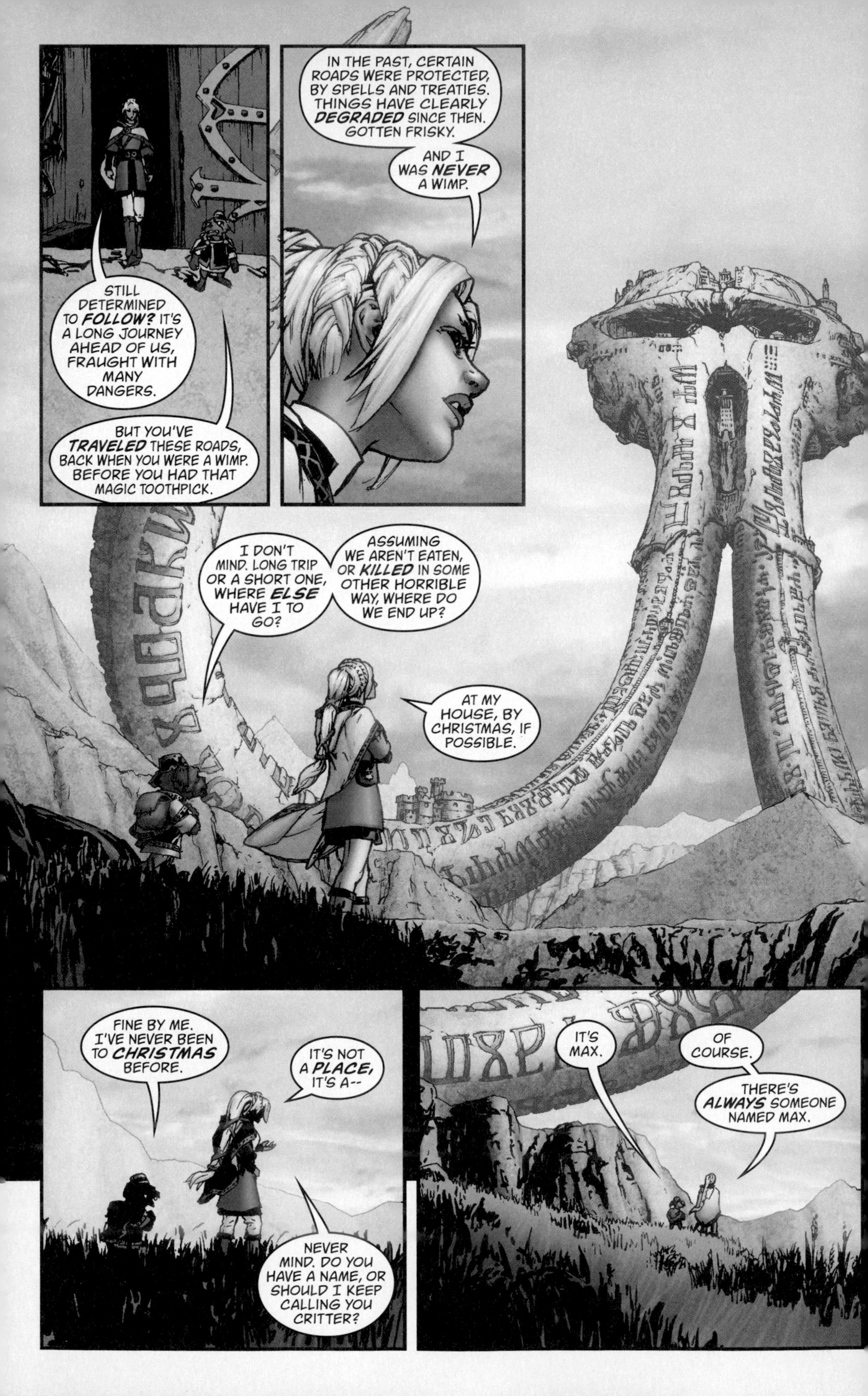
STILL DETERMINED TO FOLLOW? IT'S A LONG JOURNEY AHEAD OF US, FRAUGHT WITH MANY DANGERS.
BUT YOU'VE TRAVELED THESE ROADS, BACK WHEN YOU WERE A WIMP. BEFORE YOU HAD THAT MAGIC TOOTHPICK.
IN THE PAST, CERTAIN ROADS WERE PROTECTED, BY SPELLS AND TREATIES. THINGS HAVE CLEARLY DEGRADED SINCE THEN. GOTTEN FRISKY.
AND I WAS NEVER A WIMP.
I DON'T MIND. LONG TRIP OR A SHORT ONE, WHERE ELSE HAVE I TO GO?
ASSUMING WE AREN'T EATEN, OR KILLED IN SOME OTHER HORRIBLE WAY, WHERE DO WE END UP?
AT MY HOUSE, BY CHRISTMAS, IF POSSIBLE.
FINE BY ME. I'VE NEVER BEEN TO CHRISTMAS BEFORE.
IT'S NOT A PLACE, IT'S A--
NEVER MIND. DO YOU HAVE A NAME, OR SHOULD I KEEP CALLING YOU CRITTER?
IT'S MAX.
OF COURSE.
THERE'S ALWAYS SOMEONE NAMED MAX.

The Last Christmas Story

Bill Willingham writer - creator
Neal Adams artist
Andrew Dalhouse colorist
Todd Klein letterer
Rowena Yow assoc. ed.
Shelly Bond editor

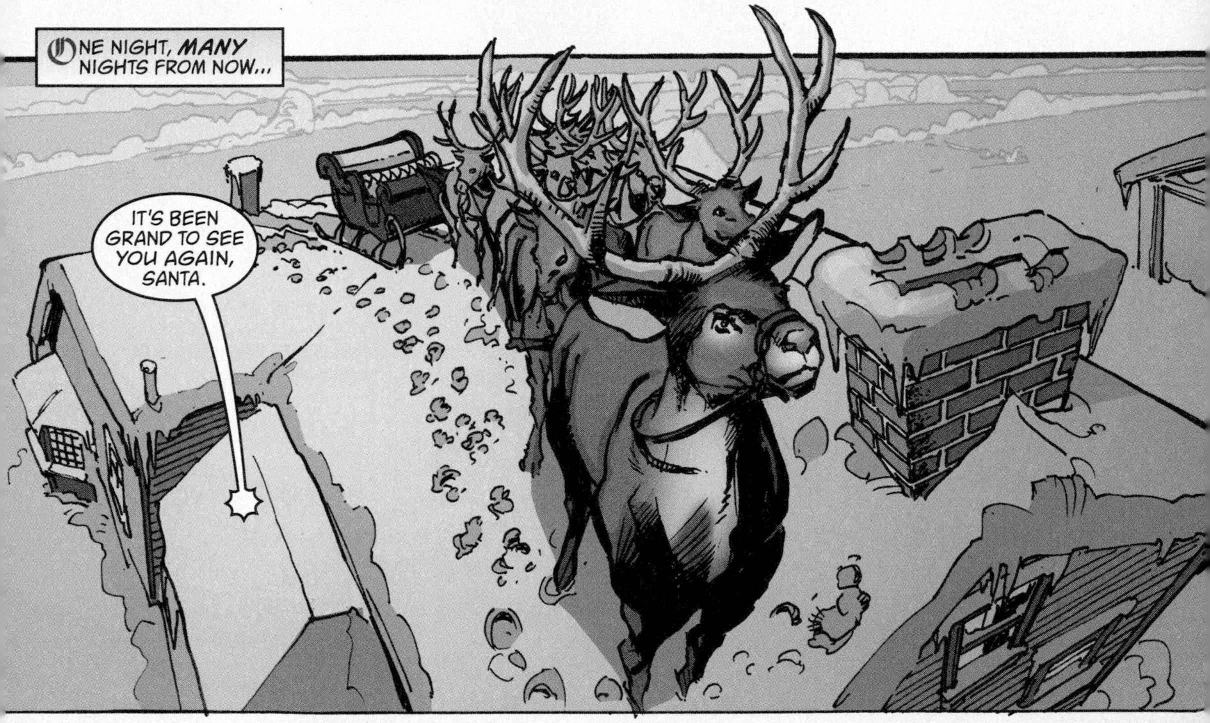
ONE NIGHT, *MANY* NIGHTS FROM NOW...
IT'S BEEN GRAND TO SEE YOU AGAIN, SANTA.

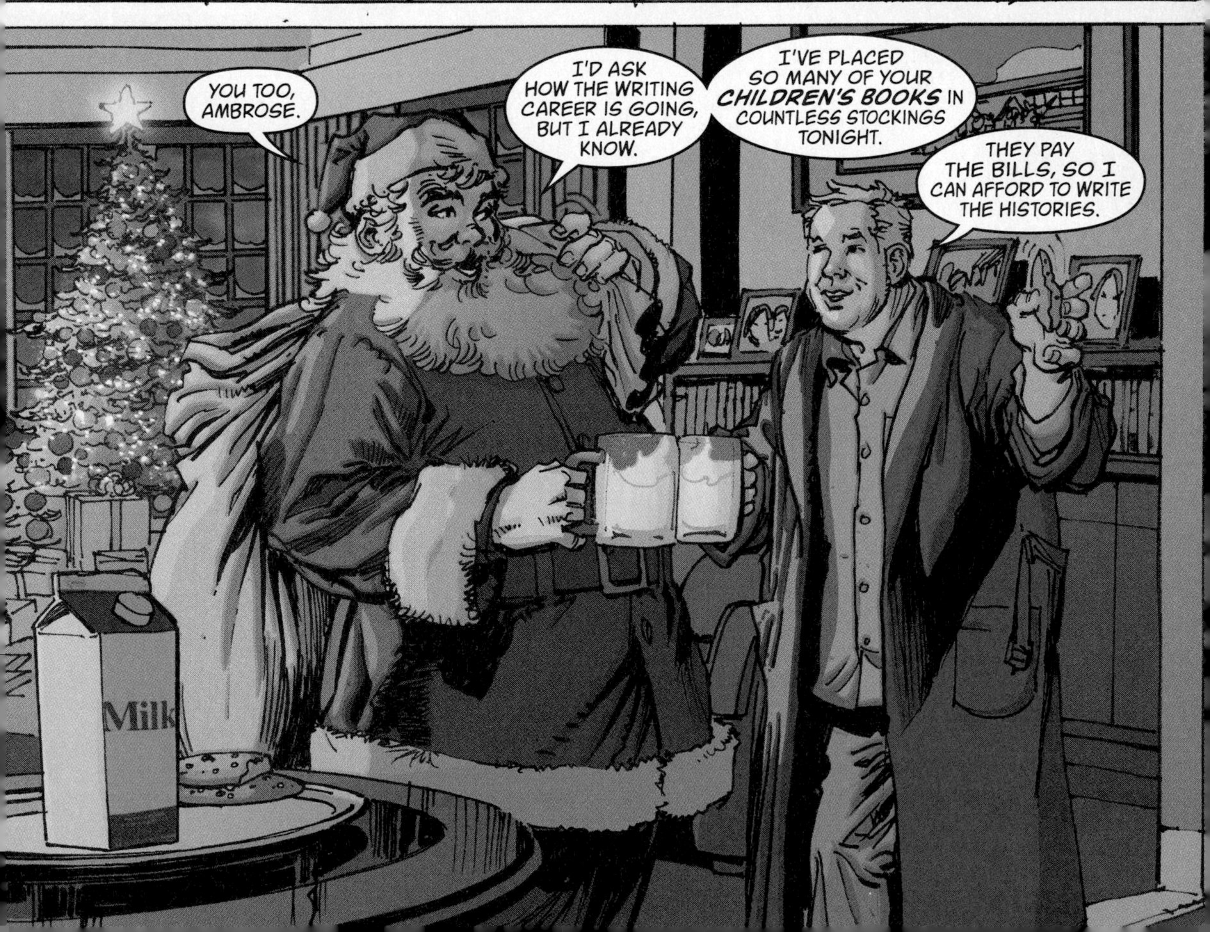
YOU TOO, AMBROSE.
I'D ASK HOW THE WRITING CAREER IS GOING, BUT I ALREADY KNOW.
I'VE PLACED SO MANY OF YOUR **CHILDREN'S BOOKS** IN COUNTLESS STOCKINGS TONIGHT.
THEY PAY THE BILLS, SO I CAN AFFORD TO WRITE THE HISTORIES.
Milk

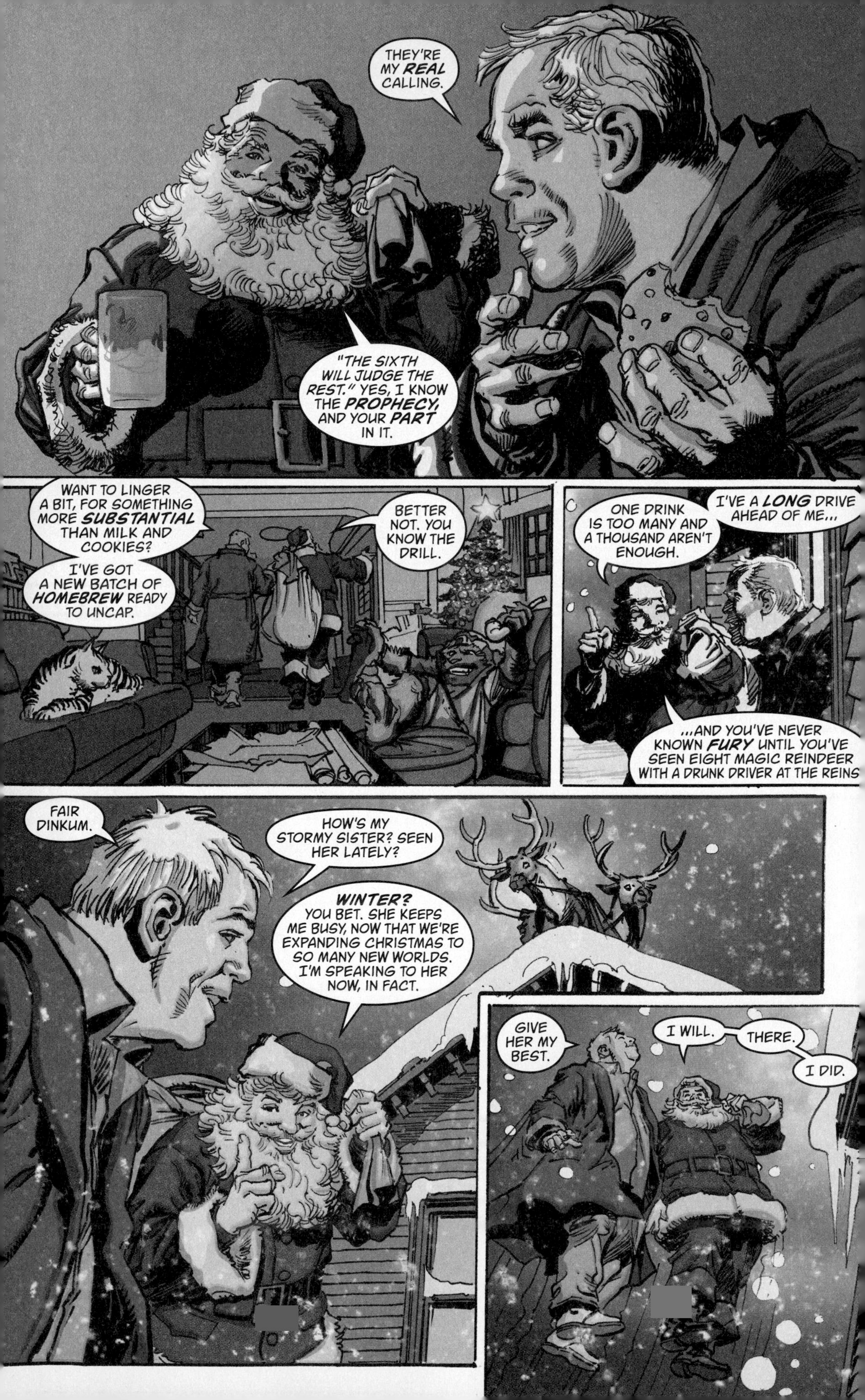

THEY'RE MY REAL CALLING.
"THE SIXTH WILL JUDGE THE REST." YES, I KNOW THE PROPHECY, AND YOUR PART IN IT.
WANT TO LINGER A BIT, FOR SOMETHING MORE SUBSTANTIAL THAN MILK AND COOKIES?
I'VE GOT A NEW BATCH OF HOMEBREW READY TO UNCAP.
BETTER NOT. YOU KNOW THE DRILL.
ONE DRINK IS TOO MANY AND A THOUSAND AREN'T ENOUGH.
I'VE A LONG DRIVE AHEAD OF ME...
...AND YOU'VE NEVER KNOWN FURY UNTIL YOU'VE SEEN EIGHT MAGIC REINDEER WITH A DRUNK DRIVER AT THE REINS
FAIR DINKUM.
HOW'S MY STORMY SISTER? SEEN HER LATELY?
WINTER? YOU BET. SHE KEEPS ME BUSY, NOW THAT WE'RE EXPANDING CHRISTMAS TO SO MANY NEW WORLDS. I'M SPEAKING TO HER NOW, IN FACT.
GIVE HER MY BEST.
I WILL.
THERE.
I DID.

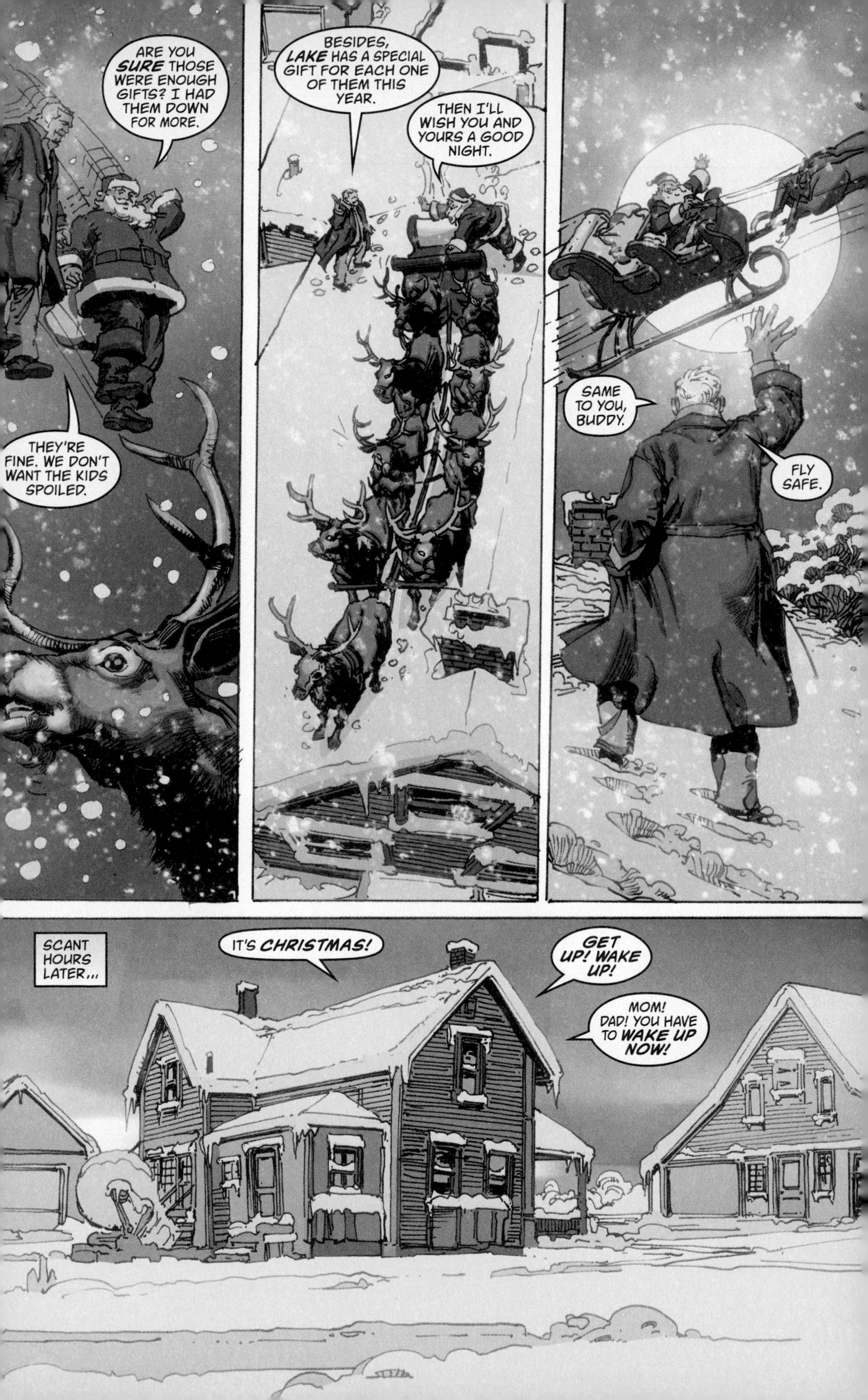

ARE YOU SURE THOSE WERE ENOUGH GIFTS? I HAD THEM DOWN FOR MORE.
THEY'RE FINE. WE DON'T WANT THE KIDS SPOILED.
BESIDES, LAKE HAS A SPECIAL GIFT FOR EACH ONE OF THEM THIS YEAR.
THEN I'LL WISH YOU AND YOURS A GOOD NIGHT.
SAME TO YOU, BUDDY.
FLY SAFE.
SCANT HOURS LATER...
IT'S CHRISTMAS!
GET UP! WAKE UP!
MOM! DAD! YOU HAVE TO WAKE UP NOW!

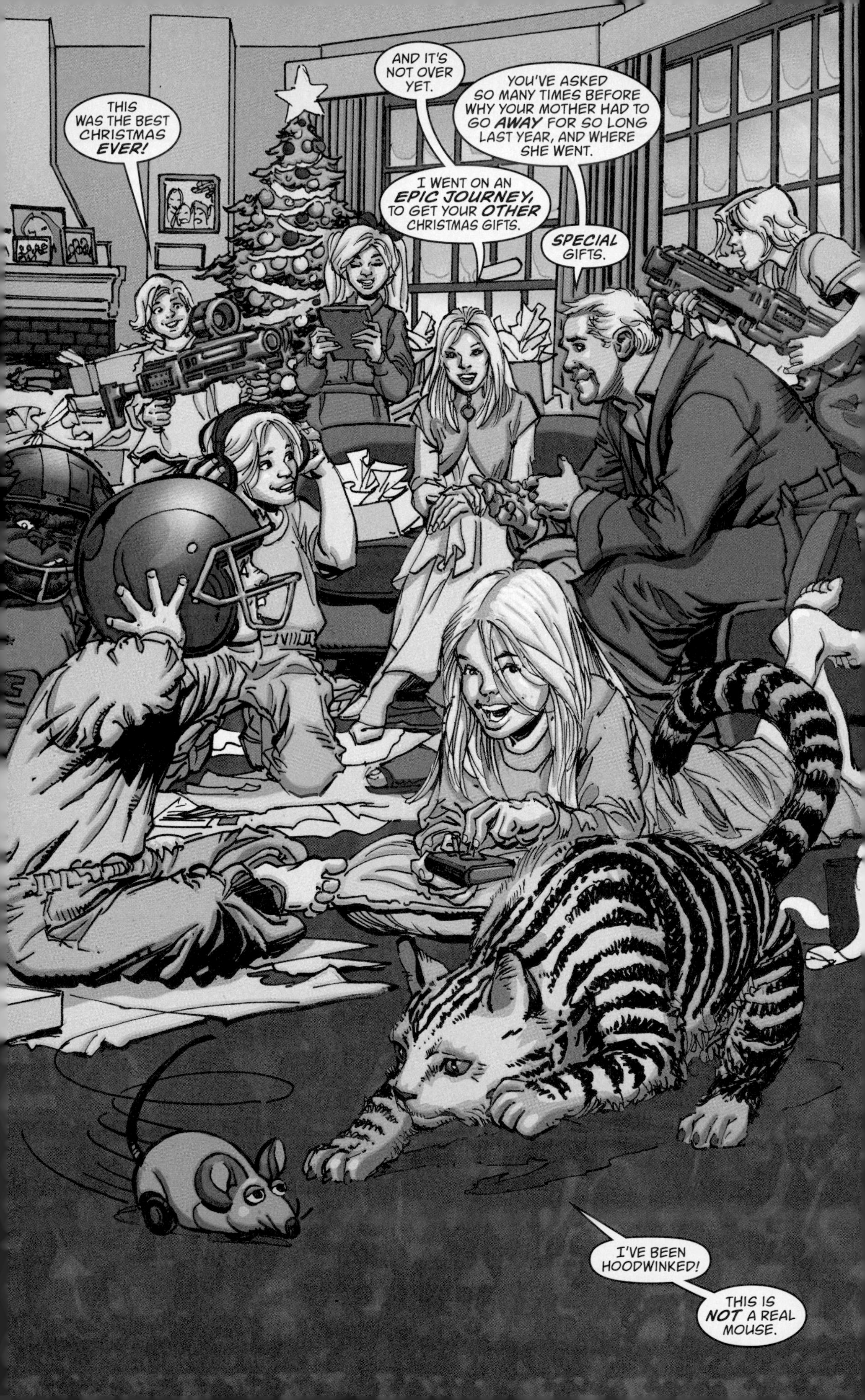
THIS WAS THE BEST CHRISTMAS **EVER!**
AND IT'S NOT OVER YET.
I WENT ON AN **EPIC JOURNEY,** TO GET YOUR **OTHER** CHRISTMAS GIFTS.
YOU'VE ASKED SO MANY TIMES BEFORE WHY YOUR MOTHER HAD TO GO **AWAY** FOR SO LONG LAST YEAR, AND WHERE SHE WENT.
SPECIAL GIFTS.
I'VE BEEN HOODWINKED!
THIS IS **NOT** A REAL MOUSE.

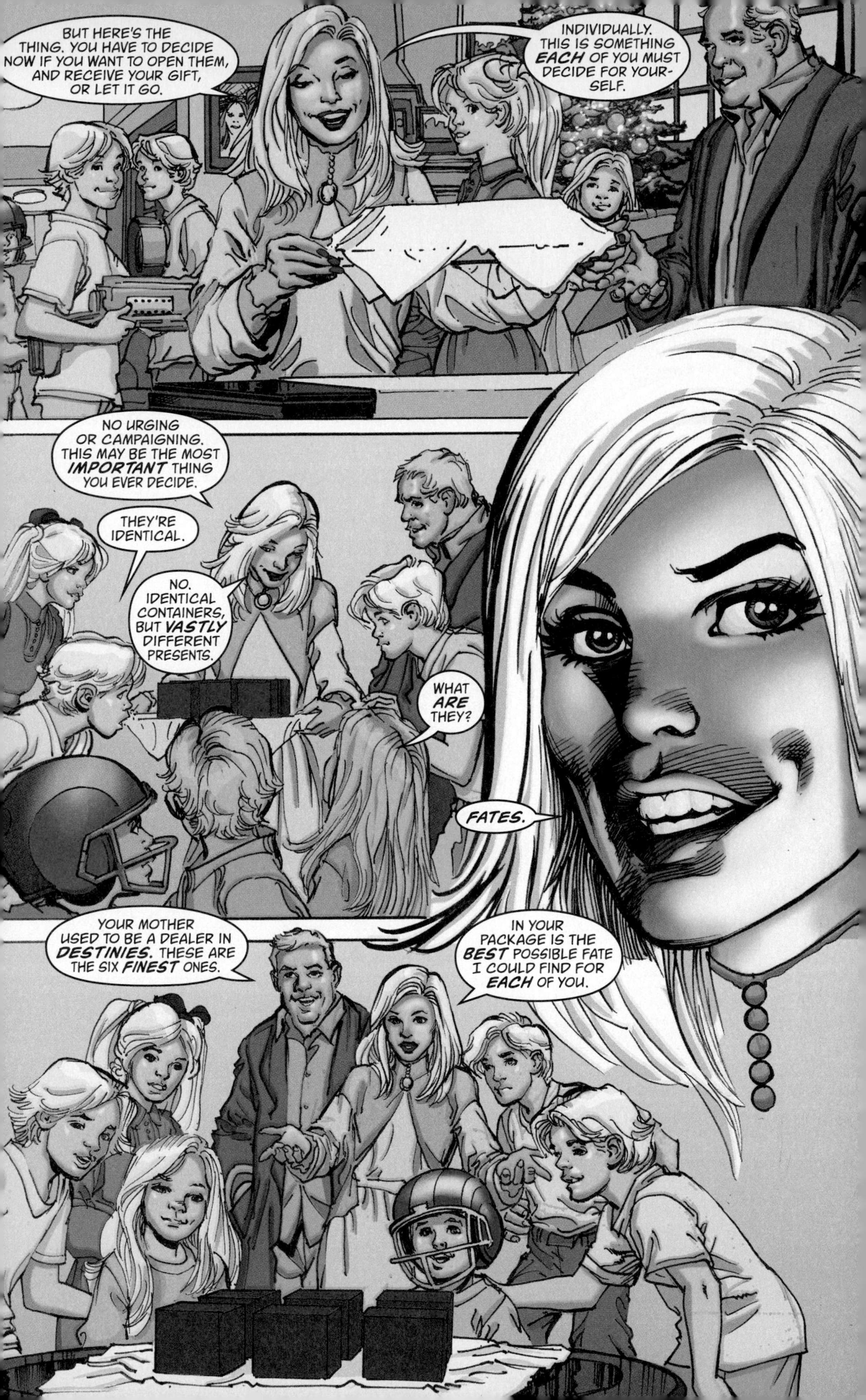
BUT HERE'S THE THING. YOU HAVE TO DECIDE NOW IF YOU WANT TO OPEN THEM, AND RECEIVE YOUR GIFT, OR LET IT GO.
INDIVIDUALLY. THIS IS SOMETHING **EACH** OF YOU MUST DECIDE FOR YOURSELF.
NO URGING OR CAMPAIGNING. THIS MAY BE THE MOST **IMPORTANT** THING YOU EVER DECIDE.
THEY'RE IDENTICAL.
NO. IDENTICAL CONTAINERS, BUT **VASTLY** DIFFERENT PRESENTS.
WHAT **ARE** THEY?
FATES.
YOUR MOTHER USED TO BE A DEALER IN **DESTINIES**. THESE ARE THE SIX **FINEST** ONES.
IN YOUR PACKAGE IS THE **BEST** POSSIBLE FATE I COULD FIND FOR **EACH** OF YOU.

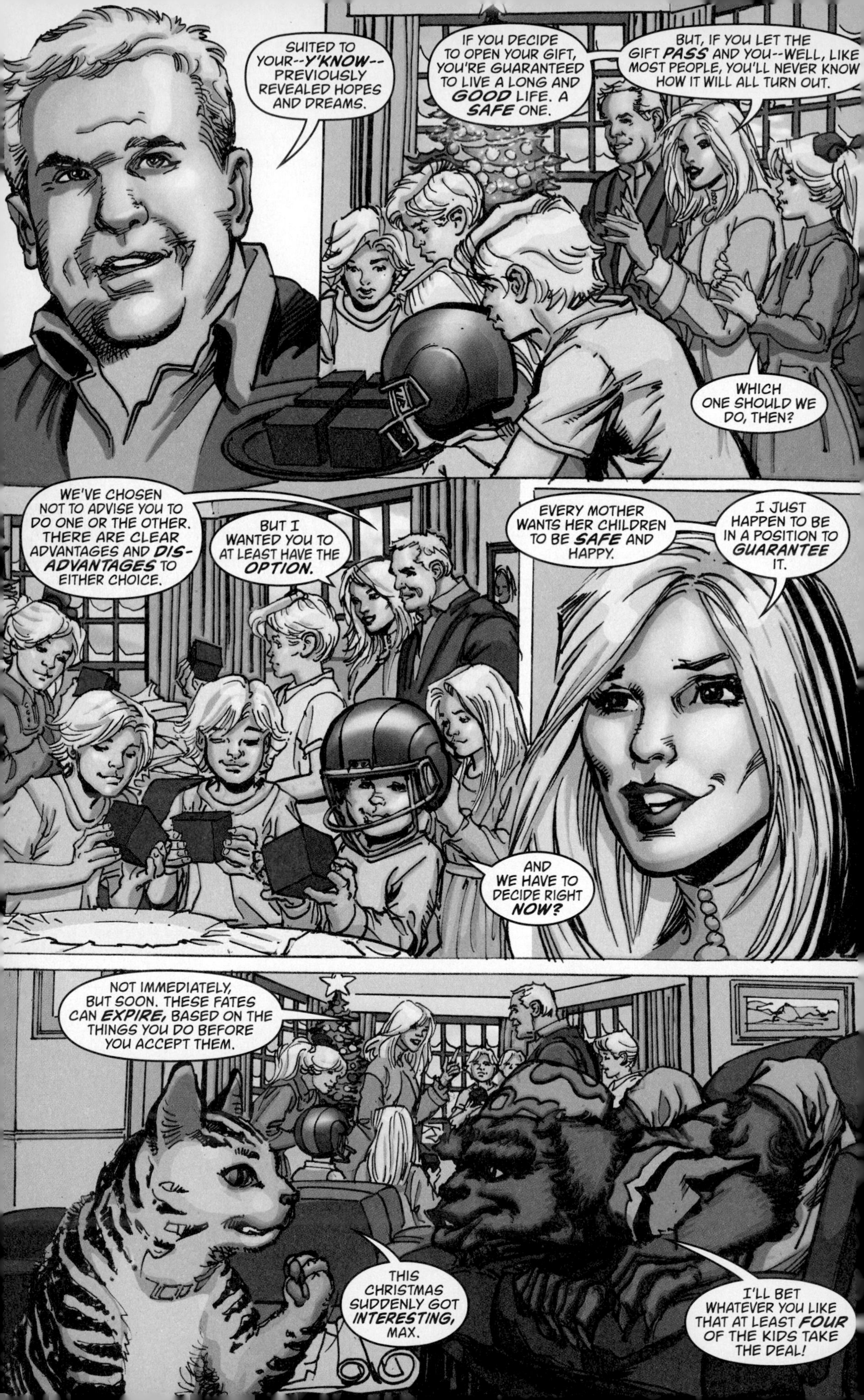
SUITED TO YOUR--Y'KNOW--PREVIOUSLY REVEALED HOPES AND DREAMS.
IF YOU DECIDE TO OPEN YOUR GIFT, YOU'RE GUARANTEED TO LIVE A LONG AND GOOD LIFE. A SAFE ONE.
BUT, IF YOU LET THE GIFT PASS AND YOU--WELL, LIKE MOST PEOPLE, YOU'LL NEVER KNOW HOW IT WILL ALL TURN OUT.
WHICH ONE SHOULD WE DO, THEN?
WE'VE CHOSEN NOT TO ADVISE YOU TO DO ONE OR THE OTHER. THERE ARE CLEAR ADVANTAGES AND DIS-ADVANTAGES TO EITHER CHOICE.
BUT I WANTED YOU TO AT LEAST HAVE THE OPTION.
EVERY MOTHER WANTS HER CHILDREN TO BE SAFE AND HAPPY.
I JUST HAPPEN TO BE IN A POSITION TO GUARANTEE IT.
AND WE HAVE TO DECIDE RIGHT NOW?
NOT IMMEDIATELY, BUT SOON. THESE FATES CAN EXPIRE, BASED ON THE THINGS YOU DO BEFORE YOU ACCEPT THEM.
THIS CHRISTMAS SUDDENLY GOT INTERESTING, MAX.
I'LL BET WHATEVER YOU LIKE THAT AT LEAST FOUR OF THE KIDS TAKE THE DEAL!

The Last Story of Many Fables

Bill Willingham writer - creator · Andrew Pepoy artist · Andrew Dalhouse colors · Todd Klein letters · Rowena Yow assoc. editor · Shelly Bond editor

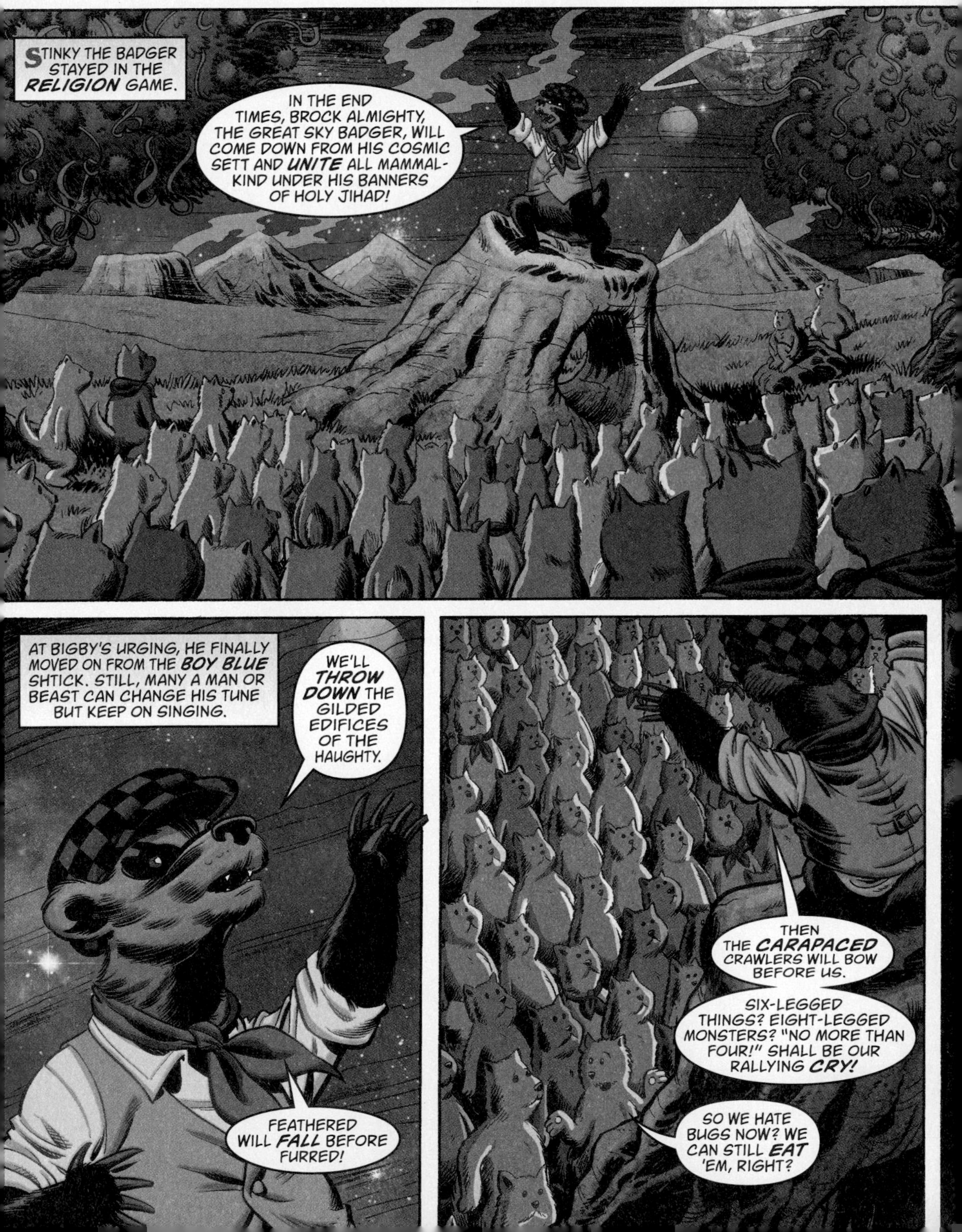
STINKY THE BADGER STAYED IN THE RELIGION GAME.
IN THE END TIMES, BROCK ALMIGHTY, THE GREAT SKY BADGER, WILL COME DOWN FROM HIS COSMIC SETT AND UNITE ALL MAMMAL-KIND UNDER HIS BANNERS OF HOLY JIHAD!
AT BIGBY'S URGING, HE FINALLY MOVED ON FROM THE BOY BLUE SHTICK. STILL, MANY A MAN OR BEAST CAN CHANGE HIS TUNE BUT KEEP ON SINGING.
WE'LL THROW DOWN THE GILDED EDIFICES OF THE HAUGHTY.
FEATHERED WILL FALL BEFORE FURRED!
THEN THE CARAPACED CRAWLERS WILL BOW BEFORE US.
SIX-LEGGED THINGS? EIGHT-LEGGED MONSTERS? "NO MORE THAN FOUR!" SHALL BE OUR RALLYING CRY!
SO WE HATE BUGS NOW? WE CAN STILL EAT 'EM, RIGHT?

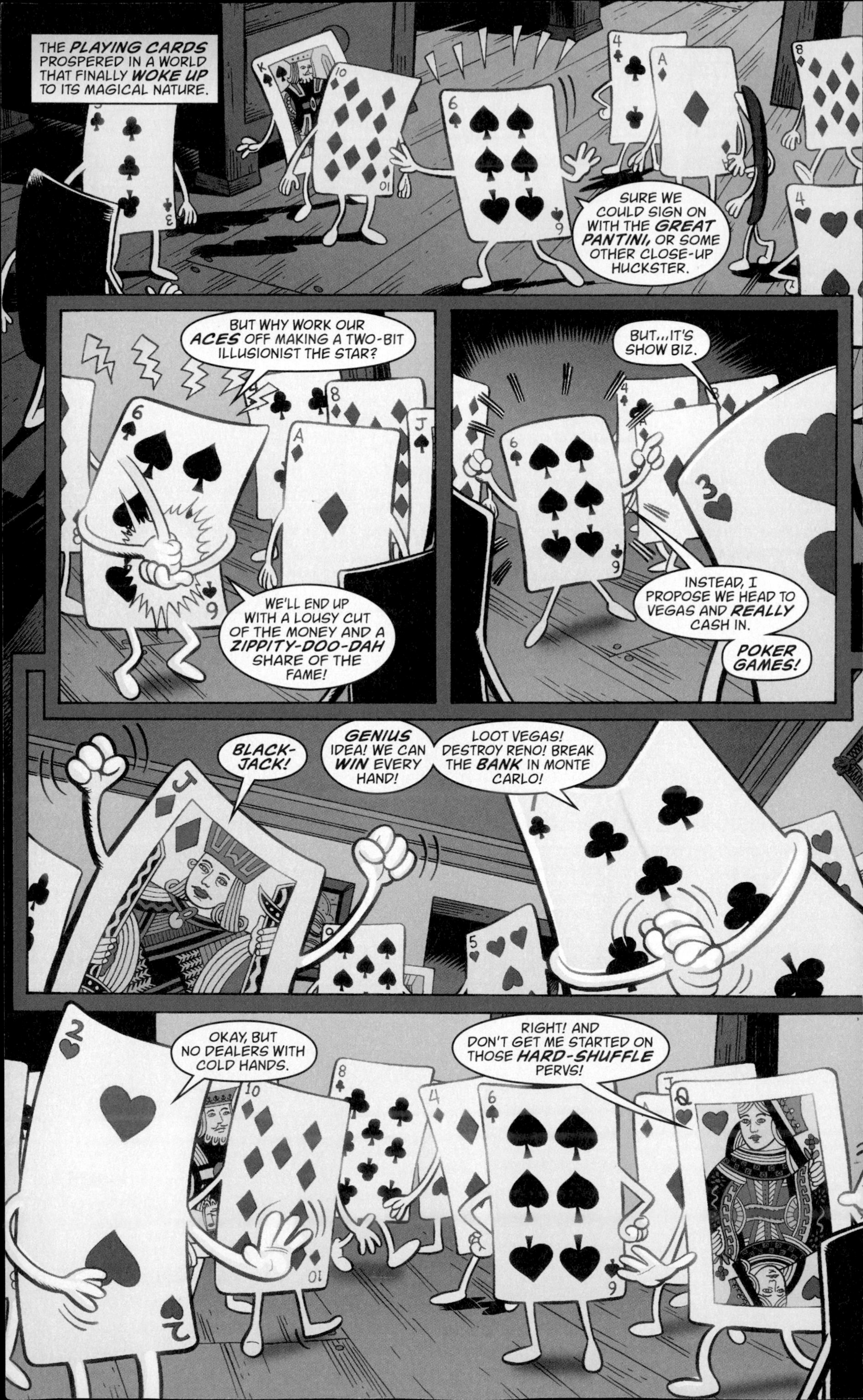

THE PLAYING CARDS PROSPERED IN A WORLD THAT FINALLY WOKE UP TO ITS MAGICAL NATURE.
SURE WE COULD SIGN ON WITH THE GREAT PANTINI, OR SOME OTHER CLOSE-UP HUCKSTER.
BUT WHY WORK OUR ACES OFF MAKING A TWO-BIT ILLUSIONIST THE STAR?
WE'LL END UP WITH A LOUSY CUT OF THE MONEY AND A ZIPPITY-DOO-DAH SHARE OF THE FAME!
BUT...IT'S SHOW BIZ.
INSTEAD, I PROPOSE WE HEAD TO VEGAS AND REALLY CASH IN.
POKER GAMES!
BLACK-JACK!
GENIUS IDEA! WE CAN WIN EVERY HAND!
LOOT VEGAS! DESTROY RENO! BREAK THE BANK IN MONTE CARLO!
OKAY, BUT NO DEALERS WITH COLD HANDS.
RIGHT! AND DON'T GET ME STARTED ON THOSE HARD-SHUFFLE PERVS!

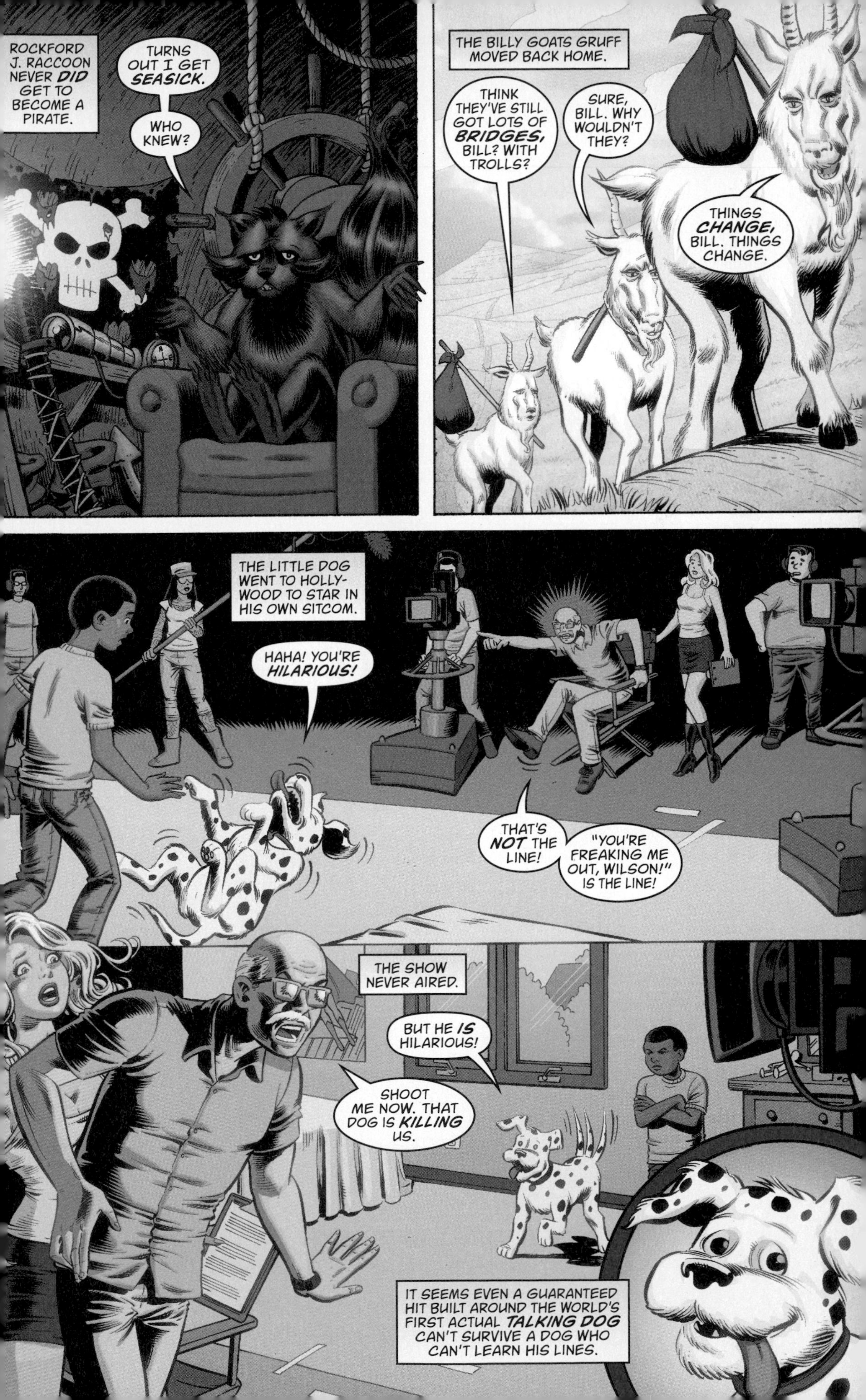
ROCKFORD J. RACCOON NEVER DID GET TO BECOME A PIRATE.
TURNS OUT I GET SEASICK.
WHO KNEW?
THE BILLY GOATS GRUFF MOVED BACK HOME.
THINK THEY'VE STILL GOT LOTS OF BRIDGES, BILL? WITH TROLLS?
SURE, BILL. WHY WOULDN'T THEY?
THINGS CHANGE, BILL. THINGS CHANGE.
THE LITTLE DOG WENT TO HOLLY-WOOD TO STAR IN HIS OWN SITCOM.
HAHA! YOU'RE HILARIOUS!
THAT'S NOT THE LINE!
"YOU'RE FREAKING ME OUT, WILSON!" IS THE LINE!
THE SHOW NEVER AIRED.
BUT HE IS HILARIOUS!
SHOOT ME NOW. THAT DOG IS KILLING US.
IT SEEMS EVEN A GUARANTEED HIT BUILT AROUND THE WORLD'S FIRST ACTUAL TALKING DOG CAN'T SURVIVE A DOG WHO CAN'T LEARN HIS LINES.

"He was one of the
pretty, pretty ones
too, and look how
HE ended up."

BLUE SKIES, BLUE MOON, BLUE SUEDE SHOES AND FOREVER BLUE

Being the last Boy Blue story

Bill Willingham writer/creator
Steve Leialoha artist
Lee Loughridge colors
Todd Klein letters
Rowena Yow assoc. ed.
Shelly Bond editor

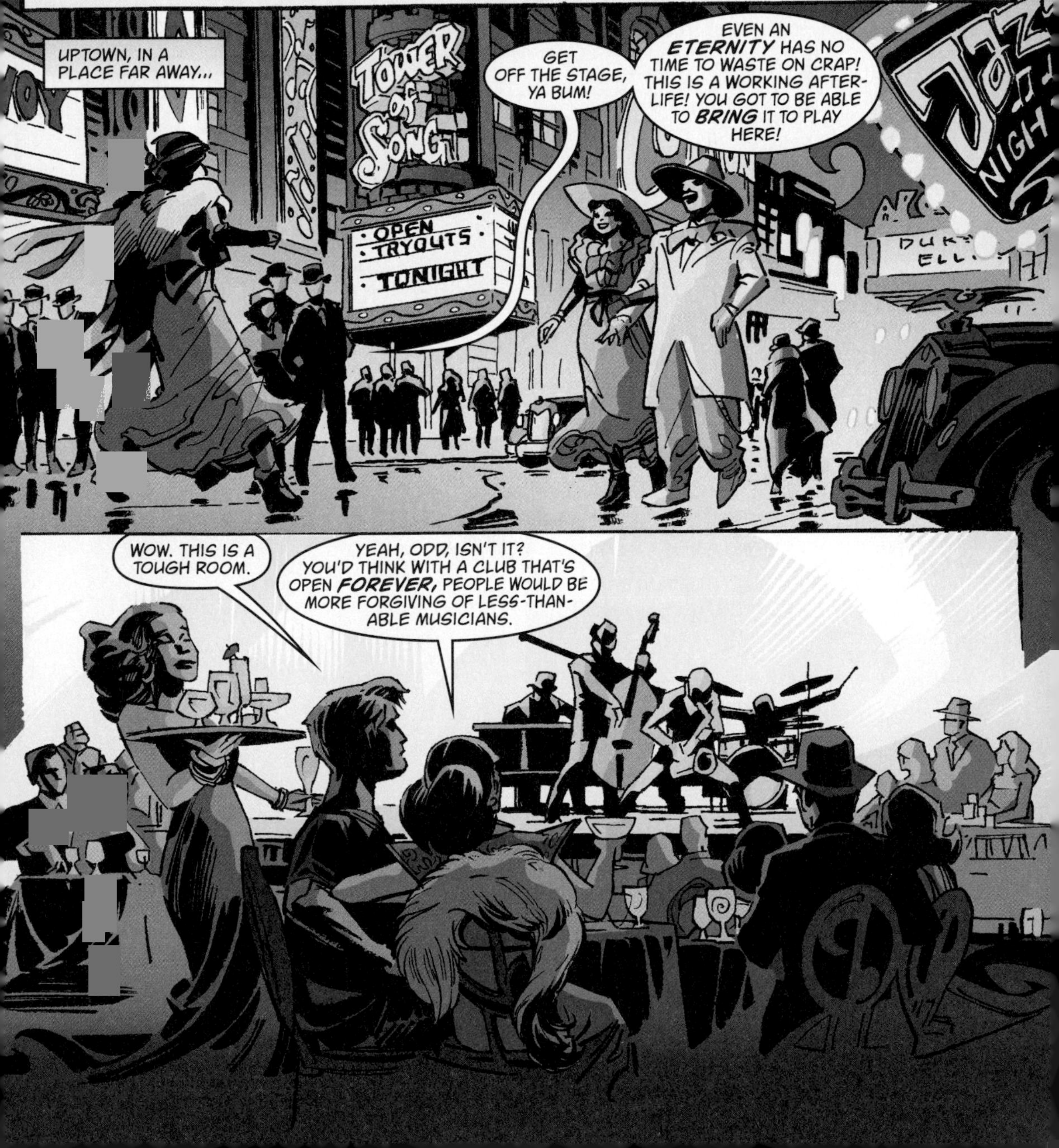

UPTOWN, IN A PLACE FAR AWAY...
TOWER OF SONG
OPEN TRYOUTS TONIGHT
GET OFF THE STAGE, YA BUM!
EVEN AN ETERNITY HAS NO TIME TO WASTE ON CRAP! THIS IS A WORKING AFTER-LIFE! YOU GOT TO BE ABLE TO BRING IT TO PLAY HERE!
JAZZ NIGHT
WOW. THIS IS A TOUGH ROOM.
YEAH, ODD, ISN'T IT? YOU'D THINK WITH A CLUB THAT'S OPEN FOREVER, PEOPLE WOULD BE MORE FORGIVING OF LESS-THAN-ABLE MUSICIANS.

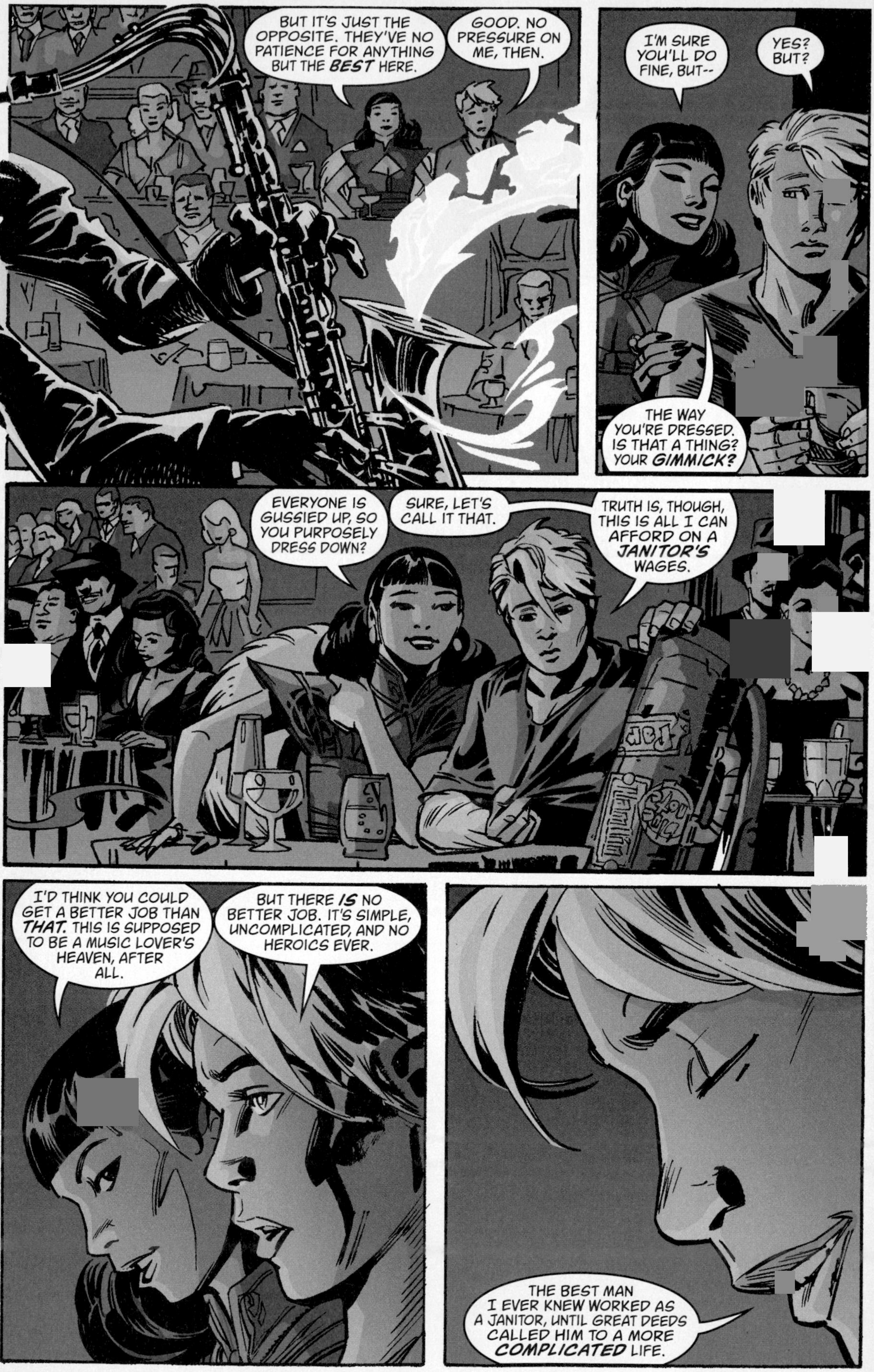
BUT IT'S JUST THE OPPOSITE. THEY'VE NO PATIENCE FOR ANYTHING BUT THE BEST HERE.
GOOD. NO PRESSURE ON ME, THEN.
I'M SURE YOU'LL DO FINE, BUT--
YES? BUT?
THE WAY YOU'RE DRESSED. IS THAT A THING? YOUR GIMMICK?
EVERYONE IS GUSSIED UP, SO YOU PURPOSELY DRESS DOWN?
SURE, LET'S CALL IT THAT.
TRUTH IS, THOUGH, THIS IS ALL I CAN AFFORD ON A JANITOR'S WAGES.
I'D THINK YOU COULD GET A BETTER JOB THAN THAT. THIS IS SUPPOSED TO BE A MUSIC LOVER'S HEAVEN, AFTER ALL.
BUT THERE IS NO BETTER JOB. IT'S SIMPLE, UNCOMPLICATED, AND NO HEROICS EVER.
THE BEST MAN I EVER KNEW WORKED AS A JANITOR, UNTIL GREAT DEEDS CALLED HIM TO A MORE COMPLICATED LIFE.

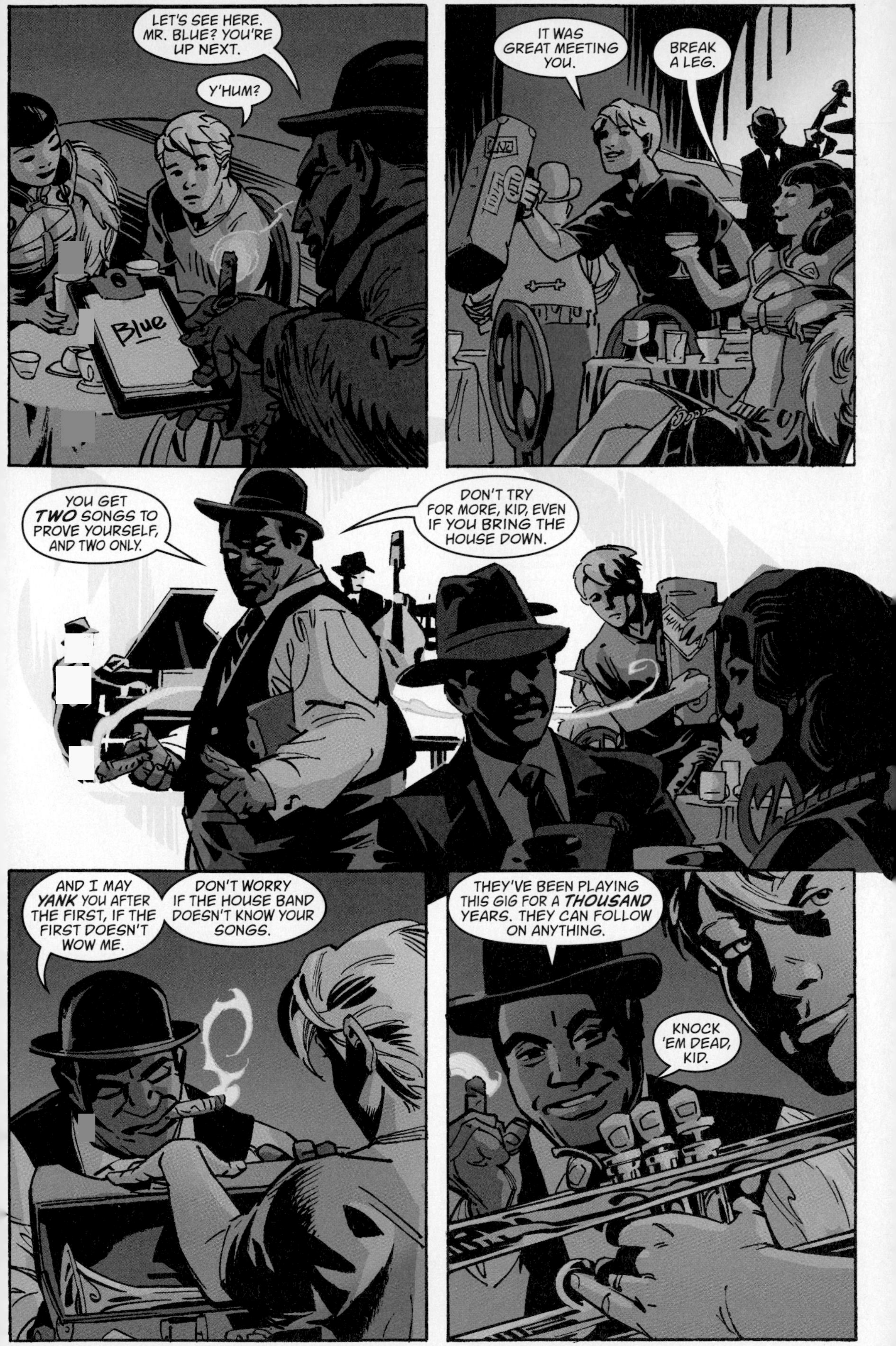

LET'S SEE HERE. MR. BLUE? YOU'RE UP NEXT.
Y'HUM?
Blue
IT WAS GREAT MEETING YOU.
BREAK A LEG.
YOU GET TWO SONGS TO PROVE YOURSELF, AND TWO ONLY.
DON'T TRY FOR MORE, KID, EVEN IF YOU BRING THE HOUSE DOWN.
AND I MAY YANK YOU AFTER THE FIRST, IF THE FIRST DOESN'T WOW ME.
DON'T WORRY IF THE HOUSE BAND DOESN'T KNOW YOUR SONGS.
THEY'VE BEEN PLAYING THIS GIG FOR A THOUSAND YEARS. THEY CAN FOLLOW ON ANYTHING.
KNOCK 'EM DEAD, KID.

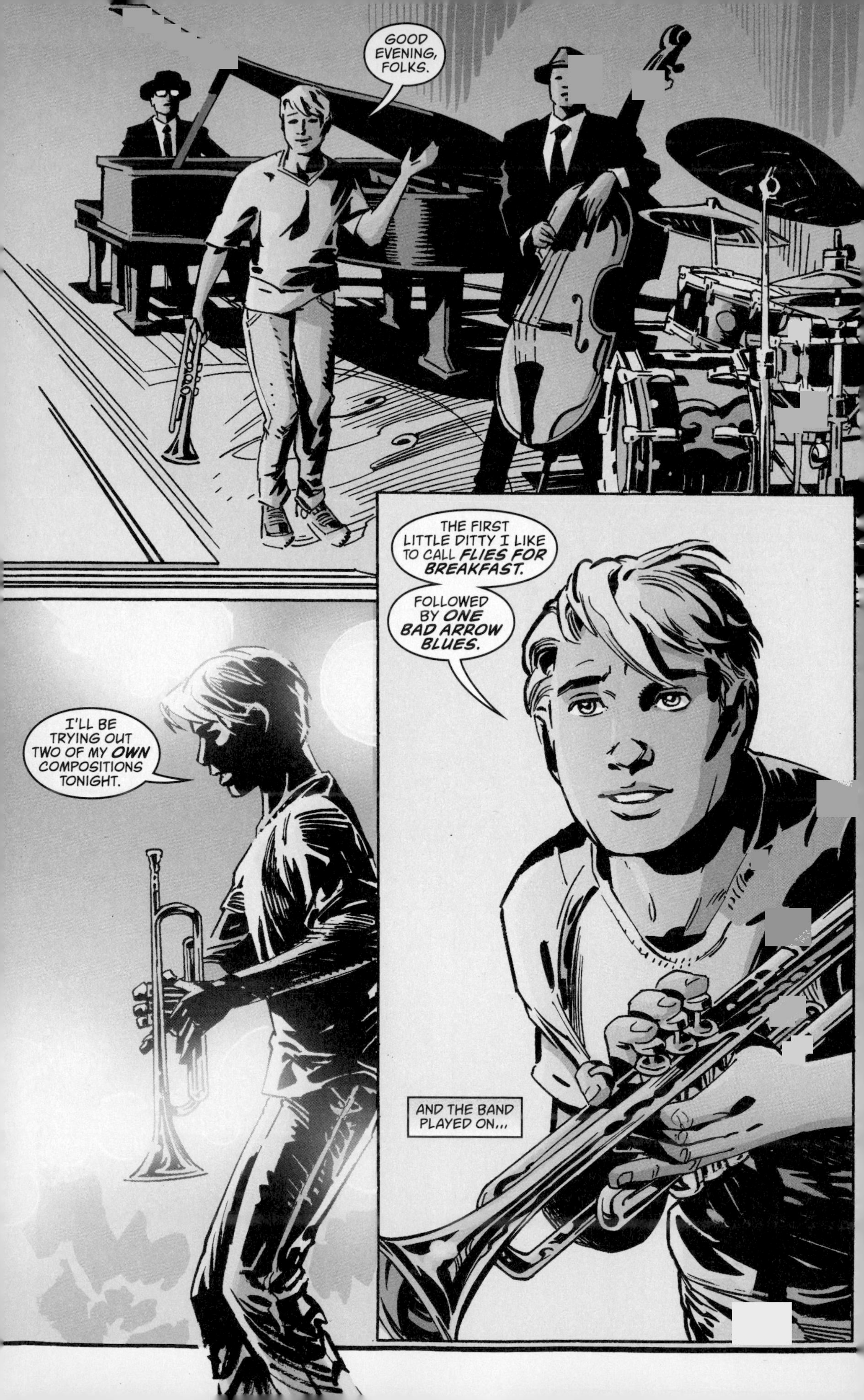
GOOD EVENING, FOLKS.
I'LL BE TRYING OUT TWO OF MY OWN COMPOSITIONS TONIGHT.
THE FIRST LITTLE DITTY I LIKE TO CALL FLIES FOR BREAKFAST.
FOLLOWED BY ONE BAD ARROW BLUES.
AND THE BAND PLAYED ON...

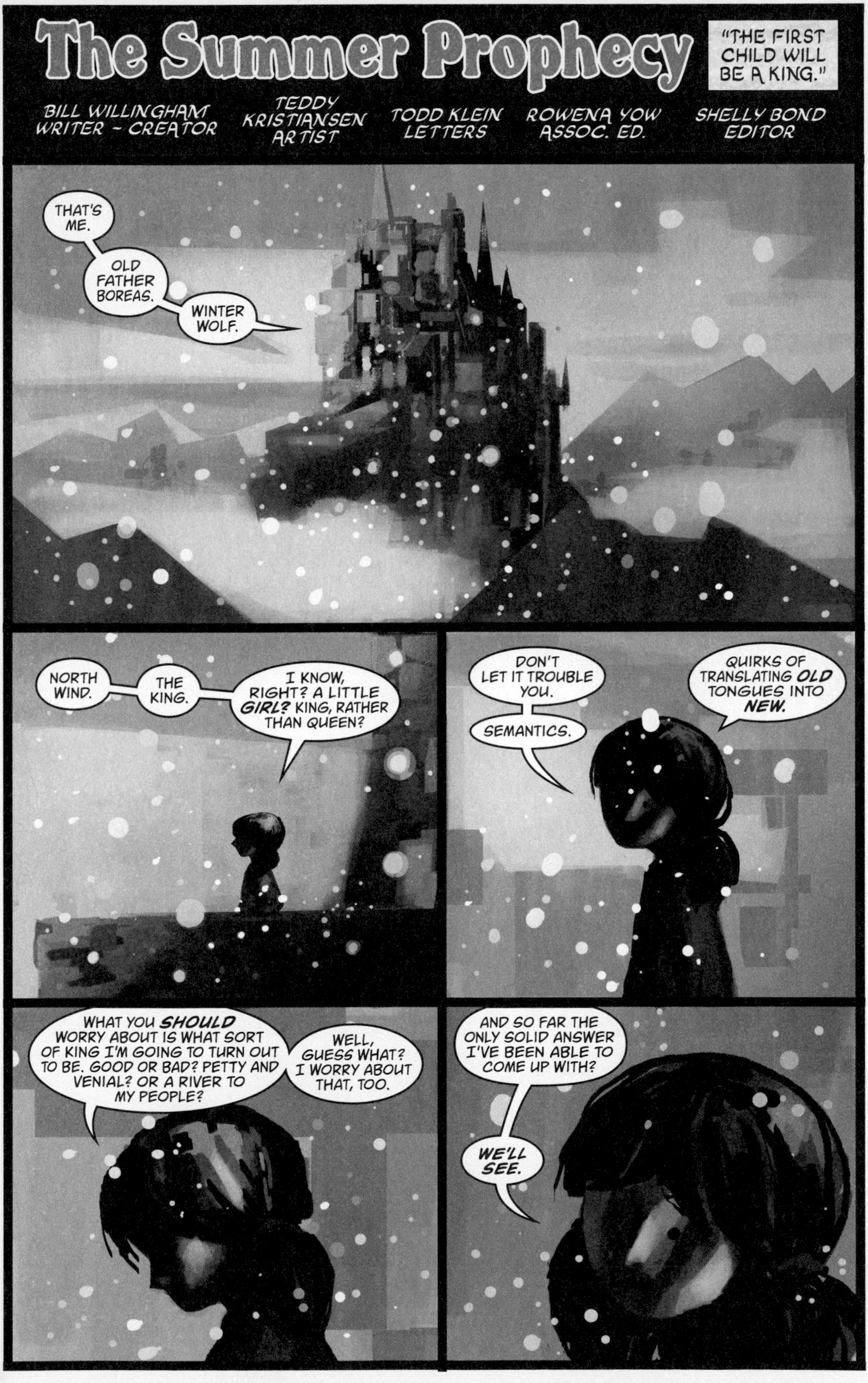
The Summer Prophecy
"THE FIRST CHILD WILL BE A KING."
BILL WILLINGHAM WRITER - CREATOR
TEDDY KRISTIANSEN ARTIST
TODD KLEIN LETTERS
ROWENA YOW ASSOC. ED.
SHELLY BOND EDITOR
THAT'S ME.
OLD FATHER BOREAS.
WINTER WOLF.
NORTH WIND.
THE KING.
I KNOW, RIGHT? A LITTLE GIRL? KING, RATHER THAN QUEEN?
DON'T LET IT TROUBLE YOU.
SEMANTICS.
QUIRKS OF TRANSLATING OLD TONGUES INTO NEW.
WHAT YOU SHOULD WORRY ABOUT IS WHAT SORT OF KING I'M GOING TO TURN OUT TO BE. GOOD OR BAD? PETTY AND VENIAL? OR A RIVER TO MY PEOPLE?
WELL, GUESS WHAT? I WORRY ABOUT THAT, TOO.
AND SO FAR THE ONLY SOLID ANSWER I'VE BEEN ABLE TO COME UP WITH?
WE'LL SEE.

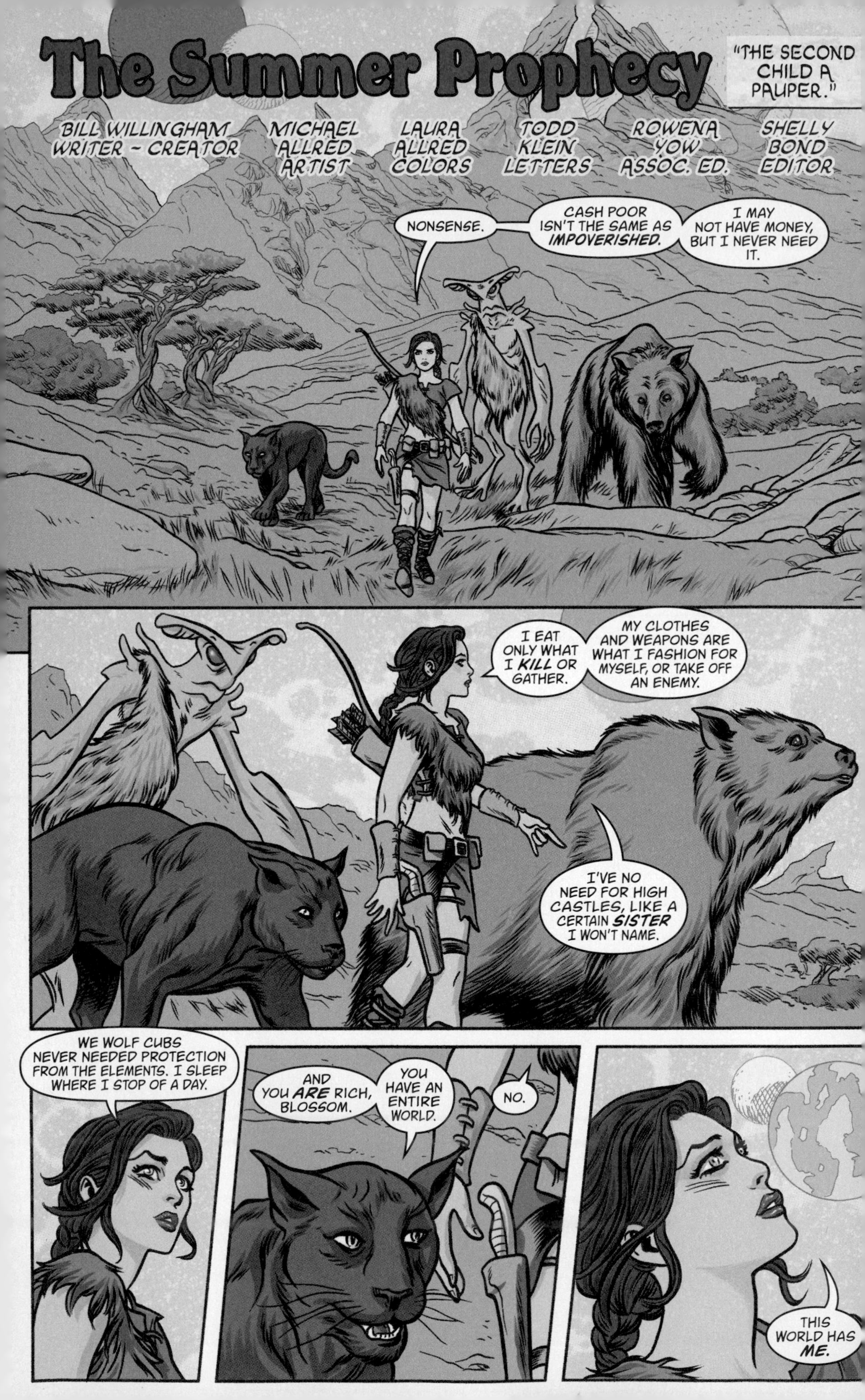
The Summer Prophecy
"THE SECOND CHILD A PAUPER."
BILL WILLINGHAM WRITER ~ CREATOR
MICHAEL ALLRED ARTIST
LAURA ALLRED COLORS
TODD KLEIN LETTERS
ROWENA YOW ASSOC. ED.
SHELLY BOND EDITOR
NONSENSE.
CASH POOR ISN'T THE SAME AS *IMPOVERISHED.*
I MAY NOT HAVE MONEY, BUT I NEVER NEED IT.
I EAT ONLY WHAT I *KILL* OR GATHER.
MY CLOTHES AND WEAPONS ARE WHAT I FASHION FOR MYSELF, OR TAKE OFF AN ENEMY.
I'VE NO NEED FOR HIGH CASTLES, LIKE A CERTAIN *SISTER* I WON'T NAME.
WE WOLF CUBS NEVER NEEDED PROTECTION FROM THE ELEMENTS. I SLEEP WHERE I STOP OF A DAY.
AND YOU *ARE* RICH, BLOSSOM.
YOU HAVE AN ENTIRE WORLD.
NO.
THIS WORLD HAS *ME.*

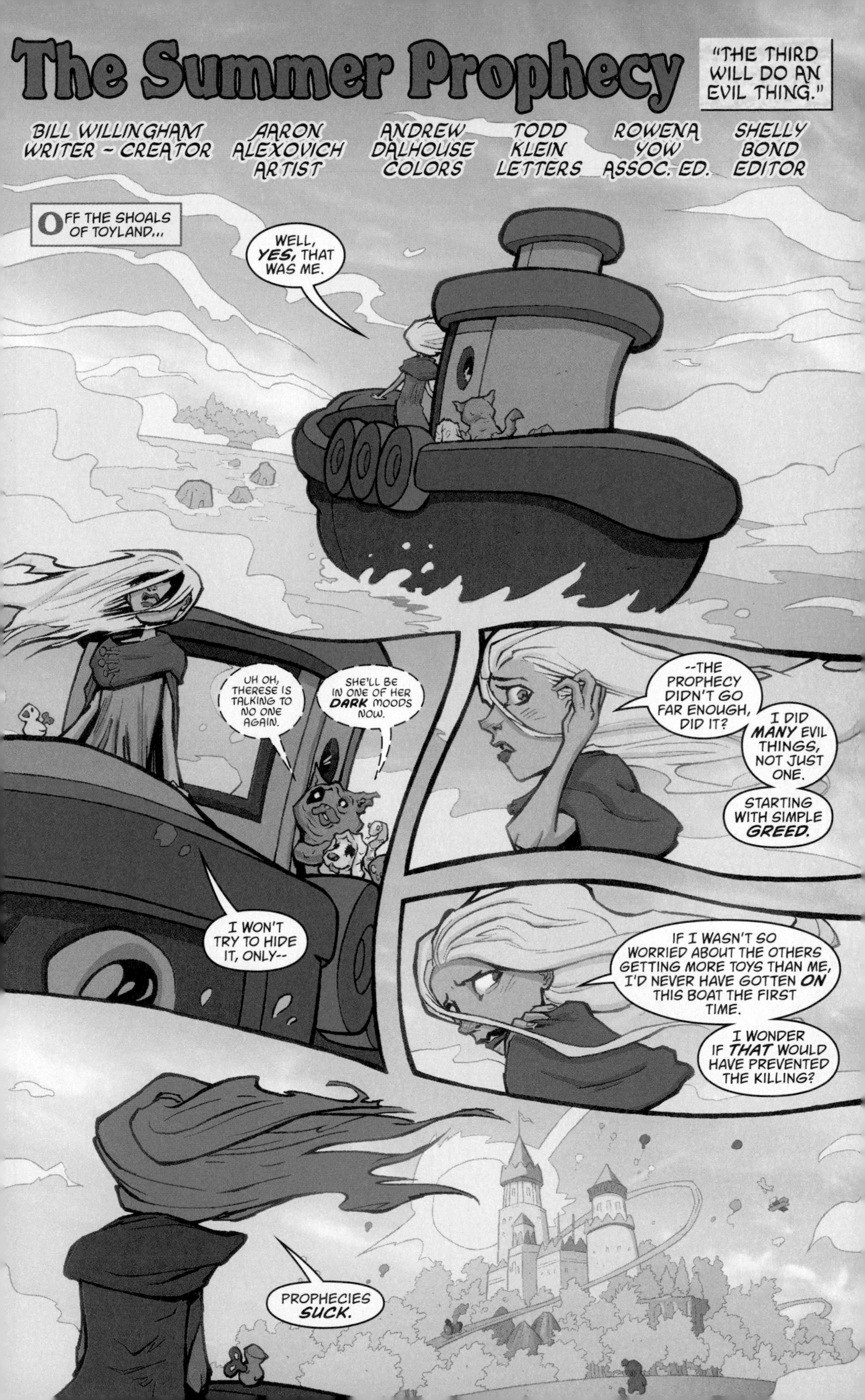
The Summer Prophecy
"THE THIRD WILL DO AN EVIL THING."
BILL WILLINGHAM WRITER - CREATOR
AARON ALEXOVICH ARTIST
ANDREW DALHOUSE COLORS
TODD KLEIN LETTERS
ROWENA YOW ASSOC. ED.
SHELLY BOND EDITOR
OFF THE SHOALS OF TOYLAND...
WELL, YES, THAT WAS ME.
UH OH, THERESE IS TALKING TO NO ONE AGAIN.
SHE'LL BE IN ONE OF HER DARK MOODS NOW.
I WON'T TRY TO HIDE IT, ONLY--
--THE PROPHECY DIDN'T GO FAR ENOUGH, DID IT?
I DID MANY EVIL THINGS, NOT JUST ONE.
STARTING WITH SIMPLE GREED.
IF I WASN'T SO WORRIED ABOUT THE OTHERS GETTING MORE TOYS THAN ME, I'D NEVER HAVE GOTTEN ON THIS BOAT THE FIRST TIME.
I WONDER IF THAT WOULD HAVE PREVENTED THE KILLING?
PROPHECIES SUCK.

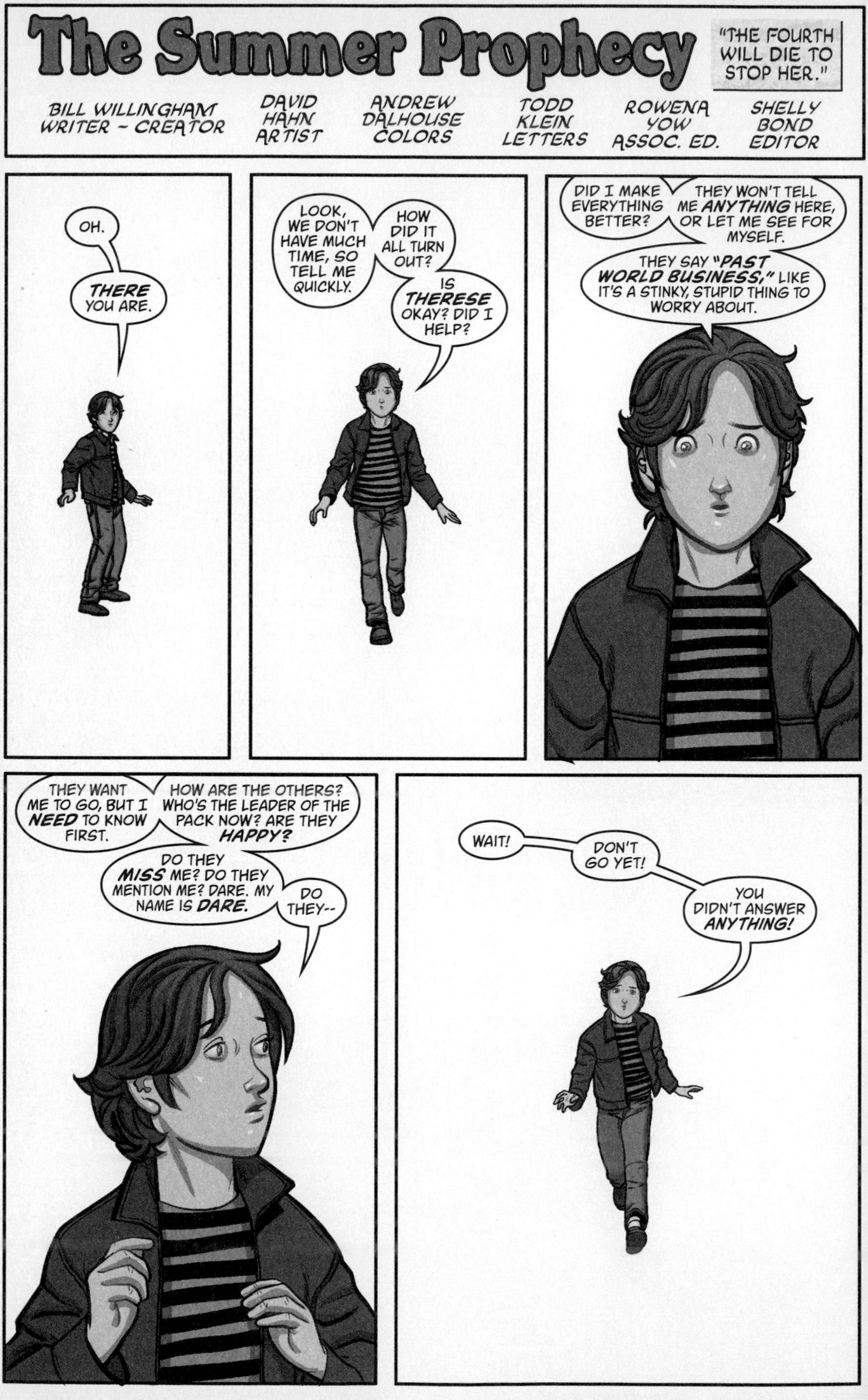
The Summer Prophecy
"THE FOURTH WILL DIE TO STOP HER."
BILL WILLINGHAM WRITER ~ CREATOR
DAVID HAHN ARTIST
ANDREW DALHOUSE COLORS
TODD KLEIN LETTERS
ROWENA YOW ASSOC. ED.
SHELLY BOND EDITOR
OH.
THERE YOU ARE.
LOOK, WE DON'T HAVE MUCH TIME, SO TELL ME QUICKLY.
HOW DID IT ALL TURN OUT?
IS THERESE OKAY? DID I HELP?
DID I MAKE EVERYTHING BETTER?
THEY WON'T TELL ME ANYTHING HERE, OR LET ME SEE FOR MYSELF.
THEY SAY "PAST WORLD BUSINESS," LIKE IT'S A STINKY, STUPID THING TO WORRY ABOUT.
THEY WANT ME TO GO, BUT I NEED TO KNOW FIRST.
HOW ARE THE OTHERS? WHO'S THE LEADER OF THE PACK NOW? ARE THEY HAPPY?
DO THEY MISS ME? DO THEY MENTION ME? DARE. MY NAME IS DARE.
DO THEY--
WAIT!
DON'T GO YET!
YOU DIDN'T ANSWER ANYTHING!

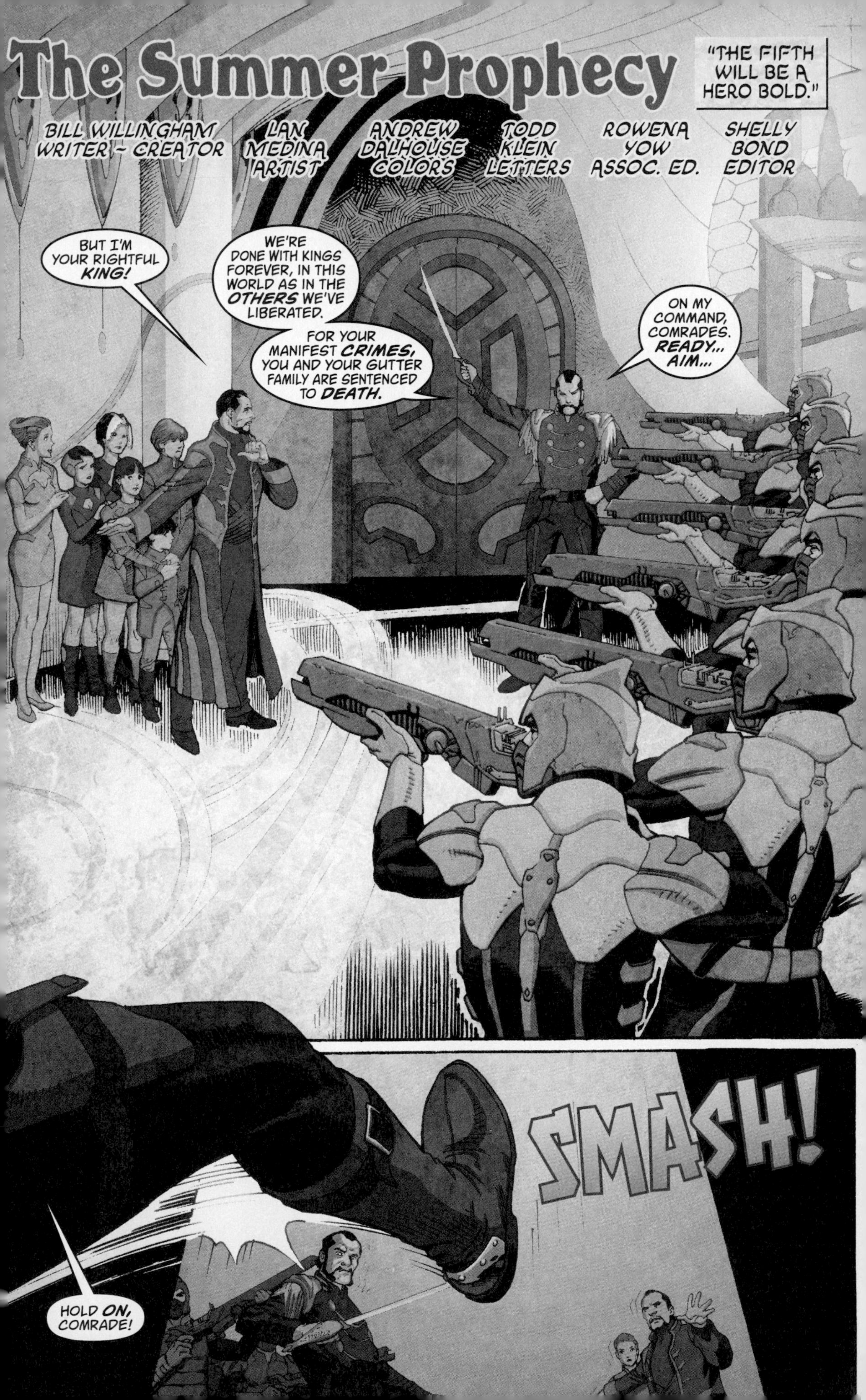

The Summer Prophecy
"THE FIFTH WILL BE A HERO BOLD."
BILL WILLINGHAM WRITER ~ CREATOR
LAN MEDINA ARTIST
ANDREW DALHOUSE COLORS
TODD KLEIN LETTERS
ROWENA YOW ASSOC. ED.
SHELLY BOND EDITOR
BUT I'M YOUR RIGHTFUL KING!
WE'RE DONE WITH KINGS FOREVER, IN THIS WORLD AS IN THE OTHERS WE'VE LIBERATED.
FOR YOUR MANIFEST CRIMES, YOU AND YOUR GUTTER FAMILY ARE SENTENCED TO DEATH.
ON MY COMMAND, COMRADES. READY... AIM...
SMASH!
HOLD ON, COMRADE!

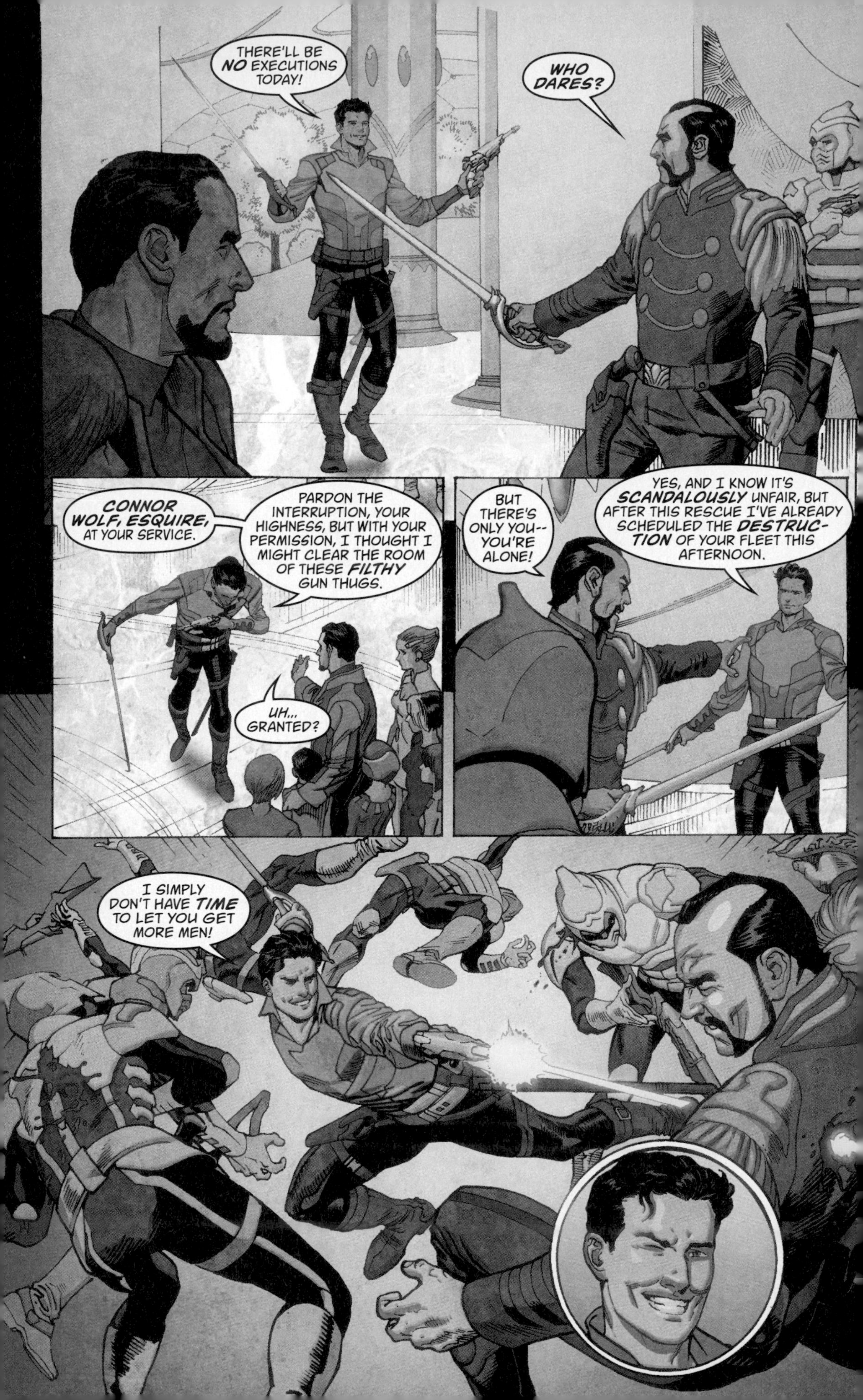
THERE'LL BE NO EXECUTIONS TODAY!
WHO DARES?
CONNOR WOLF, ESQUIRE, AT YOUR SERVICE.
PARDON THE INTERRUPTION, YOUR HIGHNESS, BUT WITH YOUR PERMISSION, I THOUGHT I MIGHT CLEAR THE ROOM OF THESE FILTHY GUN THUGS.
UH... GRANTED?
BUT THERE'S ONLY YOU-- YOU'RE ALONE!
YES, AND I KNOW IT'S SCANDALOUSLY UNFAIR, BUT AFTER THIS RESCUE I'VE ALREADY SCHEDULED THE DESTRUCTION OF YOUR FLEET THIS AFTERNOON.
I SIMPLY DON'T HAVE TIME TO LET YOU GET MORE MEN!

The Summer Prophecy

"THE SIXTH WILL JUDGE THE REST."

BILL WILLINGHAM WRITER ~ CREATOR
NIKO HENRICHON ARTIST
TODD KLEIN LETTERS
ROWENA YOW ASSOC. ED.
SHELLY BOND EDITOR

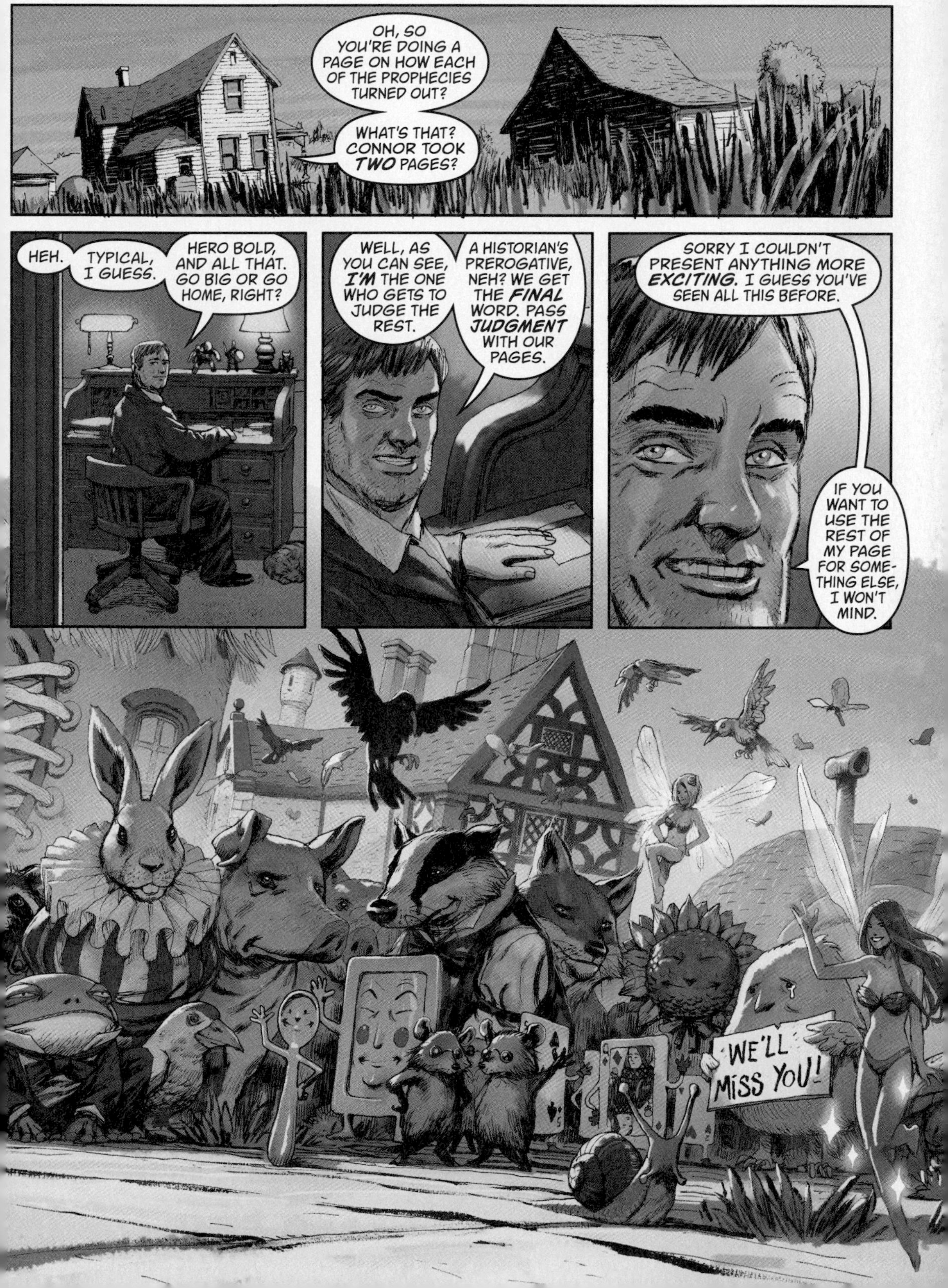
OH, SO YOU'RE DOING A PAGE ON HOW EACH OF THE PROPHECIES TURNED OUT?
WHAT'S THAT? CONNOR TOOK TWO PAGES?
HEH.
TYPICAL, I GUESS.
HERO BOLD, AND ALL THAT. GO BIG OR GO HOME, RIGHT?
WELL, AS YOU CAN SEE, I'M THE ONE WHO GETS TO JUDGE THE REST.
A HISTORIAN'S PREROGATIVE, NEH? WE GET THE FINAL WORD. PASS JUDGMENT WITH OUR PAGES.
SORRY I COULDN'T PRESENT ANYTHING MORE EXCITING. I GUESS YOU'VE SEEN ALL THIS BEFORE.
IF YOU WANT TO USE THE REST OF MY PAGE FOR SOMETHING ELSE, I WON'T MIND.
WE'LL MISS YOU!

The Summer Prophecy

BILL WILLINGHAM WRITER ~ CREATOR
TERRY DODSON PENCILS & COLOR
RACHEL DODSON INKER
TODD KLEIN LETTERS
ROWENA YOW ASSOC. ED.
SHELLY BOND EDITOR

"THE SEVENTH LIVES TO AGES OLD, AND IS BY HEAVEN BLESSED."

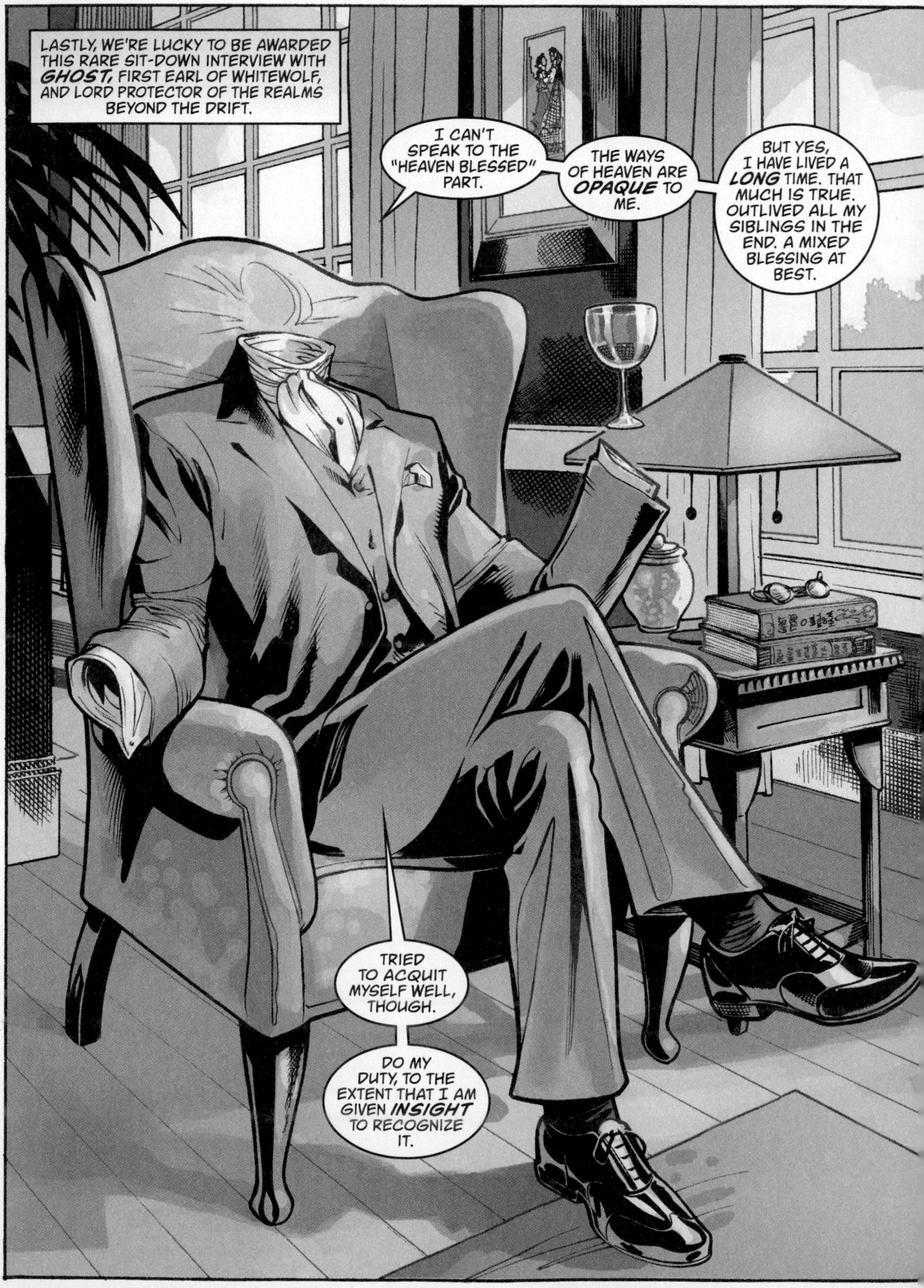
LASTLY, WE'RE LUCKY TO BE AWARDED THIS RARE SIT-DOWN INTERVIEW WITH ***GHOST,*** FIRST EARL OF WHITEWOLF, AND LORD PROTECTOR OF THE REALMS BEYOND THE DRIFT.
I CAN'T SPEAK TO THE "HEAVEN BLESSED" PART.
THE WAYS OF HEAVEN ARE ***OPAQUE*** TO ME.
BUT YES, I HAVE LIVED A ***LONG*** TIME. THAT MUCH IS TRUE. OUTLIVED ALL MY SIBLINGS IN THE END. A MIXED BLESSING AT BEST.
TRIED TO ACQUIT MYSELF WELL, THOUGH.
DO MY DUTY, TO THE EXTENT THAT I AM GIVEN ***INSIGHT*** TO RECOGNIZE IT.

THE LAST TOY STORY

Bill Willingham writer - artist - creator | Andrew Dalhouse colors | Todd Klein letters | Rowena Yow assoc. ed. | Shelly Bond editor

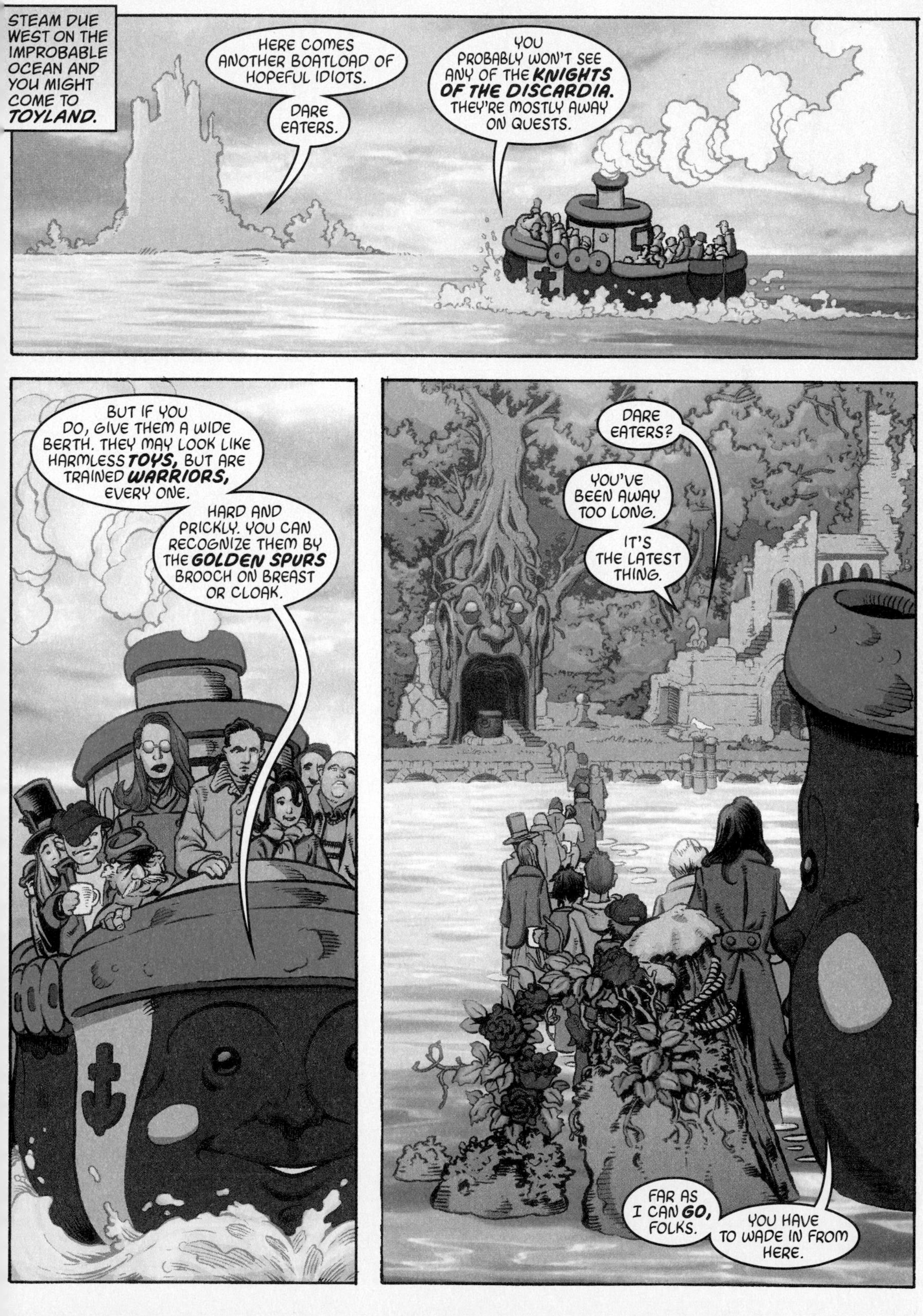

STEAM DUE WEST ON THE IMPROBABLE OCEAN AND YOU MIGHT COME TO *TOYLAND.*
HERE COMES ANOTHER BOATLOAD OF HOPEFUL IDIOTS.
DARE EATERS.
YOU PROBABLY WON'T SEE ANY OF THE ***KNIGHTS OF THE DISCARDIA.*** THEY'RE MOSTLY AWAY ON QUESTS.
BUT IF YOU DO, GIVE THEM A WIDE BERTH. THEY MAY LOOK LIKE HARMLESS ***TOYS,*** BUT ARE TRAINED ***WARRIORS,*** EVERY ONE.
HARD AND PRICKLY. YOU CAN RECOGNIZE THEM BY THE ***GOLDEN SPURS*** BROOCH ON BREAST OR CLOAK.
DARE EATERS?
YOU'VE BEEN AWAY TOO LONG.
IT'S THE LATEST THING.
FAR AS I CAN ***GO,*** FOLKS.
YOU HAVE TO WADE IN FROM HERE.

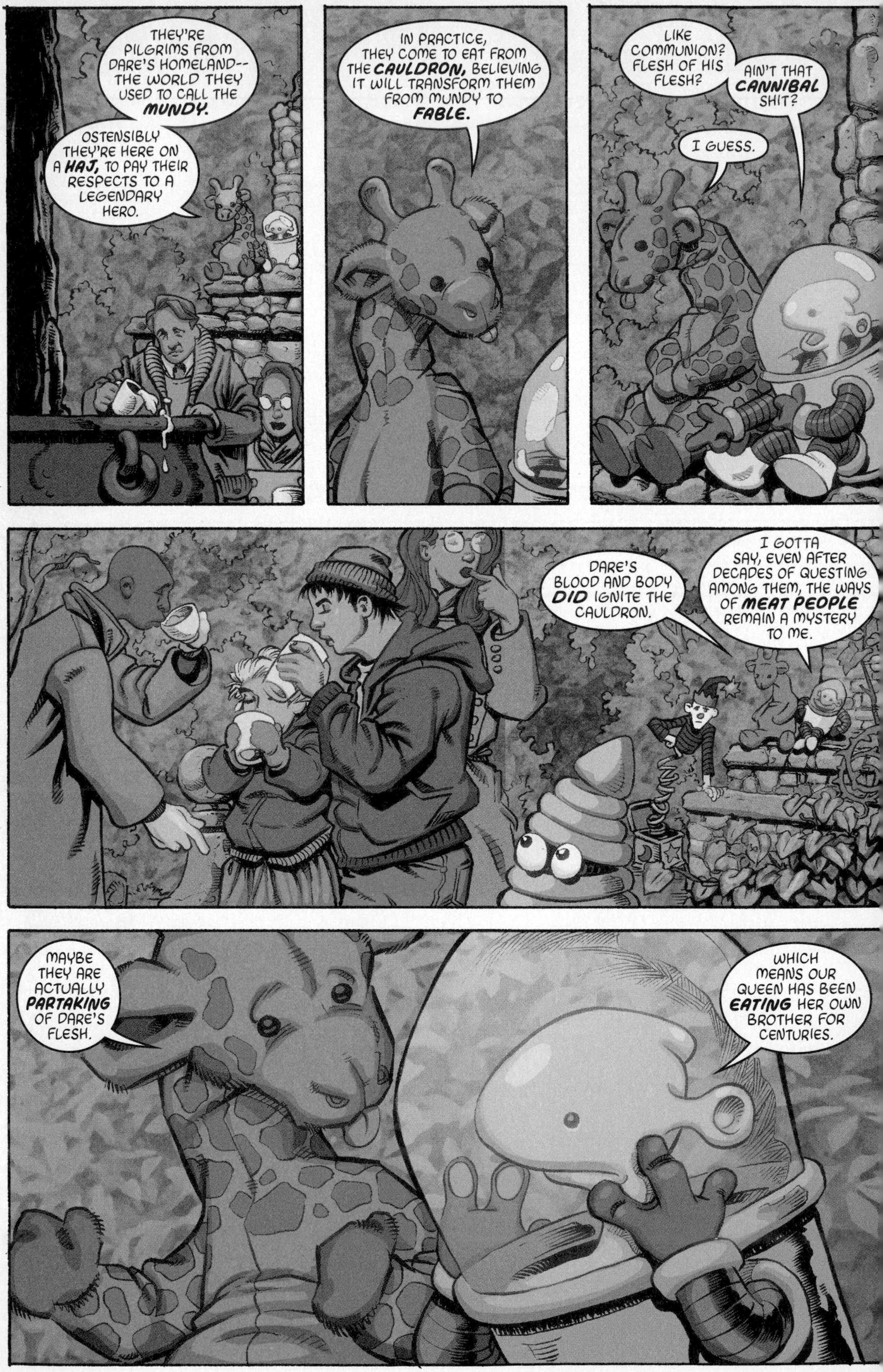
THEY'RE PILGRIMS FROM DARE'S HOMELAND-- THE WORLD THEY USED TO CALL THE MUNDY.
OSTENSIBLY THEY'RE HERE ON A HAJ, TO PAY THEIR RESPECTS TO A LEGENDARY HERO.
IN PRACTICE, THEY COME TO EAT FROM THE CAULDRON, BELIEVING IT WILL TRANSFORM THEM FROM MUNDY TO FABLE.
LIKE COMMUNION? FLESH OF HIS FLESH?
AIN'T THAT CANNIBAL SHIT?
I GUESS.
DARE'S BLOOD AND BODY DID IGNITE THE CAULDRON.
I GOTTA SAY, EVEN AFTER DECADES OF QUESTING AMONG THEM, THE WAYS OF MEAT PEOPLE REMAIN A MYSTERY TO ME.
MAYBE THEY ARE ACTUALLY PARTAKING OF DARE'S FLESH.
WHICH MEANS OUR QUEEN HAS BEEN EATING HER OWN BROTHER FOR CENTURIES.

BIG MAGIC, NO MATTER HOW IT WORKS.

THE POINT IS, THEY THINK EATING FROM THE CAULDRON WILL MAKE **THEM** MAGICAL, TOO.

IMMORTAL.

GET BACK ON BOARD AS SOON AS YOU'VE HAD YOUR TASTE.

WE CAN'T MISS THE TIDE.

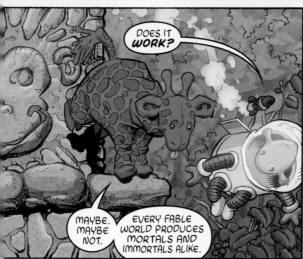

DOES IT **WORK?**

MAYBE. MAYBE NOT. EVERY FABLE WORLD PRODUCES MORTALS AND IMMORTALS ALIKE.

NO ONE KNOWS WHY OR HOW THE LUCKY ONES ARE CHOSEN--OR EVEN IF THEY **ARE** CHOSEN.

COULD BE **RANDOM.** SOME FACTOR WE'LL NEVER KNOW.

IF THESE PILGRIMS STILL LOOK YOUNG IN A HUNDRED YEARS, THEN WE'LL HAVE **SOMETHING.**

SAY GOODBYE TO TOYLAND!

"Once upon a time...
in a fictional land
called New York
City."

IN A CASTLE DARK

In which we embark on what might be called the Last Mundy Story, but also the Last Maddy Story, and the Last King Cole Story

Bill Willingham   Lan Medina   Mark Farmer
writer - creator   penciller   inker

Lee Loughridge   Todd Klein   Rowena Yow
colors   letters   assoc. editor

Shelly Bond   editor

DID YOU **SEE** THAT?

TELL ME YOU SAW THAT!

IT WAS ONLY A FEW DAYS AGO THAT THE EXISTENCE OF FABLETOWN, LURKING UNDER THEIR NOSES FOR CENTURIES, WAS FINALLY REVEALED TO THE *MUNDY* IN NEW YORK CITY.

EVERYONE SAW IT, KOWALSKI. THE GREAT BIG WINDOW-BUSTING *BOOM* SUBTLY CLUED US DIMBULBS WHERE TO LOOK.

HAND ME THOSE FIELD GLASSES.

A FEW DAYS THAT SEEM LIKE MONTHS.

YOW.

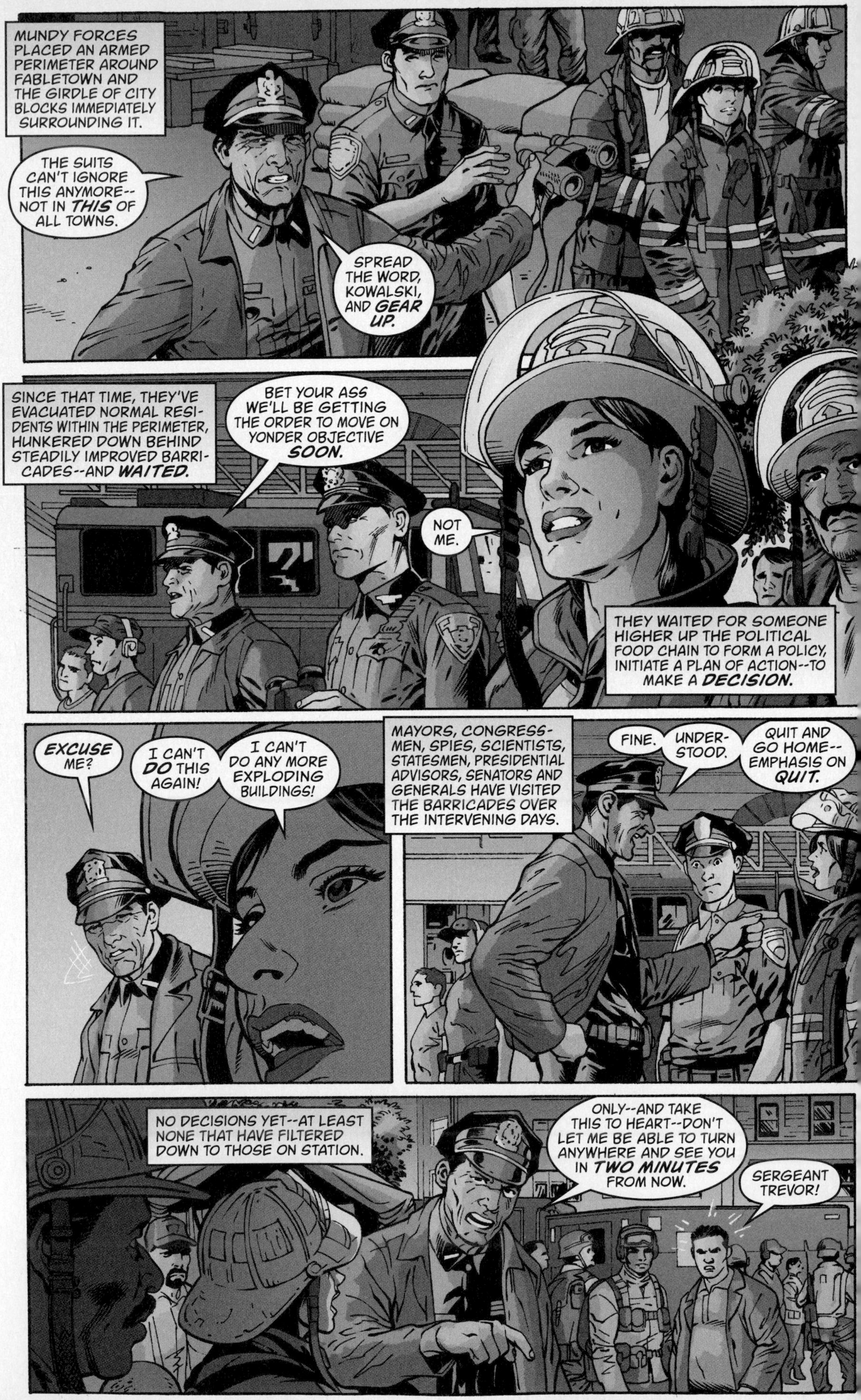
MUNDY FORCES PLACED AN ARMED PERIMETER AROUND FABLETOWN AND THE GIRDLE OF CITY BLOCKS IMMEDIATELY SURROUNDING IT.
THE SUITS CAN'T IGNORE THIS ANYMORE-- NOT IN THIS OF ALL TOWNS.
SPREAD THE WORD, KOWALSKI, AND GEAR UP.
SINCE THAT TIME, THEY'VE EVACUATED NORMAL RESIDENTS WITHIN THE PERIMETER, HUNKERED DOWN BEHIND STEADILY IMPROVED BARRICADES--AND WAITED.
BET YOUR ASS WE'LL BE GETTING THE ORDER TO MOVE ON YONDER OBJECTIVE SOON.
NOT ME.
THEY WAITED FOR SOMEONE HIGHER UP THE POLITICAL FOOD CHAIN TO FORM A POLICY, INITIATE A PLAN OF ACTION--TO MAKE A DECISION.
EXCUSE ME?
I CAN'T DO THIS AGAIN!
I CAN'T DO ANY MORE EXPLODING BUILDINGS!
MAYORS, CONGRESSMEN, SPIES, SCIENTISTS, STATESMEN, PRESIDENTIAL ADVISORS, SENATORS AND GENERALS HAVE VISITED THE BARRICADES OVER THE INTERVENING DAYS.
FINE.
UNDERSTOOD.
QUIT AND GO HOME-- EMPHASIS ON QUIT.
NO DECISIONS YET--AT LEAST NONE THAT HAVE FILTERED DOWN TO THOSE ON STATION.
ONLY--AND TAKE THIS TO HEART--DON'T LET ME BE ABLE TO TURN ANYWHERE AND SEE YOU IN TWO MINUTES FROM NOW.
SERGEANT TREVOR!

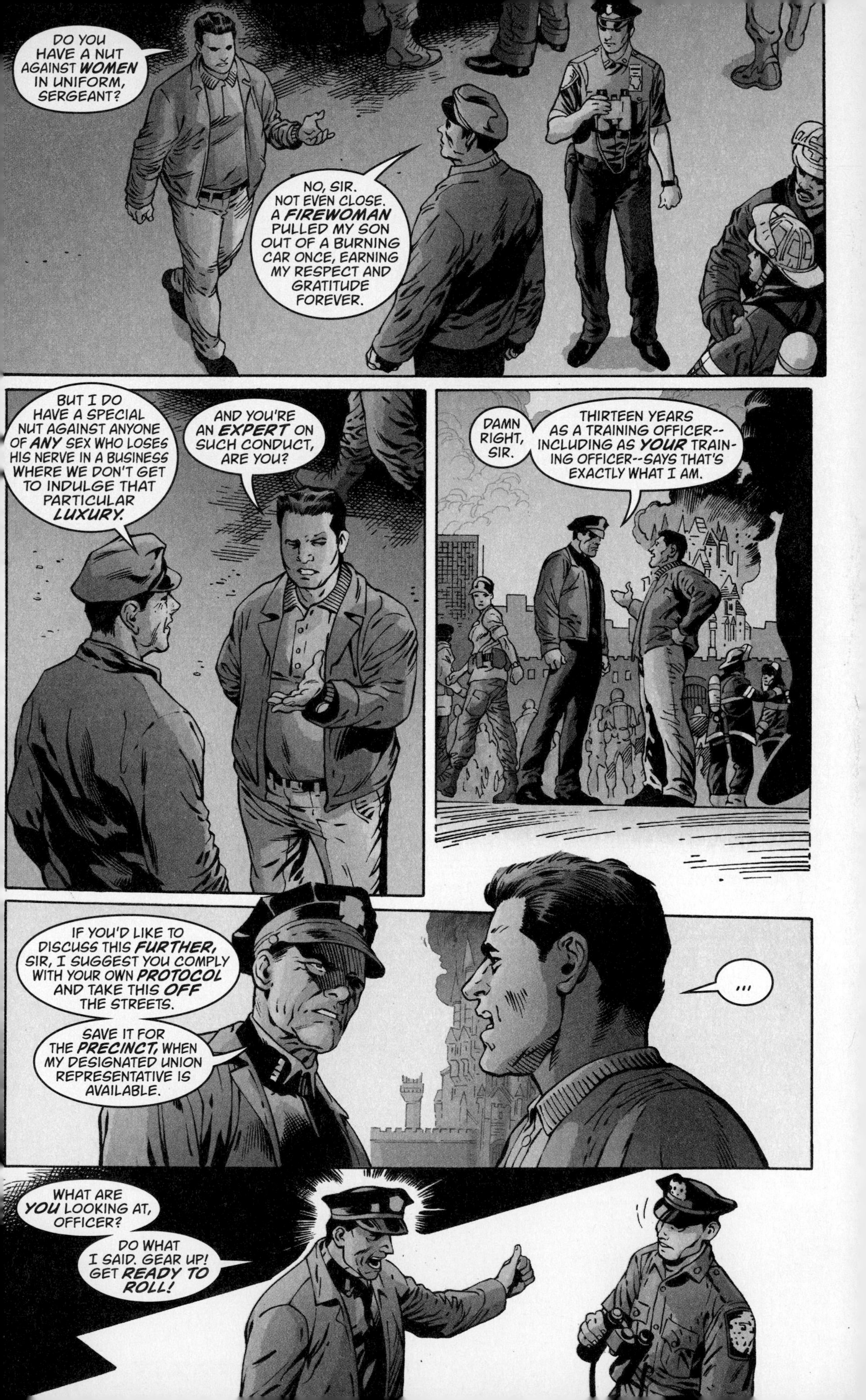
DO YOU HAVE A NUT AGAINST WOMEN IN UNIFORM, SERGEANT?
NO, SIR. NOT EVEN CLOSE. A FIREWOMAN PULLED MY SON OUT OF A BURNING CAR ONCE, EARNING MY RESPECT AND GRATITUDE FOREVER.
BUT I DO HAVE A SPECIAL NUT AGAINST ANYONE OF ANY SEX WHO LOSES HIS NERVE IN A BUSINESS WHERE WE DON'T GET TO INDULGE THAT PARTICULAR LUXURY.
AND YOU'RE AN EXPERT ON SUCH CONDUCT, ARE YOU?
DAMN RIGHT, SIR.
THIRTEEN YEARS AS A TRAINING OFFICER--INCLUDING AS YOUR TRAINING OFFICER--SAYS THAT'S EXACTLY WHAT I AM.
IF YOU'D LIKE TO DISCUSS THIS FURTHER, SIR, I SUGGEST YOU COMPLY WITH YOUR OWN PROTOCOL AND TAKE THIS OFF THE STREETS.
SAVE IT FOR THE PRECINCT, WHEN MY DESIGNATED UNION REPRESENTATIVE IS AVAILABLE.
...
WHAT ARE YOU LOOKING AT, OFFICER?
DO WHAT I SAID. GEAR UP! GET READY TO ROLL!

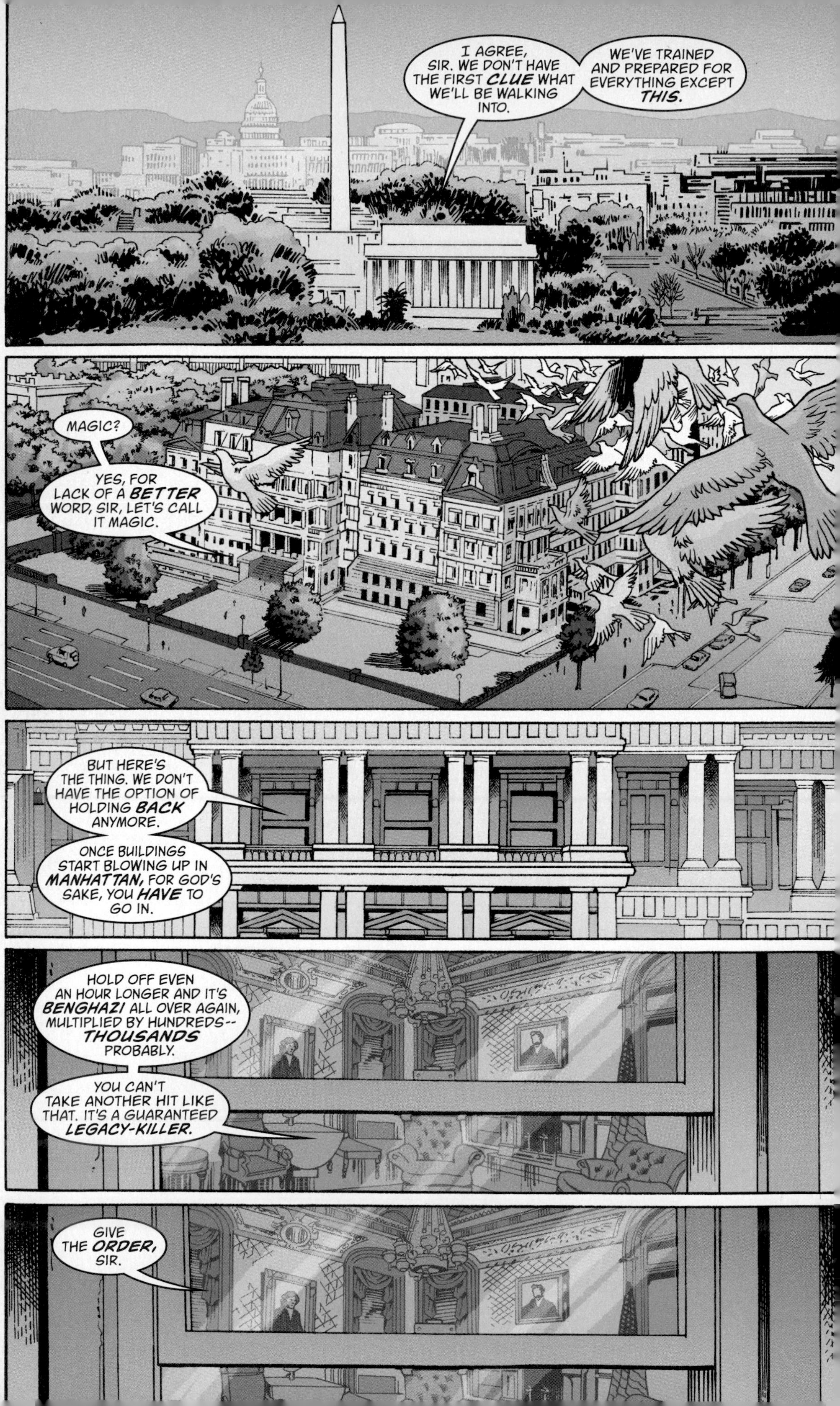

I AGREE, SIR. WE DON'T HAVE THE FIRST CLUE WHAT WE'LL BE WALKING INTO.
WE'VE TRAINED AND PREPARED FOR EVERYTHING EXCEPT THIS.
MAGIC?
YES, FOR LACK OF A BETTER WORD, SIR, LET'S CALL IT MAGIC.
BUT HERE'S THE THING. WE DON'T HAVE THE OPTION OF HOLDING BACK ANYMORE.
ONCE BUILDINGS START BLOWING UP IN MANHATTAN, FOR GOD'S SAKE, YOU HAVE TO GO IN.
HOLD OFF EVEN AN HOUR LONGER AND IT'S BENGHAZI ALL OVER AGAIN, MULTIPLIED BY HUNDREDS-- THOUSANDS PROBABLY.
YOU CAN'T TAKE ANOTHER HIT LIKE THAT. IT'S A GUARANTEED LEGACY-KILLER.
GIVE THE ORDER, SIR.

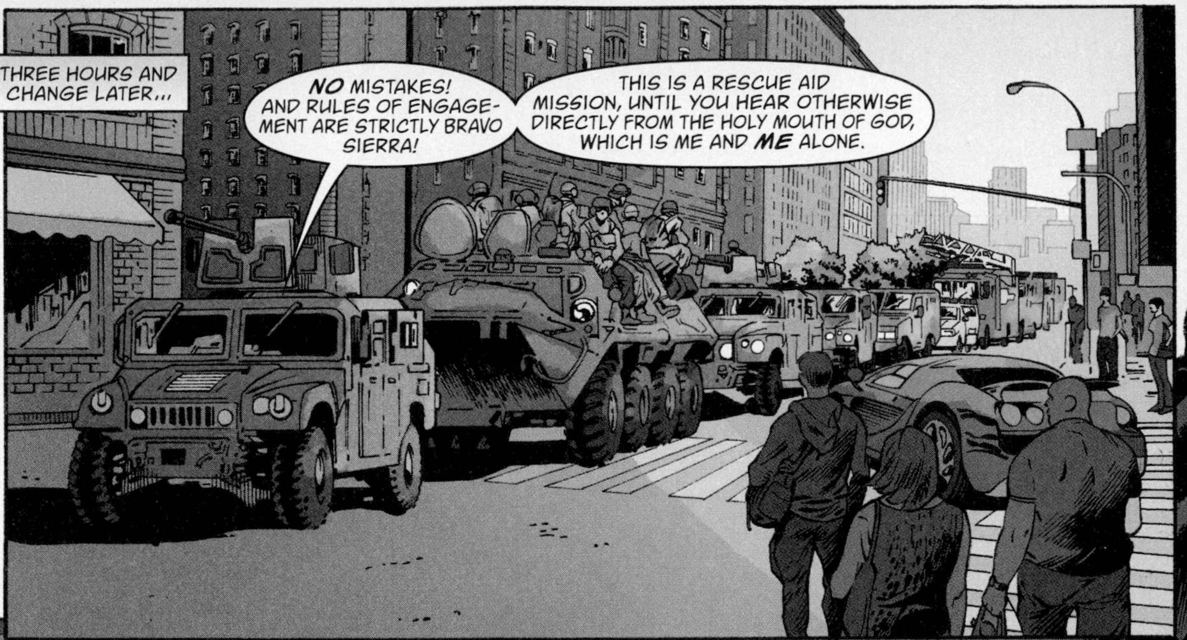
THREE HOURS AND CHANGE LATER...
NO MISTAKES! AND RULES OF ENGAGEMENT ARE STRICTLY BRAVO SIERRA!
THIS IS A RESCUE AID MISSION, UNTIL YOU HEAR OTHERWISE DIRECTLY FROM THE HOLY MOUTH OF GOD, WHICH IS ME AND *ME* ALONE.

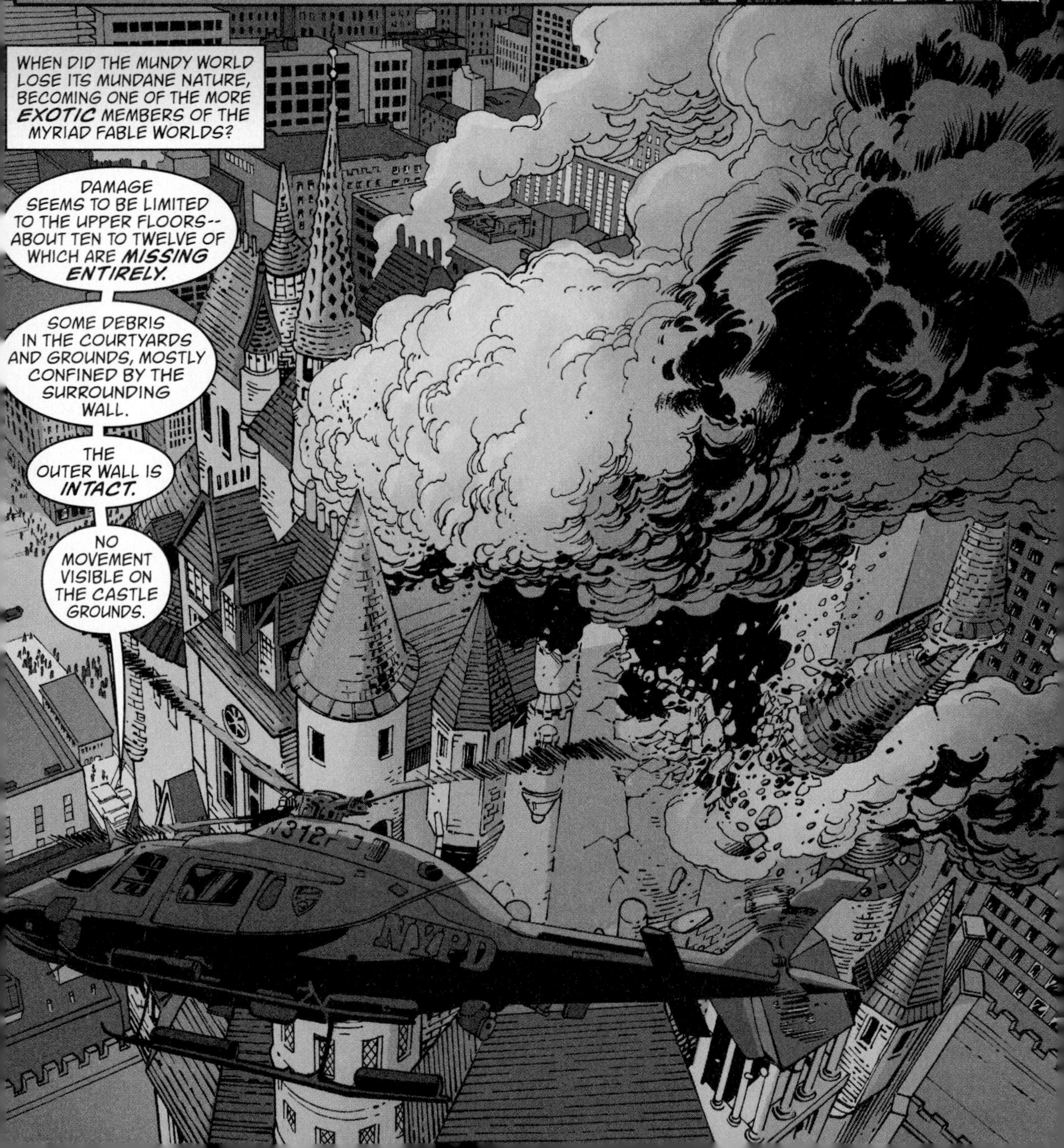
WHEN DID THE MUNDY WORLD LOSE ITS MUNDANE NATURE, BECOMING ONE OF THE MORE *EXOTIC* MEMBERS OF THE MYRIAD FABLE WORLDS?
DAMAGE SEEMS TO BE LIMITED TO THE UPPER FLOORS--ABOUT TEN TO TWELVE OF WHICH ARE *MISSING ENTIRELY.*
SOME DEBRIS IN THE COURTYARDS AND GROUNDS, MOSTLY CONFINED BY THE SURROUNDING WALL.
THE OUTER WALL IS *INTACT.*
NO MOVEMENT VISIBLE ON THE CASTLE GROUNDS.
N312F
NYPD

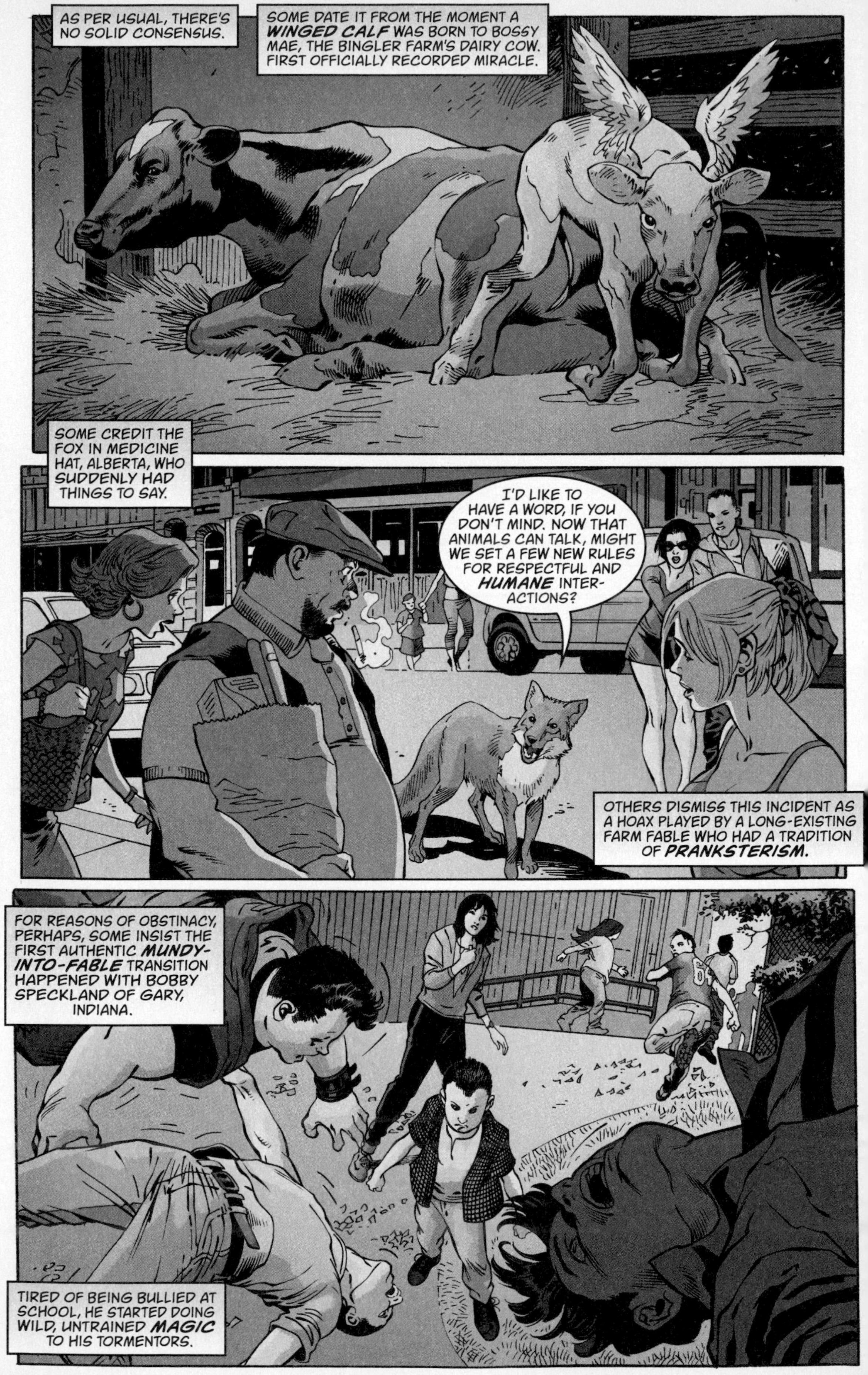
AS PER USUAL, THERE'S NO SOLID CONSENSUS.
SOME DATE IT FROM THE MOMENT A WINGED CALF WAS BORN TO BOSSY MAE, THE BINGLER FARM'S DAIRY COW. FIRST OFFICIALLY RECORDED MIRACLE.
SOME CREDIT THE FOX IN MEDICINE HAT, ALBERTA, WHO SUDDENLY HAD THINGS TO SAY.
I'D LIKE TO HAVE A WORD, IF YOU DON'T MIND. NOW THAT ANIMALS CAN TALK, MIGHT WE SET A FEW NEW RULES FOR RESPECTFUL AND HUMANE INTER-ACTIONS?
OTHERS DISMISS THIS INCIDENT AS A HOAX PLAYED BY A LONG-EXISTING FARM FABLE WHO HAD A TRADITION OF PRANKSTERISM.
FOR REASONS OF OBSTINACY, PERHAPS, SOME INSIST THE FIRST AUTHENTIC MUNDY-INTO-FABLE TRANSITION HAPPENED WITH BOBBY SPECKLAND OF GARY, INDIANA.
TIRED OF BEING BULLIED AT SCHOOL, HE STARTED DOING WILD, UNTRAINED MAGIC TO HIS TORMENTORS.

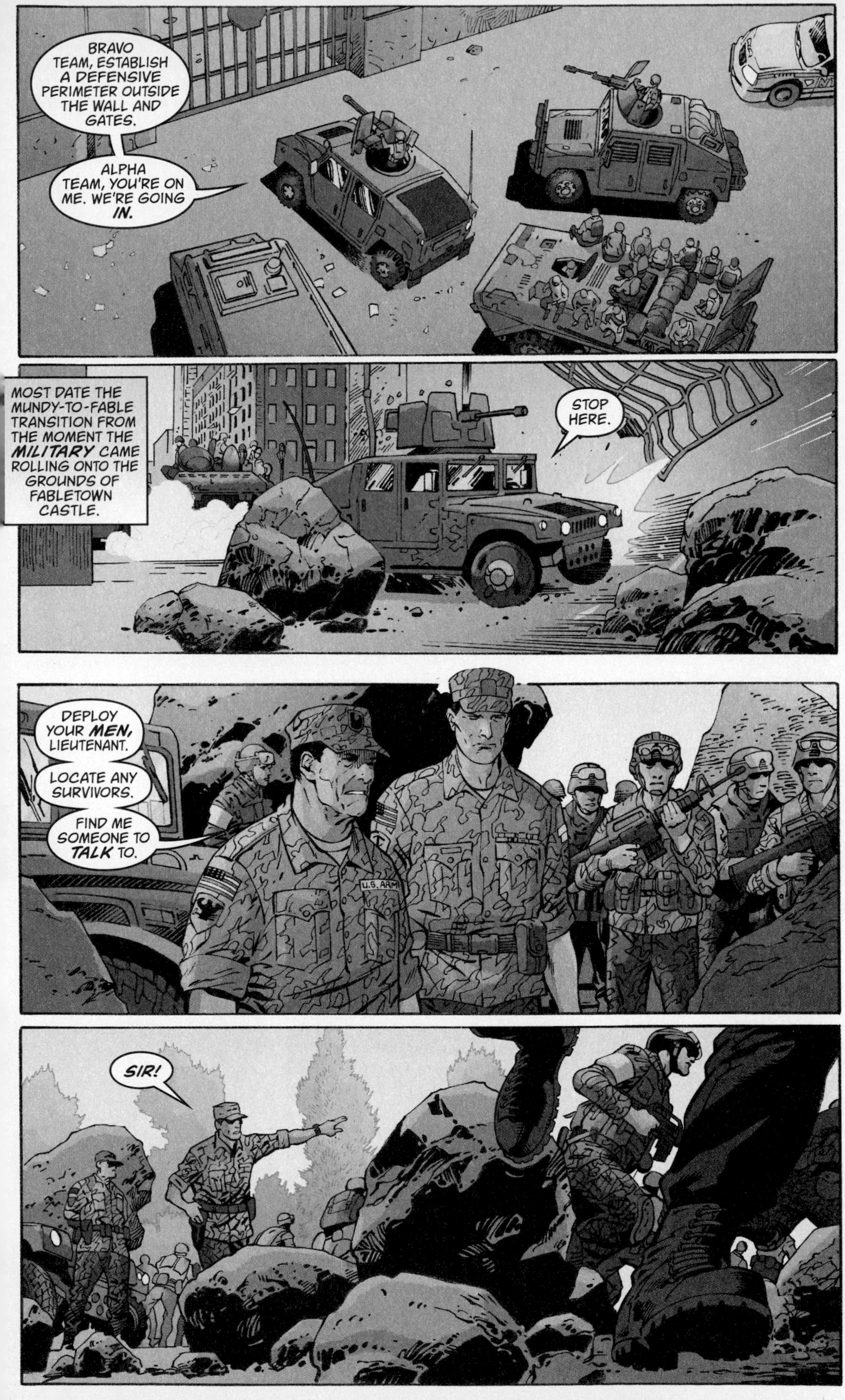
BRAVO TEAM, ESTABLISH A DEFENSIVE PERIMETER OUTSIDE THE WALL AND GATES.
ALPHA TEAM, YOU'RE ON ME. WE'RE GOING IN.
MOST DATE THE MUNDY-TO-FABLE TRANSITION FROM THE MOMENT THE MILITARY CAME ROLLING ONTO THE GROUNDS OF FABLETOWN CASTLE.
STOP HERE.
DEPLOY YOUR MEN, LIEUTENANT.
LOCATE ANY SURVIVORS.
FIND ME SOMEONE TO TALK TO.
SIR!

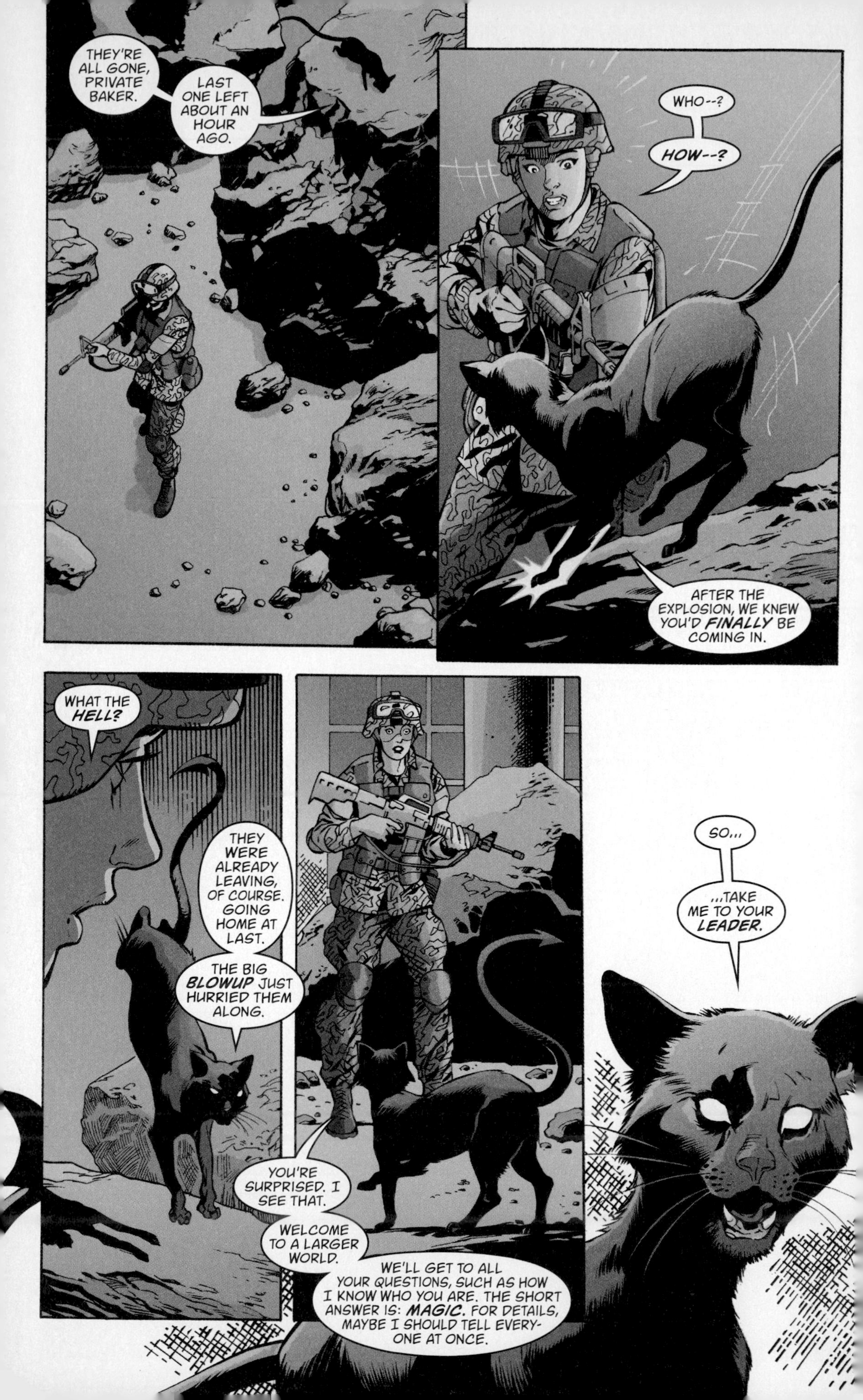
THEY'RE ALL GONE, PRIVATE BAKER.
LAST ONE LEFT ABOUT AN HOUR AGO.
WHO--?
HOW--?
AFTER THE EXPLOSION, WE KNEW YOU'D FINALLY BE COMING IN.
WHAT THE HELL?
THEY WERE ALREADY LEAVING, OF COURSE. GOING HOME AT LAST.
THE BIG BLOWUP JUST HURRIED THEM ALONG.
YOU'RE SURPRISED. I SEE THAT.
WELCOME TO A LARGER WORLD.
WE'LL GET TO ALL YOUR QUESTIONS, SUCH AS HOW I KNOW WHO YOU ARE. THE SHORT ANSWER IS: MAGIC. FOR DETAILS, MAYBE I SHOULD TELL EVERY-ONE AT ONCE.
SO...
...TAKE ME TO YOUR LEADER.

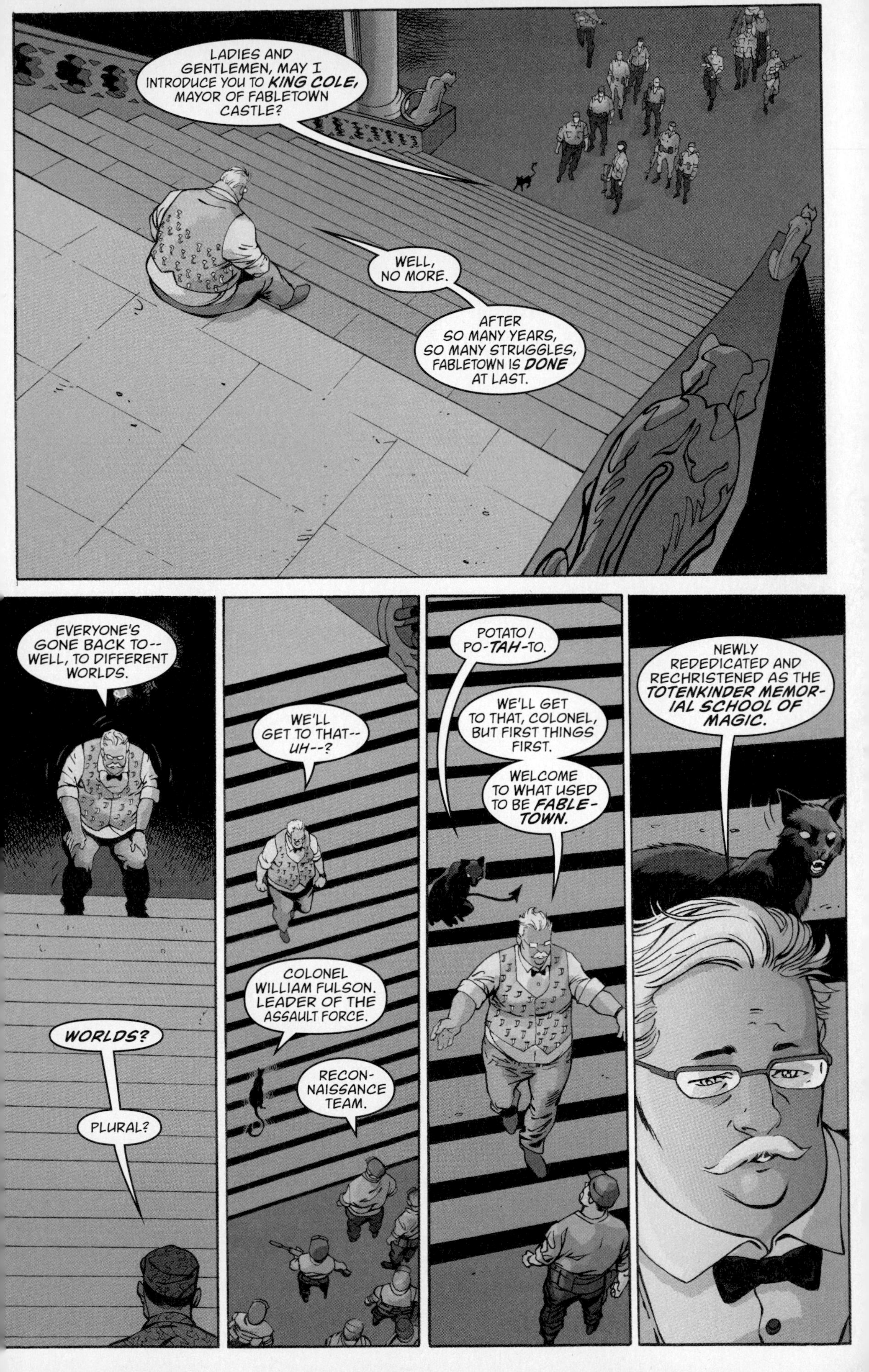
LADIES AND GENTLEMEN, MAY I INTRODUCE YOU TO KING COLE, MAYOR OF FABLETOWN CASTLE?
WELL, NO MORE.
AFTER SO MANY YEARS, SO MANY STRUGGLES, FABLETOWN IS DONE AT LAST.
EVERYONE'S GONE BACK TO-- WELL, TO DIFFERENT WORLDS.
WORLDS?
PLURAL?
WE'LL GET TO THAT-- UH--?
COLONEL WILLIAM FULSON. LEADER OF THE ASSAULT FORCE.
RECON-NAISSANCE TEAM.
POTATO / PO-TAH-TO.
WE'LL GET TO THAT, COLONEL, BUT FIRST THINGS FIRST.
WELCOME TO WHAT USED TO BE FABLE-TOWN.
NEWLY REDEDICATED AND RECHRISTENED AS THE TOTENKINDER MEMORIAL SCHOOL OF MAGIC.

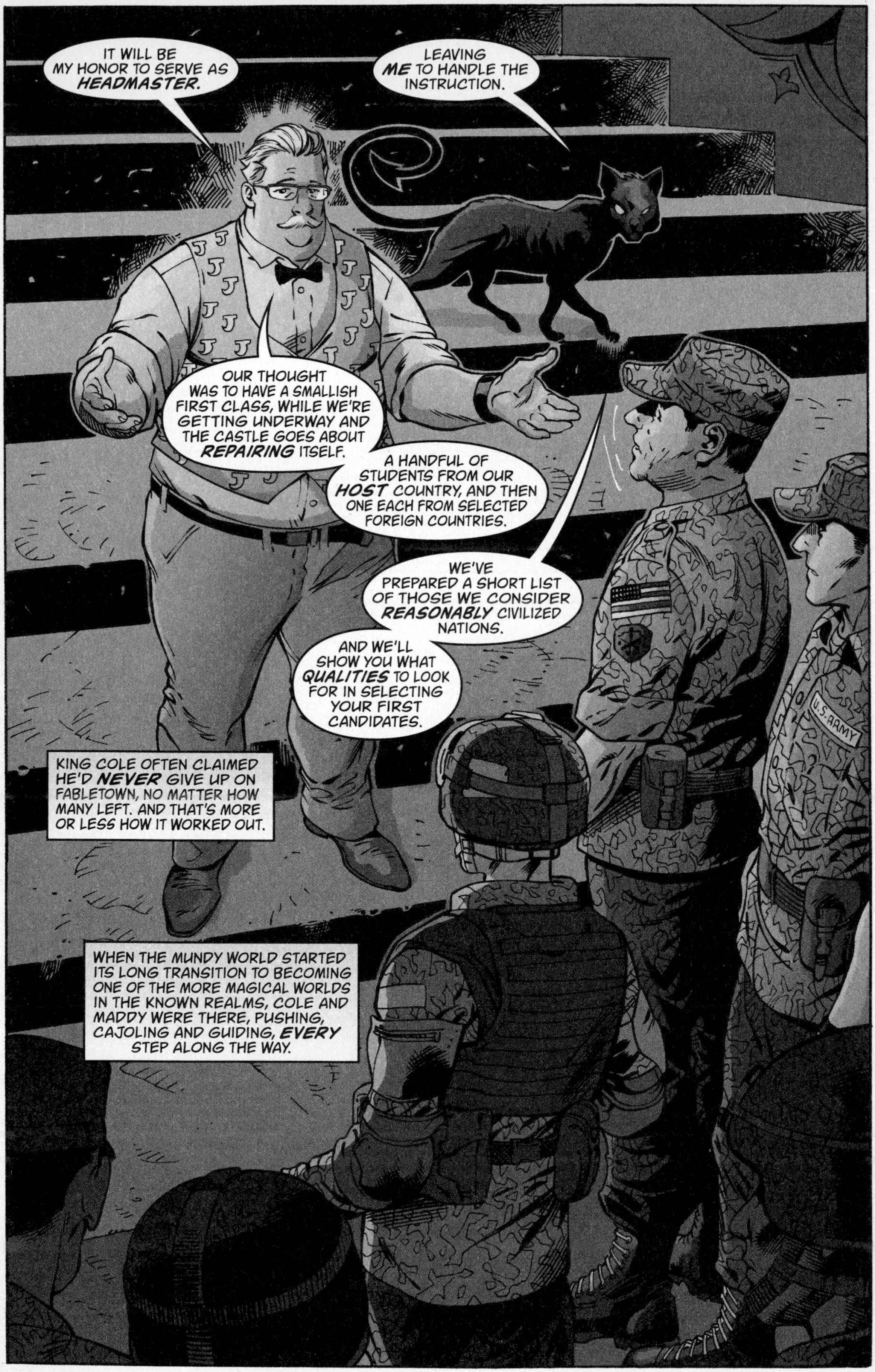
IT WILL BE MY HONOR TO SERVE AS HEADMASTER.
LEAVING ME TO HANDLE THE INSTRUCTION.
OUR THOUGHT WAS TO HAVE A SMALLISH FIRST CLASS, WHILE WE'RE GETTING UNDERWAY AND THE CASTLE GOES ABOUT REPAIRING ITSELF.
A HANDFUL OF STUDENTS FROM OUR HOST COUNTRY, AND THEN ONE EACH FROM SELECTED FOREIGN COUNTRIES.
WE'VE PREPARED A SHORT LIST OF THOSE WE CONSIDER REASONABLY CIVILIZED NATIONS.
AND WE'LL SHOW YOU WHAT QUALITIES TO LOOK FOR IN SELECTING YOUR FIRST CANDIDATES.
KING COLE OFTEN CLAIMED HE'D NEVER GIVE UP ON FABLETOWN, NO MATTER HOW MANY LEFT. AND THAT'S MORE OR LESS HOW IT WORKED OUT.
WHEN THE MUNDY WORLD STARTED ITS LONG TRANSITION TO BECOMING ONE OF THE MORE MAGICAL WORLDS IN THE KNOWN REALMS, COLE AND MADDY WERE THERE, PUSHING, CAJOLING AND GUIDING, EVERY STEP ALONG THE WAY.
U.S. ARMY

THE LAST FRANKIE STORY

Bill Willingham writer - creator
Megan Levens artist
Andrew Dalhouse colors
Todd Klein letters
Rowena Yow assoc. editor
Shelly Bond editor

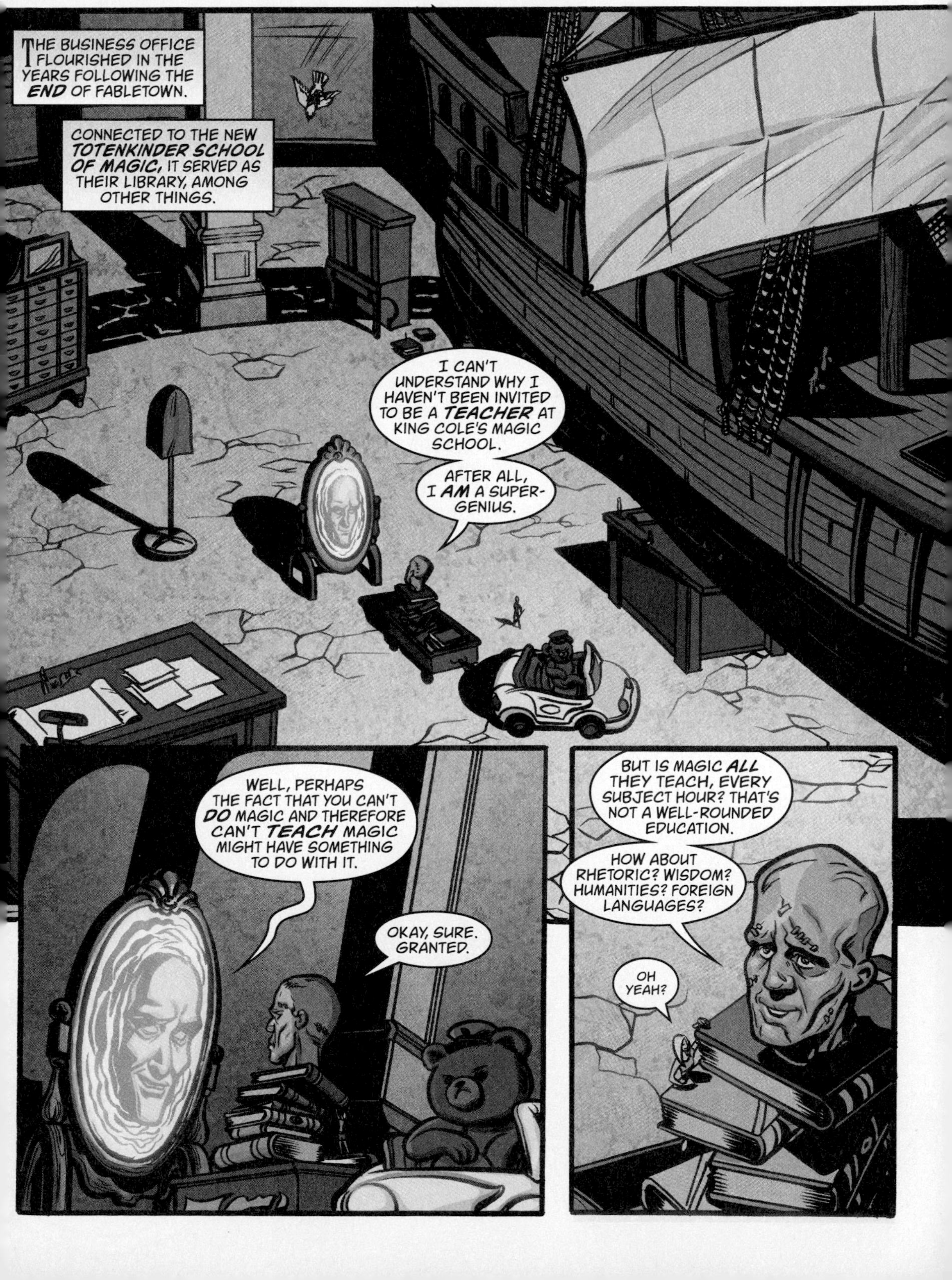
THE BUSINESS OFFICE FLOURISHED IN THE YEARS FOLLOWING THE END OF FABLETOWN.
CONNECTED TO THE NEW TOTENKINDER SCHOOL OF MAGIC, IT SERVED AS THEIR LIBRARY, AMONG OTHER THINGS.
I CAN'T UNDERSTAND WHY I HAVEN'T BEEN INVITED TO BE A TEACHER AT KING COLE'S MAGIC SCHOOL.
AFTER ALL, I AM A SUPER-GENIUS.
WELL, PERHAPS THE FACT THAT YOU CAN'T DO MAGIC AND THEREFORE CAN'T TEACH MAGIC MIGHT HAVE SOMETHING TO DO WITH IT.
OKAY, SURE. GRANTED.
BUT IS MAGIC ALL THEY TEACH, EVERY SUBJECT HOUR? THAT'S NOT A WELL-ROUNDED EDUCATION.
HOW ABOUT RHETORIC? WISDOM? HUMANITIES? FOREIGN LANGUAGES?
OH YEAH?

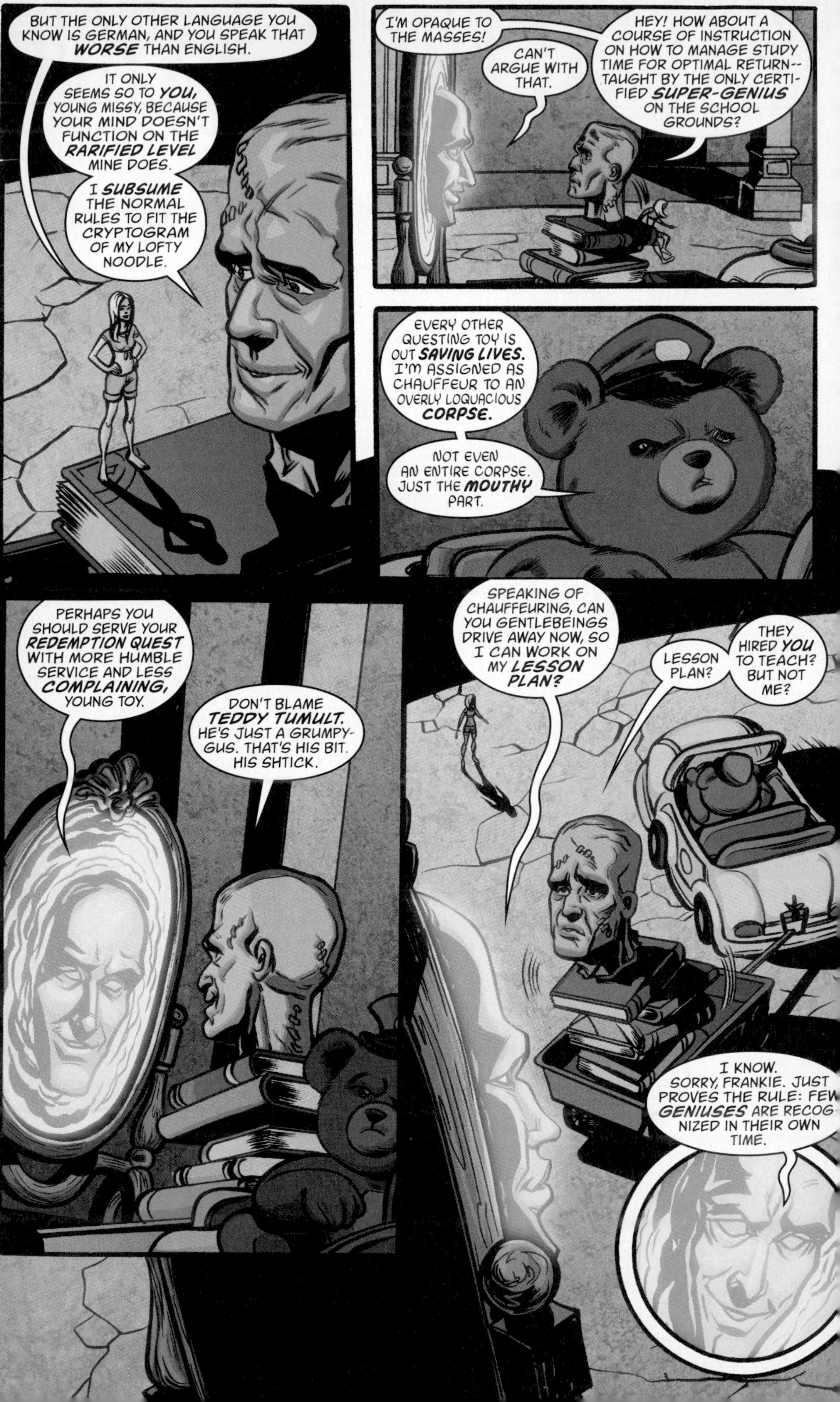
BUT THE ONLY OTHER LANGUAGE YOU KNOW IS GERMAN, AND YOU SPEAK THAT WORSE THAN ENGLISH.
IT ONLY SEEMS SO TO YOU, YOUNG MISSY, BECAUSE YOUR MIND DOESN'T FUNCTION ON THE RARIFIED LEVEL MINE DOES.
I SUBSUME THE NORMAL RULES TO FIT THE CRYPTOGRAM OF MY LOFTY NOODLE.
I'M OPAQUE TO THE MASSES!
CAN'T ARGUE WITH THAT.
HEY! HOW ABOUT A COURSE OF INSTRUCTION ON HOW TO MANAGE STUDY TIME FOR OPTIMAL RETURN-- TAUGHT BY THE ONLY CERTIFIED SUPER-GENIUS ON THE SCHOOL GROUNDS?
EVERY OTHER QUESTING TOY IS OUT SAVING LIVES. I'M ASSIGNED AS CHAUFFEUR TO AN OVERLY LOQUACIOUS CORPSE.
NOT EVEN AN ENTIRE CORPSE. JUST THE MOUTHY PART.
PERHAPS YOU SHOULD SERVE YOUR REDEMPTION QUEST WITH MORE HUMBLE SERVICE AND LESS COMPLAINING, YOUNG TOY.
DON'T BLAME TEDDY TUMULT. HE'S JUST A GRUMPY-GUS. THAT'S HIS BIT. HIS SHTICK.
SPEAKING OF CHAUFFEURING, CAN YOU GENTLEBEINGS DRIVE AWAY NOW, SO I CAN WORK ON MY LESSON PLAN?
LESSON PLAN?
THEY HIRED YOU TO TEACH? BUT NOT ME?
I KNOW. SORRY, FRANKIE. JUST PROVES THE RULE: FEW GENIUSES ARE RECOGNIZED IN THEIR OWN TIME.

"No I'm SERIOUS.
Do you want to
LIVE? What prize
would you pay to
escape DEATH
today?"

THE LAST DEATH STORY

Bill Willingham writer - creator | Bryan Talbot artist | Andrew Dalhouse colors | Todd Klein letters | Rowena Yow assoc. editor | Shelly Bond editor

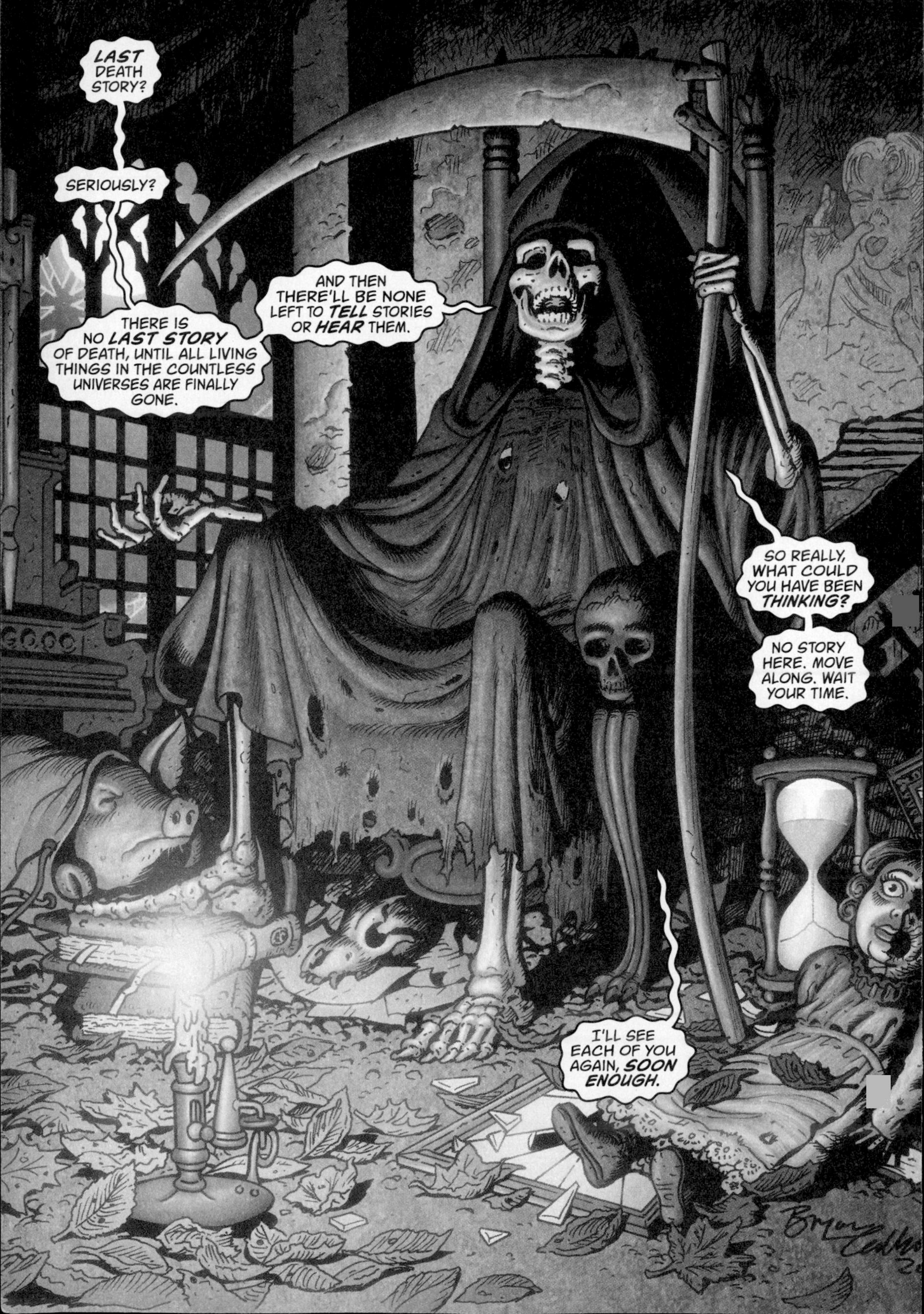
LAST DEATH STORY?
SERIOUSLY?
THERE IS NO LAST STORY OF DEATH, UNTIL ALL LIVING THINGS IN THE COUNTLESS UNIVERSES ARE FINALLY GONE.
AND THEN THERE'LL BE NONE LEFT TO TELL STORIES OR HEAR THEM.
SO REALLY, WHAT COULD YOU HAVE BEEN THINKING?
NO STORY HERE. MOVE ALONG. WAIT YOUR TIME.
I'LL SEE EACH OF YOU AGAIN, SOON ENOUGH.

"Clickety Clack!
Get into my sack!"

"I just realized something, Wolf. There was only one tent and one sleeping bag."

The Last Snow and Bigby Story

In which we take a look at the first encounter between Snow White and Rose Red since the conclusion of the Last Battle that was never actually fought.

Bill Willingham writer - creator | Mark Buckingham artist | Andrew Dalhouse colorist | Todd Klein letterer | Rowena Yow assoc. editor | Shelly Bond editor

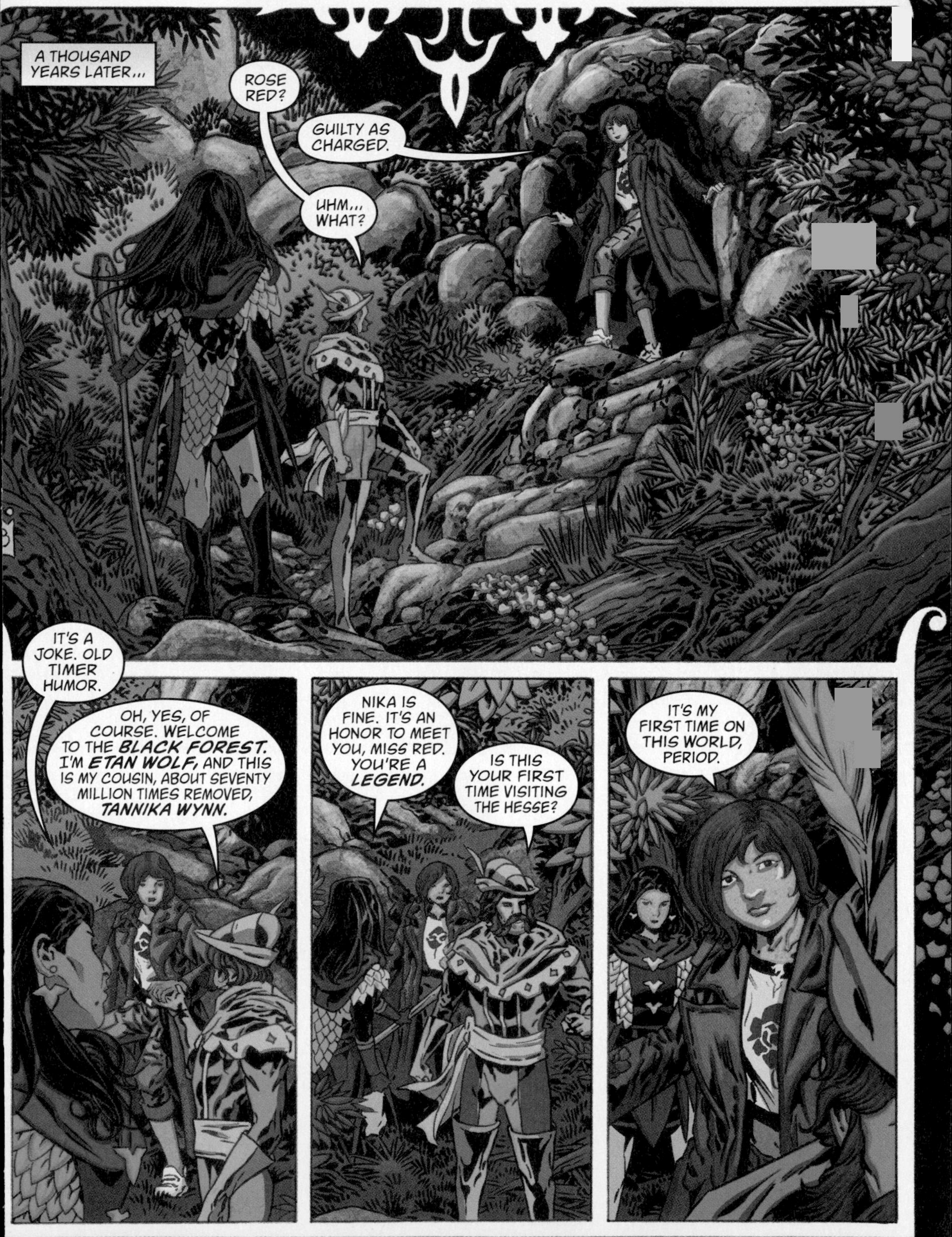
A THOUSAND YEARS LATER...
ROSE RED?
GUILTY AS CHARGED.
UHM... WHAT?
IT'S A JOKE. OLD TIMER HUMOR.
OH, YES, OF COURSE. WELCOME TO THE BLACK FOREST. I'M ETAN WOLF, AND THIS IS MY COUSIN, ABOUT SEVENTY MILLION TIMES REMOVED, TANNIKA WYNN.
NIKA IS FINE. IT'S AN HONOR TO MEET YOU, MISS RED. YOU'RE A LEGEND.
IS THIS YOUR FIRST TIME VISITING THE HESSE?
IT'S MY FIRST TIME ON THIS WORLD, PERIOD.

THE HESSE *IS* THE WORLD. WE OWN IT NOW, ALONG WITH ABOUT A DOZEN *CONNECTING* WORLDS.

WE?

THE *WOLF* FAMILY.

IT STARTED AS A PROJECT TO KEEP THE PATMAT SAFE AND COMFY, DEEP IN THEIR FOREST, WITHOUT FEAR OF BEING DISTURBED BY *OUTSIDERS.*

SORT OF GREW OUT OF CONTROL FROM THERE.

I SEEM TO KEEP ASKING DUMB QUESTIONS. I DON'T KNOW WHAT A *PATMAT* IS.

SNOW AND BIGBY. THE ORIGINAL *PATRIARCH* AND *MATRIARCH* OF OUR SPRAWLING CLAN.

OF COURSE.

I GUESS SNOW AND I HAVE *MUCH* TO CATCH UP ON.

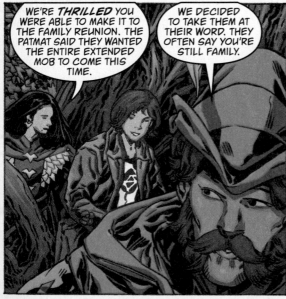

WE'RE *THRILLED* YOU WERE ABLE TO MAKE IT TO THE FAMILY REUNION. THE PATMAT SAID THEY WANTED THE ENTIRE EXTENDED MOB TO COME THIS TIME.

WE DECIDED TO TAKE THEM AT THEIR WORD. THEY OFTEN SAY YOU'RE STILL FAMILY.

WAIT.

HOLD ON.

THIS ISN'T GOING TO BE A *SURPRISE*, IS IT? YOU'RE NOT SPRINGING ME ON THEM IN SOME MISGUIDED--?

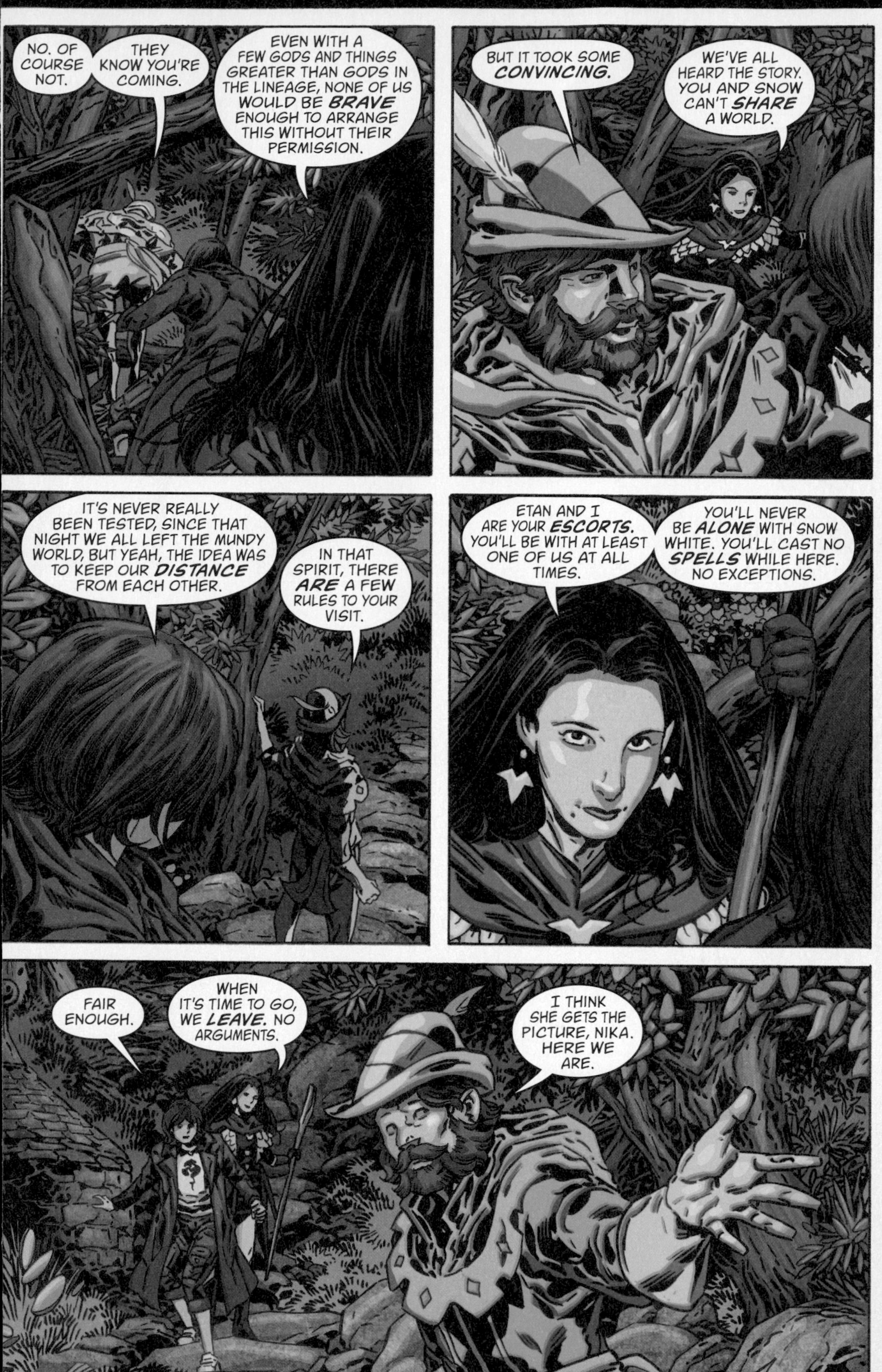
NO. OF COURSE NOT.
THEY KNOW YOU'RE COMING.
EVEN WITH A FEW GODS AND THINGS GREATER THAN GODS IN THE LINEAGE, NONE OF US WOULD BE BRAVE ENOUGH TO ARRANGE THIS WITHOUT THEIR PERMISSION.
BUT IT TOOK SOME CONVINCING.
WE'VE ALL HEARD THE STORY. YOU AND SNOW CAN'T SHARE A WORLD.
IT'S NEVER REALLY BEEN TESTED, SINCE THAT NIGHT WE ALL LEFT THE MUNDY WORLD, BUT YEAH, THE IDEA WAS TO KEEP OUR DISTANCE FROM EACH OTHER.
IN THAT SPIRIT, THERE ARE A FEW RULES TO YOUR VISIT.
ETAN AND I ARE YOUR ESCORTS. YOU'LL BE WITH AT LEAST ONE OF US AT ALL TIMES.
YOU'LL NEVER BE ALONE WITH SNOW WHITE. YOU'LL CAST NO SPELLS WHILE HERE. NO EXCEPTIONS.
FAIR ENOUGH.
WHEN IT'S TIME TO GO, WE LEAVE. NO ARGUMENTS.
I THINK SHE GETS THE PICTURE, NIKA. HERE WE ARE.

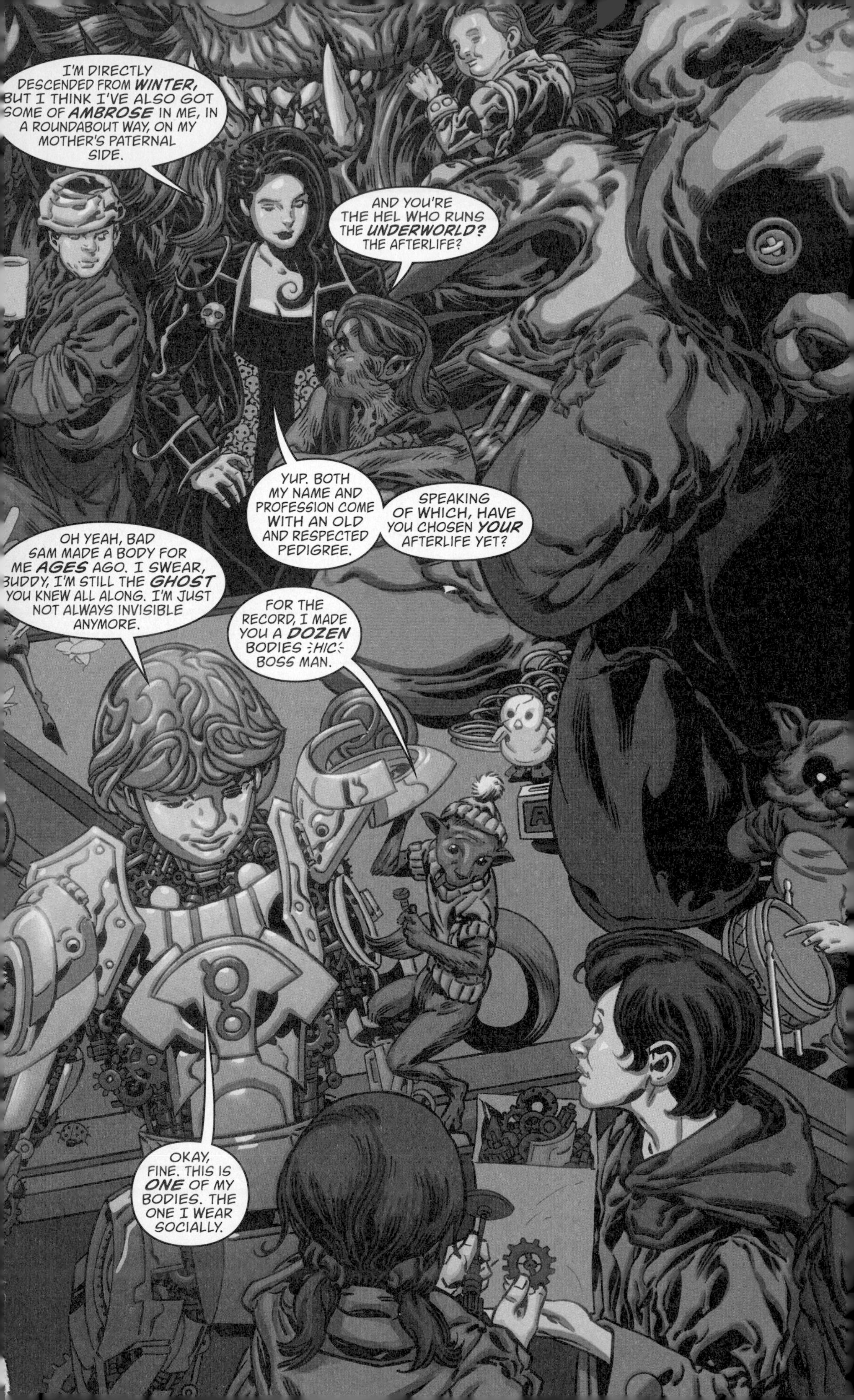
I'M DIRECTLY DESCENDED FROM WINTER, BUT I THINK I'VE ALSO GOT SOME OF AMBROSE IN ME, IN A ROUNDABOUT WAY, ON MY MOTHER'S PATERNAL SIDE.
AND YOU'RE THE HEL WHO RUNS THE UNDERWORLD? THE AFTERLIFE?
YUP. BOTH MY NAME AND PROFESSION COME WITH AN OLD AND RESPECTED PEDIGREE.
SPEAKING OF WHICH, HAVE YOU CHOSEN YOUR AFTERLIFE YET?
OH YEAH, BAD SAM MADE A BODY FOR ME AGES AGO. I SWEAR, BUDDY, I'M STILL THE GHOST YOU KNEW ALL ALONG. I'M JUST NOT ALWAYS INVISIBLE ANYMORE.
FOR THE RECORD, I MADE YOU A DOZEN BODIES -HIC- BOSS MAN.
OKAY, FINE. THIS IS ONE OF MY BODIES. THE ONE I WEAR SOCIALLY.

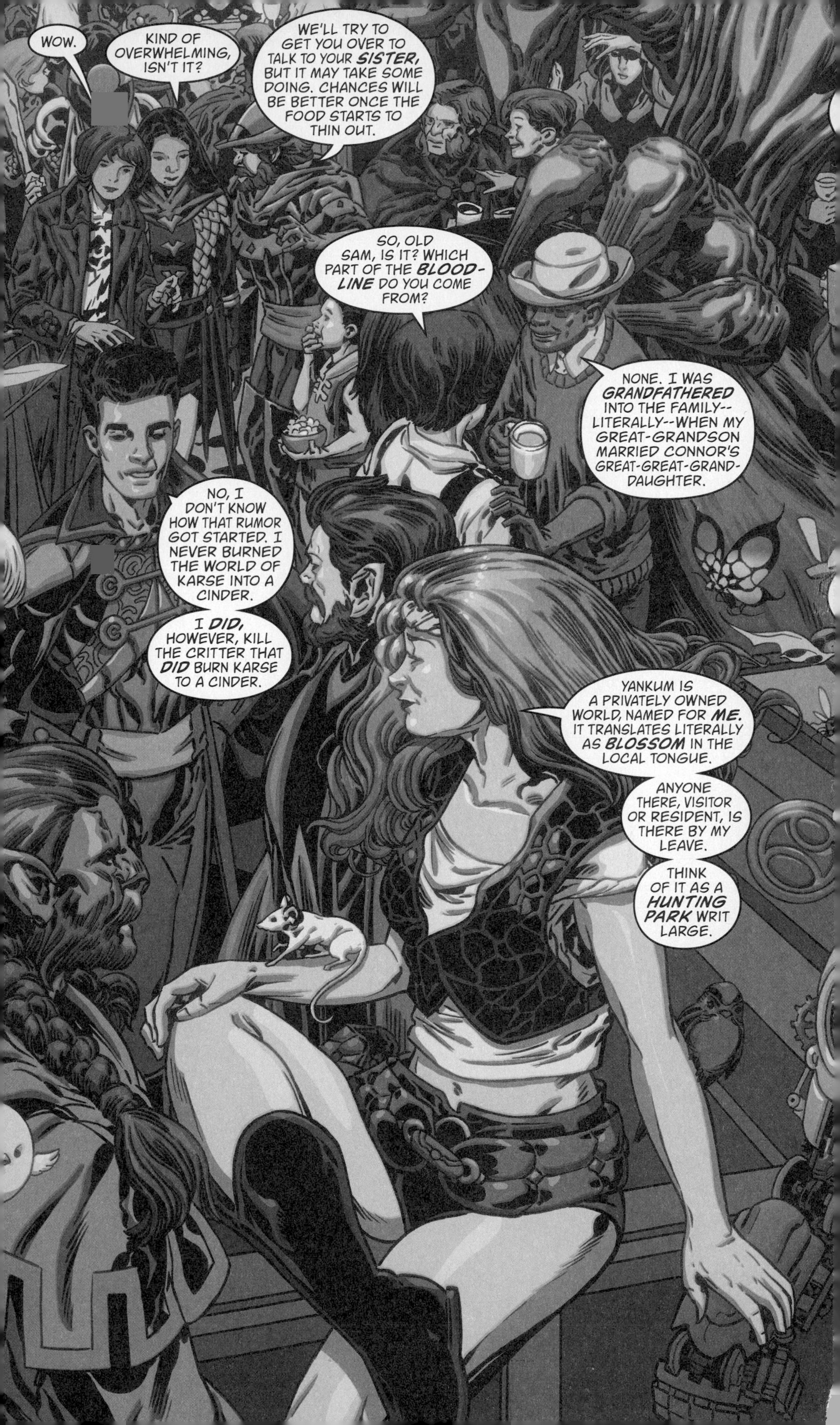
WOW.
KIND OF OVERWHELMING, ISN'T IT?
WE'LL TRY TO GET YOU OVER TO TALK TO YOUR SISTER, BUT IT MAY TAKE SOME DOING. CHANCES WILL BE BETTER ONCE THE FOOD STARTS TO THIN OUT.
SO, OLD SAM, IS IT? WHICH PART OF THE BLOODLINE DO YOU COME FROM?
NONE. I WAS GRANDFATHERED INTO THE FAMILY--LITERALLY--WHEN MY GREAT-GRANDSON MARRIED CONNOR'S GREAT-GREAT-GRANDDAUGHTER.
NO, I DON'T KNOW HOW THAT RUMOR GOT STARTED. I NEVER BURNED THE WORLD OF KARSE INTO A CINDER.
I DID, HOWEVER, KILL THE CRITTER THAT DID BURN KARSE TO A CINDER.
YANKUM IS A PRIVATELY OWNED WORLD, NAMED FOR ME. IT TRANSLATES LITERALLY AS BLOSSOM IN THE LOCAL TONGUE.
ANYONE THERE, VISITOR OR RESIDENT, IS THERE BY MY LEAVE.
THINK OF IT AS A HUNTING PARK WRIT LARGE.

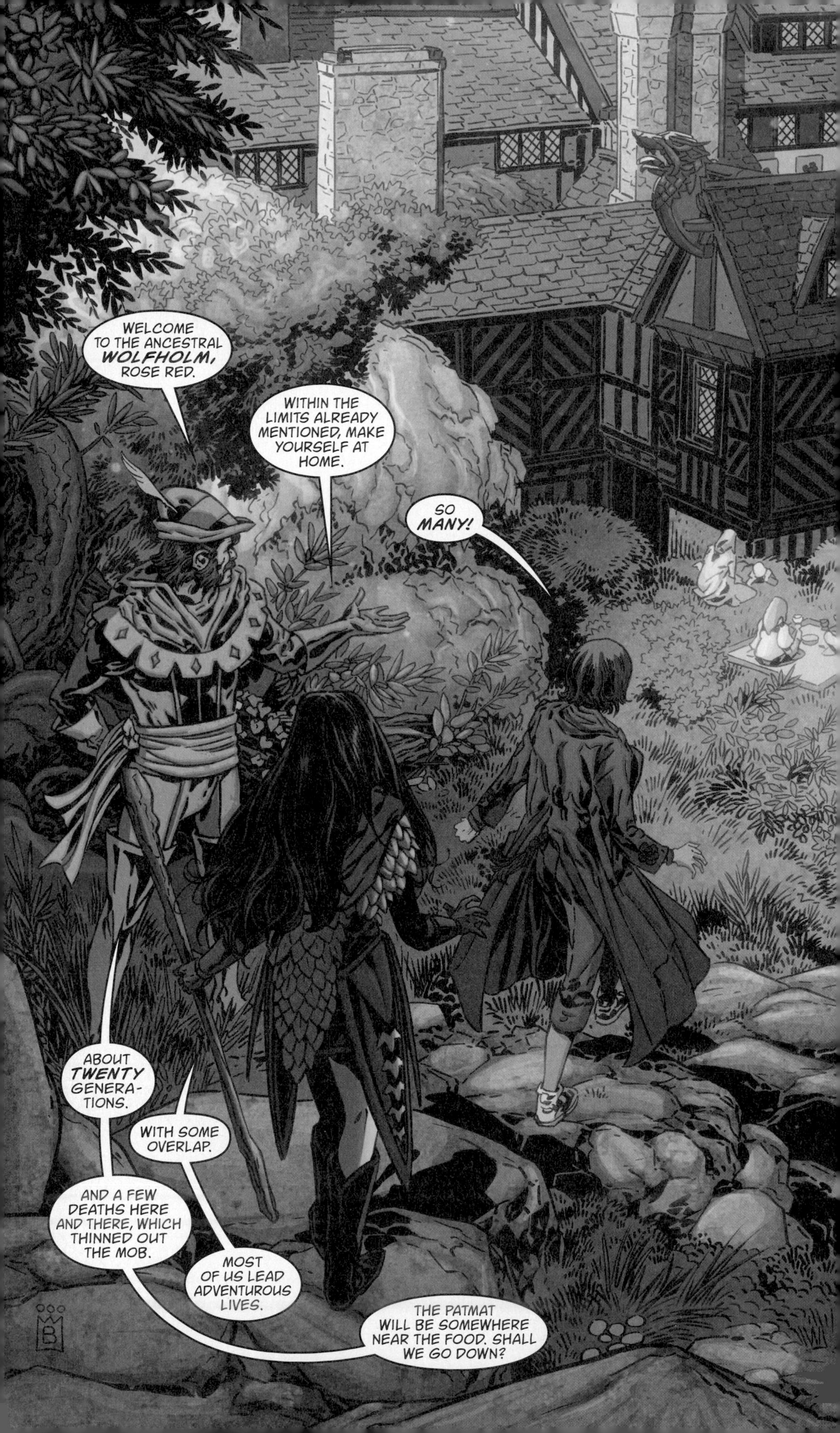
WELCOME TO THE ANCESTRAL WOLFHOLM, ROSE RED.
WITHIN THE LIMITS ALREADY MENTIONED, MAKE YOURSELF AT HOME.
SO MANY!
ABOUT TWENTY GENERATIONS.
WITH SOME OVERLAP.
AND A FEW DEATHS HERE AND THERE, WHICH THINNED OUT THE MOB.
MOST OF US LEAD ADVENTUROUS LIVES.
THE PATMAT WILL BE SOMEWHERE NEAR THE FOOD. SHALL WE GO DOWN?

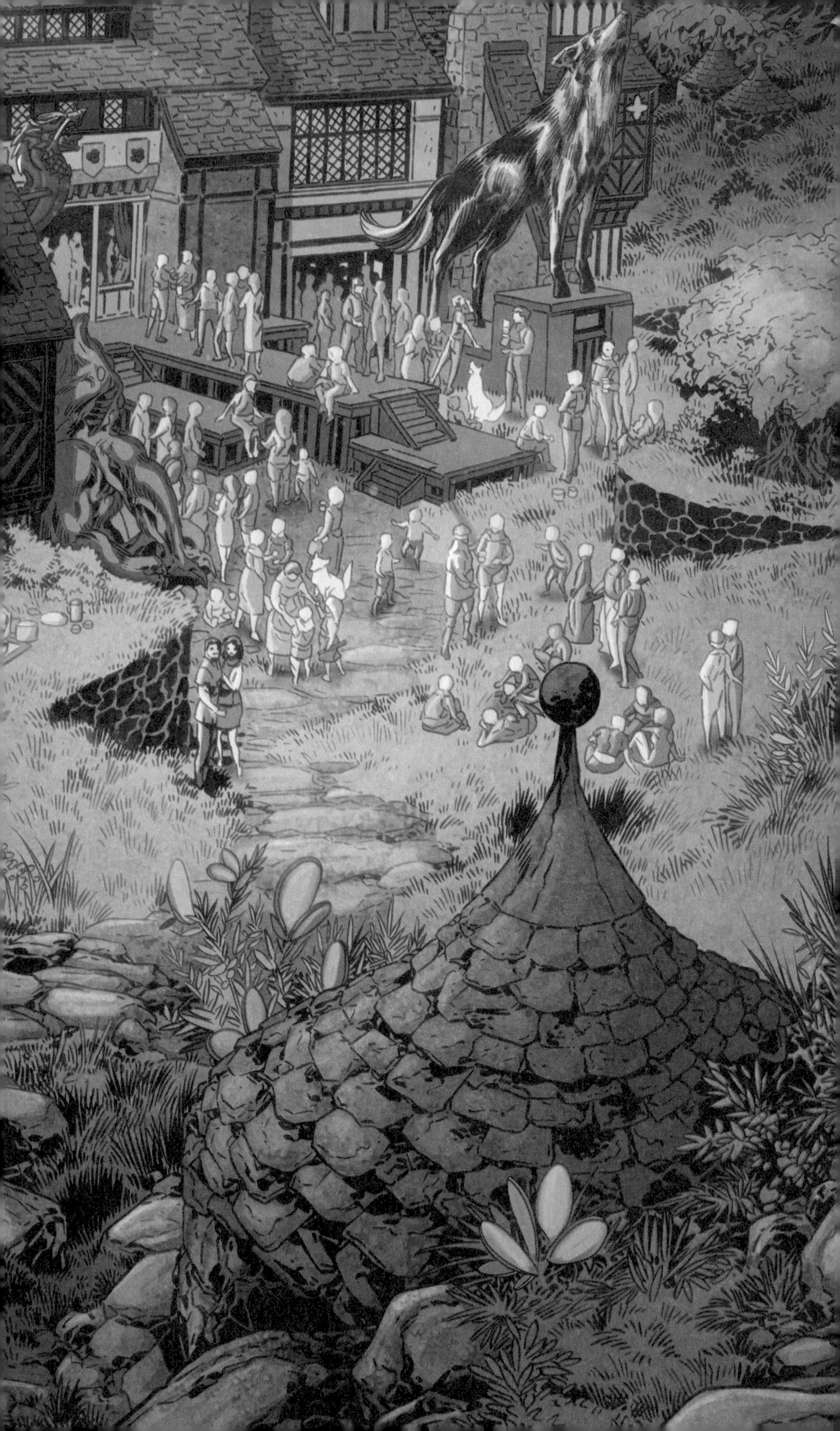

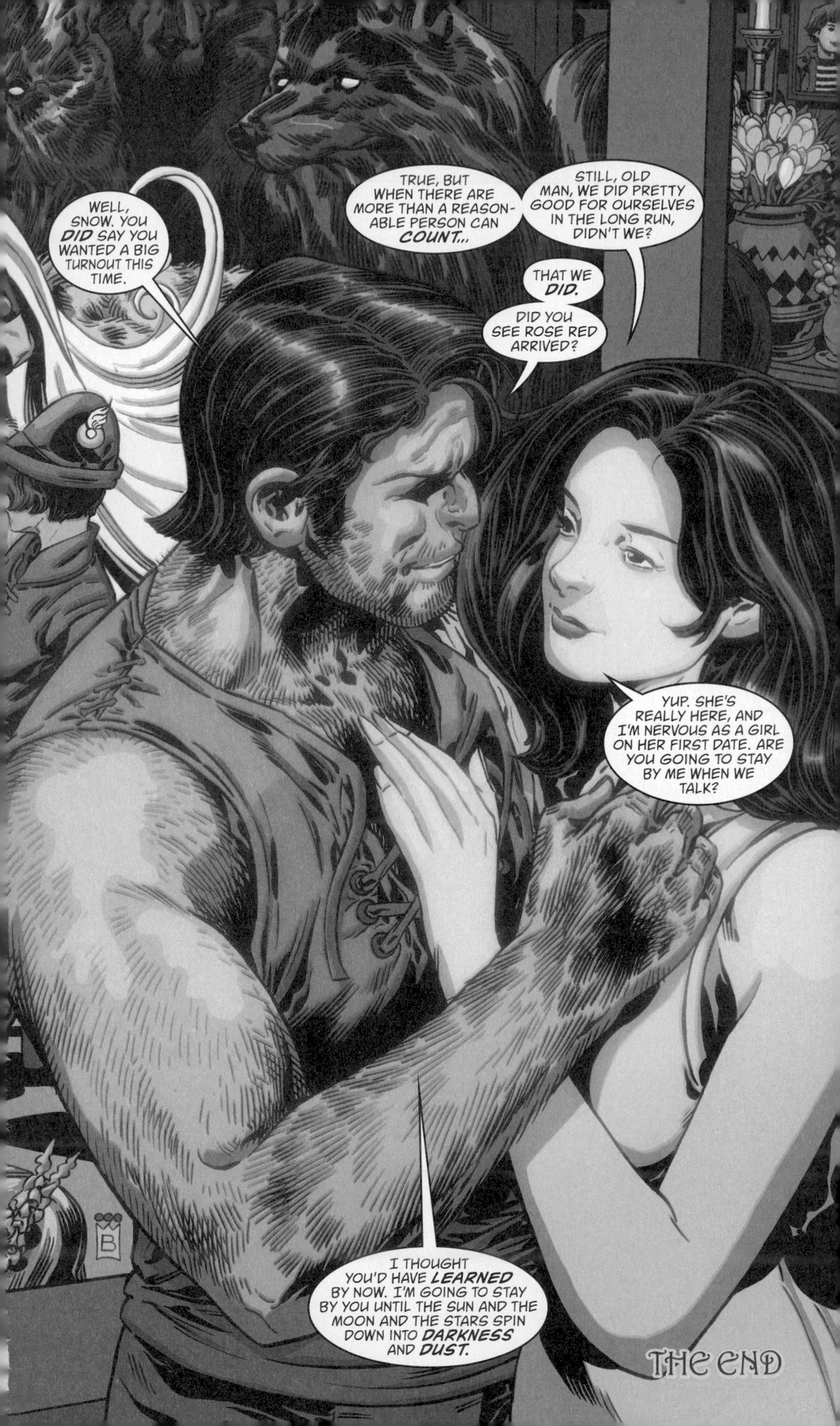
WELL, SNOW. YOU DID SAY YOU WANTED A BIG TURNOUT THIS TIME.
TRUE, BUT WHEN THERE ARE MORE THAN A REASON-ABLE PERSON CAN COUNT...
STILL, OLD MAN, WE DID PRETTY GOOD FOR OURSELVES IN THE LONG RUN, DIDN'T WE?
THAT WE DID.
DID YOU SEE ROSE RED ARRIVED?
YUP. SHE'S REALLY HERE, AND I'M NERVOUS AS A GIRL ON HER FIRST DATE. ARE YOU GOING TO STAY BY ME WHEN WE TALK?
I THOUGHT YOU'D HAVE LEARNED BY NOW. I'M GOING TO STAY BY YOU UNTIL THE SUN AND THE MOON AND THE STARS SPIN DOWN INTO DARKNESS AND DUST.
THE END

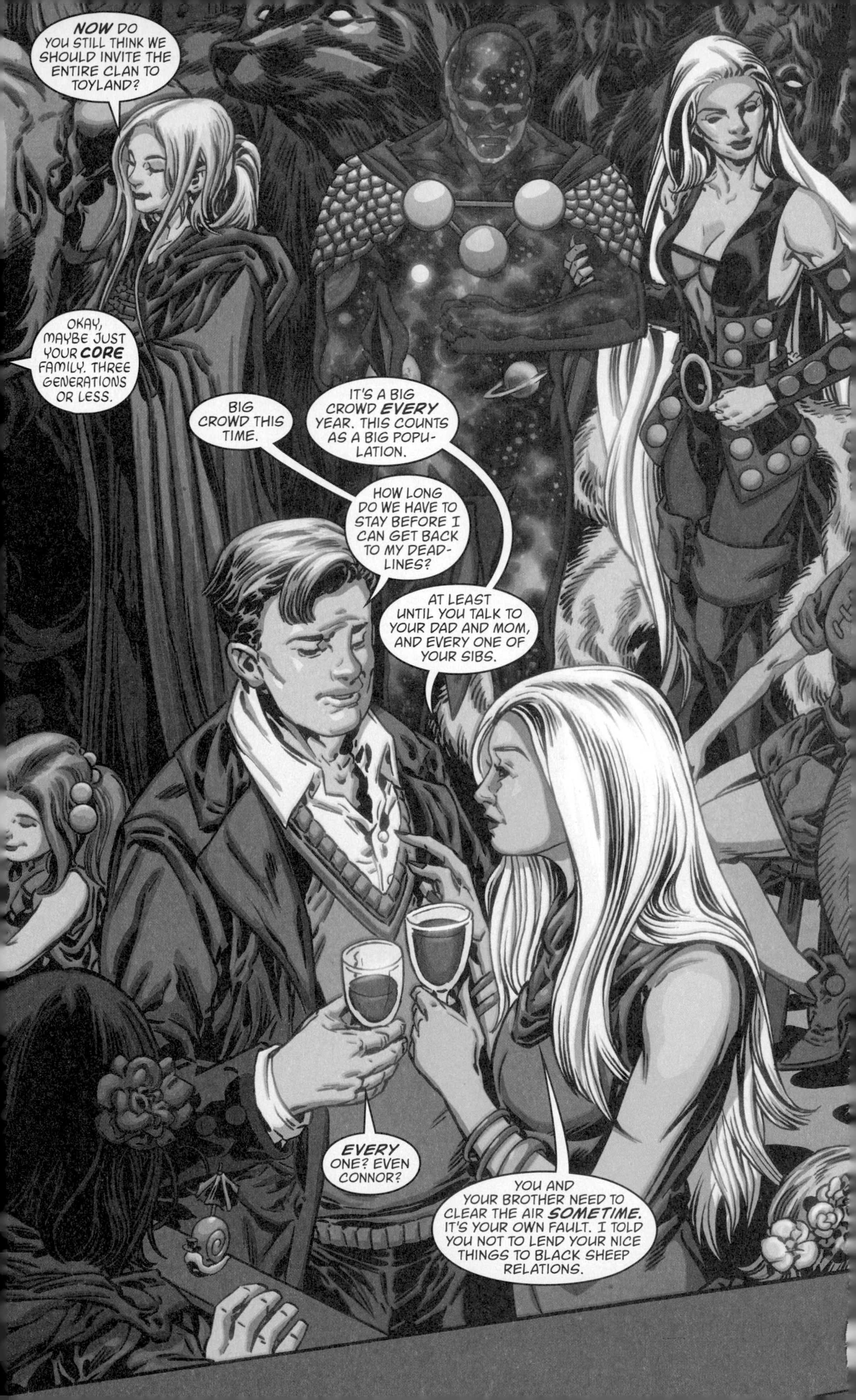

NOW DO YOU STILL THINK WE SHOULD INVITE THE ENTIRE CLAN TO TOYLAND?
OKAY, MAYBE JUST YOUR CORE FAMILY. THREE GENERATIONS OR LESS.
BIG CROWD THIS TIME.
IT'S A BIG CROWD EVERY YEAR. THIS COUNTS AS A BIG POPULATION.
HOW LONG DO WE HAVE TO STAY BEFORE I CAN GET BACK TO MY DEADLINES?
AT LEAST UNTIL YOU TALK TO YOUR DAD AND MOM, AND EVERY ONE OF YOUR SIBS.
EVERY ONE? EVEN CONNOR?
YOU AND YOUR BROTHER NEED TO CLEAR THE AIR SOMETIME. IT'S YOUR OWN FAULT. I TOLD YOU NOT TO LEND YOUR NICE THINGS TO BLACK SHEEP RELATIONS.

That's it. That's all, other than to wish you

GOODBYE and GOODNIGHT

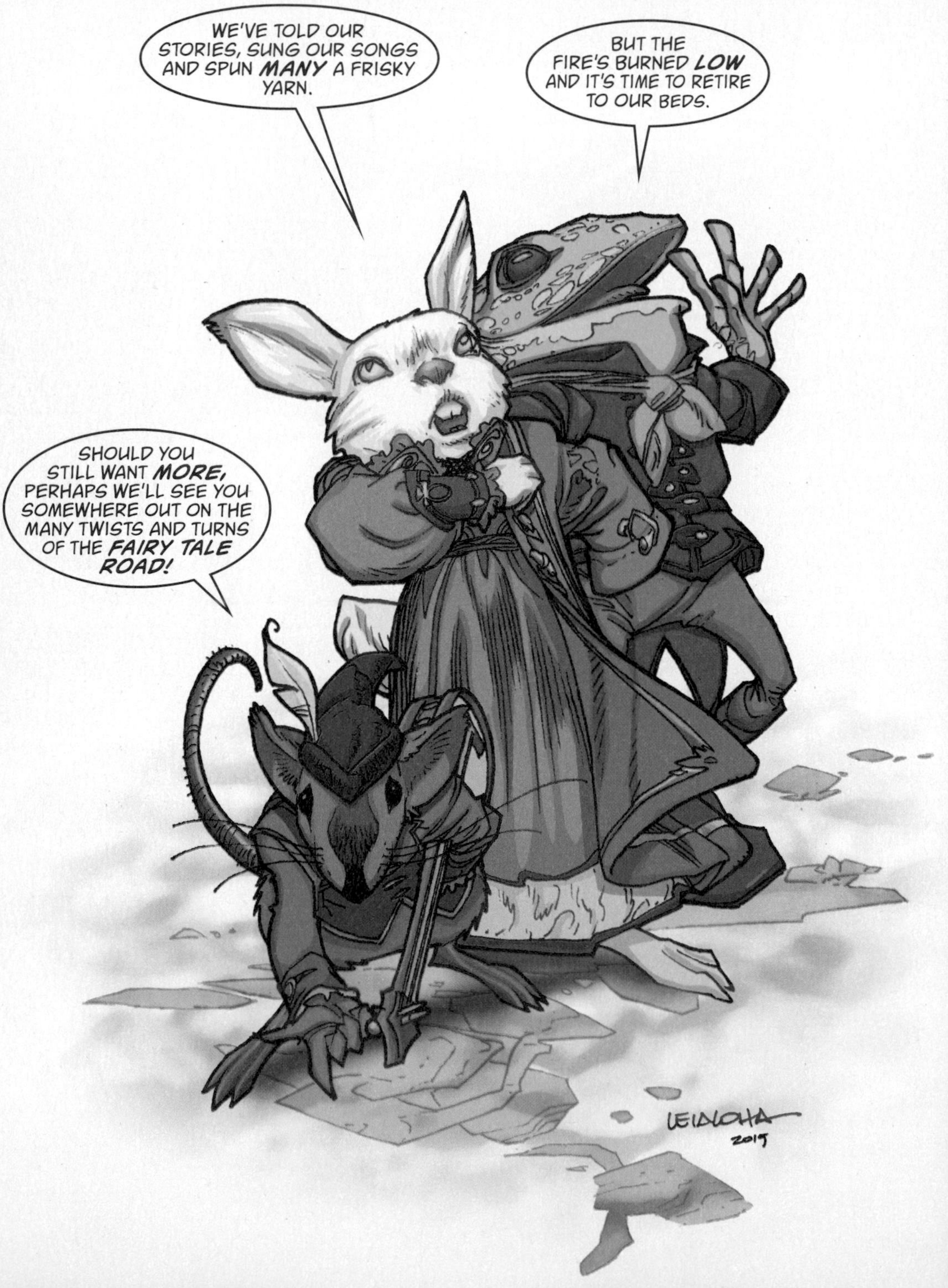

WE'VE TOLD OUR STORIES, SUNG OUR SONGS AND SPUN *MANY* A FRISKY YARN.
BUT THE FIRE'S BURNED *LOW* AND IT'S TIME TO RETIRE TO OUR BEDS.
SHOULD YOU STILL WANT *MORE,* PERHAPS WE'LL SEE YOU SOMEWHERE OUT ON THE MANY TWISTS AND TURNS OF THE *FAIRY TALE ROAD!*

LUCKY 13

A Fables Afterword in Three Parts by Bill Willingham

Part One: The Preamble

So then, a happy ending for some. In fiction and history, and (perhaps most important) in fairy tale, that's about as much as one can hope for.

Which brings us to our curtain.

The stage lights have dimmed. The house lights have come up to help you find your way out of our playhouse. Time to go home, and feel free to take the shortcut through those dark woods. Don't worry about the scary, almost monstrous, sounds you hear from deep inside. I'm certain it's only a rustling of the leaves.

There's no more story to tell.

Sure, we could go on a bit longer — hint at what happened in the Bigby and Snow family during the uncounted centuries which took place between the final page of the larger main story in this volume and the big double barreled gatefold at the end (yes, as I only recently learned, that's what you call that extraordinary single panel that sprawled languidly over four fold-out pages). We could follow Dare beyond that white nothingness, to reassure ourselves that he eventually did go on to a better world. We could detail the sixteen great crises that befell King Ambrose's Kingdom of Haven, after the closing of Fabletown and the great diaspora that followed. Or we could tell the many tales of the magic school that grew in the heart of New York, and how it changed the Mundy world into the most magical of all the worlds. I suppose we could even show you the countless misadventures of Pinocchio as President of the United States, and how his scandalous reign ended abruptly three days into his second term. But that would be just adding detail for its own sake. You already know many adventures were had. Kingdoms rose and fell. Magic was learned and forgotten and learned again. Wolf children grew up to have children of their own, and they had children, and so on, worlds without end.

Stories aren't told by the credited storytellers alone, which is why (as I've written in more detail elsewhere) I'm the one who actually wrote the complete works of Shakespeare — because I dutifully finished my parts of each of his plays, poems, sonnets and ditties, by watching them, reading them, and filling in my share of the details.

That's the secret that's never been a secret at all. Stories don't exist until they've been read or viewed or heard, and fleshed out within the minds of an audience. It's a collaboration that requires imagination and effort from both camps. We've told our bit about FABLES, and even left a few roadmarks to help you find your way from here. If anything's missing, it's left to you to keep going until you can fill it in. Who knows? Maybe in the days to come you'll let us know how it all turned out.

Part Two: Counting the (Magical) Beans

In the thirteen lucky years since the first issue, we've produced just shy of six thousand pages of story within the larger FABLES universe. Broken down further, that works out to about 26 thousand (plus) individual panels, aka individual illustrations (of which I personally produced exactly eighteen – not 18 thousand, mind you, but only eighteen). Since each panel averaged just a pinch over two captions and/or dialogue balloons per panel, which in turn average a tad less than two sentences per balloon, that gives us somewhere in the neighborhood of 102 thousand spoken lines. Throw in another four hundred or so pages of prose story and it begins to add up to something.

FABLES has been translated into 14 languages and has been published in 20 countries.

We produced one FABLES board game, which you can find in the pages of issue 100, and licensed one FABLES video game, called *A Wolf Among Us,* which you can find all over the damn place. As of this writing, we've yet to see FABLES translated into movies or a television series, but we're plugging away at that.

To my immediate knowledge we've inspired no less than two weddings (both marriages of which are meandering along just fine – thank you for asking). From other relationships, I know of a baby who was named Snow, after the FABLES Snow White, another named Dare, after the cub named Dare ("We don't intend for him to grow up timid," says Dad, as Mom nods in agreement), and a third, still not arrived at the time I met his parents, was promised to be named Ambrose Blue, after two other well-known FABLES characters. I've also met another couple wrestling with some way to name their expected girl-child some version of Totenkinder, but I recall cautioning them against it (the name does mean Child Killer after all) and never did learn the final result.

Three songs were written about FABLES. Maybe more.

At least one lawsuit occurred, going all the way to a New York court and a judge's ruling, over who gets possession of the jointly bought issues of FABLES, following a bad break-up. Maybe more.

More Fables-themed tattoos than I can guess at have been created and implemented.

Anecdotally at least (comic publishers, even the big ones, don't really have the deep pockets it takes to do exhaustive demographics research), FABLES seems to be one of the rare series to have more readers than copies sold. They're lent to husbands, wives, fathers, mothers, siblings, friends. There might be more female readers than male, but I can't swear to that.

Part Three: Gratitude

This is the tough part. So many people have helped to create, publish, distribute, sell and share FABLES with the wider world that it would be impossible to thank everyone by name. We'd have to double the size of this volume to have even a chance at publishing a full list. Hell, even those who deserve a special mention for going above and beyond are too numerous to single out.

Should I mention the nights lost, staying late at work, that Shelly and her editorial team had to endure, to make sure the next issue shipped on time, even though the writer was horribly late — thus making everyone else in the chain of production horribly late? Should I mention the legion of incredible pencillers, inkers, colorists and letterers (actually, that last job title should be singular) who've put in 20-hour days and imperiled their health and family relationships, to get last-minute work done, because the writer was horribly late yet again?

And what about the retailers who've hand-sold FABLES to customers, with such astonishing love and dedication, creating an army of loyal, returning readers, so that the afore-mentioned writer hasn't had to get a real job for more than a decade? Should I call them out for special recognition?

And what about that one artist who bore most of the weight of FABLES for the entirety of its run. Surely I should mention him at least?

I should.

But there's no room to do so. Attempting it would guarantee leaving someone — many someones, in fact — out, which would be a crime too onerous to bear.

So, instead I must thank you collectively, for sticking with us for these thirteen years. Trust that my gratitude, horribly lacking in specifics, is overflowing in volume. No matter what comes of my story-spinning career from this point on (for which I've got a few plans), I will never forget what you did for me during this wonderful time. And as for that most-of-the-weight-bearing artist mentioned a mere three paragraphs above? I see that we've a wee bit of room here, so maybe he can be persuaded to add a note of his own.

For my part, I'll end with this.

Thank you, thank you, thank you, and farewell.

— Bill Willingham   May 3, 2015

THE MOST-OF-THE-WEIGHT-BEARING ARTIST'S AFTERWORD TO THE AFTERWORD BIT
(Also known as Bucky's Wee Bit)

When you are working long hours, day after day, month after month, on a series as rich and complex and immersive as FABLES, it's very easy to miss things. Holidays with your wife. Family birthdays. Friends' parties. Life rushes by as you remain fixated on where the story goes next and you race to keep ahead of that next deadline.

You miss how lucky you are to find such an inspiring and generous collaborator as Bill, who created this universe and then shared its development with you.

You find yourself without a moment to spare to contemplate how fortunate you are to work with such talented artists as Steve, Todd, Andrew, Lee, and all the others who have been a part of the FABLES family. The best creative team in comics.

You miss the battles fought and won by Shelly, our fearless Editor, who has championed us from the start, and everything Vertigo and DC have done to help our series prosper.

There's one thing I couldn't fail to miss though, and that is the loyalty, support and enthusiasm our wonderful readers have given to FABLES for the last thirteen years. It has been both a pleasure and a privilege to work with Bill, and the rest of the amazing FABLES team, every month, to bring you these stories. We couldn't have done it without you. Thank you.

And now, I really should be getting back to work. Although I can't shake the feeling I'm missing something.

Wait a minute? Is FABLES ending?

— Mark Buckingham

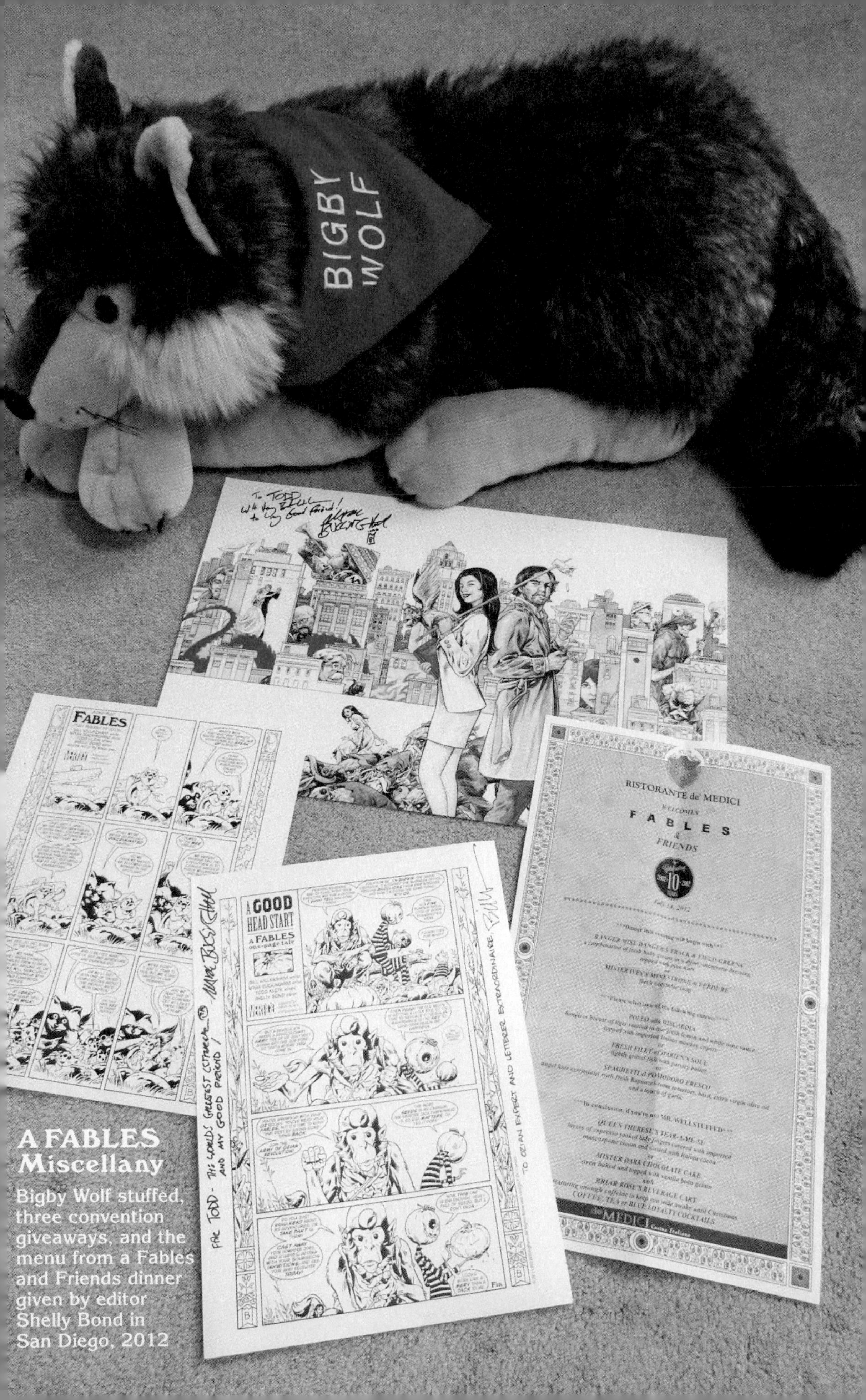
BIGBY WOLF
FABLES
A GOOD HEAD START
A FABLES one-page tale
RISTORANTE de' MEDICI
WELCOMES
FABLES
&
FRIENDS
MEDICI

A FABLES Miscellany

Bigby Wolf stuffed, three convention giveaways, and the menu from a Fables and Friends dinner given by editor Shelly Bond in San Diego, 2012

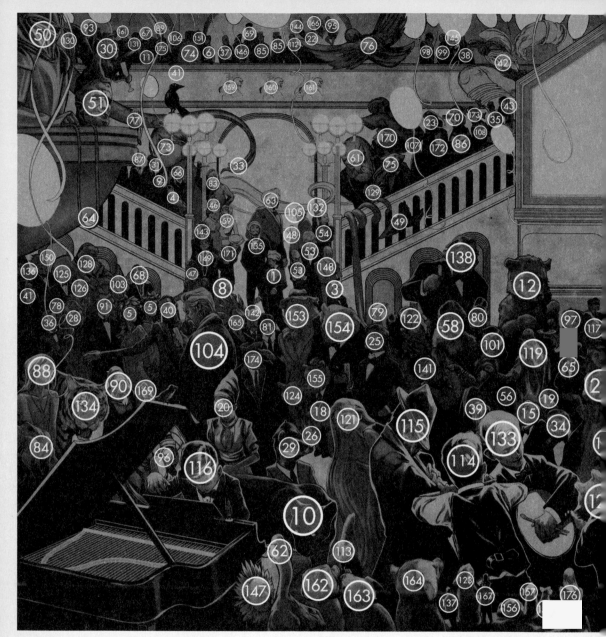

GATEFOLD COVER KEY
by Nimit Malavia

1 Aladdin
2 Flycatcher (King Ambrose)
3 Anansi
4 Commander Arrow
5 Aspen and Alder
6 Aurac
7 Ali Baba
8 Baba Yaga
9 Babcock
10 Bagheera
11 John Baker
12 Baloo
13 John Barleycorn
14 Beast
15 Ambrose
16 Beauty
17 Bigby
18 Billy Goats Gruff
19 Blossom
20 Blue Fairy

21 Bluebeard
22 General Blug
23 Thrushbeard
24 Boy Blue
25 Prince Brandish
 (a.k.a. "Werian Holt")
26 Br'er Rabbit
27 Briar Rose
28 Britomart
29 Brock Blueheart / Stinky the
 Badger
30 Bufkin
31 Chernomor
32 Cinderella
33 Clarathea
34 Conner
35 Crispin Cordwainer
36 Ichabod Crane
37 Daedalus
38 Lord Carrack
39 Darien
40 Mister Dark
41 Death

42 D'Jinn
43 Mersey Dotes
44 Leigh Duglas / Nurse Spratt
45 Lancelot Dulac
46 East Wind
47 Fairy Godmother
48 Fairy Witch
49 Mrs. Finch
50 Forsworn Knight
51 Frankenstein's Monster
52 Frau Totenkinder
53 Freddy & Mouse
54 Dorothy Gale
55 Geppetto
56 Ghost
57 Goldilocks
58 Mr. Grandours
59 Molly Greenbaum
60 Grimble
61 Grinder
62 Gudrun (The Goose That
 Lays the Golden Eggs)
63 Hakim

64 Hangy the Rope
65 Hansel & Gretel
66 Dunster Happ
67 Sergeant Harp
68 Tom Harrow
69 General Hildebrand
70 Captain Hinterfox
71 Hobbes
72 Jack Horner
73 Humberjon
74 Humpty Dumpty
75 Jack Pumpkinhead
76 Jenny Wren
77 Jill
78 Junebug
79 Kaa
80 Mr. Kadabra
81 Kay
82 King Cole
83 King Louie
84 King Noble
85 Kings of Bornegascar and
 Madagao

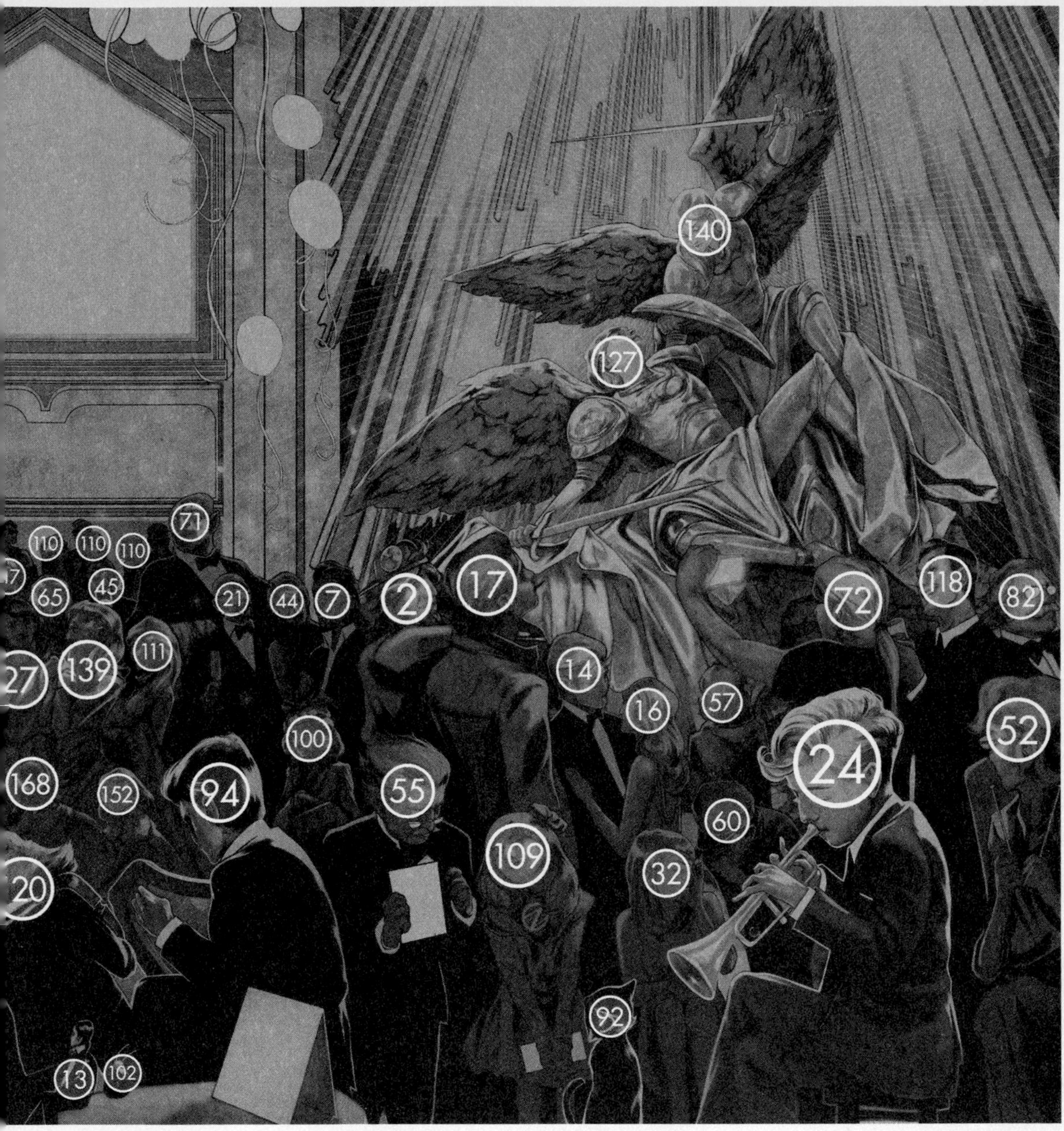
140
127
71
110
110
110
65
45
21
44
7
2
17
72
118
82
139
111
14
16
57
100
52
24
168
152
94
55
60
109
32
20
92
13
102

86 Throk / Sergeant Kroak
87 Sir Lackluster
88 Lake
89 Ronald Levine
90 Little Match Girl
91 Robin Hood
92 Maddy
93 Joey Tice
94 Seamus McGuire
95 Mistral
96 Lord Mountbatten
97 Mowgli
98 Muddlecock
99 Lord Mudsnipe
100 Miss Muffet / Mrs. Webb
101 Morgan Le Fay
102 Mustard Pot Pete
103 Nome King
104 North Wind
105 Sidi Nouman
106 Lieutenant Oakheart
107 Ogren
108 Old Woman Who Lived in a Shoe
109 Ozma
110 Page Sisters (The)
111 Bo Peep
112 Pellinore
113 Peter Cottontail
114 Peter Piper
115 Pied Piper
116 Pinocchio
117 Porky Pine
118 Prince Charming
119 Prospero
120 Puss in Boots
121 Rapunzel
122 Red Riding Hood
123 Corporal Rex
124 Reynard the Fox
125 & 126 Rodney and June
127 Rose Red
128 Santa Claus
129 Sawhorse
130 Scheherazade
131 James Schmachtenberg
132 Tommy Sharp
133 Baby Joe Shepherd
134 Shere Khan
135 Sinbad
136 Baobhan Sith
137 Robert Smallish
138 Weyland Smith
139 Snow Queen
140 Snow White
141 Mrs. Someone
142 South Wind
143 Charlene Speck
144 Squall
145 Bernard Stein
146 Sulymon the Wise
147 Mister Sunflower
148 Doctor Swineheart
149 Moss Waterhouse
150 Jack Frost
151 Jack Ketch
152 Therese
153, 154, 155 Three Bears
156, 157, 158 Three Blind Mice
159, 160, 161 Three Knights of the Rus (Bright Day, Radiant Sun, Dark Night)
162, 163, 164 Three Pigs (Posey, Dun, and Colin)
165 West Wind
166 Whiff
167 Sergeant Wilfred
168 Winter
169 Yellow Bird
170 Yoop the Giant
171 Yusuf
172 Kevin Thorn
173 Tam Lin
174 Trusty John
175 Mr. Webb
176 Thumbelina
177 Lord Carrack

Bill's Comic Writing School Lesson 67.3: The Jekyll and Hyde Syndrome

When writing a comic script, you need to be two writers in one, because you're simultaneously writing to two different readerships.

On one hand, you need to be a creative and sometimes even po-etic writer — telling a compelling story with your words, which are terse lines of dialogue and the occasional caption. This is the writing your readers will see and judge on literary merits.

On the other hand, you must be a superb technical writer, aim-ing only for clarity and nothing else. Your audience is one person — the artist who's going to draw the panels and pages you exactingly detailed, just for him.

So there you are, two writers in one: the artistic scribbler who can select just the right phrase to move and inspire a reader, and the dry and dull technical writer for whom clarity of instruction is the only goal.

But here's the trick: like Jekyll and Hyde, you must be able to switch from one to the other (and back) often and effortlessly. Schizophrenic? You bet! Welcome to the nut-house job of writing funnybooks.

Look! Here's a handy example of three script pages selected from this very volume:

Fables

Issue One Hundred and Fifty

Short Story

Title: The Summer Prophecy

Subtitle: The first child will be a king.

By Bill Willingham

1 Page

Editorial Note: This is the first of the seven one-page Prophecy stories that need to appear in direct sequence, one immediately after another, in numerical order. Each of these one-page stories will be illustrated by a different artist. Thanks.

Page One (six panels)

This isn't really a panel. It's the standardized couple of inches of space you need to leave at the top of the page for this story's titles and credits.

1) Title (display lettering): The Summer Prophecy

2) Subtitle (display lettering): The first child will be a king.

3) Credits

Panel Two

We see a daytime exterior shot of the North Wind's castle (as seen in many previous issues of Fables), high in the mountains of some world or another. As per usual, it's cold and snowy.

4) Voice (from castle): That's me.

5) Same Voice (connected balloon): Old Father Boreas.

6) Same Voice (connected balloon): Winter Wolf.

Panel Three

Same scene, but now we zoom in on one of the castle ramparts to see Winter, in her common guise as a little girl (also as seen most often in many recent issues of Fables). She is at one of the walls, overlooking her lands down below, but now she looks directly at us, breaking the fourth wall, talking to the readers. It's windy, blustery here, as it always is, and her hair blows in the wind.

7) Winter: North Wind.

8) Winter: The King.

9) Winter: I know, right? A little girl? King, rather than queen?

Panel Four

Same scene. Winter walks and talks with us, strolling along the ramparts.

10) Winter: Don't let it trouble you.

11) Winter: Semantics.

12) Winter: Quirks of translating old tongues into new.

Panel Five

Same scene. Winter strolls along, talking to us as she does. One thing is clear. She's all alone up there. Her attendants are nowhere to be seen. She should look isolated, aloof, and just a bit haughty here.

13) Winter: What you should worry about is what sort of king I'm going to turn out to be. Good or bad? Petty and venial? Or a river to my people?

14) Winter: Well, guess what? I worry about that too.

Panel Six

Same scene. Winter turns to look at us more directly, confiding a secret to us. She seems just a touch worried.

15) Winter: And so far the only solid answer I've been able to come up?

16) Winter: We'll see.

The finished page, for comparison.

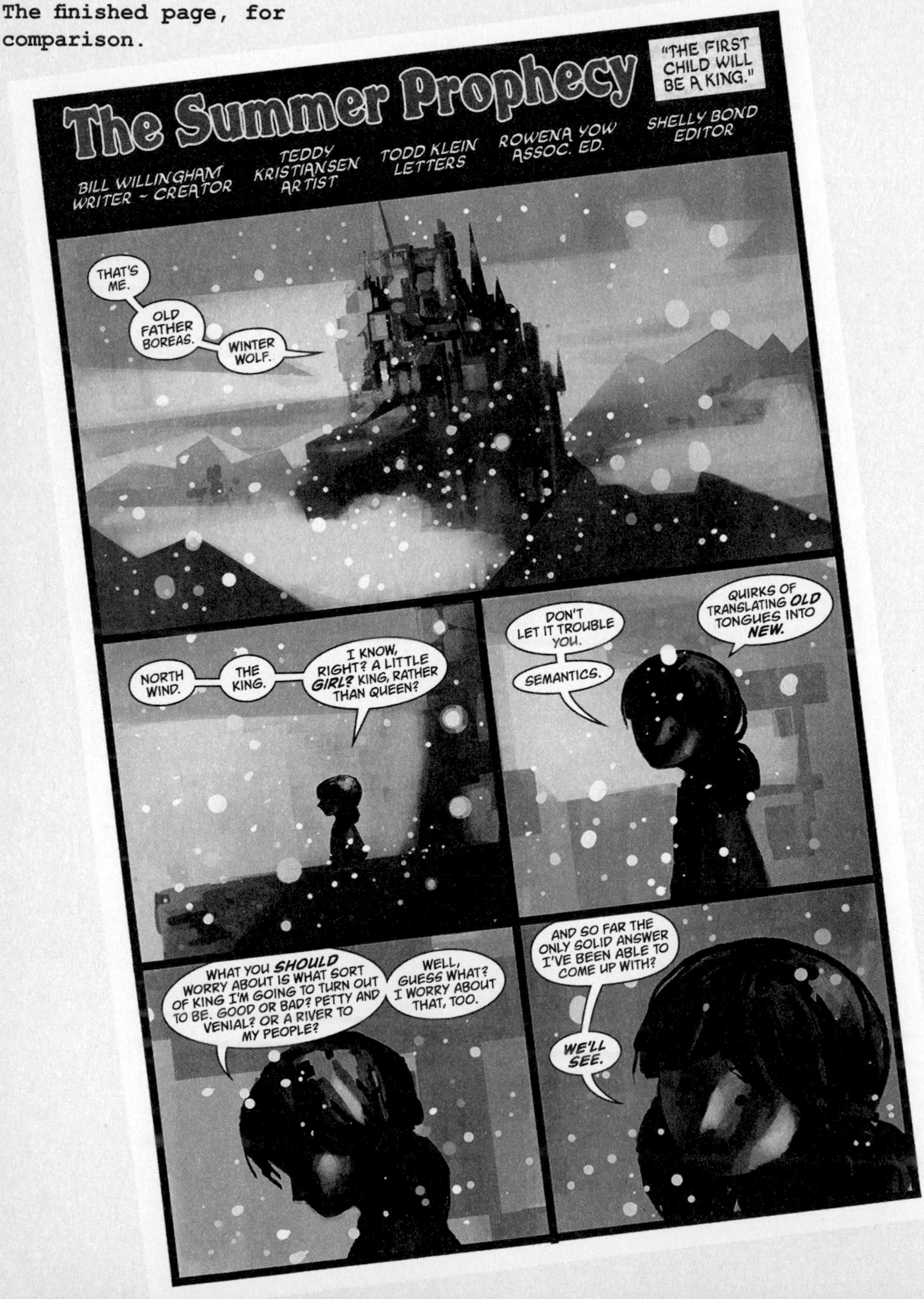

The Summer Prophecy
"THE FIRST CHILD WILL BE A KING."
BILL WILLINGHAM WRITER ~ CREATOR
TEDDY KRISTIANSEN ARTIST
TODD KLEIN LETTERS
ROWENA YOW ASSOC. ED.
SHELLY BOND EDITOR
THAT'S ME.
OLD FATHER BOREAS.
WINTER WOLF.
NORTH WIND.
THE KING.
I KNOW, RIGHT? A LITTLE GIRL? KING, RATHER THAN QUEEN?
DON'T LET IT TROUBLE YOU.
QUIRKS OF TRANSLATING OLD TONGUES INTO NEW.
SEMANTICS.
WHAT YOU SHOULD WORRY ABOUT IS WHAT SORT OF KING I'M GOING TO TURN OUT TO BE. GOOD OR BAD? PETTY AND VENIAL? OR A RIVER TO MY PEOPLE?
WELL, GUESS WHAT? I WORRY ABOUT THAT, TOO.
AND SO FAR THE ONLY SOLID ANSWER I'VE BEEN ABLE TO COME UP WITH?
WE'LL SEE.

A FABLES GALLERY

Bigby and Snow commission piece by Mark Buckingham

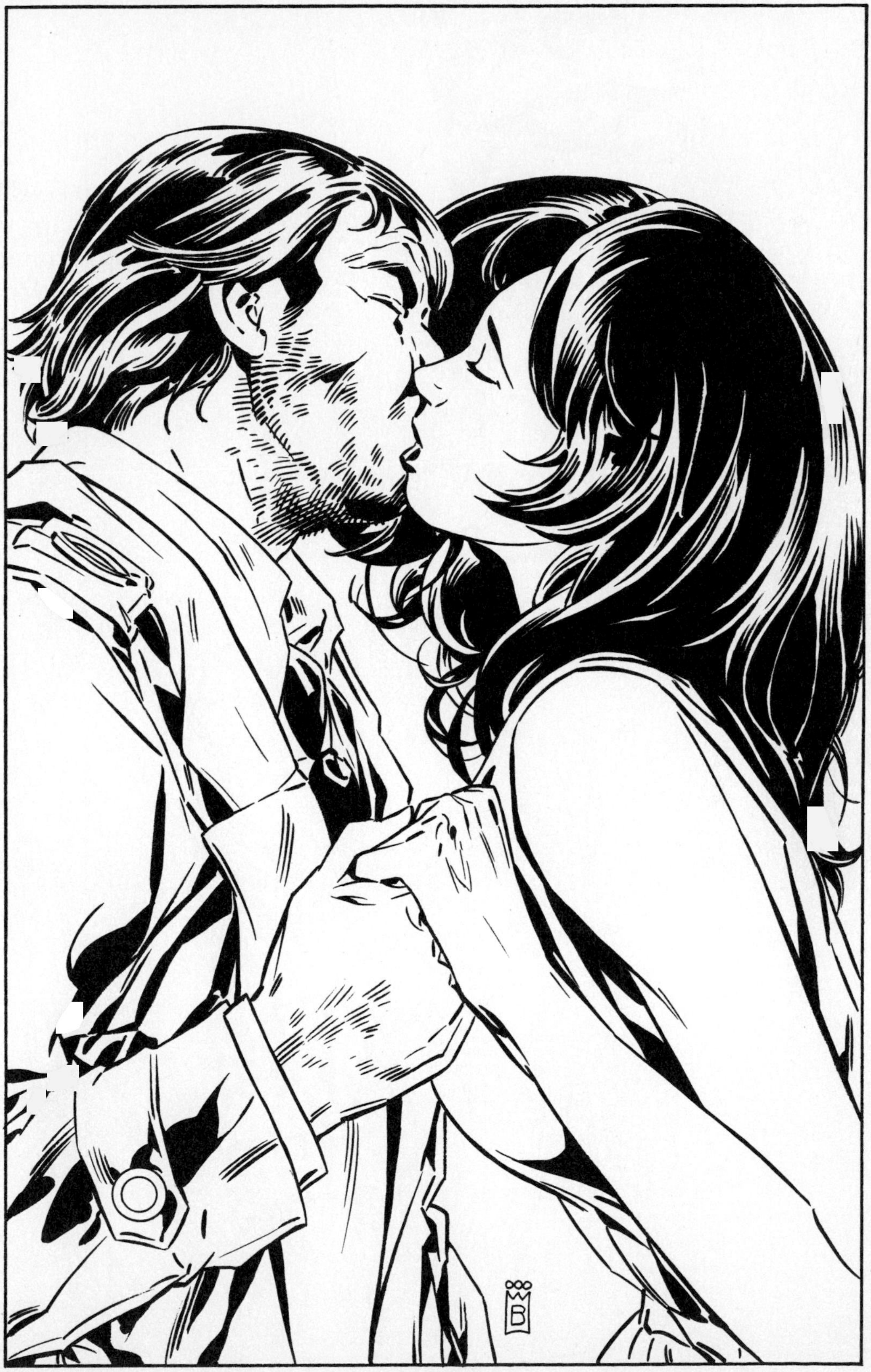

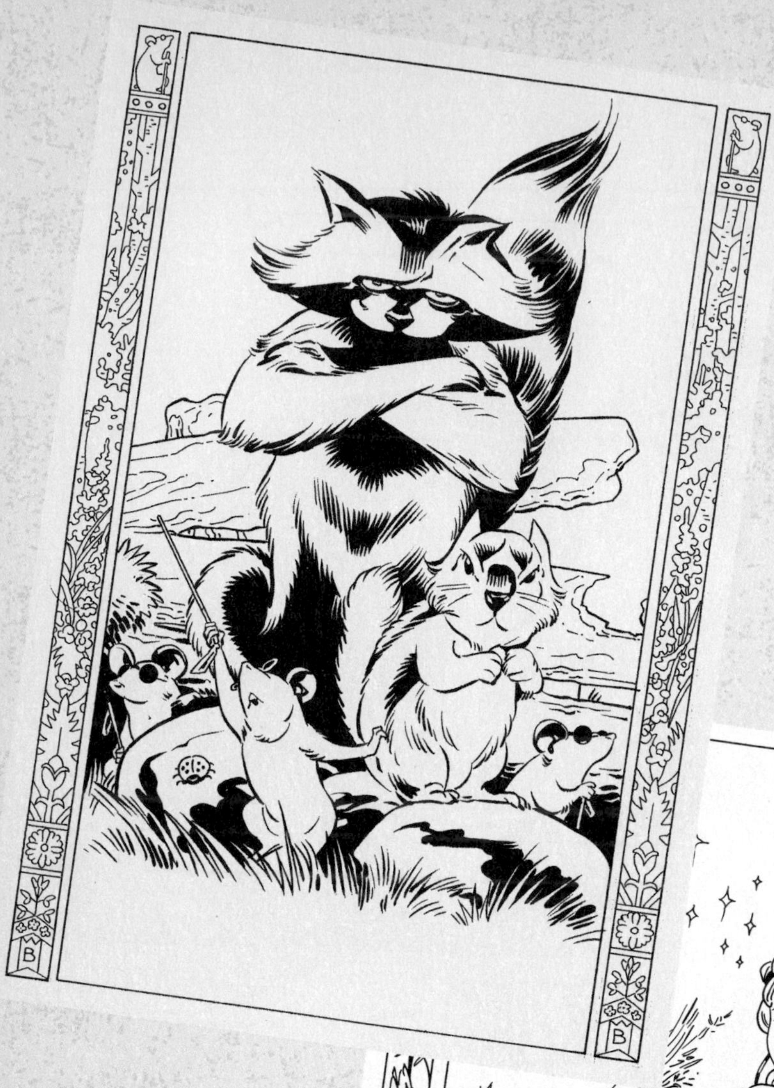

Two finished pieces by Mark Buckingham, prepared and printed by Bucky as convention giveaways

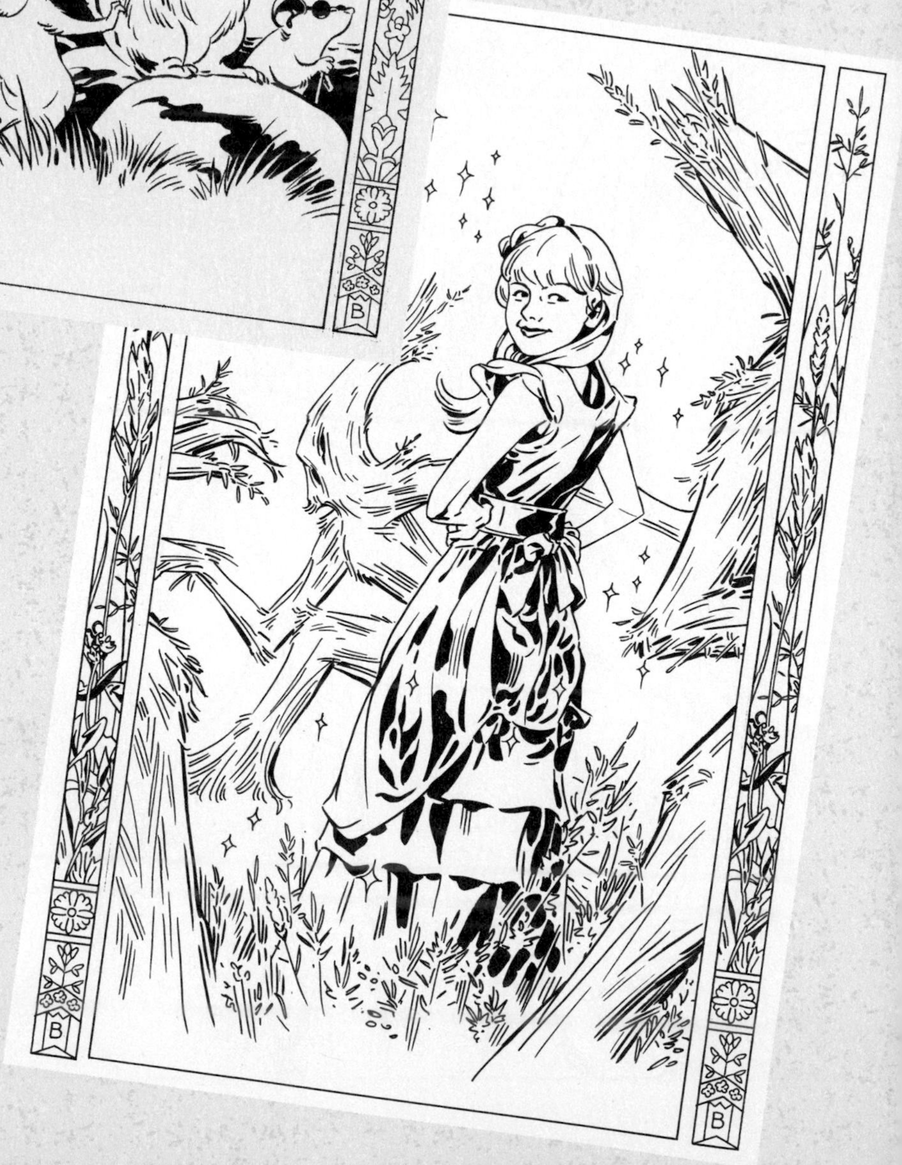

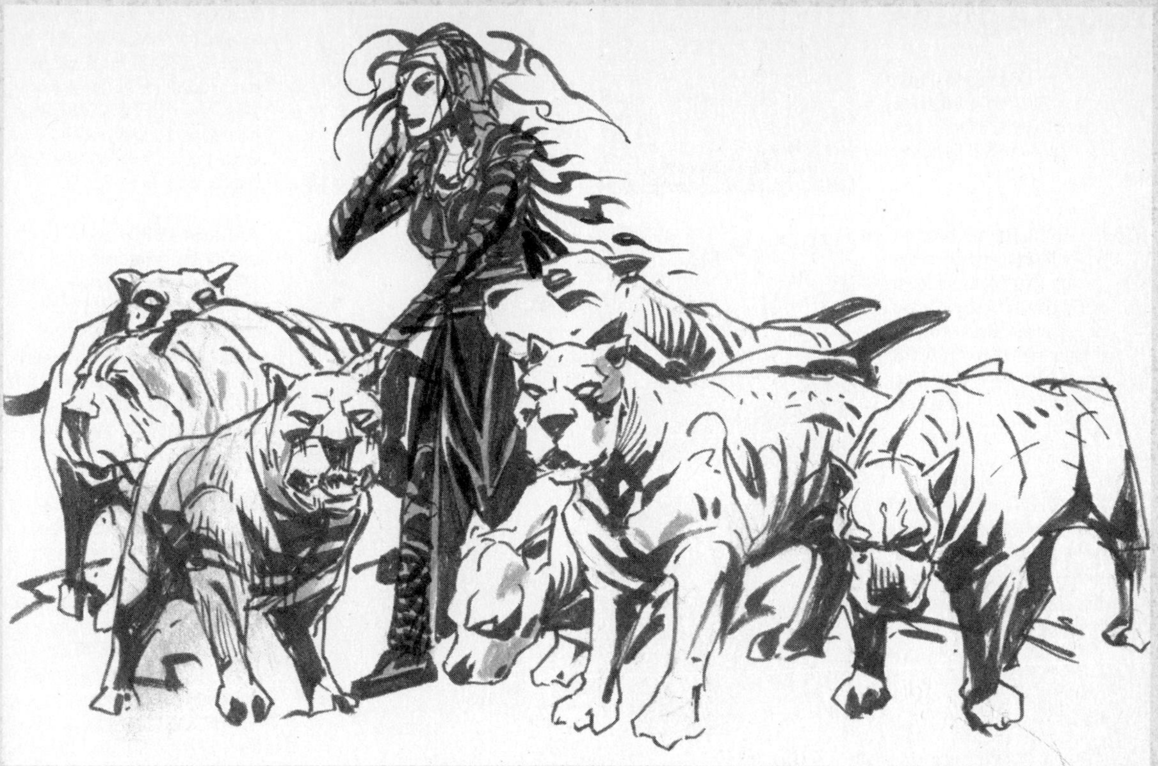

Sketches by Steve Leialoha made in preparation
for his art on FABLES #140

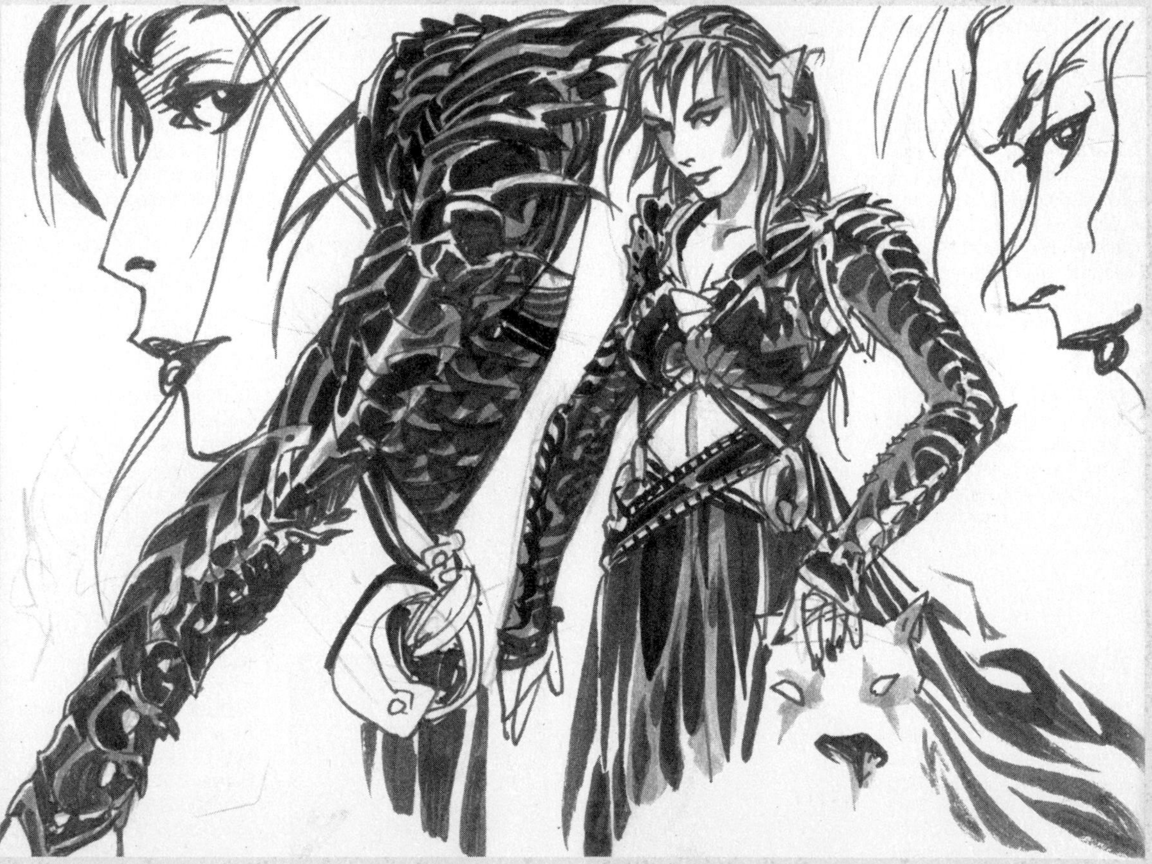

Creator Biographies

Once upon a time **BILL WILLINGHAM** used to write a funnybook series called FABLES.

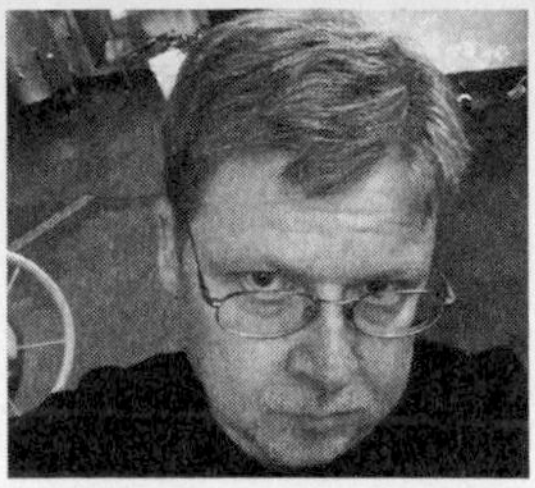

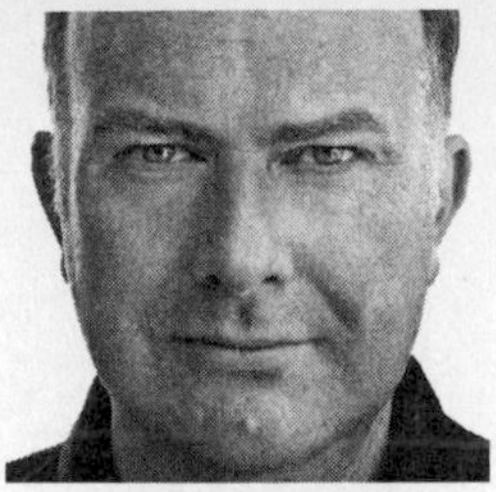

MARK BUCKINGHAM has been a constant presence throughout Vertigo's existence. "Bucky" has worked on SANDMAN, DEATH and HELLBLAZER, as well as more recent series such as DEAD BOY DETECTIVES and his writing debut on FAIREST. Since 2002, Mark has been the regular artist on FABLES.

STEVE LEIALOHA has been an artist for Marvel and DC since the '70s but has been a contributor to Vertigo for the last 20 years. Best of all, he has been part of the FABLES art team from the first issue to the last!

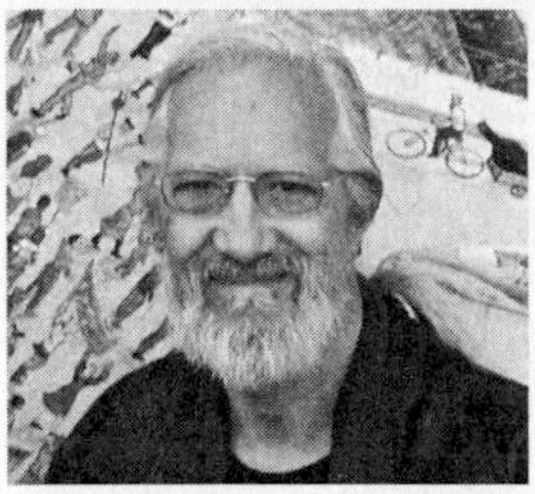

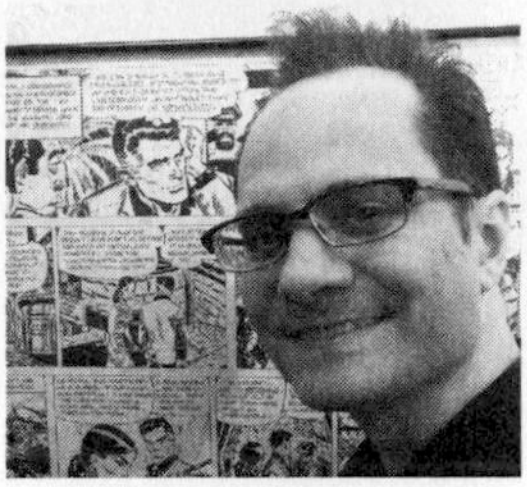

ANDREW PEPOY is an Eisner and Inkwell Award-winning artist and writer, having worked on hundreds of comics and characters. While best known for his inking on FABLES, JACK OF FABLES and *The Simpsons,* he is also the creator of *The Adventures of Simone & Ajax.*

DAN GREEN's career is long and multifaceted; penciling, inking and painting for the major comic book companies, and working as an artist, illustrator and designer in the wider world.

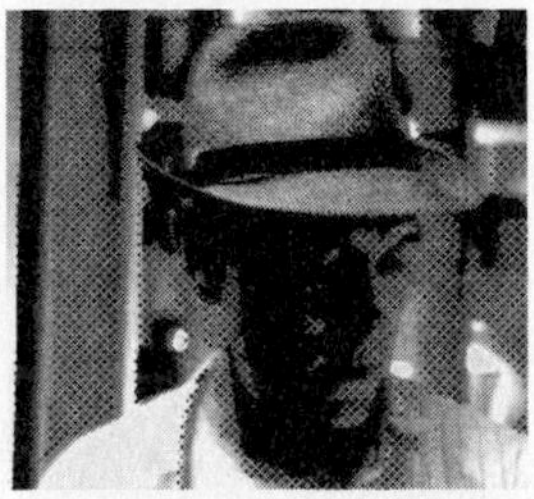

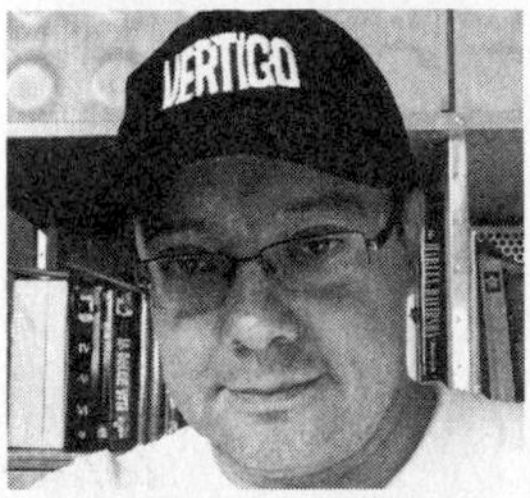
VERTIGO

JOSE MARZAN JR. is a 32-year veteran of the comic book industry, having started as an intern at Marvel Comics in 1983 at the age of 16. He began working for DC Comics in 1988, and received two 2008 Will Eisner Comic Industry Awards for his work on Vertigo Comics' Y: THE LAST MAN.

TODD KLEIN has been lettering comics since 1977, working on hundreds of titles, and recognized with awards for SANDMAN, *America's Best Comics* and FABLES, for which he has been the regular letterer since the series began.

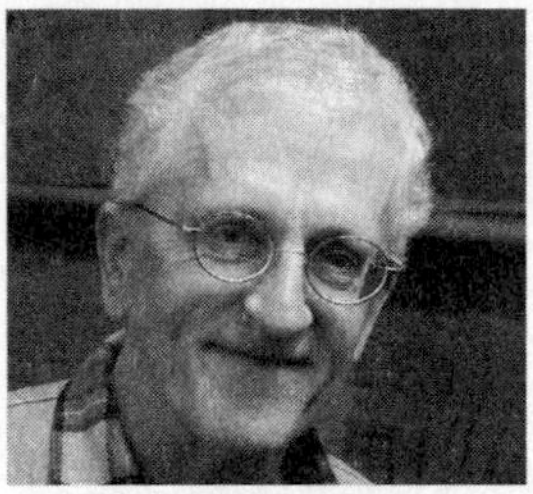

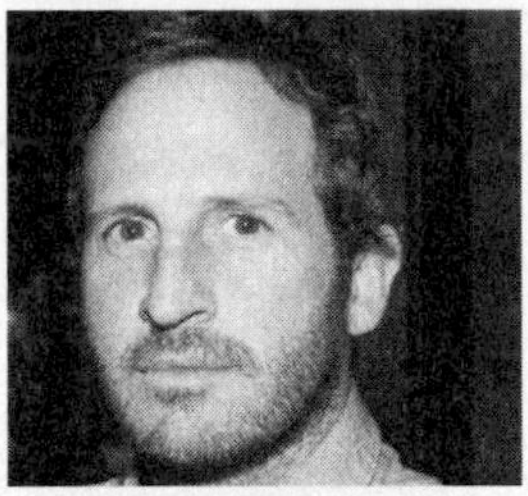

LEE LOUGHRIDGE has been the regular colorist on FABLES since 2006, and a well-respected comics colorist for over two decades.

ANDREW DALHOUSE has had a passion for coloring since high school, when he started buying comics. He pursued his passion and broke into the comic book industry over 10 years ago, and has been enjoying the ride ever since.

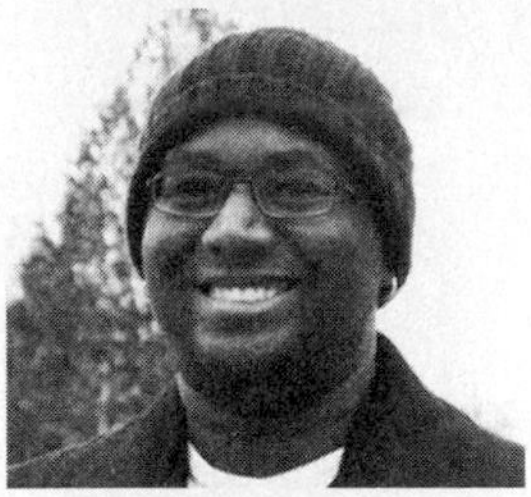

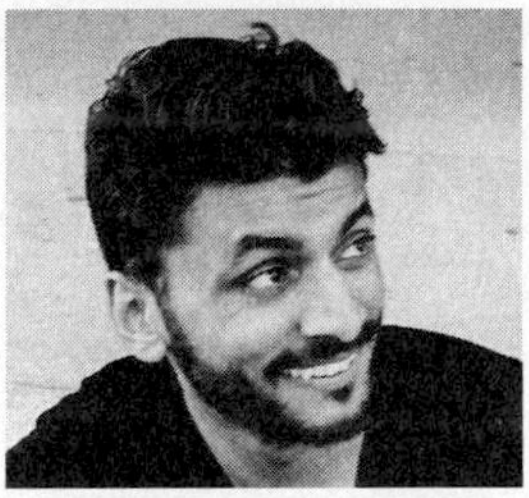

NIMIT MALAVIA is an award-winning artist living in Toronto, Canada, where he makes pictures for pleasure, profit and purpose.

NEAL ADAMS is a legend in the comics business, and an artistic inspiration to generations, not only for his superb art but for his pioneering efforts toward creators' rights.

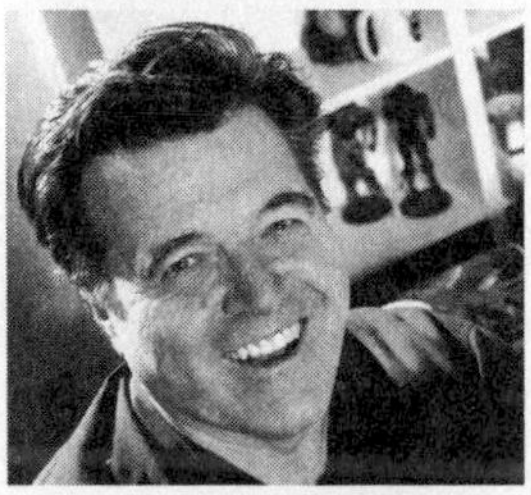

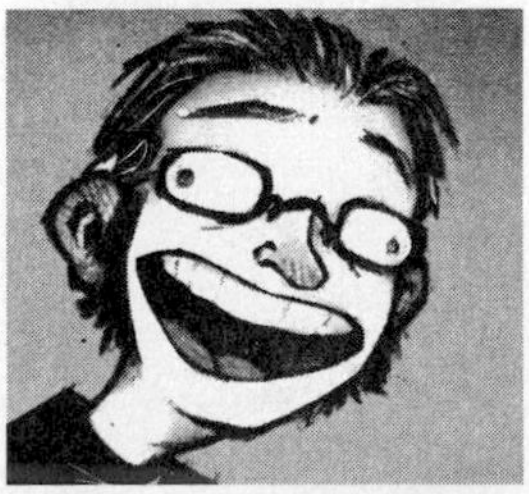

AARON ALEXOVICH's first professional art job was drawing deformed things for Nickelodeon's *Invader Zim.* Since then he's been deforming things for various projects, including *Avatar: The Last Airbender, Kimmie66, Eldritch!,* and three volumes of his own beloved *Serenity Rose.*

MICHAEL ALLRED is a writer, artist, musician and filmmaker. With intense love of the comic book world as his primary artistic outlet, he has created *Madman, The Atomics, Red Rocket 7* and co-created iZOMBIE with Chris Roberson. His work is almost always colored by his award-winning wife, **LAURA ALLRED.**

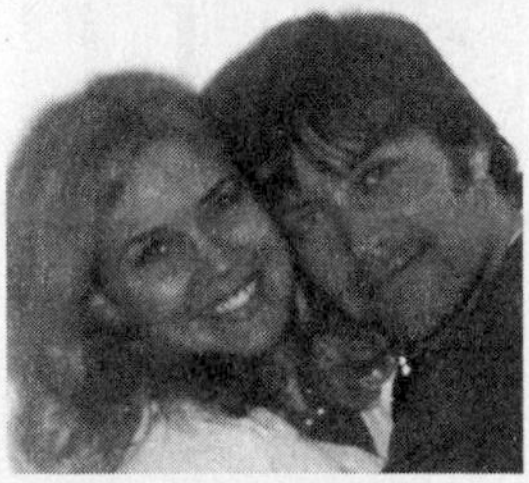

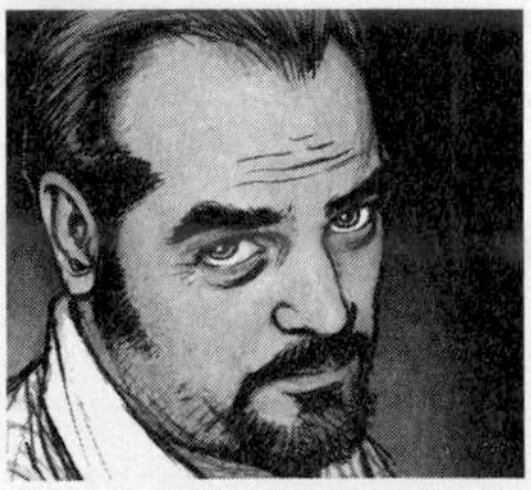

RUSS BRAUN has been in comics for over 25 years. FABLES fans will know him for his work on JACK OF FABLES, but he's done everything from *Batman* to SWAMP THING, and currently *Where Monsters Dwell* with Garth Ennis. Still waiting for Jack Horner to redeem himself...

TERRY and **RACHEL DODSON** have worked on such comics as *The Uncanny X-Men, Harley Quinn* and *Wonder Woman.* Currently they are splitting time between company-owned books like *Star Wars: Princess Leia* and creator-owned projects like *Red One,* with more to come.

MARK FARMER is best known for his renowned inking work on *The Incredible Hulk, Batman, The Avengers, The Uncanny X-Men, Green Lantern, Animal Man* and *Superman: True Brit,* the latter written by Monty Python comedian John Cleese.

LEE GARBETT is best known for his work with Grant Morrison on *Batman RIP: Last Rites* and *The Return of Bruce Wayne,* along with DC's acclaimed relaunch of *Batgirl.* Lee has also written for Vertigo's anthology CMYK: CYAN.

PETER GROSS has drawn lots of comics for Vertigo — like BOOKS OF MAGIC, LUCIFER and THE UNWRITTEN. He wishes he could have done more FABLES, but was happy he and Mike Carey got to work with Bill and Bucky on THE UNWRITTEN FABLES (An Event! Not a Crossover).

GENE HA grew up reading Bill Willingham's *Elementals* and playing two tabletop RPG adventures Bill wrote. Lately Gene got to draw Bill's stories, play through *Death Duel With The Destroyers* again, and hang out with Bill at comic cons. Gene Ha loves his life.

DAVID HAHN has illustrated BITE CLUB, FABLES and *Fringe* for DC Comics, as well as *Spider-Man Loves Mary Jane* and *The Fantastic Four* for Marvel. He is currently drawing *Dayglow,* a creator-owned graphic novel. David is a founding member of Periscope Studios.

NIKO HENRICHON has worked with writers like Brian K. Vaughan (on the acclaimed PRIDE OF BAGHDAD), Howard Chaykin, Bill Willingham and Darren Aronofsky. Currently he is illustrating the sequel to *Metabarons,* written by Alejandro Jodorowsky and Jerry Frisson.

JOËLLE JONES is currently writing and drawing a new original series called *Lady Killer,* published by Dark Horse. She has worked on various projects for *The New York Times,* Graphic Universe, Vertigo, DC, Marvel, Dark Horse and Oni Press.

TEDDY KRISTIANSEN lives and works in Denmark, with one wife, two cats, three daughters and way too many books (says his wife). When not reading, he draws stuff.

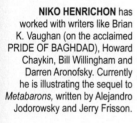

MEGAN LEVENS worked in advertising storyboards for several years before breaking into comics with *Madame Frankenstein* with writer Jamie S. Rich. She illustrated Oni Press's *Ares and Aphrodite,* and is currently working on *Buffy the Vampire Slayer* from Dark Horse.

LAN MEDINA began his comics career in the Philippines before branching into U.S. titles, including *Aquaman and the Others, District X, Punisher Max, Spawn, Aria* and *Deathlok.* He was also the enviable artist first tapped to draw the international sensation FABLES.

DAVID PETERSEN was raised on a steady diet of cartoons, comics and tree climbing that still inspires his work today. He is the creator of the *Mouse Guard* series, for which he received the 2007 Russ Manning Award for Most Promising Newcomer, and subsequent Eisner and Harvey Awards.

MARK SCHULTZ is best known for his SF-adventure comic, *Xenozoic.* He has also written or drawn many classic comics characters, including Superman, Tarzan, The Spirit, Flash Gordon and Prince Valiant. He is currently working on a new *Xenozoic* story.

BRYAN TALBOT has written and drawn comics for over 30 years, including *Judge Dredd, Batman,* THE SANDMAN, *The Adventures of Luther Arkwright, The Tale of One Bad Rat, Heart of Empire, Alice in Sunderland,* and his current *Grandville* series of steampunk detective thrillers.

VERTIGO

BILL WILLINGHAM
FABLES VOL. 1: LEGENDS IN EXILE

THE #1 NEW YORK TIMES BEST-SELLING SERIES

FABLES

Legends in Exile

"A top-notch fantasy comic that is on a par with SANDMAN."
— *Variety*

BULLFINCH STREET

Bill Willingham
Lan Medina
Steve Leialoha
Craig Hamilton

VERTIGO

VERTIGO

"It's got a little bit of everything that any sophisticated comics fan will enjoy."
—*PUBLISHERS WEEKLY*

"An unpredictable romp. It's a lot of fun." —*THE ONION*

"Sharp, quick-paced, fun-to-read stuff that is sure to impress."
—*METRO TORONTO*

FROM THE PAGES OF *FABLES*

JACK OF FABLES

BILL WILLINGHAM, MATTHEW STURGES and TONY AKINS

JACK OF FABLES VOL. 7: THE NEW ADVENTURES OF JACK AND JACK

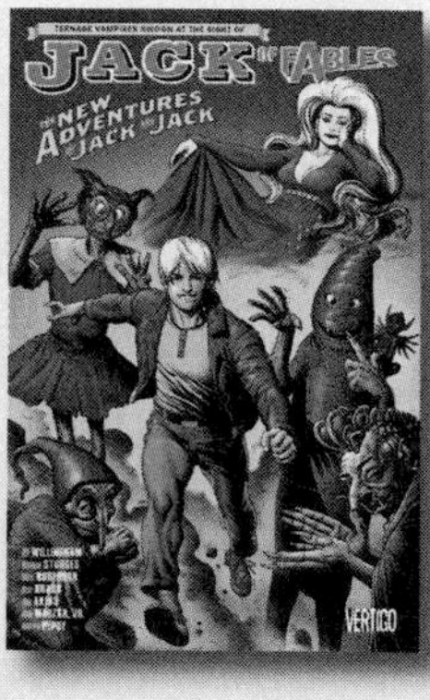
JACK OF FABLES
THE NEW ADVENTURES OF JACK AND JACK
VERTIGO

READ THE ENTIRE SERIES!

JACK OF FABLES VOL. 1: THE (NEARLY) GREAT ESCAPE

JACK OF FABLES VOL. 2: JACK OF HEARTS

JACK OF FABLES VOL. 3: THE BAD PRINCE

JACK OF FABLES VOL. 4: AMERICANA

JACK OF FABLES VOL. 5: TURNING PAGES

JACK OF FABLES VOL. 6: THE BIG BOOK OF WAR

JACK OF FABLES VOL. 7: THE NEW ADVENTURES OF JACK AND JACK

JACK OF FABLES VOL. 8: THE FULMINATE BLADE

JACK OF FABLES VOL. 9: THE END

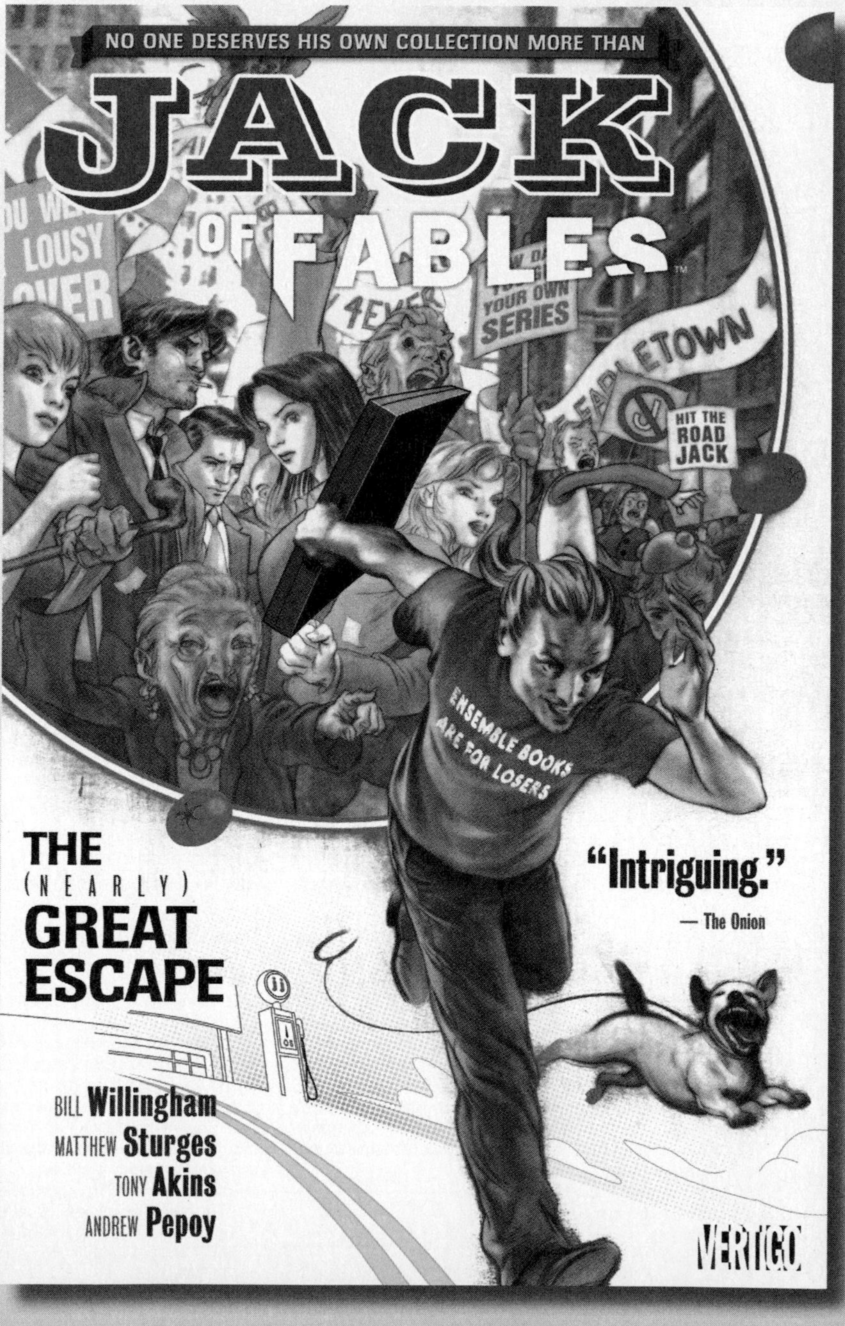
NO ONE DESERVES HIS OWN COLLECTION MORE THAN
JACK OF FABLES
LOUSY
YOUR OWN SERIES
HIT THE ROAD JACK
ENSEMBLE BOOKS ARE FOR LOSERS
THE (NEARLY) GREAT ESCAPE
"Intriguing."
— The Onion
BILL Willingham
MATTHEW Sturges
TONY Akins
ANDREW Pepoy
VERTIGO

To Shelly Bond and Shelly Roeberg, two editors who wrangled me through all of Fables and most of my writing career to date.

— Bill Willingham

To Irma. My muse (my Rose Red), my friend, my greatest champion, my one true love.

— Mark Buckingham

JUL 3 0 2015

Shelly Bond Editor
Rowena Yow Associate Editor
Kenny Lopez Cover Design
Todd Klein Publication Design

Shelly Bond VP & Executive Editor - Vertigo

Diane Nelson President
Dan DiDio and Jim Lee Co-Publishers
Geoff Johns Chief Creative Officer
Amit Desai Senior VP – Marketing & Global Franchise Management
Nairi Gardiner Senior VP – Finance
Sam Ades VP – Digital Marketing
Bobbie Chase VP – Talent Development
Mark Chiarello Senior VP – Art, Design & Collected Editions

John Cunningham VP – Content Strategy
Anne DePies VP – Strategy Planning & Reporting
Don Falletti VP – Manufacturing Operations
Lawrence Ganem VP – Editorial Administration & Talent Relations
Alison Gill Senior VP – Manufacturing & Operations
Hank Kanalz Senior VP – Editorial Strategy & Administration
Jay Kogan VP – Legal Affairs
Derek Maddalena Senior VP – Sales & Business Development
Dan Miron VP – Sales Planning & Trade Development
Nick Napolitano VP – Manufacturing Administration
Carol Roeder VP – Marketing
Eddie Scannell VP – Mass Account & Digital Sales
Susan Sheppard VP – Business Affairs
Courtney Simmons Senior VP – Publicity & Communications
Jim (Ski) Sokolowski VP – Comic Book Specialty & Newsstand Sales

Logo design by Nancy Ogami

FABLES: FAREWELL

DC Comics, 2900 W. Alameda Ave., Burbank, CA 91505
A Warner Bros. Entertainment Company.
Printed by Transcontinental Interglobe, Beauceville, QC, Canada. . First Printing.
ISBN: 978-1-4012-5233-5

Library of Congress Cataloging-in-Publication Data

Willingham, Bill, author.
 Fables. Volume 22, / Bill Willingham, Mark Buckingham.
  pages cm
 Summary: "The final volume of NEW YORK TIMES bestselling, Eisner Award-winning FABLES series is here! New York Times Best-selling author Bill Willingham delivers the end to his legendary series in Fables Volume 22. The Eisner Award-winning series sees the conclusion of the beloved stories of Bigby Wolf, Rose Red, Boy Blue, Bell, Pinnochio and countless other timeless fables. The only question left to be answered is whether or not they will have a happy ending."--Provided by publisher.
 ISBN 978-1-4012-5233-5 (paperback)
 1. Fairy tales--Comic books, strips, etc. 2. Legends--Comic books, strips, etc. 3. Graphic novels. I. Buckingham, Mark, illustrator. II. Title.
 PN6727.W52F434 2014
 741.5'973--dc23   2014010271

FSC
MIX
Paper from responsible sources
FSC® C011825
www.fsc.org